GV 14.4 .M35 1997
Mannell, Roger C.
A social psychology of
 leisure

GV 14.4 .M35 1997
Mannell, Roger C.
A social psychology of
 leisure

A Social Psychology
of Leisure

Roger C. Mannell
University of Waterloo

&

Douglas A. Kleiber
University of Georgia

A Social Psychology
of Leisure

Roger C. Mannell
University of Waterloo

&

Douglas A. Kleiber
University of Georgia

 Venture Publishing, Inc.
State College, PA

6/02 $42⁹⁵   B+T

Copyright © 1997 *oclc # 37909903*
Venture Publishing, Inc.
1999 Cato Avenue
State College, PA 16801
Phone (814) 234-4561; FAX (814) 234-1651

Printed in the United States of America

Production Manager: Richard Yocum
Manuscript Editing and Design: Michele L. Barbin
Cover Design/Illustration: Sandra Sikorski, Sikorski Design

Library of Congress Catalogue Card Number 97-60787
ISBN 0-910251-88-6

In Memory of

Lawrence La Fave, Ph.D.

Table of Contents

Chapter Four

Leisure as a Psychological State and Experience 79

Section Two—Leisure and the Person

Section Three—The Social Context of Leisure

Section Four—Cultivating Leisure and Well-Being

Preface

The social psychology of leisure is still a relatively new field. However, in the last decade or so, it has changed dramatically to become an important social science perspective adopted by leisure researchers to study and understand the role of leisure in people's lives. To add to this excitement, general social psychology itself continues to evolve. There has been a renewed interest in the practical applications of social psychology for understanding urgent social issues. Social psychological methods, theories and findings are being applied to the solution and the planning of improved arrangements for health, work, home life and, of course, leisure.

An early systematic effort to examine the potential of social psychology for understanding leisure was provided by John Neulinger in the 1974 book *Psychology of Leisure: Research Approaches to the Study of Leisure*. In 1980, Seppo Iso-Ahola published *The Social Psychology of Leisure and Recreation*, the first textbook to map out the boundaries of the field and review the social psychological theory and research available at the time. Though there have been a number of edited books and journal articles published since that time dealing with selected topics on the social psychology of leisure, there has not been a current and up-to-date textbook available. This book builds on those earlier efforts and it incorporates major new topics of research, innovative studies and contemporary examples.

The general orientation we have adopted in this book is that the *social psychology of leisure* is concerned with how people come to perceive time or behavior as free or discretionary. It is also concerned with how people choose to fill and structure this discretionary time with behavior and experience, why they make these choices, and the implications of these choices for their happiness and personal growth. Finally, the *social psychology of leisure* is concerned with the relationship between what people do during or with leisure and their experiences in the other domains of their lives, such as work, family, and interpersonal relationships. The purpose of this book, then, is to provide the student with the opportunity to examine current social psychological theory and research about leisure behavior and experience. In other words, how do people's personalities and the social situations that they encounter during their daily lives shape their perceptions, experiences, and responses to leisure? In this book we attempt to present the "basics" of the field—the core theories and findings that contribute to an understanding of leisure as it affects individuals' daily lives as well as their use of leisure services.

This book is written to serve as a textbook for undergraduate students taking a course in the psychological and social aspects of leisure and recreation. It also provides a comprehensive introduction to students in graduate courses that should be supplemented by books and journal articles focusing on specific topics. In Section I, *The Nature of Social Psychology and Leisure*, four chapters deal with the social psychological approach, the evolution of a social psychological interest in leisure, ethics and values in social psychological research, and the fascinating work that has been done by researchers to conceptualize and measure leisure. In Section II, *Leisure and the Person*, three chapters explore the role of freedom and self-determination, personality, and motivation in leisure behavior and experience. In Section III, *The Social Context of Leisure*, early-life socialization influences and the impact of changes over the lifespan on leisure are examined in two chapters, and finally, in Section IV, *Cultivating Leisure and Well-Being*, three chapters are devoted to social psychological leisure theory and research that have been applied to understanding how leisure can contribute to psychological well-being and mental health, and the quality of experience in other life domains. In the final chapter of Section IV, theories of constraints that may prevent people from taking advantage of leisure opportunities and social psychological strategies for creating "affordances" to facilitate leisure lifestyles are discussed.

The success of any text depends ultimately on its ability to communicate clearly to student readers and to spark student interest in the field of study. We have attempted to present the material simply, without oversimplifying. Special attention has been given to selecting examples that illustrate basic principles and convey our enthusiasm for the field. This book will provide the reader with the necessary social psychological background material. A previous course in general social psychology is not required. It is assumed, however, that students will have had introductory level courses in recreation and leisure studies and psychology.

We have tried to maximize the clarity and interest level of the text. Many years of teaching undergraduate and graduate courses in this area have provided a testing ground for much of the material and the methods of presentation that appear in this book. We have attempted to avoid unnecessary technical terms. Many concrete examples are used, and where appropriate, topics are introduced through the use of scenarios highlighting various types of leisure behavior for students to analyze. These illustrations are used to raise questions about such issues as:

- How do individuals know when they are having a leisure experience?

- Why do people sometimes seek danger and thrills during free time?

- Are some personality types better able to deal with leisure than others?

- Do certain childrearing methods lead to greater leisure competency?

- Is leisure important for the development of intimate relationships?

- Are there gender differences in leisure perceptions and needs?

- Can leisure help people deal with stress? and

- Are there effective ways to overcome social psychological barriers to leisure participation and satisfaction?

The bibliography at the end of the book is extensive. The discussion of each topic reflects attention to research and thinking found in the literature. We have also identified key studies that illustrate each issue and these are examined in some detail. Rather than have a separate research methods chapter, the studies selected also illustrate the various social psychological methods available to answer researchers', practitioners', and participants' questions about leisure. By posing interesting leisure questions often found in the reader's own daily life and then demonstrating how researchers have attempted to answer these same questions, it is hoped that we can demonstrate the relevance, excitement, and methods of social psychological leisure research.

Finally, in this book we discuss the potential applications of the research reviewed. These applications in some cases will have immediate implications for the provision of public and private leisure services in communities, tourism, park management, and private recreation businesses. However, there is another sense in which the book is applied. Not only can the information provided by a social psychology of leisure be used to more effectively plan leisure services, but also individuals, through an awareness of the social psychological dimensions of leisure, may be able to extend more control over their lives and better enjoy their own leisure. To this end, readers will constantly be asked to reflect on their own experiences and their personal observations of other people at leisure.

R. C. M.
D. A. K.

Acknowledgments

There are a number of people who deserve our thanks and whose interest and support have been greatly appreciated during the course of writing this book. Valeria Freysinger of Miami University, Ohio, and Seppo Iso-Ahola of the University of Maryland were requested to review an earlier version of the manuscript for Venture Publishing and provided many helpful comments and suggestions. For their comments on portions of the manuscript, we would also like to thank Linda Caldwell of the Pennsylvania State University and her social psychology of leisure graduate class, Michael Kernis of the University of Georgia, as well as University of Waterloo doctoral student Yoshi Iwasaki, and University of Georgia doctoral students Ellen Broach, Joe Garr, Eun-Ja Kim, Kevin Lyons, Sherry Malley, and Lexi McKenney. Laura Mannell merits a special acknowledgement for spending some of her summer vacation reading the manuscript and for her thoughful comments on the material from the perspective of an undergraduate student. Also, we extend a special thanks to Geoff Godbey for his ongoing support of this project.

Finally, on a personal note, our work on this book has occupied many nights and weekends, and substituted for much of our own family leisure time. Though we encountered a great deal of new information about a field that we both find fascinating, those close to us may not have found it quite so rewarding. We are very grateful to our families, and in particular Marg and Pam for enduring our mental and physical absences during this time. We promise not to do it again; at least, not for a while.

The Nature of
Social Psychology
and Leisure

Understanding Leisure with Social Psychology

Outline

Chapter ONE

Preview

This chapter introduces the reader to thinking about leisure from a social psychological perspective. We begin by looking at the need to study leisure and how psychological thinking has influenced the provision of leisure services. Then we consider how the social sciences in general, through the scientific study of people's everyday behavior and experience, differ from other ways of understanding the lifestyles people lead, and what makes their lives meaningful and happy. Next, a case study is presented that demonstrates how a social psychological approach can be used to better understand leisure issues. The social psychological approach used as a framework for this book is then described.

Social Science and the Quest for Happiness, Health and the Good Life

People have always sought the recipe for health and happiness. This search for the good life is as true today as at any time in the past—perhaps more so. Throughout history people have looked to the values of the social groups of which they are members, the folk wisdom passed down to them from their elders, religion, and philosophy as sources of the answers to these questions. During this century, social scientists have jumped into the fray in an attempt to provide answers as well.

A Question of Lifestyle: Juggling and Balancing the Demands of Daily Life

Whatever the source of the recipe for health and happiness, the answers have often taken the form of a prescription for a particular way of living. Today these prescriptions are packaged as *lifestyle*, and individuals are bombarded from all sides with suggestions for the best way to juggle and balance the various aspects of their lives. Daily newspapers feature lifestyle sections, weekly television series spotlight different and unique ways of living, and numerous self-help books on lifestyle appear on bookstore shelves. Lifestyle is typically described as a "total way of living" (Veal, 1989, 1993). Though not a new invention, people in previous generations, like fish in water, were immersed in their daily lives and for the most part oblivious to it; lifestyle alternatives were few for most people. While this lack of alternatives is still true for many people in different parts of the world, access to instantaneous electronic communication has created wide-spread awareness of lifestyle alternatives even if these choices are not available to everyone.

Commercials urge people to create their own lifestyle—with the "right" products of course. Television and magazines depict a whole range of ways to live. The food we as individuals eat, the manner in which we prepare it, our clothes, our homes, the entertainment and leisure we enjoy, the work we do, and how we raise our children all define our lifestyle. If the number of newspaper articles and popular books written recently are any indication (e.g., Crosby, 1991; Tubesing & Loving-Tubesing, 1991), most people have come to believe that their lifestyles determine their health and happiness, and just as importantly, that they can *create* their own lifestyles through how they *juggle* and *balance* the work, family and leisure aspects of their lives. Social scientists are studying the battle that people seem to be waging today to bring what are seen as runaway lifestyles under control.

People-Watching as a Science

Science is responsible for many of the lifestyle choices that modern life allows. For many people, science suggests the *physical sciences*, such as physics, chemistry and biology, and they can easily name a variety of inventions emerging from research in these sciences that have made modern life easier, for example, toasters, plastic bags, heart transplants, more resistant strains of plants and personal computers. Current problems being addressed by physical scientists are also well-known, for example, acid rain, nuclear waste disposal, AIDS, genetic disease, and environmentally harmful packaging. However, the twentieth century has also seen the development of sciences which study people.

These *social sciences*, such as psychology, sociology and anthropology, have taken the popular pastime of "people-watching" and made a science of it. When asked to identify the kinds of inventions developed by social scientists, one often finds it more difficult to come up with such a list. Yet social science has provided humanity with a number of inventions such as therapy, reinforcement, political polling, time management strategies, educational planning principles, and brainstorming. Social science is probably better known for the types of problems it attempts to address, such as child abuse, poverty, neurosis, alienation in large cities, the pain and dysfunction of drug abuse, stress reduction, unemployment and the elimination of lifestyle diseases such as poor eating habits, smoking, and lack of exercise.

As people watchers, everyone is an armchair social scientist, making predictions about the behavior of other people based on our own experiences. Everyone has theories about the best way to get a date, discipline children, organize a great party, keep New Year's resolutions, and approach the boss for a raise or a professor for a better grade—and we as individuals act on these theories. Social scientists, on the other hand, by carefully and systematically observing people in laboratories, in their homes, at work and at leisure, attempt to provide a clearer and more objective picture of human behavior than we, as individuals, can hope to achieve.

The social sciences have long been associated with the study of human problems such as mental illness. But during the latter part of this century a shift has taken place. Social scientists spend a great deal of time studying normal daily activities and the positive aspects of life as well. Altruism, creativity, humor and quality of life are only a few of the subjects that they have addressed in their research.

Much of this research by social scientists is being carried out in colleges and universities. Newer departments of health, leisure, gerontology, consumer, and family studies have emerged to provide answers to specific lifestyle issues and educate people to work in human service fields related to these. Like other sources of information and values in Western society, the solutions provided by social scientists are often controversial. However, the work of these social scientists is alerting society to important problems, sometimes confirming common sense understanding, sometimes severely challenging cherished ideas and beliefs. Hopefully, this research will contribute answers and raise social awareness about specific lifestyle issues so that as individuals we will be better able to control our lives.

What is Leisure and Why Study It With Social Science?

Leisure is an important component of lifestyle and of that lifestyle balance people seem to have difficulty achieving. As will be seen, some researchers have even suggested that an individual's leisure may have more impact on the quality of life than any other area of behavior and experience (see Kelly, 1996). Leisure has been described in a variety of ways. In fact, one of the longest-standing problems researchers have had is agreeing on how to define and measure it. Leisure has been characterized as specific types of *activity* (e.g., attending a movie); as *time* free from obligations (e.g., the amount of time not spent in paid employment and taking care of home, family and oneself); as meaningful and satisfying *experience* (e.g., feelings of satisfaction, fun, excitement, awe, belonging); or as some combination of activity, time and experience. Any of these approaches to define and measure leisure can be useful, and the approach used often depends on what questions about leisure the researcher is trying to answer. Chapters three and four will examine the issues of leisure definition and measurement in some detail.

As to why one should study leisure, many researchers do so simply because they are *curious* and would like to know more about why people chose to engage in the activities and pursue the experiences with which they fill their free time. Why do some people jump out of airplanes while others prefer quiet walks in the park? How is it that some friends never have enough time for the activities they constantly pack into their available free time, while others find their leisure empty and boring? What effects do these choices have on other aspects of life? These and many other questions are fascinating. Since leisure is based on free time or choice, most individuals have more personal control over what they do during their leisure than at any other time during their daily lives. Consequently, for those researchers who make a hobby or profession out of people-watching, what people do in their leisure may tell social psychologists more about them as people—their innermost feelings, attitudes, beliefs and personality characteristics—than what they do in any other context. Leisure is fertile ground for learning more about people as well as ourselves. It is the authors' hope that by reading this book and studying leisure behavior and experience, readers will become more aware of the factors that affect their own leisure, and consequently they will be able to extend more control over this area of their lives and better enjoy and benefit from leisure.

Many of you who read this book will be studying in recreation and leisure studies programs. Not only are you likely to be curious about leisure (both your own and others), but you will be planning to enter the leisure services field where you will be involved in developing and providing services and opportunities that will enable others to make more of their leisure time. While leisure can be rewarding, it seems to be a problem for many people as well. To work with people and help them in developing meaningful and satisfying leisure, researchers and practitioners need to constantly study and examine people's leisure behavior and experience and the factors that influence them. The resulting knowledge will hopefully sensitize leisure providers to their changing needs and better enable the provision of valued services and assistance.

Is Leisure a Problem To Be Studied With Social Science?

The use of nonwork time and leisure in our society continues to raise highly significant questions both for the individual and for society. Society is facing major social transformations with the globalization of the economy and advancing technology that are creating radical changes in the way we as individuals work, the use of our nonwork time, and the role of leisure in our lives. To make things even more exciting, there are many different views about how these changes in technology and economics are affecting the type of work individuals do, where they work, when they work, how much they work, and even if they work at all (see Best, 1988; Dawson, 1986; Schor, 1991; Reid, 1995).

What individuals do off the job, during leisure, and the lifestyles they lead are caught up in these forces of change. Social commentators who spend their time peering into the future are no more in agreement about what will happen with leisure than they are with work (McDaniels, 1990). There are even major differences of opinion about how much leisure people actually have today, whether it is increasing or decreasing, and if it can play a positive or negative role in people's lives as the opportunities for work change (Reid, 1995). For many people there is a distinct possibility of further growth in nonwork time, though it may be unevenly distributed—with some actually working longer hours and others becoming underemployed or chronically unemployed. During the past few years, there have been policy discussions by governments, employers and employee groups about the value and feasibility of job sharing and shorter work weeks in an attempt to distribute the work that is available to more people. These policies would result in more free time and possibly more leisure for many people.

While leisure occupies about one-third of the time of the average working adult (Chubb & Chubb, 1981), there are tremendous differences among people in their work and leisure lifestyle arrangements. On the one hand, unemployment and part-time work have grown at the same time that the number of people working well beyond a forty-hour week has increased (see Reid, 1995). Some of these latter individuals are doing so unwillingly; but to keep their jobs they have little choice as employers downsize and streamline their operations. Other people appear to be thriving on more work, and yet for others, work seems to be a form of addiction or workaholism driven by problems in other areas of their lives (Killinger, 1991). On the other hand, for children, retirees, the underemployed and unemployed, leisure may account for up to two-thirds or more of their time and activity. These differences and problems make the study of leisure and how people deal with it a fascinating topic. Whether this time is idle, avoided, filled with pleasure, devoted to personal growth, used in the service of others, constitutes a source of frustration and anxiety, or is used in ways that are personally or socially harmful is a matter of great academic, political, and social interest.

The Psychologization of Leisure Services

What individuals choose to do during their leisure may require few goods and services, involve no one but themselves and a few friends, and cost them nothing. However, there is an ever increasing demand for public and private leisure services. These services are provided and influenced by numerous agencies at all levels of government, by professional and advocacy groups, and by private businesses. Leisure is big business as people spend money on travel, attending sport and cultural events, collectibles from stamps to paintings, and recreational goods from sweatbands to sailboats. It is cultivated by governments for its contribution to economic growth. For example, many countries have developed strategies to promote tourism. The World Tourism Organization has estimated that the travel industry is the largest single industry in the world and since 1990 worldwide revenues have been estimated to be about three trillion U.S. dollars per year (McIntosh & Goeldner, 1990). Leisure is also seen as an effective way of fostering the quality of community and individual life through recreational, cultural and heritage activities oriented to people from childhood to old age (Searle & Brayley, 1993).

In recent years, people have shown greater concern and interest in leading healthier lifestyles. Governments have also been promoting healthier lifestyles in an attempt to reduce medical and healthcare costs which have continued to grow beyond society's ability to pay. More and more, leisure has been singled out as an important vehicle for promoting *healthy lifestyles and activities* (Godbey, 1994; Searle & Brayley, 1993). Consequently, local communities continue to build and manage recreational and cultural facilities. They provide programs for their citizens with the support of all levels of government. Public lands and forests continue to be acquired, protected as parks, and managed for recreational use.

As a consequence of the extensive resources being invested in leisure service delivery systems by all levels of government and by the private and commercial sectors, there has emerged a need for skilled professionals and practitioners to plan, develop, and manage the various service systems. To help in this enterprise, scholars and researchers in leisure studies have been concerned with how individuals, groups, and society as a whole plan, organize, and use resources for leisure. The role of leisure in meeting the health and lifestyle needs of people in various types of employment, those working at home, families, retired adults, disadvantaged groups, persons with disabilities, and the unemployed are of concern. Researchers and practitioners are concerned about policies affecting public and private sector involvement in leisure-related matters such as sport, fitness, tourism, park and heritage development, and the arts.

Leisure services have also become "psychologized" (Mannell, 1991). Many recreation providers are as concerned with the quality of the experiences provided by their recreational services as they are with the activities and settings they manage. This focus on the experience is evident in many consumer areas today. Recent research on consumer behavior in general has focused increasingly on the experience of buying in its own right, since consumers do more than simply attend to information to make purchasing choices. They also engage in imaginative and emotional consumption experiences. This growing focus on the nature of experience is reminiscent of Toffler's prediction in his book *Future Shock* (1970) that no service will be offered to the consumer until it has been analyzed by teams of *behavioral engineers* to improve the quality of the experience it creates.

Of course, this notion of experience "engineering" smacks of manipulation, and is viewed by some critics as the antithesis of the freedom of choice, personal control, and spontaneity usually associated with leisure (e.g., Goodale, 1990). In the tourism and travel industry, for example, there are those who are very concerned with the lack of authenticity of many of the travel and tourism experiences available (e.g., Cohen, 1988; MacCannell, 1973; Moscardo & Pearce, 1986). On the other hand, many leisure service providers, particularly those in the private sector, have already developed *theories* or rules of thumb through trial and error to enhance the experiences of their customers, and ensure a clientele willing to return again and again. For example, the formula for the success of theme parks is known and applied in designing and operating this type of leisure business (Cameron & Bordessa, 1981). Success is based on structuring the leisure environment in such a way as to create or encourage predictably satisfying experiences. Regardless of how researchers and service providers feel about these issues, it has become apparent that an understanding of the psychological or experiential nature of leisure must be developed.

Leisure studies scholars draw on the knowledge and approaches of the social and management sciences, and the results of their research and thinking is disseminated in a wide array of national and international journals and conferences specializing in leisure studies. Most college and university recreation and leisure studies programs encourage their students to integrate and understand the interplay between "people," "resource" and "policy" issues. In other words, leisure studies curricula require students to study individual and group leisure behavior as a function of social and cultural factors, the planning and management of natural and built resources for free time use, and policy/management issues associated with the provision of public and private leisure services. Social science can help formalize scientific planning and design principles which can provide the tools for those practitioners in the public and private service sectors who are involved with human behavior and experience during free time.

Social science research is devoted to understanding not only the antecedents and consequences of leisure choices, but also the factors that affect the quality and meaning of these choices. This knowledge hopefully will allow a better understanding of the problems people encounter in attempting to chose meaningful and enjoyable leisure; and while this knowledge may be applied in enhancing the management of human services, it may also be used to enable individuals to gain more control over their lives and better manage their own leisure.

Social Psychology of Leisure

Leisure has been studied from the perspectives of a variety of social science disciplines including sociology, anthropology and economics (see Barnett, 1988, 1995; Chick, 1987, 1995; Peterson, Driver & Gregory, 1988). During the past several decades in North America, there has been growing interest in the use of psychological, particularly *social psychological*, theory and research methods for developing an understanding of leisure (Iso-Ahola & Mannell, 1985; Iso-Ahola, 1995). What makes this theory and research social psychological? Well, consistent with the social psychological approach in the field of psychology, the focus has been on the *leisure experience and behavior of the individual*—what she or he does and feels. Also, consistent with this perspective, researchers have looked to two sources for an explanation of this behavior and experience. Leisure behavior and experience are seen to be a function of the interplay of *internal psychological dispositions* (e.g., perceptions, feelings, emotions, beliefs, attitudes, needs, personality characteristics) and *situational influences* that are part of an individual's social environment (e.g., other people, group norms, human artifacts and media).

The emergence of the social psychological study of leisure is not too surprising. Many researchers studying leisure have been committed to providing knowledge to practitioners who work with individuals to enhance their leisure participation and satisfaction. This "helping" orientation is a legacy of the *parks and recreation movement* which began at the turn of the century largely in response to the problems of industrialization and urbanization. The leisure service field is descended from this early movement and still has a responsibility for working with individuals to solve problems that are a result of both personal constraints and constraints imposed by their social environments. Thus, there has been substantial interest in understanding individual leisure behavior and experience as a function of the differences in needs, attitudes and personality that individuals carry around with them, and the social contexts and situations that they encounter during their daily lives.

We invite you, as the reader, to at least temporarily adopt this social psychological perspective in thinking about leisure and the various issues and problems that will be examined. We have found it to be a useful framework for our own thinking and understanding. Social psychology is a lively, dynamic field of enquiry. People *do* social psychology. So, before starting to examine the research on the social psychology of leisure, let's examine a "leisure problem" and observe firsthand social psychological thinking in action.

Social Psychology in Action: Trouble at the Video Arcade

Imagine that the following story just appeared in your local newspaper written by a reporter who had attended a school board meeting.

Kids Steal To Feed Video Habit, School Board Told

Educators and school board trustees want to zap students out of electronic game arcades and back into classrooms. Arcades have led to increasing problems of truancy, larceny and young students being subjected to a poor environment, the trustees of the board of education were told Monday. "There's been a marked increase in the number of youthful offenders under the age of 16 who are pouring their ill-gotten gain into these machines," the deputy police chief told the committee. His comments were echoed by the principal of a local high school, who said students are "stealing from each other and from their parents" to feed their pinball and electronic game addictions.

Arcade owners have a habit of locating near schools to attract student business and as a result some youngsters are often late returning to class after lunch or don't come back at all, the principal said. He has discussed the problems with parents, police and other county principals, and called for a bylaw that would prohibit access to the arcades to children under 16 unless accompanied by a parent, restrict hours of business so they don't coincide with school times, restrict arcade locations and license the machines to control their number.

"I think you're all overreacting," said the operator of a local arcade. "This type of business is being harassed and has been for some time."

What Is Leisure? What Is a Leisure Problem?

Is the video arcade issue raised in the article a leisure problem? Is playing video games at the arcade considered leisure? There are a number of ways of defining leisure. In fact, one of the longest-standing problems leisure researchers have had is agreeing on just exactly how to define and measure leisure. Leisure has been described at various times as an *activity*, as *time* free from obligations, as a meaningful and satisfying *experience*, or as some combination of these (Csikszentmihalyi, 1981). Leisure has also been defined *objectively* and *subjectively*. In the case of objective definitions, the judgment is made by the researcher or is the result of societal or group consensus. In the case of subjective definitions, researchers depend on the person or persons being studied to decide whether an activity, period of time, or experience is leisure; it depends on their perceptions and judgment.

Most of us would probably agree that playing video games at the arcade is a *leisure behavior* and a *recreational activity*, and there probably would be consensus about this in many groups and societies. Also, the students in the newspaper story participate during their free time (lunch and after school) and appear to find video game playing a meaningful and satisfying pursuit, even to the point of "addiction." Taken at face value, it seems plausible that the behavior discussed at the board meeting is leisure. We will return to this issue of defining and measuring leisure in chapters three and four.

It also appears that this behavior may be a *problem*. It is alleged to be causing negative outcomes: truancy, larceny, and exposure to a poor environment. As will be seen, leisure problems often take the form of barriers or constraints that prevent people from engaging in or experiencing satisfying leisure, or as may be the case in this situation, participation in leisure may result in negative outcomes for the individual or society.

How Would You Approach This Problem?

Now, imagine that you are a leisure services practitioner working for the Department of Recreation in this community. Following the school board meeting your department is approached by the board for advice and assistance in dealing with the video arcade "problem." Your director assigns you to look into the problem and asks you to provide her with some suggestions for recommendations that she can pass on to the board. How would you approach this problem? What would you do first?

In our courses, when we ask our students this question, usually their first responses are suggestions to develop a recreational program to combat the problem, that is, to provide a "constructive" alternative that will keep the high school students out of trouble, and in this case, out of the arcade. Recreation and human service students tend to be action and *solution oriented*. However, while this is admirable, there are other things one should do before stepping in with solutions.

First let's be sure of the facts. *Is there really a problem?* Has there actually been an increase in truancy and larceny in the school since the opening of the arcade? If so, is it due to the presence of the arcade and the fact that students play video games on its premises? Or is the problem that some people in the community feel adolescents playing video games in an arcade is "bad," that is, that engaging in this activity is morally wrong, much like some people may feel that gambling or abortion are wrong while others do not. The problem, then, could be primarily one of a conflict of values; the values of adolescents who like to play video games and recreation business people who wish to provide the service versus the values of adults who see them as bad. In this latter case, the link between video game playing and the deviant behavior of truancy and larceny in school may be irrelevant to this problem. We will return to this issue of values.

However, if video game playing is causing these problems, there are other questions that need to be asked if this leisure behavior is to be understood and the problem solved. Does the presence of the arcade and video game playing affect all students in the school in this negative manner? If not, why not? Which students are more "at risk?" There may be different solutions required for different students. These questions make the arcade problem much more complex. The issue involves not only what is actually going on, but what different stakeholders think or perceive is happening, and their value systems which may be in conflict. This complexity is consistent with what most people know about human life from their own experience, and this is where a *social psychological approach* comes in handy.

The Social Psychological Approach

Can the Problem Be Studied With Social Psychology?

The social psychological approach is a scientific approach. *Science* is the application of the scientific method to answerable questions. The *scientific method* is simply a way of making observations or gathering information in a systematic way; it involves the use of controlled, systematic inquiry, and a logical and rationale approach to explanation. *Answerable questions* are questions that can be answered by the use of the scientific method. While this reasoning sounds a bit circular, it simply means that the questions should have answers that can be arrived at by observing what is going on under various circumstances. As will be seen, a number of ways of observing what is going on are available with the social psychological approach. Sometimes the researcher carefully observes what is going on and records what is happening, or interviews or surveys the people involved. Sometimes the researcher may intervene and actually manipulate aspects of the situation under study and then observe what happens with field experiments. Sometimes the only way to gain some insight into the problem is for the researcher to re-create or simulate what goes on in the real world in a laboratory setting where the cause-and-effect relationships that may be at play can be more clearly examined.

If the problem cannot be answered through careful, systematic observation or the use of the scientific method, then other approaches than science may be necessary. An example of an *unanswerable question* for science is, "How many angels can dance on the head of a pin?" Many areas of human study and knowledge address questions for which science-based disciplines have no answers. Philosophy, art, literature and religious studies are devoted to exploring not only some of the same questions addressed by the scientific disciplines, but also many issues that cannot be dealt with by the scientific approach.

Many of these latter issues involve *values*. The facts may even be quite clear and agreed upon, but we as individuals have to decide whether we are in favor or against a particular practice or course of action, and no amount of research is going to help us decide (e.g., Sunday shopping, abortion, ordination of homosexuals in the church, legalized gambling, the sale of alcohol on Sundays, appropriateness of children and adolescents playing video arcade games). Novels are written, pictures painted, philosophical analyses presented, and religious and cultural standards called upon, however, which provide answers to these questions for many people.

If we decide as an individual, practitioner or researcher that the issue or problem can be clarified by observing or gathering further information then we are ready to engage in *social psychological analysis and research.* We need to determine if there is, in fact, a problem. In the present case, do the facts support the connection between video game playing, and the truancy and larceny occurring in the school suggested by the newspaper story? Several types of information can be gathered to determine the "facts." First, *descriptive information* is needed. Have incidents of "crime" in the school increased since the arcade opened? Are students from the school using their "leisure time" to hang out in the arcade? Second, as the people in charge of examining this arcade problem, we need information that would allow us to determine if there is a *cause-and-effect* relationship between these events; that is, are the two events related? Third, if there is evidence of a link, it would be useful to collect information that would clarify the *underlying linking mechanism.* That is, what are the social and psychological explanations for the link between playing at the arcade and the deviant behavior at school that might help to understand and ultimately deal with the problem?

This video arcade problem seems amenable to social psychological study and analysis, though clearly the issue of what are appropriate recreation activities for adolescents has a value judgment component as well. You could begin your study and analysis by checking school and police records to see if there has actually been an increase in thefts by students and truancy since the opening of the video arcade. Unobtrusive periodic visits for a few weeks to the arcade during the students' free time at lunch and after school, as well as during school times, would allow you to determine the extent of student participation in this activity. If you observed little student use of the video arcade and found that there had been no change in the reported frequency of truancy and school thefts since the opening of the arcade, you could conclude that there was no "leisure" problem. You might also speculate that the "problem" was really a conflict of values in the community over the appropriateness of children spending their leisure time in video arcades.

If the arcade was heavily frequented by students from the school, both during school as well as in the students' free time and thefts and truancy had increased, however, the problem would clearly warrant further study. You as the researcher do not have enough information yet to conclude that playing in the video arcade is causing or is in anyway linked to the problems at school. The increase in video playing and illegal acts could simply be a coincidence. It may be different students who play at the video arcade, on the one hand, and who are involved in truancy and larceny, on the other.

These latter problems could be due to other unidentified factors, such as an increase in drug use among students and a subsequent loss of interest in school and a need for money. Also, both video arcade participation and school problems could be due to the same unidentified factors, for example, a lack of supervision by busy, highly stressed parents. If this were the case, the video arcade would not be causing the problem. It would simply be a symptom of the problem.

The next step in this social psychological research would be to collect information that would allow you to examine the presence or absence of a cause-and-effect relationship between video arcade playing and the illegal activities at school, as well as develop some understanding of what the link might be.

Theory and Cause-and-Effect Relationships

How do the authorities cited in the article explain the relationship between video arcade playing and school problem behavior, that is, what is their *theory*? Theories are just explanations of how and why events are related. The theory suggested by the newspaper article seems to be that the presence of the arcade provides *opportunities* and causes students to engage in the *leisure behavior* of playing video games which leads to addiction which in turn leads to truancy and larceny. As we noted earlier, there is little or no evidence provided in the article to support this theory.

Let's assume for the moment that this research demonstrates that some students from the school are, in fact, regularly visiting the video arcade and that there has been an increase in truancy and stealing at school. However, as one might expect, not all students frequent the arcade, and many more students use the arcade than are involved in truancy and/or larceny. Let's also assume that this research has found that a small number of the students have been skipping school and stealing money to play video games at the arcade. This state of affairs is a more accurate reflection of what one would likely find and of the complexity of the human behavior that one typically encounters in one's daily life. Even with this knowledge, however, you do not yet have enough information to begin to understand why certain individual students seem to be adversely affected by the video arcade, let alone suggest a solution to the video arcade problem. The social psychological approach comes in handy at this point, and provides a useful framework for examining this redefined problem.

Social Psychological Ways of Looking at Problems

Throughout the development of social psychology during this century, competing views of how best to understand and predict peoples' behavior have been suggested. Within social psychology, these views can be roughly categorized into three types of approaches which differ according to the types of factors that are seen as the most useful for explaining a person's behavior and experience. These approaches differ according to the emphasis given to explanatory factors found in social situations (external factors) versus the person (internal psychological factors).

The Situation: Stimulus-Response Approach

B. F. Skinner was the best known spokesperson for the stimulus-response (S-R) approach. He was an advocate of behaviorism, an extreme form of *situationism*. Behaviorism has been on the decline as a framework for studying and explaining human behavior for several decades in all areas of psychology. Behaviorists argued that since peoples' attitudes, thoughts, feelings and motives cannot be seen, they are not worth studying or using in theories to explain human behavior. Skinner felt that the science of human behavior would be better served if psychologists focused on what they could observe with their eyes—the *circumstances* or *stimuli* in the individual's environment that triggered behavior, the actual *behavior* or *response* itself, and the *conditions* or *rewards* that led to the reoccurrence of the behavior in these circumstances.

Situationism suggests that social situations or settings act as *stimuli* to elicit a *response* (behavior) and that this predictable response occurs because it leads to positive consequences or *rewards*. In other words, if a behavior in which a person engages under particular circumstances reliably produces a reward, then the likelihood that these circumstances will lead to the behavior in the future is quite high. Consequently, social psychologists do not need to rely on unseen mental or cognitive dispositions or processes occurring within the individual to explain behavior.

If you as the researcher were to adopt this approach for understanding the video arcade–school truancy and larceny connection, you would develop explanations or theories that are restricted to identifying stimuli and rewards found in the social situations that are part of the students' daily lives. For example, you might theorize that the mere presence of the video arcade stimulates the response of video game playing. The rewards that maintain this behavior and perhaps result in it becoming excessive and "addictive" might include the admiring words of peers or the winning of free games. Video game playing at the arcade requires both the resources of time and money. You might theorize that these rewards are also responsible for students skipping school and stealing money. The reward for their deviant behavior is being able to continue to engage in the activity of video game playing. This theory would be consistent with a cause-and-effect link between the presence of the video arcade, video game playing, and students engaging in larceny and truancy.

If you follow the logic of the newspaper article and take a strict situational approach, you might expect a large number of the students at the school to be at risk and respond similarly to the video arcade situation. However, this massive increase in arcade video game playing and school crime is highly unlikely. The journalist in this article suggests that even the principal recognized that only a small number of students were likely involved. So counter to the "theory" suggested by the principal and police chief, the mere presence of the video arcade seems insufficient to explain this problematic leisure behavior.

How do you explain with situationalism why some students have become involved while others have not? You might take a closer look at other aspects of the social environment of the students and attempt to identify additional situational influences that affect some students and not others. For example, you could propose a theory that suggests that the presence of the video arcade is insufficient by itself to trigger excessive video game playing and problem school behavior. Perhaps, for the presence of the arcade to stimulate excessive video game playing and deviant activity there must be a peer subculture present that encourages and rewards such behavior. In addition to the perpetrators being members of peer groups that support this deviant behavior, you could theorize that they are likely to come from families with restricted financial resources. Consequently, students from these families do not have the money necessary to play at the arcade. Alternately, the problem students may not have part-time jobs or are uninvolved in extracurricular school activities and, therefore, have too much free time on their hands.

The Person: Organism-Response Approach

Many people would look elsewhere than the social situation for an explanation of why some students are involved in this deviant behavior and others are not. In fact, most people would want to know who these offending students were and something about them as individuals. Researchers who believe that differences among people can be measured and used to predict and explain why they behave as they do take a person or *organism-response* (O-R) approach. In contrast to situationism, the O-R approach is based on the assumption that people demonstrate stable and enduring differences in their needs, motives, attitudes and personalities, independent of the situation, which lead them to behave consistently across a wide range of situations, yet differently from one another. Consequently, if you want to understand why some students are attracted to the video arcade and engage in crime at school, you need to look for those characteristics that they carry around with them in their minds and that distinguish them from their more law-abiding peers.

A number of constructs have been used to identify and explain stable person differences, such as attitudes, needs, motives, and personality traits. These psychological dispositions may be learned, inherited, or a result of both types of influences. In the arcade example, what would be an attitudinal or personality disposition that might explain why some students are involved in the arcade and others are not, and why this activity leads to deviant school behavior for some? Perhaps some students have a greater need for excitement, what some researchers have called "sensation seeking." They may be more likely to get addicted to video playing and engage in deviant school behavior to maintain this activity and satisfy their need for excitement. There are a large number of psychological organismic or person differences that could be identified that might explain why some students are more susceptible than others. For example, you could hypothesize that the students involved in the truancy and larceny had the personality trait of being dishonest. Or perhaps those students with very negative attitudes toward authority are more susceptible to getting involved in behavior which is disapproved of by adults—in this case, playing video arcade games and school crime.

To test this theory, you could administer personality tests to the school population and ask the students to report the frequency of their video arcade playing as well as truancy and larceny. Researchers have developed paper-and-pencil tests to measure a large number of personality traits and attitudes. You could see if the personalities and attitudes of culprits differ from those of the other students.

In spite of the fact that most people rely heavily on individual differences and personality to explain and understand other people's behavior as well as their own, research has shown that people tend to overestimate the power of person factors in explaining behavior (Ross & Nisbett, 1991). In fact, people do not appear to behave as consistently in different situations as might be expected. People seen as "dishonest" are not dishonest in all situations, nor are "honest" people honest in all situations. A person's inflated belief in the importance of person factors for explaining behavior, together with the failure to recognize the importance of situational factors, has been termed the "fundamental attribution error" (Ross & Nisbett, 1991). Consequently, today most personality and social psychologists have adopted a framework that looks for explanations of people's behavior and experience in the interaction of social situation and person factors.

The Situation by the Person: Stimulus-Organism-Response Approach

Approaches that take both the *stimulus* or *situation* and the *organism* or *person* into consideration to explain *responses* or *behavior* are called *interactionism*. The assumption underlying interactionism is that people's behavior and experience can be best understood by taking into account both the influence of the social situation (e.g., the presence and behavior of other people), and the influence of what they bring to the situation (e.g., attitudes, motives, personality traits). The interaction of situation and person factors often results in different people perceiving or construing, and consequently, responding to the same objective situations quite differently. While interactionism may sound like a relatively straightforward idea, it turns out to be a complex notion with a number of versions. Not only can situation and person factors interact in different ways, but theorists differ in how they conceptualize the person factors.

One approach is based on the idea of *construal*, which refers to the personal and subjective meaning that people attach to situations (Ross & Nisbett, 1991). Social psychologists taking this approach assume that people's understanding of situations is the result of an active, constructive process, rather than a passive reception and registering of the situation. Consequently, the impact of any "objective" situation depends on the personal and subjective meaning that the individual attaches to that situation. To predict the behavior of a given person successfully, one must be able to appreciate her or his construal of the situation—that is, the manner in which the person understands the situation as a whole.

This perspective was most succinctly expressed by Lewin (1935) in his classic statement that behavior is a function of the person and the environment, that is, $B=f(P, E)$. Lewin believed that it is not the person and the environment that determine behavior, but a person-environment unit— what he called the *life space*. From this perspective the individual cannot be separated from the environment because "they interpenetrate one another in such a complex manner that any attempt to unravel them tends to destroy the natural unity of the whole and to create an artificial distinction between organism and environment" (p. 83). In the case of the video arcade problem, this approach suggests that the key to understanding the students' behavior lies in developing an idea of how they think and feel about the arcade and school settings.

Social psychological researchers who adopt the interactionist perspective differ to the extent that they feel that situation and person factors can be separated for study. On the one hand, some are interested in the general processes of social perception and construal common to all people—that is, the way people come to interpret their social environments and other people's behavior. In their research and analyses of behavior, these researchers are careful to assess how the people they are studying perceive and interpret the social contexts in which their behavior takes place. On the other hand, other researchers are interested in how the relatively stable personality, motivational and attitudinal differences that people carry around with them affect both how they perceive the social situations which they encounter and, in turn, how they respond to them. The following illustration from the video arcade problem would be an example of interactionism of the latter type. Students who are members of peer groups that value video playing expertise (social situation influence) would more likely to be addicted and commit deviant acts at school. However, only a small percentage of these students actually get addicted and are involved such deviant acts. Let's also say that a small portion of the students who are assessed as sensation seekers get involved (person influence), but again not all such students. Neither situation or person factors by themselves seem to explain very effectively the deviant behavior of concern. However, if you were to examine sensation seekers who are also members of peer groups who value video playing and find that a very high percentage of these students were hanging out at the arcade and engaging in deviant behavior at school, you would have a *situation by person interaction* and a much better explanation of the behavior in question.

This scenario exemplifies only one type or form of interactionism, that is, the *additive model of interactionism* (Endler, 1983). The behavior and experience of the individual are seen to be dependent on three sources of influence from situations, persons and their interaction. As noted previously, there was a small independent influence of the situational influence—a peer group. Also the person variable, the sensation seeker, had a small independent influence. However, it was only when these situation and person variables were both present or interacting that they have a strong influence on behavior.

Other types of interactionism differ in the way that the situation and person are seen to interact or influence a person's experience and behavior (Diener, Larsen & Emmons, 1984). For example *reciprocal interactionism* (Bowers, 1973; Pervin, 1968) is a more dynamic model. Reciprocal interactionism has been studied by researchers who believe in the importance of identifying and measuring stable individual differences (e.g., personality traits, needs, attitudes). It predicts that there is a relationship between personality and the situations people naturally choose to be in most of the time. In everyday life people usually have some freedom of choice over the types of situations in which they spend time. It might be expected that personality variables have an influence on this choice (Mischel, 1977). It also could be expected that in their everyday lives people when not constrained by situational demands would choose to spend their time in the kinds of settings that are most congruent or compatible with their personalities (Emmons, Diener & Larsen, 1986).

This model has some interesting implications for leisure researchers. In fact, a leisure researcher might expect that what people do during their leisure more accurately reflects their personalities than at any other time in their daily lives given the greater freedom to choose and fewer constraints operating in their social environments (Kulka, 1979; Pervin, 1968). High sensation seekers may choose to spend more time in video arcades and experience them more positively as a consequence of this "congruency" between their personalities and the situation. Consequently, person variables may be seen to operate at least twice. People choose to seek out specific situations and to avoid others based on differences in their personalities, and once in these situations person variables may influence their behavior and experience.

One final note on interactionism. Sometimes the situation may have more influence on a person's behavior and experience and at other times person factors may be more influential. It has been demonstrated (e.g., Mannell & Bradley, 1986; Monson, Hesley & Chernick, 1982; Price & Bouffard, 1974) that the effects of personality on behavior are likely to be greatest when situational influences are weak and consequently situations are less restrictive in terms of the possible behaviors that may be exhibited. For example, there may be circumstances in which being part of a social group or having friends who value video game playing may overpower personality differences in sensation seeking so that even people with a low need for sensation seeking become involved. When outside the peer group context, personality differences may have a stronger influence on participation or nonparticipation in this activity.

In the above discussion, the leisure problem of the video arcade has not been solved. Hopefully, the reader has arrived at a clearer understanding of social psychological thinking and analysis in action. Also, as the leisure services practitioner in this situation, you should have a better idea of where to look for answers and what types of information gathering might be useful in understanding the problem and developing effective solutions. The chapter will now be concluded by more formally defining social psychology and the social psychology of leisure.

Defining the Social Psychology of Leisure

Social psychology is the scientific study of the behavior and experience of individuals in social situations. The *social psychology of leisure* will be identified in much the same way with the addition that people's leisure behavior and experience are of specific interest. The video arcade problem demonstrated that social psychology is different than other types of knowing, including other social sciences and areas of psychology, because of its focus on the influence of social situations on the individual. Consequently, the *social psychology of leisure is the scientific study of the leisure behavior and experience of individuals in social situations.* To better understand this definition let's look at the terms in the definition and briefly summarize what was learned about the social psychology of leisure from the video arcade example.

The social psychology of leisure involves *scientific study*. As we discussed, there are many approaches to understanding how people think, feel and behave. One can learn about human behavior from novels, films, history, and philosophy. What makes social psychology different from these artistic and humanistic endeavors is the use of social science. It applies the *scientific method* of systematic observation, description, and measurement to the study of people.

The social psychology of leisure focuses on the *individual*. Many other disciplines also employ scientific techniques to study human behavior: anthropology, economics, political science, and sociology. All of these disciplines along with social psychology are called social sciences. They differ in the aspects of human behavior with which they deal. The level of analysis sets social psychology apart from other social sciences. Sociology, for instance, classifies people in terms of their nationality, race, socioeconomic class, and other social factors. Sociologists are more interested in how collectives of people, such as small groups, organizations, institutions, and societies as a whole operate. Social psychology is concerned with how individuals behave and perceive their social world: how they learn about it; remember what they experience in it; and appraise and evaluate it.

The social psychology of leisure involves the study of *experience and behavior*. Experience is a general term that refers to the awareness of the individual, and not just to past experiences. What a person perceives, feels, learns, or remembers—in a word, her or his experience—is often inferred from behavior. Researchers can also observe experience by communicating with people, that is, having people tell them what is on their minds. Behavior is comprised of those actions of the person that researchers can see and observe. However, even here a full understanding of behavior can only be achieved when a researcher knows what it means to the person who performed it. Consequently, the researcher will be interested in both leisure behavior and experience as defined "objectively" by outside observers and "subjectively" by the individual herself or himself. *Leisure*, itself, is challenging to define. There is no *one* way to define leisure. Definitions and measurements will vary depending on the nature of the leisure issue or problem. We will tackle defining leisure in chapters three and four.

Finally, the phrase *"in social situations"* refers to the social contexts in which most human behavior occurs. During the course of people's daily lives, they are constantly moving from one social context to another. Social situations refer to other individuals, groups, subcultures, cultures and even the products and creations (artifacts) of human activity such as films, books and the built environment that influence one's experience and behavior.

Limitations and Challenges

In this book, we have tried to present a reasonably coherent view of what is known about the social psychological foundations of people's leisure behavior and experience. In fact, we think it is fair to say that the social psychological study of leisure during the past 20 years or so has provided some fascinating insights into why people do what they do with their leisure, and how it impacts on the quality of their lives. We would not have written this book were we not strong advocates of the social psychological approach. However, there are some limitations of the social psychology of leisure as it is practiced today that should be kept in mind when reading this book.

First, there has been growing concern that the social psychology of leisure has been predominantly the study of male leisure behavior and experience until quite recently (see Henderson & Bialeschki, 1992; Henderson, 1994). Similarly, researchers have focused primarily on members of the dominant culture in North America and ignored cultural and ethnic differences (Gramann, 1995). It is only recently that there has been a real concern that leisure research take into consideration the impact of the different social experiences of men and women on the one hand, and of different cultural and ethnic groups on the other (Henderson, Bialeschki, Shaw & Freysinger, 1996). While there is no comprehensive social psychology of gender or cultural differences in leisure, in this book we have attempted select studies as illustrations wherever possible and appropriate that are sensitive to possible gender and cultural differences.

Second, there have been criticisms that leisure studies during the past two decades have, in fact, been too psychological; too myopically focused on the individual. This concern does not invalidate the social psychological approach. It should remind researchers, however, that many of the factors that influence people's attitudes, needs and personalities, as well as the social situations people encounter during their daily lives, are themselves influenced by broader social, political and economic forces—forces that require the perspectives of other social science and humanities disciplines if they are to be better understood (see Zuzanek, 1991a; Rojek, 1989; Kelly, 1988). For example, the question of how a society can reorganize its economy and sociopolitical institutions to better deal with the growth of automation, unemployment, and "forced" leisure requires sociological, political, and economic analyses. In fact, some issues may be outside the jurisdiction of science altogether as they deal with people's values and beliefs in what is good and bad, right and wrong.

Third, the framework of this book is strongly influenced by the social psychological traditions of North American psychology. As we will cover in the next chapter, North American social psychology is and has been strongly *quantitative* and *positivist*. This also has been largely true of research on the social psychology of leisure. Surveys, time diaries, and even experiments typically have been used by researchers to observe and *measure* leisure behavior and experience in an effort to develop and test theories about the causes and effects of leisure. A quantitative study is "an inquiry into a social or human problem based on testing a theory composed of variables, measured with numbers, and analyzed with statistical procedures in order to determine whether the predictive generalizations of the theory hold true" (Creswell, 1994, p. 2).

There are, however, social psychologies that are *qualitative* and *interpretive* (Fine, 1993; Ritzer & Gindoff, 1992), and recently leisure research from these perspectives has been increasing (Henderson, 1991a). Methods such as participant observation, unstructured interviews, case studies, and introspection are used to examine how people through their interactions with others develop shared meanings and understandings about their social worlds. A qualitative study is "defined as an inquiry process of understanding a social or human problem, based on building a complex, holistic picture, formed with words, reporting detailed views of informants, and conducted in a natural setting" (Creswell, 1994, p. 2–3). Rather than test already developed theories, qualitative researchers let their theories emerge from their observations of people.

Though a great deal of the research that has been carried out to further a social psychological understanding of leisure is quantitative, we have also drawn on qualitative leisure research in this book.

Finally, we would like to remind the reader that social science can never be completely value free. Many scientists today do not believe that science can ever be completely unbiased and objective. And indeed how could it be? Science is a human enterprise. Scientists choose what to study and how to study; their choices are influenced by their personal perspectives and values. However, good science is the effort to shake ourselves free of preconceptions, or at least become aware of them, and more clearly see what is going on around us as observers, even if never perfectly.

The Social Psychology of Leisure: Getting to Know It

Outline

Preview

In this chapter we discuss more about social psychology, the way leisure has been treated in mainstream social psychological research, and the emergence of the social psychology of leisure in the field of leisure studies. We begin by looking briefly at the history, development, and the types of questions that have been asked by social psychologists. Next, we examine the roots and emergence of the social psychology of leisure itself. After we have identified the kinds of problems and questions in which leisure researchers have been interested, and before we start looking at social psychological research on leisure, we consider the ethical issues involved in studying people scientifically.

Social Psychological Heritage

Beginnings

Psychology as a scientific field of study was created in the last quarter of the nineteenth century and has its roots in Western Europe and North America. Social psychology as a recognizable subfield did not get underway until sometime later. While not everyone agrees about who founded social psychology (Farr, 1991), generally two individuals are credited with completing the first social psychological research, American psychologist Norman Triplett and a French engineer, Max Ringelmann. Ringelmann's research was conducted in the 1880s, though not published until 1913. Triplett (1897–1898) published the first research article in social psychology at the end of the nineteenth century. The issue that Triplett was studying continues to be of interest today. Interestingly, the recreational and sporting activity of cycling was the subject of this first published social psychological study, though the focus was on the performance of the rider rather than the experience or meaning of the activity to the participant. As we mentioned in chapter one, the meaning and experience of leisure have typically been of interest to leisure researchers.

What made this a social psychological study was the fact that Triplett wanted to know what influence cycling with another person rather than alone would have on the speed of cycling. The study was also important because it demonstrated that complex social processes, in this case social influence, could be studied scientifically.

These isolated studies reported by Triplett and Ringelmann did not create social psychology as a distinct subfield of psychology. Writers of the first three textbooks in social psychology, the English psychologist William McDougall (1908) and Americans Edward Ross (1908) and Floyd Allport (1924), did much to distinguish a social psychological approach from a psychological approach and establish the boundaries of the field by identifying the topics, issues, and theories that were the subject matter of this new subfield—an area of psychology concerned with social influences on individual behavior.

Early Theory and Research

Social psychology was given a great boost through the research of a number of psychologists. One of the first important contributors was Muzafer Sherif. He was quite innovative and frequently controversial. In 1936

Sherif published an very influential study of social influence. Participants in this research observed a visual illusion (autokinetic effect)—a dot of light that was actually stationary but appeared to move. Watching alone in a darkened room, participants differed considerably in their individual estimates of the light's movement. When they watched together in groups, however, their estimates of the light's movement eventually converged. The location of the light itself never changed, but members of these groups would soon come to see the light move in the same way, that is, they developed shared norms or rules for how the light apparently moved. Sherif and other researchers have used this technique to study such processes as how groups develop and pass on norms to new group members, and the influence of the status or prestige of group members on norm development. Like Triplett's research, the research of Sherif was important for the development of social psychology because it demonstrated that it is possible to study complex behavior like social influence and norm formation in a rigorous, scientific manner.

Another important contributor to social psychology, as we have already noted, was Kurt Lewin. As we mentioned in the last chapter, Lewin's (1935) field theory specifies that *behavior* is a function of the interaction between the person and the environment, that is, B=f(P, E). Lewin also influenced the field with his strong interest in the application of social psychology to the analysis and solution of social problems. During the Second World War, it could be said that Lewin completed some of the first social psychology of health behavior research including how to promote more economical and nutritious eating habits (Lewin, 1947). Today, applied social psychology flourishes. Social psychological theory and research informs practitioners in areas such as advertising, business, education, environmental protection, health, law, politics, public policy, religion, sports and, of course, leisure.

Expansion and Enthusiasm

Following World War II and during the 1950s, the whole field of psychology grew dramatically, particularly in the United States (Benjamin, 1986). Increased government funding was available for teaching and research in universities on a whole range of issues. One of the most dramatic areas of growth was in the subfield of social psychology. There was tremendous enthusiasm and optimism that social science research and, in particular, social psychological research could help with the solutions to a wide range of social issues facing society. Major contributors carried out research in topic areas that are still of great significance, and in turn, they trained new generations of social psychologists. For example, researchers studied prejudice and stereotyping (e.g., Allport, 1954), conformity and person perception (e.g., Asch, 1956), cognitive dissonance and social comparison (e.g., Festinger, 1954, 1957), attribution and balance theory (e.g., Heider, 1958), attitudes and persuasion (e.g., Hovland, Janis & Kelley, 1953) and social exchange (e.g., Thibaut & Kelley, 1959).

This growth and enthusiasm continued into the 1960s. Social psychologists considered how people thought (Kelley, 1967) and felt (Schachter, 1964) about themselves and others. They studied interactions in groups (Moscovici & Zavalloni, 1969) and social problems such as why people fail to help others in distress (Latane & Darley, 1970). They examined aggression (Bandura, 1973), the psychological impact of physical attractiveness (Berscheid & Walster, 1974), and stress (Glass & Singer, 1972).

Crisis of Confidence

Not all social psychologists were confident of the success of social psychology. Some called it a time of crisis (e.g., Elms, 1975). Many of the disagreements among social psychologists during this period can be understood as a reaction to the dominant research method used—the laboratory experiment. Those who questioned the laboratory method maintained that certain practices were unethical (Kelman, 1967), that experimenters' expectations influenced their subjects' behavior (Orne, 1962; Rosenthal, 1966), and that the theories being tested in the laboratory couldn't be applied to understanding behavior outside the laboratory in daily life or different cultures (Gergen, 1973).

Present Day Perspectives

Though these issues continue to be debated today, social psychology has been able to progress helped by a better understanding of its strengths and weaknesses. The debate on ethics has led to more rigorous and uniform standards for research as we will point out later in this chapter (Allport, 1985). Greater attention is being given to the limitations and possible biases of frequently used research methods. Laboratory experiments continue to be done, but there has been a gradual acceptance of a wider variety of research methods (Houts, Cook & Shadish, 1986). It has been recognized that different topics require different kinds of approaches. Research techniques range from the laboratory experiment to interviews and naturalistic observation. Each technique has unique advantages and disadvantages, and any single topic can benefit from being investigated by a number of approaches. Laboratory research on leisure has been infrequent, but a variety of research approaches have been used in social psychological leisure research.

Social psychology today continues to be a dynamic field. Though certain ideas remain important to how social psychologists explain people's behavior, theories and approaches change and evolve, and go in and out of popularity. For example, important *theories about attitudes and attitude change* were developed and tested in the 1950s. In the 1960s *consistency theories* dominated. They were developed to explain when inconsistencies among a person's cognitions (i.e., beliefs, attitudes and values) or between cognitions and actions would motivate them to change either their beliefs or their behavior (Berkowitz & Devine, 1989). *Attribution theory* emerged in the 1970s and the theory helps explain the kinds of causal explanations people give for the events in their lives and the effects these causal inferences have on their social behavior (Weiner, 1986). Beginning in the late 1970s and continuing to the present, *social cognition* (the study of how people perceive, remember, and interpret information about themselves and others) has proven very influential (Devine, Hamilton & Ostrom, 1994). Now in the 1990s, theories that attempt to explain people's behavior in a more holistic manner by accounting for emotions and motivations, on the one hand, and cognitions, on the other, are being proposed (Boggiano & Pittman, 1992).

North American social psychology has dominated the field. Consequently, it has been open to the criticism that its theories and research findings may not be applied across gender, ethnic, and cultural lines. Fortunately, social psychology is developing greater international and multicultural scope and there is an increased recognition of alternative social psychological approaches emerging in cultures other than those of North America and Western Europe (Moghaddam, 1987). An interest in women and gender issues has emerged. Also, there are growing numbers of women in the field and social psychologists can be found in may different countries (Berscheid, 1992). Hopefully, social psychological principles and theories applicable to a wider range of people will result from this greater diversity.

Finally, the new diversity in social psychology is reflected by the many applied areas to which social psychologists contribute research and theory. The value of social psychology for understanding contemporary life has been recognized by psychologists and nonpsychologists alike. Many fields (e.g., business, education, health, social work, journalism, recreation) now require courses in social psychology for their students. Many researchers trained in professional or applied disciplines, though not social psychologists, have a substantial research training in the social psychological approach, its theories, and research methods. Social psychology often finds itself "hyphenated to reflect its alliances with other areas of psychology and fields outside of psychology: social-development, social-clinical, social-personality, social psychology and law, social-health, social-organizational, social-educational, social-environmental, and social-community" (Berscheid, 1992, p. 531). Social psychologists "have become the vanguard of the movement to extend the boundaries of traditional psychology into the realms vital to contributing solutions for real-world problems—the areas of health, ecology, education, law, peace and conflict resolution, and much more" (Zimbardo, 1992, p. xiv).

Treatment of Leisure in Social Psychology

Social psychologists have been interested in what they consider the *basic social psychological processes* which underlie all human behavior across all types of social situations and settings. For example, the processes of norm formation, interpersonal attraction, or learned helplessness would seem to operate regardless of the social context—whether it be a work, leisure, education, or health context. However, a number of specialized areas have evolved, for example, the social psychology of work (Argyle, 1990), the social psychology of health (Rutter & Quine, 1994), and the social psychology of leisure (Iso-Ahola, 1995). In these subfields, not only have major social psychological theories been applied to understanding the issues of interest, but theories specific to these subfields have been developed.

Leisure researchers began to draw on social psychology in the late 1960s and deliberate attempts to develop and promote a social psychology of leisure emerged in the early to late 1970s (see Iso-Ahola, 1980a, 1988; Mannell, 1984a). With his 1980 textbook, Seppo Iso-Ahola contributed to the development of the social psychology of leisure by identifying theory and research from mainstream social psychology that had very direct relevance for understanding leisure behavior. This widely used book also demonstrated that in spite of the small amount of social psychological research done on leisure at the time, there were many interesting questions to be studied and good potential for further development.

Mainstream social psychology, itself, during the past 80 or 90 years has paid relatively little attention to leisure. However, as we suggested in our brief historical overview of social psychology, researchers have occasionally studied the social processes that interested them in leisure and play contexts. For example, William McDougall (1908) in the first textbook on social psychology, identified play as a basic human instinct or tendency. A few years later G. T. W. Patrick (1916) wrote a book on the *Psychology of Relaxation*. Floyd Allport (1924) in his social psychology text argued that leisure serves as a form of need compensation—compensation for oppressive work. Since the emergence of these early works, a number of social psychological studies have been reported which have implications for understanding leisure, though their focus was not to study leisure specifically.

Social Influence on Cycling and Football Spectators

Leisure settings have provided a useful testing ground over the years for numerous studies of basic social psychological processes. The 1898 bicycle experiment reported by Triplett is a good example. He was a bicycle enthusiast and a social scientist. On the basis of his own experience, he theorized that cyclists ride faster over a given distance when in the presence of other riders than when alone, even when the cyclists in both situations are trying to perform their best. To test his theory, he devised an experiment in which some riders attempted to cycle as fast as they could alone while others cycled in the presence of other cyclists.

Triplett found that those individuals who performed in the presence of others cycled five seconds per mile faster than lone cyclists. He described this phenomenon as the *dynamogenic* or the *rabbit effect*. The influence of the presence of other people on performance has continued to interest researchers and today this phenomenon is known as the *social facilitation effect* (Zajonc, 1965). However, Triplett's study was not an attempt to understand cycling as a leisure behavior, but rather to examine or discover an underlying principle of general human behavior—the influence of other people on an individual's performance.

A second research study that can be used to illustrate the use of leisure contexts to examine general social psychological principles was based on a rather infamous college football game (Hastorf & Cantril, 1954). The Dartmouth and Princeton football game, played during the 1940s between the two rival schools, was billed as a grudge match. It has been called the dirtiest and roughest game in the history of the two schools. Dartmouth was out to get Princeton's all-American, Dick Kazmaier, and eventually did as he was forced to leave with a broken nose. A player on the other team received a broken leg and there were fist fights throughout the game.

In this study, the researchers showed film clips of the game to students from each school some months later. The objective for the students was to spot infractions of the rules. Students from both schools observed and reported twice as many violations by players from the opposing team during this study, demonstrating the way in which social perception can be influenced by group membership or reference group loyalty.

Social Perception and Group Behavior at Camp

The *Robbers' Caves Studies* of Muzafer Sherif and his associates (Sherif, Harvey, White, Hood & Sherif, 1961) were carried out in the leisure setting of a summer camp to study general social psychological principles. These studies took place at Connecticut, New York, and Oklahoma camps. Sherif and his colleagues selected psychologically normal 9-year-old to 13-year-old boys from middle-class backgrounds. The boys were randomly assigned to two groups and each group was sent to different areas and facilities at the camps and for first week were unaware of the presence of the other group.

The researchers used the boys' involvement in camp and outdoor recreation activities to study the formation of norms and leadership in groups. Eventually, the two groups of boys were made aware of each other and a series of competitive games were staged. The researchers observed the impact that this intergroup competition had on the group norms and leadership structures that had already developed. For example, they found that in some groups norms for toughness evolved to the point where the boys would not report injuries to camp counselors. Also, the leadership structure of the groups often changed. Now that the tasks facing the groups shifted from noncompetitive and friendship-oriented activities to competing successfully and winning against other groups, different boys, often those with good athletic skills and toughness, became the leaders.

Sherif and his research team also built experiments into the camping experience through the use of games. To study how group membership affected perceptions of other people, the researchers had the boys participate in a game that required them to estimate the number of beans collected by themselves and the other boys. They were asked individually to judge how many beans each of the other boys had collected in the game. The researchers found that both group membership and the leadership structure of the groups influenced these perceptions. For example, the boys tended to judge boys who were members of their own group, the in-group, as more competent at the task than members of an out-group. Also, the higher the status of a boy in his own group, the more competent at this task he was judged to be by the other group members. These judgments were actually unrelated to how well each of the boys had done at the task.

Finally, the researchers were interested in the impact of getting these, by now, antagonist groups of boys involved in cooperative activities. They found that by presenting the boys with a common problem that required them all to work together, for example, finding a leak in the camp waterline that came down from the surrounding hills, the boys eventually decreased their competitiveness, aggressiveness, and dislike of the members of other groups. Establishing such a "superordinate goal," which required cooperation for its achievement, worked better than rewards and church sermons.

Rewards in the Playroom and Altruism at the Beach

Social psychologists continue to use leisure settings or situations to study basic social psychological processes. The first major study of intrinsic motivation and the factors that undermine it, the *overjustification effect*, involved studying children playing with colored markers in a "play room" (Lepper, Greene & Nisbett, 1973). As we will present in a later chapter, these researchers found that rewarding people to do things that they already enjoy can reduce their motivation to engage in activities for the enjoyment and personal satisfaction they offer.

A study of altruism or helping behavior by Moriarity (1975) took place in a leisure setting on a beach with sunbathers. In this study, a confederate of the researcher would spread out her blanket and put an expensive radio on it near an unsuspecting sunbather. A short time later, the confederate would get up and leave for a few minutes. After leaving, a second confederate of the researcher would approach, grab and "steal" the first confederate's radio. The researcher then observed how the sunbather reacted. In some cases, the first confederate would ask the sunbather to watch her possessions. As one might expect, getting a commitment from the sunbather was more likely to result in this person engaging in some kind of helping behavior. Only 20 percent of the bystanders attempted to help when they had made no commitment to do so, whereas 95 percent intervened when the commitment had been established. When individuals feel personal responsibility, they are significantly more likely to act in an altruistic way.

Emergence of Personality During Leisure

The last example we will present is based on two studies reported by Ed Diener, Robert Emmons and Randy Larsen (1984; 1986). In these studies, the researchers did not start out with any particular interest in leisure, nor were they interested in contributing to a social psychological understanding of leisure. However, their research examined certain social psychological processes that underlie human behavior, and interestingly, they found that these processes were more likely to be seen in recreational contexts. Essentially, they found that people's personalities were more likely to influence their behavior and experience in recreational settings. For example, they measured how outgoing and extroverted the university students in their study were. They then had these students carry diaries with them every day for a number of weeks. The students recorded their activities, the different social settings in which they became involved and how they felt when involved (moods). When the researchers analyzed this information, they found that the students' personalities were more likely to affect the choice of activities and settings in which they participated during their leisure. For example, extroverts were more likely to choose to be involved in social activities and introverts solitary activities in recreational situations. Such differences did not appear in other contexts such as work. Extroverts also had more enjoyable experiences when with other people than when alone, whereas those subjects who were more introverted experienced greater enjoyment in solitary activities. This personality difference in choice of activities and level of enjoyment was not found for nonrecreational situations. It would seem that the effect of personality on behavior and experience is likely to be greatest when situations are less restrictive and allow greater freedom of choice. Of course, freedom of choice is central to notions of leisure.

These types of studies, though not carried out to further knowledge of leisure behavior per se, do provide an idea of how the basic social psychological principles of human behavior can be used to explain leisure behavior. A number of studies referred to in this book will be of this sort and contribute to the understanding of not only leisure but behavior in general. The last study mentioned, however, suggests that there may exist social psychological principles that are more likely to operate in leisure contexts.

Social Psychological Approaches to Leisure Studies

Though efforts to study leisure as a topic in its own right with psychological science have a short 20 to 25 year history, the social psychological approach has emerged to be an influential framework guiding leisure research in North America. From the mid-1960s to the early 1970s research studies using social psychological concepts began to appear. Systematic efforts to develop the social psychology of leisure as a distinct field began in the mid to late 1970s.

However, prior to this "psychologization" of leisure studies, there was much written about leisure-related issues by people in the recreation field, as well as those outside of it, dating back to the first quarter of the twentieth century (Zuzanek, 1982, 1991a; Barnett & Wade, 1988). As community and government agencies became more involved in leisure services, and university programs in recreation and leisure studies developed in the United States and Canada, recreation practitioners, educators and researchers contributed to the development of applied recreation research dealing with the management and provision of leisure services. Much of this early work attempted to justify and promote the need for leisure services and resulted in a great deal of uncritical, highly speculative and moralistic writing about the benefits of these services. These types of publications found their way relatively quickly into the curricula of the newly emerging university recreation degree programs of the time and to a large extent contributed to the formulation of the social philosophy of the recreation profession (Zuzanek, 1982; Kelly, 1988).

Of the social sciences, sociology was the major contributor of both theory and research on the role and nature of leisure in modern industrial society. While the emergence of a social psychology of leisure is relatively recent, the recognition of the importance of the social context and the person in understanding leisure can be found in the writings of a number of early leisure scholars.

Applied Recreation Research

The development of leisure research was driven by the need of providers of leisure services for information to improve and justify these services. In the United States, the social reform movement arising in response to social conditions at the end of the last century stimulated investigations of the recreational needs and interests of people living in industrial cities, particularly children. The first published experimental study in the recreation field explored play and playground use in the 1890s, and was conducted by Joseph Lee, the first president of the Playground Association of America (Barnett & Wade, 1988). At the turn of the century, Lee had set up his own experimental playground to determine the best type of administration, leadership, design, and programs for play areas (Knapp & Hartsoe, 1979).

Educators concerned with the physical health of school children were the first to conduct systematic studies on the physical activity participation and preferences of children. The growth of recreation and leisure research was given a significant boost by the formation of the Playground Association of America in 1906, which later became the National Recreation Association in 1926. Numerous nationwide surveys were conducted in the United States to learn what public, private, and commercial facilities were available, what people needed for recreation, and what types of administration were needed in communities for public recreation (Barnett & Wade, 1988). This type of applied, practitioner-oriented research lead to the publication of *Parks: A Manual of Municipal and County Parks* (1928) by L. H. Weir, considered by many authors (e.g., Zuzanek, 1982; Allen, 1988; Barnett & Wade, 1988) to provide the first comprehensive introduction to park management and recreation administration.

In the United States and Canada, municipal parks and outdoor recreation soon began to attract the support of different levels of government. These developments, particularly in the United States, stimulated applied leisure research. Beginning in the 1930s and continuing into the 1940s and 1950s, a number of local and national studies were completed to obtain information on existing recreational facilities and areas, to analyze existing plans and problems, and to determine future needs so that plans and policies could be formulated to meet recreational needs (Barnett & Wade, 1988).

The 1930s also saw attempts to promote leisure as a form of therapeutic intervention. Little research was carried out, but a great deal of writing in this area was educationally oriented and discussed how to educate or prepare different groups within the population for more efficient use of the growing amount of leisure time available (Zuzanek, 1982). However, the field of therapeutic recreation as a clearly defined field did not develop until much later. Empirical research began to emerge in the late 1960s and 1970s with an increase in efforts to evaluate and test the principles and practices used to guide interventions with the recipients of therapeutic services. However, much of this research has not built on previously completed research and there have been few efforts to systematically develop programs of research focused on important themes or problems in therapeutic recreation (Witt, 1988; MacNeil, 1995).

Improving recreation management practices was a theme of early empirical studies. During the 1930s, investigations were undertaken to describe, evaluate and improve services. These studies were concerned with such issues as the role of supervision in play areas on delinquency among boys, financial support of playground and recreation activities in different areas, and the relationship between public and private recreation agencies to name only a few (Allen, 1988). Interest in specific areas of management such as finance, personnel, and policy development grew in the 1950s and 1960s. Also, a more concerted effort was made to evaluate management principles and programs. During the past several decades there has been considerable growth in the number and sophistication of researchers and in the quality of leisure management research related to marketing, personnel, finance, evaluation and planning (Allen, 1988).

Social Science Efforts

Although the first pioneering works that explore the role and meaning of leisure in the life of society can be placed in the late 19th to early 20th century (e.g., Thorstein Veblen's, *The Theory of the Leisure Class* in 1899), the beginnings of truly systematic social science research, primarily sociological, began in the late 1920s. Sociologists examined leisure as a social phenomenon rather than as a moral issue, an object of social reform or a management issue.

For example, Lynd and Lynd (1929, 1937) examined the structure of everyday community life based on well-designed surveys and thorough observation. As well as examining people's work, family life, community activities, and religious practices, the Lynds' research provided extremely interesting insights into the changing patterns of leisure involvement and attitudes during a ten-year period. Lundberg, Komarovsky and McInerny's (1934) sociological study attempted to examine leisure behavior as part of the social structure of U.S. society. Leisure behavior and community participation were examined as a function of social class, race, ethnicity, political affiliation, family structure, and community recreation institutions (Zuzanek, 1982).

Sociologists have continued to contribute to the study of leisure. The Chicago Center for the Study of Leisure established in the 1950s served as a catalyst for social science research on leisure phenomena. Examples of this work include the study of leisure as part of more general trends of social and cultural change (e.g., Riesman's *Lonely Crowd*, 1950), the relationship between leisure and social stratification (e.g., Smigal, 1963), and sociocultural meanings of leisure behavior (e.g., de Grazia, 1964). Some commentators have argued that the sociology of leisure has not lived up to the exciting expectations created during the 1950s and 1960s (Zuzanek, 1982) and that there has been a lack of theory building and conceptual linkage with mainstream sociology (Godbey, 1988).

"Psychologization" of Leisure Studies

Prior to what we have been calling the "psychologization" of leisure studies, one can find in the writings of various authors, attempts to explain leisure behavior in terms that are social psychological. Many texts and influential writings on leisure have speculated about the psychological effects of leisure on the individual, in particular personality development (Iso-Ahola, 1980a). Authors have claimed that play and recreation are good for children since they promote a sense of justice, decision-making ability, self-control, perseverance and initiative, as well as social skills such as kindness, friendliness and tolerance. However, as Iso-Ahola noted, though leisure philosophers and writers acknowledged the importance of social psychological variables, little theory development and research was carried out.

Some of the earliest empirical work that can be labeled social psychological was done by researchers in the United States interested in understanding why people participate in outdoor recreation. Interest in the motivations and satisfactions associated with outdoor recreation emerged in the 1960s, blossomed in the 1970s, and continues to flourish today (Manning, 1985). Early studies (e.g., Bultena & Taves, 1961; Burch 1965, 1969; LaPage, 1974) found diverse motivations for participation in camping and wilderness use.

The founding of the *Journal of Leisure Research* in 1969 gave an important push to the development of the social psychology of leisure. Although, it was not exclusively psychologically oriented, the journal did provide an outlet for contributions in this area (Iso-Ahola, 1995). Early published research on leisure used such social psychological concepts and approaches as attitudes (e.g., Neulinger & Briet, 1969; Brown, 1970; Heberlein, 1973), motivation and satisfaction (e.g., Bultena & Klessig, 1969; Burch, 1969; Mercer, 1973), group behavior (e.g., Field & O'Leary, 1973; West & Merriam, 1970), environmental influences (e.g., Witt & Bishop, 1970; Knopp, 1972), socialization (e.g., Bishop & Chace, 1971;

Yoesting & Burkhead, 1973; Kelly, 1974) and interactionism (e.g., Bishop & Witt, 1970). A number of studies were also published that began to explore social psychological strategies for measuring leisure (e.g., Bishop, 1970; Bull, 1971; Kelly, 1973; Witt, 1971).

In the 1970s, Driver and his associates began laying a more systematic social psychological foundation for the study of motivations in outdoor recreation (e.g., Driver & Toucher, 1970; Driver & Brown, 1975; Driver, 1976). To better understand why people choose to participate in particular activities, the rewards they receive from participation and the factors that enhance the quality of the experience derived from participation, a psychological approach was proposed where recreation was defined as "an experience that results from recreation engagements" (Driver & Tocher, 1970, p. 10).

Calls for the systematic development of social psychological approaches for the study of leisure emerged early in the 1970s. Driver (1972) argued for the potential contributions that social psychology could make to recreation resource management. John Neulinger, in his book *The Psychology of Leisure* (1974), also argued for the importance of psychology for studying and understanding leisure. Like Driver and his associates, Neulinger argued that the subjective nature of leisure requires the theories, methods and tools of psychology if it is to be studied effectively. Neulinger's well-known book was the first written on the psychology of leisure and he contributed substantially by outlining important issues that could be studied. He also drew the attention of researchers to a variety of social psychological theories and research areas that had relevance to the study of leisure. For example, Neulinger suggested that the social psychological concepts of *time perception, boredom, sensory deprivation, locus of control, perceived freedom* and *intrinsic motivation* might prove useful for understanding leisure. He also advocated a "person-environment" interaction approach for the study of leisure experiences (Neulinger, 1974, p. 110), and for the use of laboratory experiments (p. 132–133). In subsequent chapters, the reader will discover that a number of these suggestions have been picked up and explored by leisure researchers.

Most of the research and theory in the psychological study of leisure has been done from a social psychological perspective (Mannell, 1984a; Ingham, 1986; Iso-Ahola, 1995). In 1978 the first Psychology/Social Psychology of Leisure Session was held in Miami, Florida, and organized by Seppo Iso-Ahola as part of the Leisure Research Symposium associated with the National Recreation and Parks Association. This symposium session is today a major annual meeting place of researchers working in the social psychology of leisure area. Also, the other sessions such as management, human development, therapeutic recreation, and sociology have become psychologized with the frequent reporting of studies focusing on social psychological variables (Iso-Ahola, 1995).

Another significant contribution to the development of a social psychology of leisure, as we suggested earlier, was provided by Iso-Ahola with the publication of his 1980 textbook, *The Social Psychology of Leisure and Recreation.* As an introductory textbook for several generations of students, it has contributed to the definition of the boundaries of the emerging field and provided students with an idea of what it is like to examine leisure from a social psychological perspective.

There has been a 17-year gap between the publication of the Iso-Ahola textbook and the next textbook—this one. Social psychology, itself, went through a 13-year hiatus in textbooks from the early 1950s to the mid-1960s (Berscheid, 1992, p. 529). However, a great deal of social psychological leisure research has occurred since the Iso-Ahola textbook was published. In 1980, two edited books on the psychology and social psychology of leisure were published (Iso-Ahola, 1980b; Ibrahim & Crandall, 1980). Phillip Pearce published a textbook on social psychology of tourist behavior in 1982. A number of edited works have reviewed significant advances in the field. Gaétan Ouellet edited a special issue of the journal, *Society and Leisure* in 1984 on the social psychological study of leisure. In the same year Peter Stringer edited a special issue of *Annals of Tourism Research* on the social psychology of tourism. Most of the chapters in Wade's edited book the following year, *Constraints on Leisure* (1985), were social psychological analyses of leisure, as were many of those in Edgar Jackson and Thomas Burton's 1989 edited book, *Understanding Leisure and Recreation.* Also, the major journals in the field of leisure studies publish a great deal of research done from a social psychological perspective.

Today, research on leisure motivation and satisfaction continues in the outdoor recreation area and has been applied to many types of leisure behavior (see Manning, 1985; Mannell, 1989; see chapter six). Innovative research methods and concepts have lead to advances in researchers' ability to conceptualize, measure and understand leisure experiences and states, as well as behavior, from a psychological perspective (see Shaw, 1985a; Mannell & Iso-Ahola, 1987; Samdahl, 1991; Dattilo & Kleiber, 1993; Mannell & Dupuis, 1994; see chapters three and four). Coupled with these developments, considerable research has been done in the area of understanding the role that perceived freedom and intrinsic motivation play in leisure (see Barnett, 1991; Iso-Ahola, 1989; see chapters five and seven).

Individual differences in leisure behavior and personality were barely addressed in the early years with a few exceptions (e.g., Driver & Knopf, 1977; Iso-Ahola, 1976; Kleiber, 1979), but with the development of leisure-specific personality constructs, it has become an active area of study (see Kleiber and Dirkin, 1985; Iso-Ahola, 1995; see chapter six). Early interest in measuring leisure attitudes cooled, and only recently has there been a renewed interest in how to influence and change leisure attitudes (Manfredo, 1992; see chapter eleven). Interest in leisure socialization and the influence of life cycle changes on leisure (and vice versa) has continued to grow (see Kleiber & Kelly, 1980; Osgood & Howe, 1984; Freysinger, 1990; see chapters eight and nine), as has the concern for the relationship between work and leisure, and how people organize and balance the work, leisure and family domains of their lives (see Kabanoff & O'Brien, 1986; Kirchmeyer, 1993; Freysinger, 1994; see chapter ten).

Also, there has been a growth in interest in gender and leisure in recent years (Henderson, Bialeschki, Shaw & Freysinger, 1989, 1996) and there appears to be an emerging interest in sociocultural and cross-cultural factors, and ethnicity as they affect leisure (see Allison, 1988; Ammassari, 1991; Floyd, McGuire, Shinew & Noe, 1994). Recently, a concern for the health benefits of leisure has grown (e.g., Coleman & Iso-Ahola, 1993) as well as other leisure benefits. In fact, several organizing frameworks with a social psychological basis have emerged in the field of leisure studies that are concerned with enhancing leisure. The constructs of *leisure benefits* (see Driver, Brown & Peterson, 1991b; see chapter ten) and *leisure constraints* (see Jackson, 1988; see chapter twelve) have been developing and providing a means of organizing and thinking about much of the social psychological research that has been done as it applies to recreation practice. Identifying the benefits and costs of leisure behavior will likely emerge as a research priority during the next decade. In the case of constraints research, the focus of the research has expanded to include the identification of factors that encourage leisure involvement (i.e., affordances) and negotiation strategies employed by people to overcome constraints.

The Ethics of Studying People

We have now outlined the *social psychological approach* and suggested that many researchers have found it to be useful for developing an understanding of leisure. An important aspect of the approach is the belief that people's behavior and experience can be understood as a result of their *interactions* with the social settings they encounter in their daily lives. The social psychological approach is also a *scientific* way of knowing. This means that to study leisure, researchers must systematically and carefully observe people's behavior and assess their feelings, perceptions, beliefs, and attitudes. Typically, when researchers study and observe people, they intrude on or intervene in their lives in some way. This raises *ethical concerns*. Before moving on to examine what leisure researchers have come to know about leisure using social psychology, we briefly examine the ethics of studying people.

Just as social psychology and the social psychology of leisure have evolved and developed, so have views about how the people who participate in social psychologists research should be treated. Although researchers in all fields have a moral and legal responsibility to abide by ethical principles, discussions about ethical standards for studying people have been particularly intense in social psychology (Diener & Crandall, 1978; Greenberg & Folger, 1988). For the most part, concerns about the treatment of research participants has been created by the frequent use of deception that is often built into laboratory studies (Baumrind, 1985; Kelman, 1967). Also, in many nonexperimental studies, participants often are not fully informed about the purpose of the research, at least not until after it is completed.

Studies have been published in which those people participating, though not in danger physically, may have been at risk psychologically. For example, studies have examined the conditions under which people will obey orders to harm an innocent person (Milgram, 1963), and act brutally as part of a social role (Zimbardo, 1973). Though these studies addressed issues of social concern, the question remains, "Does the significance of research topics such as these justify exposing people to the possibly harmful psychological effects?"

Today, none of these studies could be conducted in their original form. But even with current provisions for safeguarding the welfare of human research participants, some research still raises ethical concerns. For example, in the study by Moriarity (1975), was it fair for people sunbathing on a beach to be approached by a collaborator of the researcher and asked to keep an eye on an expensive radio, and then be faced with the stress of seeing it "stolen" and having to make a decision about what to do about it? Mannell (1986) conducted an experimental laboratory study some years ago in which the participants were mislead as to how much choice they had to engage in a leisure activity. The deception was fully described to them following the study, yet, was even this minor deception warranted? Not everyone will agree on the answers to these questions. However, there has emerged agreement about the process investigators must follow in examining the ethical aspects of their research.

In Canada and the United States, there are government regulations requiring review boards at institutions where researchers seek government funding for research involving human participants. At most colleges and universities researchers, including student researchers, must get their research proposals and plans approved by committees set up to ensure that the welfare of research participants is protected. Complaints about additional bureaucracy are sometimes heard, though these review procedures have become widely accepted among researchers. Also, the likelihood of a proposal being accepted is not always based on ethical considerations (Ceci, Peters & Plotkin, 1985). Researchers worry that these committees can censor their right to do what they consider to be important research on the basis of political and social issues unrelated to ethical problems.

Researchers are also required to abide by their profession's code of ethics. For example, the American and Canadian Psychological Associations have developed codes of ethics that affect research procedures and practices. These codes stipulate that researchers are to carefully weigh the benefits of research to the development of knowledge and society against any mental or physical costs involved for the participants (Cook, 1976).

To protect the welfare of the people in their research, researchers are typically required to obtain *informed consent*. People must be asked whether they wish to participate in the research and must be given enough information to make an informed decision. They must be told that they can withdraw from the research at any time. But what about informing the participants about all of the procedures to be used in the research? Many of the studies of leisure behavior reviewed in this book would have been impossible if the participants had been told about the study beforehand. Even if social psychologists do not "deceive" research participants, it is often necessary to delay full disclosure of the purpose of the research until after the study is over so that participants will *behave naturally*.

Should informed consent be obtained from people observed in a public place like a shopping mall, a playground, or an auction? Should the purpose of research involving anonymous questionnaires or naturalistic observations require full disclosure of the purpose of the research and informed consent? Most researchers believe that the most important factor in protecting the welfare of research participants is to guarantee their *anonymity* (Babbie, 1992). The individual's privacy must be strictly guarded by keeping her or his identity completely hidden in any report on the study.

Have you ever been a participant in a social psychology study of leisure or some other type of behavioral study? Did you find it interesting and did it provide you with any insights into your own or other people's behavior? Did the researcher tell you about the study after your involvement? Another ethical standard is that researchers *debrief* all study participants. Debriefing is a process that occurs after all the research data has been collected. At this time, the researcher goes over all the procedures used, explaining exactly what happened and why. Any deceptions are revealed, full details on the purpose of the research are discussed, and the researcher makes every effort to help the research participants feel comfortable about their participation. Debriefing can be effective in both getting the facts straight and making the experience less stressful. Participation in research can also be an interesting and informative experience. Research participants are often treated as collaborators; they and the researcher are on a mission of discovery together. The research also may encourage participants to recall and think about what they do or feel in response to events in their daily lives. For example, research methods that have people record what they do during the course of a day may provide them with the opportunity to examine how they spend their time and the relative benefits of different activities to their well-being. Sometimes participation in a study can encourage people to systematically consider issues of relevance to their lives, but issues that they had not clearly articulated or would have taken the time to think about (Mannell, 1990).

In the following chapters leisure research is reviewed that varies widely in terms of its purpose, the setting in which it was conducted, the research techniques used, and the measures employed. The reader will have an opportunity to assess the researchers' abilities to treat the people they studied ethically and, at the same time, make the systematic observations needed to understand leisure from the social psychological perspective.

Leisure as Behavior, Setting and Time

Chapter THREE

Outline

Preview

The Challenge of Defining and Measuring Leisure: Mapping the Terrain

Classifying Leisure Definitions and Measures
Type of Phenomena
Definitional Vantage Point: External and Internal
Back to the Video Arcade

Measuring Leisure Behavior and Time
Leisure Behavior Inventories
Time Diaries
Direct Observation
Strengths and Limitations of These Approaches

Internal Vantage Point of the Participant

Progress in Definition and Measurement

Preview

One of the most actively written about and researched areas in the social psychology of leisure is the *nature of leisure* itself. The story of the quest to understand the nature of leisure from a social psychological perspective is also the tale of the ways that researchers have attempted to translate various philosophical, historical, and sociological notions of leisure into constructs that can be observed, measured, and studied scientifically. There is not necessarily a right or wrong way to conceptualize and define leisure. Different approaches have their advantages as well as limitations. Some strategies work better for certain types of questions researchers want answered, and other strategies are more useful for a different set of problems. In this chapter, we will begin examining the definitional terrain of the various approaches to conceptualizing and measuring leisure, and attempt to provide a road map to help the reader find her or his way. Next, we will examine how leisure has been conceptualized and measured as behavior, setting and time while assessing the strengths and limitations of the approaches used. The next chapter will pick up the story and discuss attempts to conceptualize and measure the experiential nature of leisure. To help in understanding each of these approaches, selected research studies will be presented and used to illustrate how these conceptual and measurement approaches differ, and can be used to study the nature, quantity, and quality of leisure.

The Challenge of Defining and Measuring Leisure: Mapping the Terrain

In the *video arcade problem* examined in chapter one, the reader faced the challenge of deciding whether playing a video game in an arcade is leisure. Deciding what is and what is not leisure is an ongoing issue that researchers must deal with in their studies. Before a researcher can look at the factors that affect people's leisure and how leisure in turn affects people, a researcher must have some sense of what it is, what it looks like, and how to observe or measure it.

Most people with some interest in leisure, at one time or another, have tried their hand at defining leisure. Finding a way to define and measure leisure has been the holy grail of leisure scholars, although some observers feel it is about as unattainable, and that little progress has been made (e.g., Sessoms, 1986, p. 110). The difficulties of defining leisure, as well as measuring it, have long been regarded as the major challenge and impediment to progress in the study of leisure.

It is easy to see why this assessment has been made. Many definitions of leisure abound. Researchers and theorists often view leisure as participation in recreational or cultural activities such as sports, hobbies and dance. Leisure also is identified by the setting in which it is experienced such as parties, theaters, and parks. It is described as time free from obligation, the freedom to do whatever one wants to do, or as simply doing something for its own sake. Certain feelings or experiences are considered leisure. A sense of freedom, relaxation, enjoyment, and even intense concentration have been used to characterize leisure.

However, as we will explain in this and the next chapter, a great deal of thinking and research has increased the researchers' ability to measure and study leisure from a social psychological perspective, and we will examine a wide variety of strategies that researchers have used to confront this challenge. They have used a wide variety of strategies. Researchers have taken the question of the nature of leisure to people from many walks of life. They have had them respond to questionnaires, they have observed and interviewed people in settings where leisure takes place, and they have tracked people as they negotiate their way through their daily lives. Researchers have even involved people in experiments in the psychological laboratory to study the nature of their leisure.

Approaches to defining and operationalizing leisure can be classified according to two criteria (see Figure 3.1, p. 54). The first is the *type of phenomena* taken as an indicator of the occurrence of leisure. Two types of phenomena are typically distinguished—*objective* and *subjective* (Neulinger, 1974; Ellis & Witt, 1991; Lawton, 1993). Objective definitions equate leisure with certain types of activity and/or time. In contrast, according to subjective definitions, leisure is associated with the occurrence of certain types of mental states, perceptions, meanings, needs satisfied, and/or experiences. In the former case, leisure can be defined and measured as behavior, i.e., as something people do. It can be defined by setting, i.e., by what is going on in the individual's immediate social and physical environment. Leisure also can be a psychological state, i.e., an attitude, experience, cognition, emotion, or a sense of satisfaction.

The second way to distinguish among leisure definitions and measures is according to the *definitional vantage point* taken by the researcher when studying leisure. In other words, regardless of whether the researcher is studying behavior, settings or mental states, what is defined as leisure can be based either on the viewpoint of the researcher (*external*) or that of the person being studied (*internal*). These issues are examined in more detail in the following sections.

Type of Phenomena	Definitional Vantage Point	
	External	Internal
Objective	*Activity, setting or time period* is defined by the *researcher* as leisure or nonleisure.	*Activity, setting or time period* is defined by the *participant* as leisure or nonleisure.
Subjective	*Experience, satisfaction or meaning* associated with involvement is defined by the *researcher* as leisure or nonleisure.	*Experience, satisfaction or meaning* associated with involvement is defined by the *participant* as leisure or nonleisure.

Figure 3.1 Research Approaches to Defining Leisure

Classifying Leisure Definitions and Measures

Type of Phenomena

When social psychologists study individuals, they can focus on what they do, the situation they are in, or what they think and feel. When leisure is defined as "what people do," researchers have used measures based on the *activities* in which they participate and the amount of *time* they spend engaged in these activities. This approach generally involves measuring the number of specific activities (e.g., skiing, watching a movie, doing crossword puzzles) or general categories of activities (e.g., social, sport, cultural) participated in by individuals, the frequency of participation in these activities, and the amount of time they are involved.

Leisure can also be defined according to the setting or environment likely to support activities or evoke experiences thought to be leisure. Tennis courts, beaches, and theaters are among the more obvious settings for leisure. Often it is difficult to disentangle leisure activities and settings. Some activities can only occur in specific settings. For example, a party or visiting a park can be viewed as both leisure activities and settings for leisure. Consequently, leisure settings are frequently not distinguished from leisure activities though the importance of distinguishing between the impact of settings and activities has been noted (Manning, 1985). Deem (1986) and Henderson (1990a) have suggested that activities and settings can be thought of as "containers" for leisure.

When leisure is defined in terms of what people think and feel, researchers use measures that reflect *mental experience* while engaged in leisure activities and the *satisfactions* or *meanings* derived from these involvements. The mental or phenomenological world of leisure is populated by conscious experiences including emotions, moods, satisfactions, cognitions, attitudes, and beliefs. While these can be inferred from behavior, researchers typically "observe" them from what people tell them about their experience. These self-reports can be obtained in interviews or with standardized rating scales.

These various ways of defining and measuring leisure are not in conflict or competition. Questions about leisure require the use of a variety of approaches. A full understanding of leisure often requires that researchers simultaneously use several of these approaches. For example, assume that some researchers are interested in the relationship between people's leisure and their ability to cope with the stress in their lives. In fact, also assume they have a theory that suggests that people who are more actively involved in leisure are more immune to stress, that is, they experience less stress and consequently less illness. In order to study this relationship, leisure and stress need to be measured. Consider leisure. If these researchers measure leisure as an objective phenomenon, they could observe how many activities people are participating in, the types of leisure settings they encounter during their daily life, how frequently they participate and/or how much time they are involved in these activities and settings. They could then see if those people who have greater leisure are less stressed.

However, as the reader will discover, it is likely that this objective approach to defining and measuring leisure would provide an incomplete picture. If the researchers also knew what the people being studied were experiencing when they were involved in leisure activities and settings, that is, how enjoyable, challenging, relaxing and satisfying, the researchers would have a better idea of the impact that these leisure involvements have on the people's ability to cope with the stressful events in their lives.

Definitional Vantage Point: External and Internal

You have probably noticed that though we have suggested that leisure has been defined by researchers in terms of people's behavior, the setting in which the behavior takes place and their mental experience, we have not identified how researchers decide whether a behavior, setting, or experience is leisure or something else. In other words, who decides?

In leisure research who decides what leisure is depends on the *definitional vantage point* used by the researcher in a particular study. The definitional vantage point can be *external* or *internal* to the person or people being studied. If an external vantage point is adopted, what constitutes leisure is determined by the researcher and is based on viewpoints other than those of the individual or people being studied. External definitions of leisure are based on what people in a social group or society actually agree to be leisure and researchers often share these beliefs if they are members of the same group or society. When studying people who are members of societies or groups that differ from their own, researchers must first develop an understanding of what leisure is for these social collectives. In a sense, the researcher predetermines or imposes a definition of leisure on the people being studied and hopefully this is informed by a thorough knowledge of the social groups to which the people being studied belong or identify.

This approach is not quite as dictatorial as it sounds. Researchers may be interested in how an individual becomes involved in activities typically seen as leisure in that person's social group or culture, what keeps them involved and the psychological, and social costs and benefits of their involvement (e.g., Fine, 1987; Stebbins, 1992a). Other researchers, as well as leisure service providers, may be interested in how accessible certain leisure opportunities are for the members of a group or community. These leisure opportunities likely consist of the activities (e.g., children's organized sports), settings (e.g., urban parks), and experiences (e.g., appreciation of beauty in an art gallery) generally seen by the people comprising this community to be leisure, and that are made available through the efforts of both public and private leisure service agencies. Consequently, it makes sense to use an external, socially derived definition of leisure in studying these types of equity issues.

If an internal vantage point is adopted by the researcher, the definition of leisure is based on the perception or construal of the behavior, setting or experience as leisure by the individuals being studied. In other words, the researcher leaves it up to the individuals in the study to determine if an activity, setting, or experience is leisure for them personally. An early study by Johnson (1978) demonstrates this distinction between what we have called the external and the internal vantage points. Adults and children were found to often have very different ideas about whether a particular physical setting was a recreation or nonrecreation space. By using the individual's own definition of leisure, researchers will get a more accurate picture of how much leisure people feel they have and what is meaningful to them, which in turn may also allow a clearer understanding how leisure impacts on their lives. Personal definitions of leisure can be expected to be influenced by and consistent with the values and beliefs of the group and society of which people are members. However, while externally and internally based definitions of leisure are frequently in agreement, they can be and are often at odds.

The distinction between definitions and measures based on the definitional vantage point adopted by the researcher is not only an issue in defining leisure. As we mentioned in chapter one, social psychologists studying all types of behavior and experience attach a great deal of importance to how individuals perceive or construe their own behavior, the behavior of others, and the situations in which they find themselves. *Construal* is an important idea for understanding all aspects of human behavior and experience and the influence of the social environment. Ross and Nisbett (1991) have stated the "impact of any 'objective' stimulus situation depends upon the personal and subjective meaning that the actor attaches to that situation. To predict the behavior of a given person successfully, we must be able to appreciate the actor's construal of the situation—that is, the manner in which the person understands the situation as a whole" (p. 11). The social psychological perspective is based on a belief in the importance of taking into account both socially derived or external, as well as personal or internal definitions of behavior, settings and experiences to fully understand human behavior (Diener, Larsen & Emmons, 1984).

Back to the Video Arcade

Let's return to the video arcade example we discussed in chapter one. How does one decide if the involvement is leisure for these adolescents? As observers and researchers, one has a variety of options available to her or him for defining and measuring leisure and they can be distinguished and classified on the basis of the *type of phenomena* used and the *definitional vantage point* adopted by the researcher.

For example, an external definitional vantage point can be adopted based on the knowledge that video game playing is a popular recreational activity and video arcades are a leisure setting for many adolescents. In fact, it would be fairly safe to say, at least in North America, that video game playing and arcades are seen by most people as leisure behavior and settings. If researchers wanted to survey all of the adolescents who were students at the school with truancy and larceny problems about their leisure by sending them a questionnaire that asked them to indicate how frequently or how much time they spent playing video games in an arcade each week, researchers would likely feel confident they were getting valid information about how they use some of their leisure. This strategy would be a relatively quick and inexpensive way in which to measure how much of the adolescents' leisure was spent playing video games.

However, observers cannot be absolutely certain that video game playing is experienced as leisure for each of the adolescents at the school or even for a particular adolescent each time he or she plays. If researchers are trying to understand the impact that video game playing has on the lives and daily school experience of these adolescents, they may feel it is important to adopt a research strategy that allows them to measure the extent to which each of the adolescents they are studying construe video game playing as leisure as well as how much of it they do.

Of course, a researcher could also examine the subjective nature of leisure. Experiences of fun and enjoyment are often taken as signs that people are engaged in leisure. However, even when observing and measuring mental experiences or states, a researcher can take an external or internal vantage point. Not all individuals may construe themselves to be engaged in leisure simply because they are enjoying themselves, or construe an activity as leisure because it is experienced as enjoyable. For some individuals, leisure might be better indicated by other feelings such as a feeling of relaxation or escape.

In actual practice, a combination of these approaches is often used for determining if someone is engaged in leisure. If an observer were to see a person in a video arcade and playing a video game (objective) and overheard this individual say she was having a good time (subjective), the observer would likely assume that this engagement was leisure for that person. Of course, the observer could confirm the observation and external definition by approaching the player and asking if she felt that what she was doing was "leisure"—adopting an internal definitional vantage point.

It is no longer accurate to criticize the field of leisure studies for a lack of advancement in conceptualizing and measuring leisure. Approaches have been developed that utilize not only objective and subjective approaches when studying the leisure of individuals, but that also define leisure from the external and internal vantage points. In the remainder of this chapter, we will describe research that illustrates objective approaches to the definition and measurement of leisure from both external and internal vantage points. In the next chapter we will focus on subjective approaches.

Measuring Leisure Behavior and Time

In recent years, there has been an increase in the number of studies reported that examine people's involvement in specific leisure activities and settings, for example, television (Kubey & Csikszentmihalyi, 1990), youth baseball, and role-playing games like "Dungeons and Dragons" (Fine, 1983, 1987), the use of shopping centers for socializing (Graham, Graham & MacLean, 1991), contract bridge (Scott & Godbey, 1992), amateur science as serious leisure (Stebbins, 1981), fishing and hunting among urban youth (Dargitz, 1988), participation in adult baseball camps (Brandmeyer & Alexander, 1986), and involvement in the world of auctions (Glancy, 1988). However, when researchers have attempted to conceptualize and measure leisure, they have more frequently been interested in assessing overall patterns of leisure activity engagement and time usage; what we might call the *leisure style*. Underlying this more usual practice of not focusing on a specific *activity* is the assumption that factors such as the range of activities and the frequency of participation are more important to understanding the impact of leisure on people than the specific activities in which they engage. As well, there has been an assumption that the needs and motivations people seek to satisfy during their free time can be fulfilled by different combinations and types of activities, making no one type of leisure activity unique or singular in importance for quality of life, health, or well-being (see Mannell & Iso-Ahola, 1987). As we will suggest, this is a questionable assumption.

Leisure as *time* is also an objective measure and has been conceptualized in several ways. Leisure is sometimes defined as the time left over after people have taken care of the necessities of life. Paid work, household chores, caring for others, school work, personal maintenance, and other obligations are usually seen as necessities. This residual time approach views leisure as freedom from obligation. However, when leisure time is of interest, researchers typically measure the amount or duration of the time spent by people engaging in leisure activities or settings.

As data collection strategies, *behavioral inventories* and *time diaries* have been used most frequently when leisure style is defined as activity, setting, or time. Recently however, with the growth of studies of single specific activities, there has been a corresponding growth in the number of studies reported using *direct observation* with *qualitative* research methods. While researchers using these methods have, for the most part, used external definitions of what constitutes a leisure activity or setting, some innovative approaches have been developed to assess whether the individuals being studied are in agreement with researcher definitions and construe the activities, settings, or time periods in which they are involved as "leisure."

Leisure Behavior Inventories

The most frequent measurement approach used by researchers has been the leisure behavior inventory. Typically, external vantage point definitions are used. Comprised of a list of activities, respondents are asked to check if they have participated in these activities and sometimes how often during a specified time period (e.g., week, month, season, year), or to rate their relative frequency of participation on Likert scales (see Figure 3.2).

Researchers typically custom design inventories to suit their research purposes and the lifestyles of the people they are studying. For example, bungee jumping is not likely to be included in the list of activities used to measure the leisure participation of people who are frail. Consequently, the types and numbers of activities vary substantially from study to study.

Indicate the number of times you participate or engage in each of the following activities during a typical week. Write your answer on the line provided.

_____ Listening to records, stereo, tapes
_____ Reading books for pleasure
_____ Reading magazines and newspapers
_____ Walking a dog or pet
_____ Fitness exercise (e.g., jogging, aerobics, walking, weight-training)

In the following list, circle the number of those activities in which have you participated *at least once during the last year.*

1   Taking a vacation trip
2   Visiting a national or regional park
3   Visiting a fair or festival
4   Visiting an art gallery
5   Attending a live theater performance (e.g., drama, comedy, musical)
6   Attending a rock concert
7   Attending a sporting event (e.g., baseball, football, hockey)
8   Dining out at a restaurant
9   Going to the movies
10   Visiting a public library
11   Attending a club meeting
12   Working for a church group or charity
13   Taking general interest or art courses

For each of physical activities listed below rate how frequently you participated during the *last year.* If you *"never"* participate in the activity circle the *"0."* If you participated *"infrequently"* circle the number *"1."* If you participated *"occasionally"* or *"frequently"* circle the numbers *"2"* or *"3"* respectively. In the case of seasonal activities (e.g., water-skiing) rate your frequency of participation on the basis of when the activity could be engaged in.

0 1 2 3   Swimming
0 1 2 3   Water-skiing, surfing, scuba diving
0 1 2 3   Playing tennis, squash, other racquet sports
0 1 2 3   Golfing
0 1 2 3   Bowling
0 1 2 3   Team sports (e.g., baseball, football, ice hockey)
0 1 2 3   Gardening
0 1 2 3   Fishing or hunting
0 1 2 3   Camping or visiting a private cottage

Figure 3.2 Typical Leisure Behavior Inventory Items
What activities would you include?

While this tailoring of inventories provides flexibility, the lack of widely-used, standardized scales makes comparisons between studies difficult (Bull, 1982; Mannell & Dupuis, 1994).

A customized leisure behavior inventory was used by Ragheb (1980) to study the influence of a variety of attitudinal and sociodemographic factors on the leisure participation of 383 adolescents and adults in the southern United States. The behavioral inventory was part of a questionnaire and consisted of 41 activities. The participants in the study were asked to indicate their frequency of participation in each activity using a five-point Likert-type scale by selecting one of the following alternatives: 1 = never, 2 = seldom, 3 = some of the time, 4 = often, and 5 = very often. For the analysis of the information collected with the inventory, the leisure activities were examined individually and grouped into six categories by the researcher which included mass media, social activities, outdoor activities, sports activities, cultural activities, and hobbies (see Figure 3.3). These ratings provided a score on each activity for each participant ranging from 1 to 5. Also, the researcher was able to calculate an average score for each category of activity and an overall leisure participation score for each participant by averaging the ratings of the activities in each category and the ratings for all 41 activities respectively. With these measures of leisure, Ragheb was able to determine that individuals who were more active were also more satisfied with their leisure. This relationship was strongest for hobbies and cultural activities. Gender and educational differences were also found in levels of leisure participation.

One of the few standardized leisure behavior inventories available is the *Leisure Activities Blank*, or LAB (McKechnie, 1974, 1975) developed for use with an adult population. The LAB includes 120 leisure activities that were chosen because of their high participation rates in the United States. These activities were then grouped into a smaller number of activity types. For each activity, the respondent indicates separately the extent of his or her past involvement and expected future participation. This instrument can be unwieldy to administer and tabulate because of its length and classification scheme, and few researchers use the scale today. Those who do use the scale tend to modify it for their own purposes, usually making it shorter (e.g., Lounsbury & Hoopes, 1988; Ragheb & Griffith, 1982).

Time Diaries

The measurement of leisure time could be done by following people around with a stopwatch and recording the amount of time they spend involved in

Mass Media Watching TV Reading newspapers or magazines Going to movies	**Cultural Events** Attending concerts, singing, etc. Attending ballet, opera, dance Visiting art museums Folk or square dancing Attending theater
Sports Activities Spectating at sports events Fitness activities (e.g., jog, swim) Team sports (e.g., softball, soccer) Individual sports (e.g., golf, fencing) Dual sports (e.g., tennis, squash)	**Outdoor Activities** Picnicking Fishing, hunting Gardening Day outings (e.g., zoo, museums) Hiking Boating Nature study Camping
Social Activities Visiting friends Entertaining friends Dating Attending parties Social dancing Indoor game parties	**Hobbies** Painting/drawing/sketching Woodwork, furniture refinishing Collecting (e.g., stamps, coins) Needlework, sewing, knitting Floral arranging, plant care Waving, pottery, sculpture Photography, movie-making

Figure 3.3 Example of Grouping of Leisure Activities into Larger Categories

Adapted from Ragheb (1980)

leisure activities and settings. Perhaps a trench coat and dark sunglasses would be useful as well! This method would be similar to "time-and-motion studies" done in industrial settings where the amount of time spent on various tasks by workers is studied by direct observation (Steers & Porter, 1991). However, this approach would be time-consuming and rather intrusive. Instead, researchers have asked people on questionnaires to estimate how much time they spend engaged in leisure during a specified period of time, for example, the past day, month, or year. More typically, researchers have people record in a diary the sequence and duration of the activities in which they engage over a specified period, most typically the 24-hour day. This time diary or time budget approach allows the researcher to estimate the amount of time that the participant spends in various daily activities including leisure (Zuzanek & Box, 1988). Other researchers (e.g., Moss & Lawton, 1982) have collected time diary-type data by asking respondents to recount each sequential activity in which they were engaged during the previous day. In a study reported by Zuzanek and Smale (1992) this information was collected in a telephone interview. Again, the definition of what is leisure is typically determined by the researcher.

Time-budget studies have been used since the 1920s, though wider use has been made of them during the past 30 years. They have been used to examine how much time people in different segments of society and at different life-cycle stages spend at paid work, leisure, housework and family obligations, and how these patterns change from workdays to weekends (Szalai, 1972; Robinson, 1977; Zuzanek, 1980).

In its simplest form, the time diary requires participants to record the main activities in which they engage during the course of the day and when they engage in these activities (see Figure 3.4). Other types of information may also be requested (e.g., if doing two things at once indicating the secondary activity, where doing the activity, with whom). Following the completion of the study, the researcher then sums up the time spent in various types of activities to measure the amount and proportion of time the participants spent in these activities during their daily lives. Typically, respondents carry the diaries for one or two weekdays and one weekend day. The entries can be weighted to provide time-use estimates for a complete week of 168 hours. Sometimes a typical weekday and weekend day are described from the data.

The use of time budget data to examine leisure defined from an external definitional vantage point is illustrated by a study reported by Zuzanek and Smale (1992) on the "rhythms of the week." These researchers were interested in how time spent engaged in leisure and other activities varied across the days of the week. They also wanted to know how participation time in these activities was influenced by being employed, married, and/or having small children, and if this impact differed for men and women. Data for these analyses came from a national study carried out by the Canadian government in 1986. The time-budget data were collected over the telephone. A total of 9,946 households all over Canada were randomly dialed by a computer, and individuals 15 years of age and older who answered were interviewed. In addition to demographic characteristics, the respondents provided information on their time use for a 24-hour period encompassing a randomly selected day from the previous week. They reported the primary activity in which they were involved, the total duration of each

| Day Filled Out: | Mon | Tue | Wed | Thur | Fri | Sat | Sun |

Date: _____

Evening: page 3

What was the main thing you were doing?	Time began	What else were you were doing?	Where?	With whom?
	6:10			
	6:20			
	6:30			
	6:40			
	6:50			
	7:00			
	7:10			
	7:20			
	7:30			
	7:40			
	7:50			
	8:00			
	8:10			
	8:20			
	8:30			

Figure 3.4 Example of a Time Diary Page

activity in minutes, where the activity took place, and with whom they were involved. This information was recorded on a time-diary form by the interviewer. Activities identified by the respondents were classified into one of 99 activity types. Zuzanek and Smale then grouped these activities into the general categories of work, domestic activities, childcare, personal care, and leisure. They also specifically examined the leisure activities of dining out and television viewing. The amount of time in minutes each respondent spent engaged in these types of activities was calculated.

For the sample as a whole, the researchers found time spent in leisure activities was relatively similar from Monday to Thursday, then, as would be expected, increased on Friday and was highest on Saturday and Sunday. Saturdays and Sundays differed substantially, however. Saturdays were days of domestic work and shopping as much as they were days of leisure. Much of Saturday's leisure was taken up with outings. On the other hand, Sundays were days of sleep, rest, family contacts, childcare, and mostly passive leisure. For men, this meant watching television.

Employed mothers seem to be the major losers when it comes to leisure, particularly on Sundays. When time at paid work, domestic work, and childcare were added together, employed mothers with small children reported 2.0 to 2.5 hours greater workloads, a half-hour less sleep, and one to two hours less leisure compared to mothers at home on workdays. This difference decreased on Saturdays, but deepened again on Sundays, when employed mothers reported 1.5 hours higher overall workloads, and two hours less leisure time than mothers at home. When employed mothers were compared with employed fathers, workloads balance out on workdays. However, they had about a half-hour less leisure per workday. This difference was amplified on the weekend days. Employed fathers reported workloads which are 1.0 to 1.5 hours lower than those reported by employed mothers, and their leisure exceeded that reported by employed mothers by two to 2.5 hours per weekend day. Employed mothers with small children were the only group who increased rather than reduced their domestic work and childcare on weekends relative to workdays. Employed women with small children appear to have less opportunity than other groups, including employed men with small children, for the break in a busy week that leisure provides. In other words, being employed, married and having young children amplified the difference between the amount of leisure available to men and women.

Of course, it would be interesting to see if this difference remained if an internal definitional vantage point was adopted in defining leisure. It is possible that the women with small children in this study may have defined childcare on Sundays as leisure. For example, Bella (1989) has theorized that some of the time that women spend in role-related activities and caring for family members may be experienced as leisure. She argues that there are significant differences in the way men and women define leisure that are due to their different social roles.

Direct Observation

Probably the most obvious method to use in studying leisure is the way people gather information every day of their lives. In other words, if one wants to know about an individual's leisure, why not just go "where it's happening" and watch it happen? As we suggested earlier, a growing number of studies have been based on the direct observation of people's behavior. Rather than examining the full range of their leisure activities, these studies have typically focused on the individual's involvement in specific leisure activities. This trend is due to the greater interest researchers are showing in how people become involved in or are recruited into leisure activities, why they drop out or remain involved, and the development of an ongoing, career-like commitment to the activity.

Direct observation may take the form of in-depth interviews, participant observation and case studies. These approaches are often termed *field research*. In a sense, social psychologists do field research whenever they observe or participate in social behavior and try to understand it, whether in a leisure setting or some other setting. Information collected through direct observation can be *quantitative* or *qualitative*. Quantitative leisure data resulting from direct observation is converted into numerical form, such as the number of activities participated in, the frequency of participation in an activity, or the duration of participation. Leisure settings can be measured in terms of the number and types of choices or alternatives for participation available to an individual, the extent to which rules or norms are present that constrain or guide behavior, and so forth. For example, in the study of the play of children, a variety of scales have been developed for directly observing and quantifying children's activity in natural settings. Rubin, Watson and Jambor (1978) developed the Parten/Piaget scale that allows an observer to record the frequency with which children in various settings engage in different types of play (e.g., constructive, functional, symbolic) as well as the type and frequency of their social play (e.g., solitary, parallel, interactive).

Most of the leisure research on adults using direct observation, however, has been qualitative. This qualitative field research produces data which are not reduced to numbers. Written notes are made by the researcher describing what the people being observed are doing or saying. The basic tools of field research are a notebook or field journal and a pencil. If possible, qualitative researchers take notes as they are observing. When this is not possible, notes are written as soon as possible afterward. Notes typically include both empirical observations and interpretations of them. In other words, researchers record what they "know" has happened as well as what they "think" has happened. In field research it is also appropriate for the researcher to take a more active role than passive observer; consequently, the researcher questions the people being studied. Researchers' notes also consist of a record of these *unstructured interviews*, including the questions and responses.

Researcher Robert Stebbins has used direct observation in a number of studies during the past decade and a half to examine what he calls *serious leisure*. He has studied participants in various types of sport (baseball, football), art (music, theater), variety art (magic, stand-up comedy), science (archaeology, astronomy) and hobby (barbershop singing) activities (see Stebbins, 1992a, 1992b, 1992c). He defines serious leisure as "the systematic pursuit of an amateur, hobbyist, or volunteer activity that is sufficiently substantial and interesting for the participant to find a career there in the acquisition and expression of its special skills and knowledge" that endures for a considerable part of a person's life (Stebbins, 1992a, p. 3). Stebbins sees serious leisure as distinct from casual or relaxing leisure in its demands for perseverance, personal effort in the development of specially acquired knowledge and skill, the development of a career in the activity, and strong attachment to or identification with the activity. Serious leisure often involves membership in or identification with a group of participants with distinct beliefs, norms, values, traditions and performance standards.

Stebbins has taken an external definitional vantage point in defining what constitutes serious leisure. The various activities he has labeled serious leisure and chosen to study may or may not be perceived as leisure by the participants. He also recognizes that the participants likely do not see their participation in these activities as leisure all the time (1992a, p. 3–6). In fact, in a recent doctoral study of "serious runners" using Stebbins' theoretical framework (Major, 1994), the respondents only saw their active running as leisure when they were doing it socially and for fun (i.e., noncompetitively).

Stebbins' (1983) research on amateur magicians provides a good example of the direct observation approach. Thirty amateur magicians ranging in age from sixteen to seventy-three, and living in Calgary, Alberta, Canada were observed and interviewed over a one-year period. The interviews were preceded by approximately eight months of participant observation of all social aspects of the practice of magic which included performances, monthly gatherings and executive committee meetings of an amateur magicians' association, its annual banquet, a festival, television taping sessions, and informal gatherings of magicians whenever these occurred. Each amateur was interviewed by Stebbins. While the interviews were unstructured, he used an interview guide that listed the types of information and questions he wished to pursue with his respondents. The participant observations and interviews provided a rich and detailed picture of what amateur magicians do, the various settings in which they pursue their activity, and the amount of time they invest in the activity.

In addition to developing an understanding of the nature of this leisure activity, Stebbins was able to gather information about how the participants became interested in and committed to regular participation. He found that the process of becoming an amateur magician looked very much like the process of developing a job career. He was also able to determine the psychological rewards and costs of participation, as well as the impact of this type of leisure involvement on their other leisure involvements, and the work and family domains of their lives. On the basis of his research on serious leisure, Stebbins theorized that participation in serious leisure activities can and does contribute to life satisfaction and well-being. The hard work and perseverance required by amateurs, hobbyists, and volunteers to meet the challenges of their leisure was predicted to engender feelings of accomplishment and provide psychological benefits that include self-enrichment, self-actualization, self-expression, positive social identity, re-creation and escape from personal problems, social belonging, and a feeling of contributing to a group (Stebbins, 1992a, p. 17). Stebbins also speculated that serious leisure can be important to the quality of older retired adults' lives by expanding their social circle, promoting transcendence, constituting a theme in the life review, fostering responsibility, and creating the opportunity to feel needed by other people (p. 127).

Strengths and Limitations of These Approaches

Direct observation, behavior inventories and time diaries all have their place in the observation and measurement of leisure behavior, settings and time. All have their strengths and limitations. The strength of direct observation lies in the ability of the researcher to provide rich detail about all aspects of the activity under study. Also, direct observation, like the time diary, gives researchers a sense of how these activities are embedded in the setting of daily life and other activities. Another advantage of direct observation is related to the opportunity that it affords the researcher to develop an understanding of what these activities mean to the participant (Henderson, 1991a) and to determine if they are, in fact, leisure from the internal vantage point of the individual.

With direct observation, the researcher is able to study only a relatively small number of individuals in any one study who are typically not randomly selected. Consequently, care must be taken in generalizing the research findings to other individuals or groups. Although in-depth, direct observation can also be extremely time-consuming for the researcher and field research observations are very personal. Consequently, they can be difficult for other researchers to confirm or replicate. A variety of strategies are available to help field researchers using direct observation assess the reliability of their observations (Creswell, 1994). These limitations or challenges are well-recognized among those researchers using direct observation and are more than made up for by the detailed descriptive information obtained on the activities and how they are connected to other aspects of the participants' lives. As Stebbins and many other researchers using qualitative approaches have suggested, direct observation provides an excellent opportunity to explore new issues and develop new ideas and theory that can guide future research.

Carefully designed inventories and time-budget methods continue to be useful research strategies and provide a picture of how people structure their lives with activity. They are cost-effective and can be used to collect information from a large number of randomly selected people providing a representative picture of their leisure behavior. The two methods if used effectively have been shown to provide similar and consistent information if the time period for recalling the type and level of participation is not too lengthy. Bishop, Jeanrenaud, and Lawson (1975) had people complete time diaries and also asked them to fill out a behavioral inventory about their participation during the preceding month. The two methods provided similar estimates of the frequency of participation in 35 different leisure activities. Other researchers investigating the comparability of data gathered with the time-budget diary relative to the behavioral inventory suggest that *infrequent activities* may be more accurately measured with the inventory rather than the time diary approach (Cosper & Shaw, 1985). For example, a sporting event, the theater or a vacation are not likely weekly events and may be missed in time-diary studies. On the other hand, when measuring *daily or frequently occurring activities* (e.g., exercising, watching television), the time diary appears to be the superior approach (Zuzanek, 1991b).

However, the measures obtained with both inventories and diaries have been described as imprecise indicators of leisure behavior and style for a variety of reasons. There is no standard list of activities that researchers agree constitute leisure, and inventories differ substantially on the specificity of the activities they include. Some researchers use a large number of very specific activities (e.g., McKechnie, 1975), whereas in other studies, researchers have used only a small number of very broad activity categories such as mass media, reading, social, outdoor, sports, spectator, cultural and hobby activities (e.g., Ragheb & Griffith, 1982). Also, when analyzing data gathered with leisure behavior inventories and time-budget diaries, it is standard practice to group specific leisure activities into a smaller, more manageable number of activity classifications. However, researchers have not been consistent in how they have done this grouping. They often have classified the same activities in different leisure behavior categories. For example, team sports can be classified as social activities or physical activities.

An extensive activity classification scheme that has been influential was developed by an international group of researchers for use in analyzing large time-budget studies (Szalai, 1972). This type of time-budget classification scheme is typically based on distinctions between economically motivated behavior (e.g., work for pay), biologically or physiologically determined behavior (e.g., sleep, eating, personal hygiene), and family role-oriented and house maintenance activities (e.g., childcare, house chores).

Classifying leisure activities are even more challenging than classifying other types of behavior. The principal criterion for defining leisure is often a "negative" one, that is, that part of the day which is not occupied by paid employment or the meeting of physiological or other needs. Most researchers agree that leisure activities serve a number of personal and social functions, and consequently activities are sometimes grouped on the basis of the needs that the researcher feels participation in them satisfy (e.g., self-actualization, rest/respite, spiritual renewal, entertainment, social). Other researchers prefer to use conceptual approaches to classify activities tailored to meet the needs of their research. Statistical procedures such as factor analysis that group activities on the basis of how frequently the people in a study participate in them have also been used (e.g., Witt, 1971). However, in Lawton's (1993) review of the research, he concluded that there was "little empirical evidence for a common set of activity categories" (p. 27) developed with the use of statistical strategies.

Inventories typically require that respondents report participation at a time substantially removed from the actual involvements themselves or over lengthy periods of time. Research has demonstrated that inaccuracies in recall are quite likely if the recall period is lengthy. Chase and Godbey (1983) surveyed two groups of people who were members of either a tennis club or a swim club. The swimmers were asked to indicate the frequency of their participation during the preceding season and the tennis players for the preceding two seasons. The researchers had access to the sign-in records for the people in these two clubs. They found that over 75 percent of the people in each of the groups overestimated their frequency of participation and at least 43 percent overestimated it by at least 100 percent. The time diary gets around this potential problem by having the respondent record their behavior as it occurs or shortly after. However, time diaries usually require more of a time commitment from the respondents, (typically two or three days) making it more difficult to recruit participants. Time diaries require more time and effort to administer as the respondents have to be trained in their use, and it also takes much more time to code and analyze the data. As mentioned earlier, less frequent events, such as vacations, will likely be missed. The researcher also has to assume that the week and days studied are typical in the life of the respondents.

Internal Vantage Point of the Participant

As we have explained, these approaches, particularly inventories and time diaries rely heavily on what we have called the *external definitional vantage point*. In spite of their utility, they fail to consider the way individuals construe these activities and the subjective meanings that they associate with them. Researchers typically assume that specific activities have a common meaning or are defined as leisure by everyone in the study. However, activities that constitute leisure are likely to differ by culture and subculture, gender, age, and perhaps even personality. Also, the same individual may view an activity to be leisure on one occasion and something else on a second occasion. Knowing what the people being studied personally define as leisure, rather than relying on researcher-imposed judgments, provides a more sensitive approach to measuring the quantity and quality of leisure experienced. This ability may be particularly important when researchers are interested in understanding individual behavior and how involvement in the same activities and settings can have a different impact on various individuals, their quality of life, well-being, work and so on.

Recently, researchers have been developing methods and measurement strategies to allow the assessment of leisure behavior, time, and settings from the *internal definitional vantage point* of the participant. This ability to determine whether the individual sees the activity and setting in which they are involved as leisure (with its various meanings) is an integral part of qualitative research and a variety of direct observation methods. Even though Stebbins defined being an amateur magician as leisure (serious leisure), his observations and interviews made it clear that the participants sometimes experienced their activities as very work-like when rehearsing and practicing, having to perform when ill, or the time pressures from other domains of their lives were heavy. However, at other times, particularly, during a good performance, the activity was described as very leisure-like.

Behavioral inventories can be designed to allow respondents to identify and record activities that they perceive as leisure which are not included on the list provided by the researcher. Several studies have been reported where the respondents, rather than rating a list of activities, were asked to write in their most frequent, important, or favorite leisure activities (e.g., Hirschman, 1984).

Shaw (1984) has demonstrated an innovative way of using the time-diary method to simultaneously measure leisure behavior, setting, and time from both external and internal definitional vantage points. She used a modified time-diary approach to measure how much leisure time a group of 60 married couples had during the course of a normal week in their lives. These study participants filled out the time diary on one typical weekday and a weekend day. After the completion of the time diaries, during a follow-up interview, her research participants were asked to classify all the activities they had listed in their diaries as "work," "leisure," "a mixture of work and leisure," or "neither work nor leisure." Mannell and Reid (1996) added a column to the time diary they had their respondents fill out. In this column the respondents were asked to check one of the four categories used by Shaw to indicate their definition of the activities they were recording in their diaries.

In Shaw's study, the activities recorded in the diaries were categorized using the 37 activity codes from the multinational time-budget study mentioned earlier. She then grouped these activities further into five main types: paid work, housework and household obligations, childcare, personal care, and leisure. In other words, leisure was defined from an *external vantage point*. However, Shaw was also able to define and measure leisure from the *internal vantage point* of her respondents. Not only was she able to compare the extent to which her respondents' internal perceptions corresponded to the external definitions used by time budget researchers, but she was also able to determine if the people in her study encountered situations where they perceived externally defined "nonleisure" activities and settings as leisure.

In this study, Shaw found significant differences in the amount of leisure reported by her respondents when their internal psychological definitions of leisure were used compared to the use of the external activity definitions. Fourteen percent of the externally defined leisure activities were judged as something other than leisure. Studying and participation in religious, community, and cultural organizations were frequently not defined as leisure, and even active sports, reading the paper, and social events were not always defined as leisure. However, reading a book was defined as leisure 100 percent of the time. Interestingly, 35 percent of all work and obligated activities were actually defined as leisure. While paid work and home chores were rarely perceived to be leisure, activities such as eating, childcare, and gardening were rated as leisure quite frequently.

Shaw also found differences in what was seen as leisure by men and women. The men in her study were much more likely than the women to perceive externally defined obligated activities as leisure. Cooking, shopping, and childcare were defined as leisure more often by males. Shaw suggests that men feel less obligation and more freedom of choice with respect to these activities than do women. The women in the study perceived a few externally defined leisure activities, such as gardening and social events as leisure more often than men.

One final point that Shaw's study illustrates is the fact that the same individual can perceive the same activity differently at different times—an activity whether externally defined as leisure or nonleisure can be perceived as leisure on one occasion and nonleisure on another. For example, 22.1 percent of the respondents' perceived their paid work activities as leisure on one occasion and work on another. The same was found for home chores (37.5%), television (12%), cooking (69.1%) and childcare (85.3%).

The implications of using definitions of leisure based on the external or internal vantage point is nicely demonstrated in a follow-up analysis of her data (Shaw, 1985b). The 60 married couples studied were randomly selected from working and middle class areas of Halifax, Nova Scotia, Canada, with the criterion that the husband worked full-time. The women in the study were full-time employed, part-time, or not employed outside the home (33 employed, 27 housewives). The mean age of the respondents was 39.6 years; 19 couples had children over 18 years of age, 41 couples had at least one child at home, 21 couples had at least one preschool child. The paid employment engaged in by the men varied from unskilled blue collar to professional work. Over half the women were employed in clerical and sales occupations.

Given the assumption that having leisure is important to the quality of life, Shaw argued that it is important to determine if different groups in society have equal access to leisure, much as society is concerned about whether people have equal access to employment, education, and health services. In this analysis, she wanted to determine if the men and women in her study had access to equal amounts of leisure time. Additionally, Shaw was interested in the effects that employment status, time devoted to employment, and family work load had on the availability of leisure time. The research reported on gender differences in leisure time has typically defined leisure from an external vantage point and as we described earlier may be insensitive to what men and women see as leisure. However, Shaw's time-budget data allowed her to also define leisure activities and time from the internal vantage point of her respondents.

When using their perceptions of leisure, no significant difference in the leisure time available to the men and women (men's mean = 6.37 hours, women's mean = 6.02 hours) was found for weekdays. However, a highly significant difference between the leisure time available to men and women (men's mean = 11.77 hours, women's mean = 8.10 hours, a difference of 3.67 hours) was found on weekend days.

Female and male respondents who had high family workloads, as defined by the number and age of their children and spouses who worked longer hours, were found to have significantly less leisure time available. The impact was, however, much greater for women. For example, having a wife with a high work load decreased leisure time on a weekend day by 2.15 hours for men, whereas for women having a husband with a high work load decreased leisure time by 4.88 hours. Also, husbands' work time was found to negatively impact on wives' leisure time during the week, but wives' work time did not impact on husband's leisure time during the week. There was little difference in the leisure time available to housewives and employed women. These results are similar to those we examined earlier in this chapter reported by Zuzanek and Smale (1992). Even when the male and female respondents' own perceptions of what was leisure were taken into account these differences persisted.

Progress in Definition and Measurement

Deciding what is and what is not leisure is an ongoing issue with which researchers must deal in their studies. The difficulties of defining leisure, as well as measuring it, have long been held up as the major challenge and impediment to progress in the study of leisure. Some commentators still feel that researchers have made little progress. However, it is no longer accurate to criticize the field of leisure studies for a lack of advancement in conceptualizing and measuring leisure. Approaches have been developed that treat people's behavior, the social and physical setting, and their mental states as indicators of the presence of leisure.

The definitions and measures used by researchers to study the leisure of individuals can also be distinguished according to whether they are based on external, socially-derived views of what constitutes leisure or the internal vantage point of the participant. Social psychologists studying all types of behavior and experience attach a great deal of importance to how individuals perceive or *construe* their own behavior, the behavior of others, and the situations in which they find themselves. Advances have been made in modifying traditional measures of leisure to allow researchers to assess what people construe as leisure. *Behavioral inventories* and *time diaries* have dominated research when leisure style as defined by activities, settings, and time is of interest. Recently, with the growth of studies of single specific activities, there has been a corresponding growth in the number of studies reported using *direct observation* and *qualitative* methods. Researchers using these methods have typically used external definitions of what constitutes a leisure activity or setting, however, some innovative approaches have been developed to assess whether the individuals being studied are in agreement with researcher definitions and construe the activities, settings or time periods in which they are involved as "leisure." Behavioral inventories can be designed to allow respondents to identify and record activities that they perceive as leisure that are not included on the list provided by the researcher. The time-diary method can also be used to simultaneously measure leisure behavior, settings and time from both external and internal *definitional vantage points*.

This measurement capability is important because the activities that constitute leisure for various groups of people are likely to show cultural and subcultural, gender, age, and possibly attitudinal and personality differences. As well, the same individual may view an activity to be leisure on one occasion and something else on a second occasion. Knowing what the people being studied personally define as leisure, rather than relying on researcher imposed judgments, provides a more sensitive approach to measuring the quantity and quality of leisure experienced and may better allow researchers to establish the relationship between leisure and other aspects of their lives, such as mental health, the quality of life, work, successful retirement and so forth.

In this chapter, research has been reviewed that illustrates the *objective approach* to the definition and measurement of leisure from both external and internal vantage points. In the following chapter, we will focus on the *subjective approach*, as well as examine what social psychological leisure research has discovered about the characteristics that distinguish leisure from other human involvements.

Leisure as a Psychological State and Experience

Chapter FOUR

Outline

Preview

In this chapter, we continue our story of the efforts of researchers to conceptualize and measure leisure, particularly leisure's subjective aspects. The notion of a leisure experience or state has different meanings and usages. There is interest in the attributes that people must perceive as being present in an activity or setting for it to be construed as leisure, the psychological satisfactions derived and experienced from participation, and the properties and quality of the experiences that accompany leisure participation. Some theorists and researchers see any state or experience that accompanies participation in leisure activities and settings as leisure, whether exceptional or mundane, positive or negative. Other researchers reserve the label "leisure" for those states and experiences that have special and unique properties. We will examine different types of subjective definitions of leisure, as well as research studies that illustrate the various measurement and research strategies used.

In the last chapter, we noted that researchers study leisure as it is defined internally by the people under study, or as it is defined external to the participant. As will be explained the same two approaches are possible when studying leisure experiences and states. What constitutes a leisure state or experience has been left up to the study participants' judgment by some researchers and based on external criteria by others.

Studying Leisure States and Experiences: A "Mind" or a "Mine" Field?

In a combination theme park and shopping mall, in a community not too far from where one of the authors lives, stands a machine looking not unlike a flight simulator. When it was first observed, it periodically spun, bumped, and twisted. When it stopped, two people emerged with slightly bemused smiles on their faces. The machine had just dispensed a *simulated leisure experience*—with accompanying sounds, sights and feelings of disequilibrium. This virtual reality environment produced an *engineered* experience that was advertised to duplicate that of an actual ride on the world's largest roller coaster located 800 or 900 hundred kilometers distant.

Leisure experiences, whether occurring in simulated, virtual or real, authentic or nonauthentic settings, have come to be seen not only as important but, perhaps, as the primary outcomes of leisure and recreational behavior. Many researchers believe that to understand the impact of leisure on health, well-being, and other domains of daily life, they not only need to be able to assess what people do in their leisure but also how they construe and feel about what they do.

The social psychology of leisure had its beginnings in part due to the attempts of researchers to translate philosophical and speculative ideas about the special nature of leisure experiences and states into constructs that could be studied by social science. Social psychology provided this opportunity because of its focus on what goes on in the head of the individual relative to what is going on the social environment, and because a number of existing social psychological theories and constructs dealt with elements of leisure that philosophical inquiry (e.g., de Grazia, 1964; Pieper, 1952) and social analysis (e.g., Dumazedier, 1967; Marcuse, 1964; Marx, 1970) suggested were important. For example, the idea of "freedom," often seen as the essence of leisure, has been translated into the social psychological constructs of *perceived freedom, freedom of choice* (Neulinger, 1974) and *freedom from social role obligations* (Kelly, 1972). Importantly, these constructs were part of already developed social psychological theories. Brehm's (1972) theory of psychological reactance deals with the impact of losing freedom on behavior and experience, and Rotter's (1966) locus of control theory attempts to explain how people differ in their beliefs about how much freedom and control they have in their lives, and the impact these differences have on their behavior. And just as important, methods for measuring and studying these phenomena had been developed.

The roller coaster simulator episode described previously allows the illustration of three major sets of questions and measurement problems that have drawn the attention of researchers who have been studying the subjective or experiential nature of leisure. *First*, what is the actual nature of the experience that accompanies participation? That is, what are the participants feeling and thinking during an episode and how can researchers observe and measure the texture and quality of their experience? *Second*, is the involvement construed as leisure by the participants, or does an observer of the incident only think they are experiencing leisure? If the former, what are the criteria used by the participants to judge the activity, setting, or experience to be leisure, and again how do researchers observe and measure these criteria? *Third*, what satisfactions are derived from this activity, setting, or experience? Are they distinct from the satisfactions that could be experienced through participation in another type of recreational activity (or in this case the "real" roller coaster ride)? How can these satisfactions be observed and measured?

These questions have in turn led to three strategies for conceptualizing and measuring leisure experiences and states—the immediate conscious experience, the definitional, and the *post-hoc* satisfaction approaches (Mannell, 1986; Mannell & Iso-Ahola, 1987). The three approaches are similar in that leisure is viewed to be most profitably understood by assessing the psychological state or experience of the participant; yet they differ in how they treat or conceptualize this experience. The *immediate conscious experience* approach involves monitoring the actual, on-site, real-time nature of experiences accompanying engagement in leisure activities or settings. The *definitional* approach focuses on the criteria used by participants in judging or construing activities, settings, or experiences to be leisure. The *post-hoc satisfaction* approach deals with the satisfactions associated with the experience based on the extent to which the needs and expectations of the participants are met by involvement in an activity, setting, or by the experience itself.

In this chapter, we will examine the immediate conscious experience and definitional approaches and the measurement issues involved. The discussion of how researchers have conceptualized and measured the satisfactions experienced from participation in leisure activities and settings will be taken up in chapter seven.

Immediate Conscious Experience Approach: The Texture of Leisure

The most direct research approach to study the *subjective* dimension of leisure is to measure the quality or texture of what people experience during leisure. Following the lead of such writers as de Grazia (1962), social psychologically oriented leisure researchers proposed that leisure be defined as "an experience that results from recreation engagements" (Driver & Tocher, 1970, p. 10). Researchers who have adopted this approach have attempted to examine the actual experiences accompanying involvement in leisure activities and settings. In other words, there is interest in the anatomy of the experience, its evaluative components (e.g., moods, emotions, feelings), cognitive components (e.g., thoughts, images), intensity, and duration. Also, researchers became interested in identifying the features of situations, activities, and persons which inhibit or enhance the quality of these experiences (Mannell, 1980).

Properties of a Leisure Experience

Immediate conscious experience is the experience of the present moment. The metaphor "stream of consciousness" used by William James (1890) probably best describes mental experience and suggests that conscious states are perceived as continuous and constantly changing. The stream of consciousness can be described as "the flow of perceptions, purposeful thoughts, fragmentary images, distant recollections, bodily sensations, emotions, plans, wishes, and impossible fantasies...[it] is our experience of life, our own personal life, from its beginning to its end (Pope & Singer, 1978, p. 1).

A number of properties have been proposed by theorists and researchers as important features to measure when studying the experiences accompanying leisure engagements. In Table 4.1 (pp. 84–85), these properties have been listed and described. Also, research in which these properties have been examined and the types of research methods used are noted.

Moods that reflect positive and negative feelings or emotions have been most frequently measured when studying the experiences accompanying leisure. The level of intensity, relaxation, arousal, or activation felt by the individual have also been assessed. Only a few studies have actually attempted to assess the cognitive components of the experience, that is, what people are actually thinking or imagining, when engaged in leisure. In addition to these basic emotional and cognitive features of conscious

Table 4.1 Immediate Conscious Experience Approach: Properties of Leisure Experiences and Examples of Research

Property	Description	Studies & Techniques
Emotions, moods	Affective component of experience, typically seen to vary along a positive-negative dimension, though research suggests that there may be independent positive and negative dimensions to our experiences (e.g., affection, elation vs. anxiety, sadness).	*On-site survey:* Hammitt (1980); Hull, William & Young (1992); Hull & Michael (1995); More & Payne (1978) *Laboratory:* Mannell (1979); Mannell & Bradley (1986) *ESM:* Chalip & Csikszentmihalyi (1984); Ellis, Voelkl & Morris (1994); Evans & Haworth (1991); Kleiber, Larson & Csikszentmihalyi (1986); Mannell, Zuzanek & Larson (1988); Samdahl (1988, 1991, 1992) *Qualitative:* Lee, Dattilo & Howard (1994)
Arousal, activation, relaxation	Feelings of mental and physical activation or arousal seen to vary in intensity (e.g., alert-drowsy, active-passive, energetic-tired, excited-bored).	*On-site survey:* Hammitt (1980); More & Payne (1978) *ESM:* Graef, Csikszentmihalyi & Gianinno (1983); Mannell, Zuzanek & Larson (1988); Zuzanek & Mannell (1993a, 1993b) *Qualitative:* Lee, Dattilo & Howard (1994)
Cognitions	Ideas, beliefs, thoughts and images.	*On-site survey:* Stewart (1992) *ESM:* Larson, Mannell & Zuzanek (1986) *Qualitative:* Lee, Dattilo & Howard (1994)
Time duration	Characteristic of involvement in an activity. Perception of how much time has passed during participation in an activity or context. The perception may or may not correspond to the actual amount of clock time that has passed. The more involved the faster time is perceived as passing.	*Laboratory:* Mannell (1979); Mannell & Bradley (1986) *ESM:* Ramos & Folkers (1994)

Table 4.1 Immediate Conscious Experience Approach: Properties of Leisure Experiences and Examples of Research *(continued)*

Property	Description	Studies & Techniques
Concentration, focus of attention, absorption	A characteristic of involvement in an activity. The more involved and more absorbed, the narrower the focus of attention, the higher the level of concentration and the less aware the participant is of anything else than the activity engaged in.	*On-site survey:* Hammitt (1980) *Laboratory:* Mannell (1979); Mannell & Bradley (1986) *ESM:* Kleiber, Larson & Csikszentmihalyi (1986); Mannell, Zuzanek & Larson (1988)
Self-consciousness, self-awareness, ego-loss	A characteristic of involvement. More involved less self-conscious and self-aware the participant. Ego-loss is the loss of awareness of one's sense of self when highly involved in an activity or context.	*ESM:* Samdahl & Kleiber (1989); Samdahl (1991)
Sense of competence	Feeling of the participant that they are knowledgeable or skilled in the activity	*ESM:* Csikszentmihalyi & Larson (1984); Csikszentmihalyi & LeFevre (1989); Ellis, Voelkl & Morris (1994); Graef, Csikszentmihalyi & Gianinno (1983); Mannell, Zuzanek & Larson (1988) *On-site survey:* Priest (1992)
Sense of freedom	The feeling of freedom that may accompany participation in an activity or event.	*ESM:* Csikszentmihalyi & Graef (1980); Kleiber, Larson & Csikszentmihalyi (1986)

experience, other properties that have been suggested or studied include perceptions of how quickly time is passing, and how self-conscious or self-aware people are when engaged in a leisure activity or setting. Also, the level of absorption or concentration, feelings of competence, and sense of freedom experienced have been measured.

Good or Optimal Leisure Experiences

By observing and measuring leisure experiences with the use of these properties one can begin to get a idea of the quality of the experiences people have while engaged in various leisure activities and settings. Supposedly, this will allow participants, or those providing leisure services, to improve and make leisure experiences better. Good leisure experiences may better contribute to well-being and happiness. However, this raises a rather important question: *"What is a good leisure experience?"* Is it characterized by higher positive moods, greater intensity or a relaxed feeling, the experience of time going quickly or slowly, greater absorption, lesser or greater self-consciousness, or other criteria?

When discussions in the leisure studies literature refer to "leisure experience," often more is being suggested than simply the experience accompanying an engagement or episode. For example, some theorists have conceptualized the existence of *unconditional* (Kelly, 1983) and *pure* (Neulinger, 1974) leisure. From this perspective, then, to qualify as a legitimate and high quality leisure experience, the fact that it is derived from a leisure activity is not sufficient. Rather, certain features or properties must be present before the experience can be properly viewed as leisure. The most frequently cited example of this approach is de Grazia's (1964) view of leisure as a special state of being. He argued that the possession of free time, or participation in a recreational activity, is no guarantee that one will experience leisure.

> Leisure and free time live in two different worlds. Anybody can have free time. Not everybody can have leisure.
> Leisure refers to a state of being, a condition of man, which few desire and fewer achieve (de Grazia, 1964, p. 5).

Similarly, the best or true tourist experiences have been characterized as having special qualities. For example, the ultimate travel experience has been compared to a religious experience and to be the result of pilgrimage, where the tourist searches for something less tangible than the trip and more rewarding than just being there (Cohen, 1979a). The search for this ultimate tourist experience has also been described as a quest. MacCannell (1976) refers to it as a quest for authentic experiences; Cohen (1979b) calls it a quest for center; Meyersohn (1981) suggests it is a quest for meaning; and Przeclawski (1985) considers it a quest for values. Not unlike de Grazia, Cohen (1979a, p. 194) suggests that these more profound modes of experience are hard to realize for all but a special few.

Though many people might not agree with what seems to be an elitist view of what constitutes a good, or at least a legitimate leisure experience, most people would probably be comfortable with the idea that a higher quality leisure experience would be associated with more positive and less negative moods. However, even here there is not complete agreement. For example, some leisure may be accompanied by negative moods at the time of participation due to the difficult challenges, the effort required, or other conditions in the setting, such as poor weather. However, there seems to be general agreement that the experience of leisure is pleasant in anticipation and recollection (Mannell, 1980; Stebbins, 1992a; Tinsley & Tinsley, 1986). It seems quite likely that good leisure experiences can take on many shapes and forms and that there is a need for researchers to explore leisure experiences and states based on a wide variety of properties and using a number of different measures.

Though what constitutes a legitimate leisure experience is debatable, the view that good leisure leads to an *optimal experience* has been a prevalent theme in theory and research during the past decade. Optimal experiences are states of high psychological involvement or absorption in activities or settings. From this perspective, a high-quality leisure experience is seen to be similar to a variety of highly involving psychological states, for example, peak, mystical, flow, and intense sport experiences (Kleiber & Dirkin, 1985; Mannell, 1980). Maslow's (1968) notion of *peak* experience and Csikszentmihalyi's (1975) concept of *flow* have been particularly attractive conceptualizations for leisure researchers, since they identify a variety of features or characteristics of conscious experiences that can be used to define and measure optimal experiences.

Maslow (1968, p. 73) describes peak experiences as "moments of highest happiness and fulfillment" often achieved through the nature experience, aesthetic perception, creative movement, intellectual insight, organismic experience, athletic pursuit, and the like. Csikszentmihalyi (1975) suggested that flow is the experience individuals frequently seek in their various activities and that leisure and play activities and settings can be excellent sources of flow. However, involvement in leisure activities and settings does not guarantee flow will be experienced. The correct choices must be made and certain conditions must be present in the activity or setting.

Csikszentmihalyi (1975) originally developed the *flow model* on the basis of extensive interviews with people engaged in their best leisure (i.e., rock climbers, basketball players, recreational dancers, chess players) and work (i.e., surgeons). The model provides insight into how the activities of everyday life come to be invested with meaning and experienced as optimal. Episodes that provided intensely absorbing experiences, challenges that matched participants' skills, and in which the participants lost track of time and their awareness of themselves were best remembered and experienced as most rewarding. Csikszentmihalyi's subsequent studies have led him to suggest that these flow experiences are "the best moments of people's lives" and "occur when a person's body or mind is stretched to its limits in a voluntary effort to accomplish something difficult and worthwhile" (Csikszentmihalyi, 1990, p. 3).

Csikszentmihalyi (1975, 1990) has summarized the basic features and operation of his flow theory with a simple diagram (see Figure 4.1). Assume that the diagram represents an involvement in a leisure specific activity, for example, a new video game. The two most theoretically important dimensions of the experience, *challenges* and *skills*, are represented on the two axes of the diagram. The letter C represents Christie, a girl who has just purchased a video game she has never played. The diagram shows Christie at four different points in time. When she starts playing (C_1), Christie has limited knowledge and skills for this particular game, and the major challenge she faces is getting the game character she controls with her joystick to move in the direction she wants. This is not a very difficult feat, but Christie is likely to enjoy it because the difficulty is just right for her rudimentary skills in the new game. So at this point she will probably be in flow. But she cannot stay there for long. After a while, if she keeps practicing, her skills will improve, and then she will grow bored with just being able to control the character (C_2). Also, being an experienced video game player, she likely realizes that there are harder challenges for her than just moving the character around on the screen—at which point, she will feel some anxiety (C_3) concerning her "poor" performance.

Neither boredom nor anxiety are positive experiences, so Christie will be motivated to return to the flow state. How is she to do it? Glancing again at the diagram, one sees that if she is bored (C_2) and wishes to be in

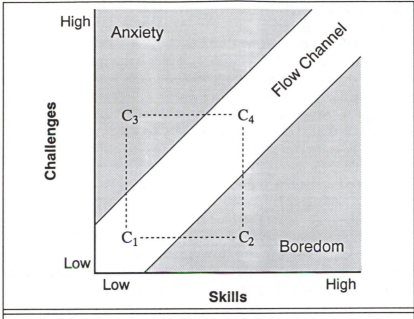

Figure 4.1 Csikszentmihalyi's Flow Model

Adapted from Csikszentmihalyi (1990)

flow again, Christie has essentially only one choice: to increase the challenges she is facing. (She also has a second choice, which is to give up playing altogether—in which case C would simply disappear from the diagram.) By setting herself a new more difficult goal that matches her skills—for instance, to avoid the traps and pit falls that are blocking her mission in the game and to move onto the next level—Christie would be back in flow (C_4). If Christie is anxious (C_3), regaining flow requires that she increase her skills. Theoretically, she could also reduce the challenges she is facing, and thus return to flow where she started (C_1).

The diagram shows that both C_1 and C_4 represent situations in which Christie is in flow. Although both are enjoyable, the two states are quite different in that C_4 is a more *complex* experience than C_1. It is more complex because it involves greater challenges, and demands greater skills from the player.

But C_4, although complex and enjoyable, does not represent a stable situation, either. As Christie keeps playing, either she will become bored by the stale opportunities she finds at that level, or she will become anxious and frustrated by her relatively low ability. So the motivation to enjoy herself again will push her to get back into the flow channel, but now at a level of complexity even *higher* than C_4.

Csikszentmihalyi (1990, p. 75) feels that it is this dynamic feature that allows flow activities to lead to psychological growth and discovery. One cannot enjoy doing the same thing at the same level for long. People grow bored or frustrated; and then the desire to enjoy themselves again pushes them to stretch their skills, or to discover new opportunities for using them. Herein lies the reason for the attractiveness of video games for participants. Because of the multiple levels of difficulty of the games, no sooner has the player succeeded in mastering one set of tasks than she or he is faced with a new more challenging level of difficulty. While sports and games provide good opportunities for this constant matching of challenges and skills, the interactive nature of computer-based games allow this challenge-skill matching process to occur over and over automatically.

Csikszentmihalyi's model is more useful for understanding the involvement dimension of leisure experiences than the notion of peak experience. The model allows for the recognition that the experience does not have to be "all-or-nothing" and that the degree of flow can vary from modest involvement (microflow) to intense peak-like involvement. The flow model provides an idea of the factors that contribute to the achievement of this state. While it suggests that some activities have greater potential for being high involvement activities (such as we described with the video game), the source of this high involvement is as much in the mind of the individual as it is in the activity. It is not only the "real" challenges presented by the situation that count, but those that the person perceives. It is not the skills people actually have that determine how they feel, but the ones they think they have.

Mannell (1979, 1980) demonstrated that a number of the characteristics of flow can be readily measured and studied in the psychological laboratory and that experiences accompanying leisure engagements vary in level of flow or absorption. Flow is also the central element in Tinsley and Tinsley's (1986) theory of leisure experience and its benefits. In their theory, they agree that the experiences accompanying leisure activities can vary in level of involvement; however, they regard true leisure, what they call the "leisure state," as occurring only when an intense flow experience is achieved.

Other theorists, including Csikszentmihalyi himself, do not equate flow states with leisure states since it has been demonstrated that flow experiences can occur in a wide variety of activities and settings. On the one hand, it seems reasonable to hypothesize that there may be more potential for achieving flow states in leisure than other domains. The greater freedom allowed by leisure to select and control individual activities should allow one to maintain or achieve a match between challenges and skills. On the other hand, if people regularly select relaxing and passive involvements devoid of challenges for their leisure, these choices will not likely promote the experience of flow. In fact, studies of adult workers (Csikszentmihalyi & LeFevre, 1989) and retired older adults (Mannell, Zuzanek & Larson, 1988) found that flow was experienced more frequently in work or obligatory nonwork tasks than in leisure. The respondents typically chose passive activities for leisure, and the things they "had to do" frequently were more challenging and demanding of higher levels of skill.

The reader has an idea of the features or properties that have been used in studying the experiences accompanying leisure engagements. In the following discussion, we will examine several types of research to get an idea about how these leisure experiences have been defined and measured, and the research methods used. In spite of the fact that researchers have examined the subjective or experiential nature of leisure, they typically have used an *external vantage point* in defining experience as leisure. Two strategies have been used. First, researchers ahead of time may decide that experiences are leisure only if the people they are studying perceive them to be "leisure," or if the experiences have certain properties (e.g., are characterized by positive moods, are absorbing). Second, researchers may choose an activity or setting they judge to be leisure and examine participants' experiences in this "leisure" engagement. These experiences may turn out to be positive or negative, exciting or boring, intensely involving or not involving, satisfying or unsatisfying, and so forth. In other words, from this perspective, leisure can be positive and satisfying or negative and unsatisfying. The following are some examples of how leisure experiences have been studied.

On-Site Surveys of Moods:
Leisure in Outdoor Areas and Other Settings

One of the first studies to attempt to monitor on-site leisure experiences was reported by More and Payne (1978). The leisure activity and setting studied by these researchers was a day trip to one of three wildlife sanctuaries near several cities in Massachusetts. While at these nature centers the participants viewed nature exhibits, picnicked, observed wildlife, and hiked. The moods accompanying this engagement were measured by having the visitors fill out a *survey questionnaire* when they entered and then again when they left the park. Besides asking for background information about the participants, the questionnaire contained a mood adjective checklist which required respondents to indicate on a four-point Likert scale the extent to which each of 33 adjectives described how they were feeling at the moment. In this study, the leisure experience was defined as the change in visitors' moods over the course of their visit to the nature center.

More and Payne predicted that negative moods (e.g., aggression, anxiety) would decline and positive moods (e.g., elation, vigor) would increase based on the theory that visitors to natural areas from cities should experience temporary escape from the pressures and tensions of urban life. They found that negative moods did decrease significantly, however, they also found positive moods decreased (see Figure 4.2). The researchers explained these findings by suggesting that the on-site experience is just the *"tip of the iceberg,"* the most visible part of the total leisure episode, and that what goes on before and after the event needs to be taken into consideration.

In other words, the researchers saw the leisure experience as a *multiphase experience* (Clawson & Knetsch, 1966). According to Clawson and Knetsch, the phases include:

(1) *anticipation*—a period of imagining and planning the trip or event;

(2) *travel to*—getting to the recreation site;

(3) *on-site*—the actual activity or experience at the site;

(4) *travel back*—the return trip home; and finally

(5) *recollection*—the recall or memory of the activity or experience.

More and Payne suggested that the participants arrived in high spirits with very positive moods and low levels of negative moods in anticipation of the outing, and that they likely chose to leave the park when they had had enough and were feeling tired and less enthusiastic.

In a subsequent study, Hammitt (1980) examined all of the five phases of the recreation experience by measuring the moods of 61 students during a trip to Mud Lake Bog (a small marsh or swamp) in Michigan. The *anticipation* phase moods were measured after students had received a one-hour lecture on their upcoming trip to the bog environment. Moods for the *travel to* phase were measured when the bus arrived at the bog, *on-site* moods

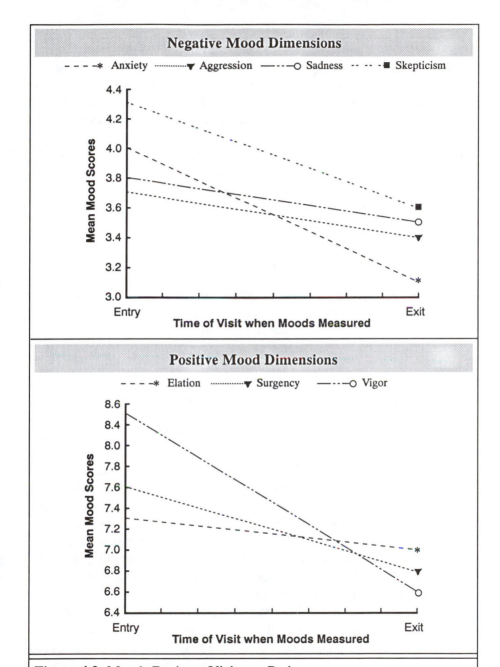

Figure 4.2 Moods During a Visit to a Park

Adapted from More and Payne (1978)

were assessed part of the way through their presence at the site, and *travel from* moods were assessed when the students returned to the buses. The *recollection* phase was measured two days after the bog trip. Levels of positive moods tended to increase during the "anticipation" and on into the "on-site" phases of the recreation experience, but then rapidly declined during the "travel from" phase. Negative moods showed the opposite trend.

Hammitt (1980) points out that there is a need to consider many recreation engagements as a "package deal; all parts having a potential role..." (p. 114). Depending on the length or nature of the leisure activity—for example, vacations and going to the movies would be quite different—the various phases may take on greater or lesser importance in influencing the leisure experience.

Experiments: Leisure Experience in the Laboratory

The flow or absorption aspect of the leisure experience has been examined in the *psychological laboratory* in a series of studies by Mannell and his associates (Mannell, 1979; Bradley & Mannell, 1984; Mannell & Bradley, 1986). In these studies, the laboratory was used to *simulate* the periods of free time that for most people are sandwiched between the obligatory activities of their everyday lives and that provide potential leisure settings. Waiting in a physician's office or for a bus, engaging in a 45-minute workout during lunch, and taking a coffee break are typical of these relatively brief free time or leisure interludes. With the use of the laboratory, the researchers were able to: (1) engineer a period of "free time" during the course of the experiment that the participants would perceive, at least within certain limits, was their own time and separate from the "obligatory" activities under study; (2) manipulate the independent variables, that is, vary the setting; (3) hold constant all other features of the physical and social environment for all participants in the study; (4) measure the dependent variables used to operationalize psychological absorption or flow; and (5) disguise the purpose of the experiment so that the participants would behave as normally as possible.

In one study (Mannell, 1979), the amount of freedom participants had in choosing a game to play during the free time period and the level of competitiveness of the game were manipulated. It was predicted that those participants who had greater freedom of choice and were in a more competitive situation would become more absorbed (higher level of flow) than participants who were given no choice and in a less competitive situation.

The participants in the study were 60 university students. An appointment was made with each individual to visit and participate in a "learning experiment." Each participant was randomly assigned to one of four treatment conditions (see Figure 4.3): (1) low choice of game/low competitive game; (2) low choice of game/high competitive game; (3) high choice of game/low competitive game; (4) high choice of game/high competitive game. Consequently, fifteen students participated in each one of these four sets of conditions.

Freedom of Choice	Competitiveness of the Game	
	Low	High
Low	15 participants	15 participants
High	15 participants	15 participants

Figure 4.3   Experimental Conditions in Leisure and Flow Study

Each participant arrived and was met individually by a graduate research assistant. The laboratory consisted of two adjoining rooms. In the first room, all participants performed a tracking task on a pursuit rotor requiring them to follow a moving light on a screen with a pencil-like wand. Whenever they lost contact with the light the electronic equipment made a beeping sound and recorded a miss. The participants were led to believe that their performance on the pursuit rotor task was the major focus of this "learning" study. They were asked to remove their watches and all jewelry, supposedly to prevent interference with the electronic equipment in the laboratory. However, the real purpose was to collect their watches and prevent them from keeping track of how much time they were involved in playing a game in the "free time" phase of the experiment in the second room. They performed on the pursuit rotor for five minutes, then were ushered into the second room of the laboratory which was furnished to look like a waiting room with comfortable furniture and pictures and posters on the walls. In this adjoining room the participants were told that the people in the study waited for various lengths of time before returning to perform again on the pursuit rotor learning task. Every effort was made to make the participants feel that what happened in this waiting or "free time" period had nothing to do with the actual purpose of the experiment.

Once in the waiting room, those participants who had been assigned to either of the two *high choice conditions* were told by the graduate student assistant that her advisor, whose experiment this was, was allowing her to ask them to help her by choosing to play one of two games she was developing for people who were hospitalized and by filling out an evaluation form while they were waiting for the next phase of the experiment. It was stressed that they were under no obligation to play. In addition to the choice of playing one of the two games, the high choice participants could choose to sit and read magazines. (Actually, the two games were just one game packaged in two different boxes with different names to create the perception of choice. Having only one game ruled out the possibility that any differences in flow levels among the experimental groups could be due to the influence of different games.) Participants in each of the *low choice conditions* were made aware of these alternatives but were told that they had to play a specific game since the other one had been fully tested and evaluated. They were not given the choice of sitting and reading.

The research assistant demonstrated the game. The game itself allowed the participants to pace themselves, and required them to create a series of patterns on specially designed cards and then match them from memory with a tray of red and white cubes. Participants in each of the two *high competitive conditions* were instructed to record their scores and place them in an envelope that they would be required to sign so that comparisons could be made with the other participants' scores. Participants in the *low competitive conditions* were instructed to record their scores, but that these would not be collected and used by the experimenter.

The participants were then left to play the game for 30 minutes. Following this free time period, they were taken back to the first room of the laboratory where they completed scales used to assess their level of absorption or flow in the game. Flow was operationalized in two ways. The first was as *perceived time duration*. High levels of flow result in people experiencing time as passing very quickly (Csikszentmihalyi, 1975). By measuring the length of time the participants perceived that they had spent playing the laboratory game during the standard time period of 30 minutes, the researchers were able to measure their experience of "loss of time." A *time duration scale* was devised consisting of two horizontal lines displayed on a sheet of paper (see Figure 4.4a). The participants were instructed that the top line represented the time they had spent performing on the five minute pursuit rotor task when they arrived at the laboratory. They were requested to draw a line through the second longer horizontal line at a point which represented their estimate of the time duration of the waiting period. The shorter the time duration was judged, the more absorbing the experience during the free time period.

Time Duration Scale

Two lines are displayed below. The shorter line represents the *amount of time* you spent performing on the pursuit rotor learning task before the waiting period. *Please draw a vertical line through the second longer line to indicate your estimate of the amount of time you spent in the waiting room.*

├────────┤

Time performing on the pursuit rotor

├──────────────────────────

Time spent in the waiting room

Figure 4.4a Time Duration Scale

Adapted from Mannell (1979)

The second characteristic of flow measured was the participants' focus of attention or level of concentration on the game. Focus of attention was measured by testing the participants' memories of the features of waiting room environment. A *situational memory test* was devised consisting of ten five-item multiple choice questions (see Figure 4.4b, p. 98). It was assumed that the less remembered about the waiting room, the greater the focus of attention and absorption in the game. Two additional trials on the pursuit rotor (to ensure the participants perceived the learning task as the central purpose of the study) were followed by a partial debriefing to determine if they had any suspicions about the hypotheses or actual purpose

Waiting Room Situational Memory Test

For each of the following questions about the waiting room, *circle* the correct answer. If you don't remember, please circle *e*.

1. *What type of flooring did the room have?*
   a. tile
   b. hardwood
   c. carpet
   d. scatter rugs
   e. don't remember

2. *How many windows did the room have?*
   a. 1
   b. 2
   c. 3
   d. 4
   e. don't remember

3. *What did the curtains on the window look like?*
   a. solid color
   b. flowered pattern
   c. checkered pattern
   d. vertical strips
   e. don't remember

4. *How many posters were on the wall?*
   a. 2
   b. 3
   c. 4
   d. 5
   e. don't remember

5. *What was the predominant color in the poster above the game table?*
   a. blue
   b. red
   c. green
   d. yellow
   e. don't remember

6. *What was the year and month on the calendar above the coffee table?*
   a. October 1976
   b. December 1976
   c. August 1977
   d. January 1978
   e. don't remember

7. *How many bookcase shelves were filled with books?*
   a. 0
   b. 1
   c. 2
   d. 3
   e. don't remember

8. *How many pencils were in the cup of the game table?*
   a. 1
   b. 2
   c. 3
   d. 4
   e. don't remember

9. *What did the painting in the sitting area depict?*
   a. a ship
   b. fruit
   c. portrait of a man
   d. flowers
   e. don't remember

10. *What was written on the black-board?*
    a. a date (14/02/78)
    b. an arithmetic sum $(2+2=4)$
    c. a time (12:45 p.m.)
    d. a temperature (67°)
    e. don't remember

Figure 4.4b   Waiting Room Situational Memory Test

Adapted from Mannell (1979)

of the study. None of the participants suspected the real nature of the experiment. A month later a full debriefing was given to the participants and the purpose and deceptions involved in this study discussed.

As predicted, participants in the high choice and high competitive conditions experienced more flow than those in the low choice and low competitive conditions. In Figure 4.5, it can be seen that those participants who perceived they had more choice in playing the game, remembered less about the waiting room environment, that is, they were more focused and involved in the game. The same was true of those participants in the high competitive conditions. Out of the ten items they were asked to recall, on average the high choice/high competitive participants only correctly identified one feature of the waiting room. In comparison, the low choice/low competitive group on average recognized three features of the waiting room. These participants did not become as fully involved in the game. The time duration estimates followed the same pattern. A conversion of

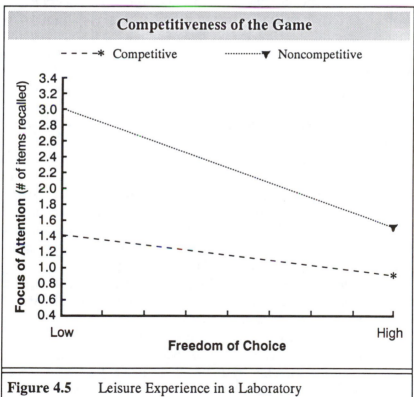

Figure 4.5   Leisure Experience in a Laboratory

Adapted from Mannell (1979)

the time scores (centimeters) into minutes suggests that the low choice/low competitive participants perceived the duration of the 30-minute waiting period reasonably accurately, that is, about 29 minutes in length. The participants in the high choice/high competitive condition experienced the 30-minute period to be only about 10 minutes in duration.

This study demonstrates that perceiving a leisure activity as freely chosen has a strong influence on the quality of the resulting experience, here defined as the level of flow. The more competitive conditions in this experiment also caused the participants to become more involved.

Experiential Sampling Method: Experiencing Leisure in Daily Life

As noted earlier, a large portion of people's leisure time and activity is embedded within the everyday activities that make up their lives. Csik-szentmihalyi and his colleagues developed the *experiential sampling method,* or ESM (Larson & Csikszentmihalyi, 1983) to monitor not only what people do during their everyday lives, but to measure the psychological states and experiences that accompany this daily activity. This method is used to uncover the regularities in perceptions and feelings of happiness, self-awareness, concentration, and other characteristics of conscious experience in various settings including work and leisure. The goal is to develop a "systematic phenomenology," to "carry out a science of internal experience" (Csikszentmihalyi & Larson, 1985).

Typically, respondents carry electronic pagers with them and are randomly signaled seven to nine times throughout the day for a period of one week. Each time the pager emits a signal (an audible beep), the respondents take out a booklet of brief questionnaires (experiential sampling forms, or ESF) and complete a series of open- and close-ended items indicating their current activity, the social and physical context of their activity, and their psychological state (see Figure 4.6, pages 102–103).

Though the ESF has been varied slightly across studies, the types of variables and scales included have been fairly standard. The ESF includes items that require respondents to: write in the time of the pager signal and the time that they actually filled out the ESF (usually, the questionnaire data are dropped if too much time elapses between the signal and response.); write down what they were thinking about at the time of the signal; record the main thing/activity they were doing; check on a list who they were with; rate on Likert scales several items that measure the level of psychological involvement in the activity (e.g., level of concentration, personal skills and challenge, perception of the passage of time); rate mood states on semantic differential scales assessing affect and arousal; and indicate the reasons or motivations for participation. Some researchers have included additional scales or items on the ESF that require respondents to rate their feelings of self-esteem when signaled (Wells, 1988), perceptions of leisure (Samdahl, 1988) and willingness to engage in alternative activities (Mannell & Zuzanek, 1991). The reliability of the multiple item mood scales has been shown to be consistently high in most studies reported. In analyses of the reliability of the ESF measures over a week of repeated use, the participants' responses have been shown to change only slightly from the first to the second half of the study week. Differences between individuals were also found to be stable (Csikszentmihalyi & Larson, 1984; Wells, 1988).

The ESM has been used to address a number of leisure-related research questions. Studies have examined the intrinsic satisfactions resulting from participation in recreational compared to nonrecreational activities (Graef, Csikszentmihalyi & Gianinno, 1983), the meaning and quality of experiences derived from the leisure activities engaged in by adolescents (Kleiber, Caldwell & Shaw, 1993; Kleiber, Larson & Csikszentmihalyi, 1986), leisure activities as a context for social relationships (Larson, Mannell & Zuzanek, 1986), and the experiential outcomes of conditions predicted to foster optimal leisure states (Mannell, Zuzanek & Larson, 1988; Samdahl, 1988).

In a study of the leisure experiences of adolescents (Kleiber, Larson & Csikszentmihalyi, 1986), ESM data were collected and allowed the authors to identify those leisure activities and settings in which adolescents experienced the most positive moods and became most psychologically involved. A sample of 75 male and female high school adolescents volunteered to participate in the study. Over the course of the study week the students responded to 69 percent of the signals. The total number of self-reports completed was 4,489.

The activities engaged in by the adolescents when they were signaled were determined by their response to the question: "What was the *MAIN* thing you were doing (as you were beeped)?" These responses were coded into 16 basic activity categories. The mood and affective properties of their experiences were measured by having them rate how happy–sad, irritable–cheerful, lonely–sociable and angry–friendly they were feeling. These ratings were combined for an affect score. The involvement dimension of the experience was measured by having the adolescents rate the level of concentration and challenge they experienced in the activity. The

Experiential Sampling Form   page 1 of 2

Date: _____ Time beeped: _____ am/pm Time filled out: _____

As You Were Beeped:

What were you thinking about? _____
_____

What was the main thing you were doing? _____
_____

Who were you with? ❑ Spouse/Partner   ❑ Alone
                    ❑ Your Children   ❑ Other _____
                    ❑ Friends/Neighbors   _____

How well were you concentrating? _____
_____

Was it hard to concentrate? _____
_____

Were you in control of the situation? _____
_____

How much did you like what you were doing? _____
_____

Describe How You Felt As You Were Beeped:

	Very	Quite	Some	Neither/ Not Sure	Some	Quite	Very	
Alert	—	—	—	—	—	—	—	Drowsy
Happy	—	—	—	—	—	—	—	Sad
Irritable	—	—	—	—	—	—	—	Cheerful
Energetic	—	—	—	—	—	—	—	Tired
Upset	—	—	—	—	—	—	—	Calm
Active	—	—	—	—	—	—	—	Passive
Worried	—	—	—	—	—	—	—	Carefree
Excited	—	—	—	—	—	—	—	Bored
Confused	—	—	—	—	—	—	—	Clear
Relaxed	—	—	—	—	—	—	—	Harried
Good	—	—	—	—	—	—	—	Bad

Figure 4.6   Experiential Sampling Form (ESF)

From Zuzanek & Mannell (1993)

Experiential Sampling Form page 2 of 2

	0	1	2	3	4	5	6	7	8	9

Did you feel lonely when beeped?

— — — — — — — — — —
Not at all Very much

Challenges of the activity:

— — — — — — — — — —
Low High

Your skills, knowledge, or competence in the activity:

— — — — — — — — — —
Low High

Do you wish you had been doing something else?

— — — — — — — — — —
Not at all Very much

How free were you to choose this activity?

— — — — — — — — — —
Not at all Very much

Did you do it primarily:
- ☐ for your immediate enjoyment or pleasure
- ☐ because it was good for you
- ☐ for the benefit of others
- ☐ because you had to
- ☐ because there was nothing else to do

At this moment, would you feel like watching TV?

— — — — — — — — — —
Not at all Maybe Very much

Why/Why not? _____

_____

★★
Great thoughts, wise cracks

Figure 4.6   Experiential Sampling Form (ESF)—continued

From Zuzanek & Mannell (1993)

intrinsic motivation and perceived freedom associated with the activity in which they were engaged at the time were measured on similar scales.

In Figure 4.7, the reader can see the relative frequency with which the adolescents were involved in the 16 basic types of activities over the course of a typical week in their lives. Figure 4.8 summarizes the average levels of freedom, affect, concentration, and challenge they experienced in the three major activity categories created by classifying the 16 activities (i.e., productive, maintenance, leisure). Those activities defined as leisure by the authors were experienced as more positive and free. However, when considering the involvement indicators of concentration and challenge, a different picture emerges. As seen in Figure 4.8, leisure activities had only slightly higher levels of concentration and perceived challenge than maintenance activities and considerably lower levels than productive activities. The researchers point out that these findings are consistent with the view that leisure is relaxing, but it also suggests that the leisure activities of adolescents rarely require much in terms of effort and attention or what might be called flow.

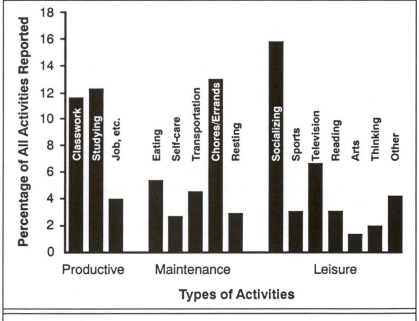

Figure 4.7 Frequency of Daily Activities Reported by Adolescents

Adapted from Kleiber, Larson and Csikszentmihalyi (1986)

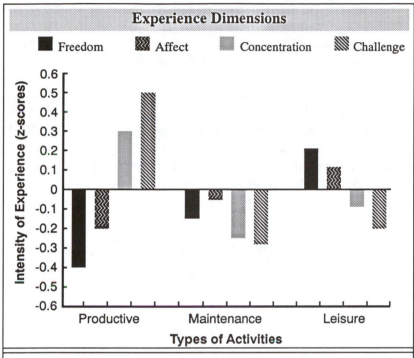

Figure 4.8 Experiences of Freedom, Affect, Concentration, and Challenge

Adapted from Kleiber, Larson and Csikszentmihalyi (1986)

However, when the researchers examined different types of leisure activities they found evidence for two categories of leisure experience. One, *relaxed leisure,* was found in the leisure activities of socializing, watching television, reading and listening to music, as well as the maintenance activities of eating and resting. The authors suggest that this type of leisure provides pleasure without high levels of involvement. The second set of activities included sports, games, artwork, and hobbies. These activities were experienced as freely chosen, intrinsically motivated and very positive, yet also as challenging and demanding of effort and concentration. The authors argued that participation in these *transitional leisure* activities offers adolescents a bridge between childhood and adulthood by demonstrating that the enjoyment found in the activities of childhood can also be found in the more demanding activities required of them as they move into adulthood.

It is important to note that even though the researchers in these studies of leisure experiences are entering into the subjective and experiential world of the participants, leisure is still typically defined from the *external definitional vantage point* of the researcher on the basis of the activity and setting—visits to natural outdoor recreation areas, participation in a laboratory game, and a variety of recreational activities occurring in the daily lives of a group of adolescents. The focus of these studies was on the quality and texture of the experiences accompanying these externally defined leisure activities and settings. It is not clear from these studies if and to what extent the participants construed all or any part of these outings to be leisure. We will take up this issue of the construal of activities, settings, and experiences as leisure in the next section.

Definitional Approach: Leisure in the Eye of the Beholder

How do you know if you are experiencing leisure? Is it based on the presence of certain features or characteristics you feel are part of the activity or setting in which you are involved? If so, what are these characteristics? Or is leisure independent of activities and settings, and instead a special feeling or experience? How would you describe this feeling? Does leisure have any properties that distinguish it from other types of experiences? As we noted in the last chapter, people differ in their assessments of what constitutes leisure, and even something seen as leisure on one occasion may not be perceived as leisure on another. The search for what people mean by leisure or the personal criteria they use in deciding whether something is leisure has also taken us into the minds of people.

Earlier, we argued that if researchers want to know how much leisure people have in their lives, it is important to measure not only how much time they spend in socially defined leisure activities and settings (external vantage point), but in activities and settings that they as individuals construe as leisure (internal vantage point). However, does it really matter if researchers know what people define as leisure and why they see it this way? If two people are both participating in the same activity, and if they both find it rewarding and enjoyable, does it matter whether one of them construes the activity as leisure and the other as something else? Will this perception affect the impact of their involvement on stress levels, well-being, or quality of life? Will it affect the nature and quality of their social interactions? Is it important that people perceive that they have "leisure" in their lives? These questions have not been directly addressed by leisure researchers. However, knowing what people define as leisure and what criteria lead them to make this attribution is still of importance to the study of leisure and its application.

When researchers ask people questions about their leisure (e.g., whether it be about how much they have, their attitudes toward leisure, their level of satisfaction with their leisure, how bored they are with it), the researcher often assumes that the word "leisure" has the same meaning for their subjects as it does the researchers themselves. This assumption is certainly not always the case as discovered in Shaw's (1984) modified time-diary study. Consequently, researchers need to continually check that the definitions used by the people they study are the same as the conceptual and theoretical definitions used and understood by researchers (Samdahl, 1991). If the factors that lead people to label something as leisure can be identified and understood and these factors are relatively similar for most people, researchers have a much better chance of accurately predicting and anticipating when activities, settings and experiences will, in fact, be construed as leisure by the people they are studying.

Criteria Necessary for Something To Be Construed as Leisure

The *definitional approach* to the study of the leisure experience, then, is characterized by theory and research which attempt to identify the attributes or properties of an activity, setting or experience that lead people to construe it as leisure. A number of *leisure attributes* with a variety of names have been proposed (see Table 4.2, pp. 108–109). The most central and commonly agreed upon set of attributes is associated with *freedom* or a *lack of constraint*. This lack of constraint is a quality typically attributed to situations or settings; the setting is free of requirements that one has to do anything. Lack of constraint has been called by many names (e.g., freedom of choice, freedom *from* constraints, the freedom *to* do something, self-determination, lack of role constraints, low work-relation, and "final" goal-orientation), but from a psychological perspective the common element suggested by these labels is that an activity or setting is more likely to be construed as leisure when people attribute their reasons for participation to themselves (i.e., it is freely chosen) rather than the social situation.

There is a second set of attributes commonly identified as being important. Activities, settings and experiences construed as leisure are likely to be perceived as providing opportunities for the development of competence,

Table 4.2 Definitional Approach: Attributes of Events Construed as Leisure and Examples of Research

Attribute	Description	Studies & Techniques
Freedom of Choice / Reduced Role Constraint	Perceived freedom to chose to participate or freedom from role constraints resulting from our interactions with others.	*Experiment:* Iso-Ahola (1979, 1980), Unger (1984); *Qualitative:* Gunter (1987), Henderson (1990), Lee, Dattilo & Howard (1994); *Diary + Qualitative:* Shaw (1985); *ESM:* Samdahl (1988, 1991), Samdahl & Kleiber (1989)
Intrinsic Motivation / Goal-Orientation	Perception that participation in an activity is for its own sake or enjoyment and as a final end in itself and not as instrumental for gaining something else.	*Experiment:* Iso-Ahola (1979, 1980), Unger & Kernan (1983); *Diary + Qualitative:* Shaw (1985)
Work-Relation	Perception that an activity or context is independent of paid work activity or employment activity.	*Experiment:* Iso-Ahola (1979); *ESM:* Samdahl (1992), Samdahl & Jekubovich (1993)
Opportunity for Self-Realization / Self-Expression	Perception that activities and contexts provide the opportunity to explore, understand and express one's true or core self. Opportunity for the development of self-identity.	*ESM:* Samdahl (1991); *Qualitative:* Gunter (1987)
Relaxation	Perception of a state of low tension and effort with the absence of strong emotions.	*Diary + Qualitative:* Shaw (1985); *Qualitative:* Henderson (1990), Lee, Dattilo & Howard (1994)
Enjoyment / Pleasure / Affect	Perception that activities or context provides positive affect and moods.	*Qualitative:* Gunter (1987), Henderson (1990), Lee, Dattilo & Howard (1994); *Diary + Qualitative:* Shaw (1985); *ESM:* Samdahl (1988), Samdahl & Kleiber (1989)
Sense of Separation	Perception that participation in an activity or context provides escape from the everyday mundane, routine world and its pressures.	*Qualitative:* Gunter (1987)

Table 4.2   Definitional Approach: Attributes of Events Construed as Leisure and Examples of Research (cont'd)

Attribute	Description	Studies & Techniques
Spontaneity	Perception that participation in activities or contexts are or allow spur-of-the-moment, impulsive or unexpected reactions.	*Qualitative:* Gunter (1987)
Timelessness	Perception that participation in an activity or context contributes to an experience of the absence of time, lack of awareness of the passage of time or a focus on the present moment.	*Qualitative:* Gunter (1987)
Fantasy / Creative Imagination	Perception that an activity or context provides an opportunity to achieve an openness to new things, that requires both the opportunity and necessity for creative imagination or fantasy.	*Qualitative:* Gunter (1987)
Adventure / Exploration	Perception that an activity or context provides a sense of adventure or the opportunity to satisfy one's curiosity.	*Qualitative:* Gunter (1987)
Lack of Evaluation	Perception by participant that the outcome of an activity is or will not be judged or tested.	*Diary + Qualitative:* Shaw (1985)
Definition of an Activity or Setting as Leisure	Perception that an activity or context is considered leisure by the participant (internal vantage point).	*Experiment:* Iso-Ahola (1979), Unger (1984); *ESM:* Samdahl (1992), Samdahl & Jekubovich (1993); *Qualitative:* Henderson (1990); *Diary + Qualitative:* Shaw (1984)

self-expression, self-development, or self-realization. When people engage in activities and settings that provide these opportunities, they are said to be *intrinsically motivated*. This attribute is clearly not completely independent of the freedom of choice attribute; self-determination is theorized to be an essential ingredient of intrinsic motivation. Intrinsic motivation is usually seen as an important secondary leisure attribute. We will examine the theories underlying the importance of freedom and intrinsic motivation to human behavior and experience, and consequently leisure in the next chapter.

A third major set of attributes that has been identified is based on the nature and quality of experiences derived from participation. When an engagement is experienced as *enjoyable, fun or pleasurable*, it is more likely to be construed as leisure. The feeling of *relaxation* as well as its antithesis, *intense involvement,* have also been suggested as attributes of leisure experiences; as have feelings of *separation or escape* from the everyday routine world; a sense of *adventure, spontaneity*, and *loss of time*. Additionally, experiences with cognitions involving *fantasy* and *creative imagination* have been suggested as attributes leading to perceptions of leisure.

Though in recent years researchers have developed a much clearer picture of what people mean when they use the word "leisure," there are some questions that remain. For example, must an individual perceive the presence of all of these attributes before they construe an activity, setting, or experience as leisure, or are there core attributes that are critical and others that contribute to, but do not necessarily trigger, the perception of leisure? Is the construal of some involvement as leisure an all-or-nothing perception? Can something be construed as slightly or moderately leisurely? The following sections examine research approaches that have been used to explore these and other issues with the definitional approach.

Qualitative Approaches: Participants Talk About Leisure

Researchers have directly observed and interviewed people about their leisure experience (e.g., Fine, 1983; Gunter, 1987; Henderson, 1990a; Henderson & Rannells, 1988; Roadburg, 1983; Shaw, 1985a). For example, Gunter (1987) asked 140 students in a self-report essay to describe both their most *memorable* leisure experience and the most *typical* leisure they normally experienced during the routine conduct of their daily lives. He then analyzed these stories to discover if the leisure experiences that stood out in their minds shared a common set of characteristics or attributes.

Consequently, the analysis did not focus on the specific activities reported (e.g., travel, music, reading for pleasure, visiting, meditation, drug use, isolation on an island, romantic liaisons, sitting on the bottom of the ocean). The most common attributes were: a sense of *separation* from the everyday world; *freedom of choice* in one's actions; a feeling of pleasure, or *pleasurable involvement* in an event; *spontaneity*; *timelessness*; *fantasy* (creative imagination); a sense of *adventure* and *exploration*; and *self-realization.*

The importance of taking individual definitions of leisure into account *(internal vantage point)* and looking at the factors that influence whether something is construed as leisure is nicely demonstrated in an interview study reported by Henderson (1990a). She carried out one to three hour life-history interviews with women who were 60 or more years old and had lived on a farm for the majority of their married lives. The interviews were carried out in the participants' homes, and they were asked to reflect on their total lives. Henderson was interested in understanding the types of activities and the social and physical settings that were seen by this group of women as leisure, as well as how changes over the life span affect these perceptions. She found that these women, who had worked hard all their lives, typically found leisure-like experiences in their work and family obligations even though the women saw themselves as having had little or no leisure. Even an outside observer at first glance may not have judged their involvements to be leisure. However, they had found opportunities to experience *freedom of choice, enjoyment* and *satisfaction* in a variety of activities, social settings, and physical locations—what Henderson called *"containers for leisure."* For example, many family obligations and community activities with other women had elements of leisure for the women even though they involved work-like activities. The home was also found to be a primary location or container for leisure.

As mentioned in the last chapter, Shaw (1984) used the time-budget diary to allow the people she was studying to indicate whether the activity or setting in which they were engaged was leisure for them or something else. Additionally, in follow-up interviews she had her subjects explain why they labeled their activities "leisure" or "nonleisure." Activities labeled "leisure" were characterized by the perception that they had been *freely chosen* and *intrinsically motivated.* She also found that feelings of *enjoyment, relaxation,* and a *lack of evaluation* by other people were associated with those activities her respondents construed as leisure.

Quasi-Experiments: Imagining Leisure

Researchers also have used quantitative methods to determine whether various attributes influence whether an activity or setting is construed as leisure (e.g., Iso-Ahola, 1979a, 1979b; Samdahl, 1988, 1991; Unger & Kernan, 1983; Unger, 1984). Iso-Ahola (1979b) used a quasi-experimental design and had the participants in his study imagine themselves engaging in a recreational activity during their free time. They could choose to imagine any recreational activity they wished. He then had them read eight hypothetical stories (see Figure 4.9) and further imagine themselves engaging in that activity in the different set of conditions described in the each of the hypothetical situations described in the stories. These situations differed in terms of the amount of freedom they had in choosing the activity (low vs. high), type of motivation for engaging in the activity (intrinsic vs. extrinsic) and degree to which the activity was work-related (related vs. unrelated). For each hypothetical situation, the 81 male and female university student participants rated to what extent they perceived the activity to be leisure (1 *"Not leisure at all"* to 10 *"Leisure at its best"*).

The analyses indicated that the perception of leisure was significantly greater when perceived freedom was high than when it was low, when participation was intrinsically rather than extrinsically motivated, and when the leisure activity was unrelated rather than related to work. Iso-Ahola also found that when the respondents imagined their participation to be their own choice (i.e., high freedom of choice), they construed the situation as leisure even when they perceived the activity to extrinsically motivated and work-related. These findings led Iso-Ahola (1979b) to suggest that "perceived freedom is the critical regulator of what becomes leisure in people's minds and what does not" (p. 313).

Experiential Sampling Method: You Call It—"Leisure or Nonleisure"

In the earlier discussion of the experiential sampling method, we described how researchers used the technique to monitor the experiences that accompanied activities they judged to be leisure (e.g., sport, artwork, television viewing, socializing). In other words, they took an external definitional vantage point. Samdahl (1988), however, used the ESM to examine the experiential attributes of leisure from the internal vantage point of her respondents. She added several items to the experiential sampling form that followed Iso-Ahola's procedure of asking study participants to rate the

---

Instructing Study Participants to Imagine Leisure

For a moment, *assume* that the present time represents your free time (i.e., free from your daily work and from other necessary activities such as sleeping and eating) and that you are presently participating in an activity X (e.g., playing tennis, reading, watching TV). In short, you are doing something during your free time. Then, at the same time, you are aware of the fact that the activity X has certain meaning to you. That is, (1) it is or is not related to your daily work, (2) you have or have not participated in it freely, and (3) it is intrinsically or extrinsically motivating. (Note that intrinsic motivation refers to behaviors which are motivated by intrinsic rewards, such as feelings of competence and self-determination and for which there are no apparent extrinsic rewards such as money. On the other hand, extrinsic motivation refers to behaviors which are motivated by extrinsic rewards such as money and for which there are no apparent intrinsic rewards).

Next you will be presented with the eight situations which are characterized by the above three elements. Your task is to rate what the activity X means to you as leisure in each case. To do this, circle one number that best represents your opinion in each case. In sum, place yourself in each of the following eight situations and then indicate by circling what your current participation in activity X means to you *as leisure*, under the specified (hypothetical) conditions. Note that each situation has three predominant characteristics.

Example

One of the eight hypothetical situations the study participants were asked to imagine:

> *You are not participating freely in the activity* X *(i.e., you did not have an opportunity not to participate) —the activity* X *is unrelated to your daily work—the activity* X *is intrinsically motivating.*

Rating scale:

1	2	3	4	5	6	7	8	9	10

Not leisure   Leisure
   at all   at its best

Figure 4.9 Instructing Study Participants to Imagine Leisure

Adapted from Iso-Ahola (1979b)

extent to which what they are involved in is leisure for them. Of course, Samdahl's respondents were assessing an actual activity or setting in which they were involved when "beeped" rather than an imaginary situation.

Similar to other ESM researchers, she used an experiential sampling form that required her respondents to indicate their moods, perceptions of freedom or constraint, motivation, and so on. Samdahl also included items that asked her respondents to rate on seven-point Likert scales (1 *"Strongly disagree"* to 7 *"Strongly agree"*) the extent to which they construed the activity or situation as leisure.

The participants were 18 women and men from a variety of backgrounds between the ages of 18 and 60 who volunteered to participate in the week-long study. These individuals reported 695 moments in their lives in response to the "beeps" emitted by the electronic pagers they carried. Samdahl was able to demonstrate that when people perceived that they had chosen to participate in an activity independently of the expectations of other people (low role constraint) and they felt that they were expressing their true selves (high self-expression), they were more likely to construe and rate the activity or situation as "leisure" and experience positive moods (see Figure 4.10).

In a more recent study, Samdahl and Jekubovich (1993) combined the ESM and a semi-structured qualitative interview to achieve a more com-

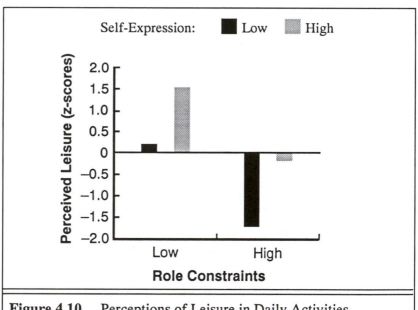

Figure 4.10 Perceptions of Leisure in Daily Activities

Adapted from Samdahl (1988)

prehensive understanding of the leisure experience. In their study of 83 adults between the ages of 30 and 65, the researchers were not only able to identify with the ESM when, where, and in what settings their respondents construed their activities as leisure, but the qualitative interviews provided insights into how these people actively organized their lives to make room and take advantage of opportunities for leisure. Not surprisingly, leisure in daily life was typically experienced "in the evenings and on weekends, at home, with family and friends, and within recreation or informal conversation" (Samdahl & Jekubovich, 1993, p. 137). However, based on their qualitative interview data, the researchers found that leisure was not a passive occurrence that emerged after other activities were done. "Leisure was not left to chance" (p. 138). Some of the ways the people in this study made room for leisure included getting up before family members, going to a motel in their hometown, arranging family dinners, and altering work schedules. Leisure was found to be important to many of the respondents, and positive leisure experiences occurred as a result of active negotiation and interaction with the social contexts that comprised their daily lives.

A Final Note on the Subjective Nature of Leisure

The experiential nature of both the daily routine events of life, as well as special and rare episodes, are becoming of greater interest to social scientists. In personality and social psychological research, there has been a substantial increase of interest in data that will allow psychologists to investigate the meaningful aspects of people's lives and experiences. There is increasing use of case studies, psychohistories, logs, diaries, and the experience sampling method (Pervin, 1985). As pointed out in this chapter, this trend is also evident in the social psychological study of leisure. A great deal of research and a wide variety of research methods have been focused on understanding the nature of leisure experiences in people's daily lives, and not only as some rare and special state. In light of the theory and research on the nature of leisure reported during the past decade and a half, it is no longer accurate to criticize the field for its inability to define, observe, and measure leisure. A wide range of methods and measures are available to researchers who wish to study specific leisure-related issues, and there are many examples of excellent investigations in which they have been used.

Different individuals do not necessarily see the same activity, setting, or experience as leisure. A given individual does not always construe the same activity, setting, or experience as leisure. However, researchers have found that people do tend to use similar criteria or rules in "deciding" if their engagements are leisure. In other words, activities, settings and experiences construed as leisure share in the perception of most people a limited number of attributes, such as perceived freedom, intrinsic motivation, enjoyment, and lack of evaluation.

Theories about what people see as leisure and how they develop their personal views are interesting in themselves. However, the research in this area is more than merely an interesting scholarly exercise. While people may not agonize over whether what they have done is leisure or not in the course of their daily lives, knowing how the people researchers study personally define leisure, rather than relying on researcher-imposed judgments, provides a much more sensitive approach to measuring the quantity and quality of leisure experienced by individuals. Today there is a great deal of interest in establishing the relationship between leisure and other areas of people's lives, such as mental health, the quality of life, work, and successful retirement. Policy makers and service providers want to know how equitably the opportunities for leisure are distributed among the members of society, what the barriers are to equitable distribution, and what constraints people feel to participation in meaningful leisure. Any attempt to assess the impact of leisure on the quality of life will be more successful if researchers are able to observe and measure the actual amount of leisure experienced, as opposed to simply the amount of externally defined leisure in which people engage.

The restriction of the term "leisure experience" to the positive or "upbeat" side of these experiences tends to divert attention away from factors that may inhibit the achievement of meaningful states (Goodale, 1990). A more useful approach is to not equate leisure experiences with more psychologically involving and positive experiences, but to examine what it is about leisure activities that seems to make them more likely to produce meaningful experiences. One way of thinking about or defining leisure experience, then, is simply as the contents of the stream of consciousness that accompanies a leisure activity or occurs in a leisure setting, either externally or internally defined. This approach leaves the way open to discuss and examine leisure experiences that are, among other things, positive and negative, involving and uninvolving, profound and not profound, and authentic and inauthentic. This approach differs from approaches to defining and conceptualizing leisure in which theorists only apply the term leisure to a special subset of those experiences that accompany leisure, recreation, travel, and cultural activities or engagements. Some time ago, Brightbill (1960) cautioned against an overemphasis on leisure as being automatically "positive" since this would prevent and inhibit a true understanding of leisure. He suggested that leisure can be used for good or bad; it can be used to improve or destroy ourselves, and to help or harm others.

It is also worth noting that leisure service professionals cannot structure, engineer, or provide leisure experiences directly. As a practitioner, one is limited to fostering, encouraging, and facilitating meaningful leisure experiences through the management of the recreation environment and setting, and the provision of concrete opportunities. Leisure service providers also can help people develop the skills and attitudes necessary to allow them to take advantage of these opportunities. Hopefully, research will help leisure service professionals understand the personality and social situational factors that not only affect the quality of experience but the links between the objective environments they manage and the way they are construed and perceived by the individual participant.

One of the most consistent findings to emerge from research on subjective leisure phenomena is that for something to qualify as leisure for most people, it must be perceived as freely chosen and intrinsically motivated. Interestingly, these two phenomena have been of great interest to social psychological researchers in many fields. Perceived freedom and intrinsic motivation seem to be extremely important to human mental and physical health, and they also just happen to be at the core of what people see as leisure. We will present some of these theories and examine research on these two central psychological processes in the next chapter.

Leisure and the Person

Perceived Freedom and Intrinsic Motivation: The Psychological Foundations of Leisure

Chapter FIVE

Preview

As we have discussed in previous chapters, researchers have found a variety of characteristics that distinguish leisure from other human activities and experiences. Two defining characteristics that have turned up repeatedly and are central to social psychological understanding of leisure are *perceived freedom* and *intrinsic motivation*. These characteristics reflect two well-studied social psychological processes that researchers see as extremely important in understanding human behavior. In this chapter, we will explore these constructs in more detail and discover why they are the conceptual pillars upon which a great deal of leisure theory has been built. Factors that influence perceived freedom and intrinsic motivation are identified, and the implications for leisure behavior and experience are discussed.

Imagine you are caring for two young children. They have had their breakfast and while you are cleaning up the dishes they gravitate to the television. They are now deeply engrossed in a television program. It's a beautiful day and you want them to go outside and play in the nearby park. Experience tells you that depending on how you approach the children, you may be in for some conflict and a poor start to a potentially pleasant day. You may also end up with children who are less than enthusiastic about an activity they typically enjoy. How do you handle this situation? What are your options?

* * * * *

You could tell the children that "they must go outside and play." They may resist, argue, perhaps refuse, or at best drag themselves out of the house with the look of martyrs, only to return within minutes to report that there is nothing to do.

In an effort to avoid this outcome, you may resort to what is sometimes called "reverse psychology." You can tell the children that though it is a beautiful morning and their friends are likely already at the park, they "cannot go out and play right now." Sometimes this strategy actually works and the children might lose interest in the television program and lobby you to let them go and play at the park. In this case, you "reluctantly" give in and let them "have their way." Unfortunately, it doesn't take children very long to develop immunity to this strategy. If the children are experienced with adults and their ways, they are likely to look at you with contempt and perhaps some pity.

You may decide to take a more direct approach—bribery! You promise them a visit to the corner store for some candy later in the day if they go out and play in the park. This may work in the short term. However, experience tells you that this approach sets a precedent and may result in the children expecting to be rewarded for everything you suggest they do, even when it is something that they usually enjoy.

There is a final strategy that you can consider. Though requiring the children go outside and play, you could allow them to decide for themselves when they will do so, at least, within certain limits. You tell them that they have to go outside and play, but they can watch another half-hour of television before they go out, or they can go outside now and come in before lunch to watch the television. If the play at the park is an attractive option, and you remind them of this, they may go along with this suggestion. On the other hand, this may not work either and you will have to decide whether to use your authority as an adult and dictate what they do.

The children's behavior and reactions in this hypothetical situation and the strategies for dealing with them revolve around the importance of having *choice*, feeling in *control*, and experiencing behavior as *self-determined*. When an authority figure tells someone that they "have to do something," such as "you have to go out and play," she or he restricts their choices. This may result in individuals feeling that they have little control over what is going on and it prevents them from feeling that they are the "cause" or "origin" of their own behavior. The importance of choice, control, and self-determination is reflected in the children's resistance to doing what they are told, and their less than enthusiastic response to the request that they go outside and play in the park.

When you use a "reverse psychology" you were attempting to take advantage of the children's desire for choice and self-determination. By appearing to restrict or eliminate the option of "going outside to play in the park," you expected them to react negatively and try to increase the amount of choice and control they have by lobbying to do what has been forbidden. Of course, the children will eventually come to realize that they are being controlled and really have no choice. Consequently, they are not likely to experience their behavior as self-determined. At this point, the strategy looses its effectiveness.

The issues of choice, control, and self-determination are also at work when you resort to bribery. It may lead to compliance with your wish that the children play in the park. However, the use of rewards may result in the children feeling that "playing in the park"—something they have enjoyed in the past—is no longer self-determined behavior. After all, they now see themselves as doing it for a reward. This may have long-term implications for their willingness to participate in the future when there are no adults around to reward them.

With the final strategy, you are attempting to give the children a feeling of choice that will hopefully allow them to feel that playing in the park is self-determined behavior. Obviously, the amount of choice available to the children is somewhat limited by the guidelines and conditions you have established. However, it may be sufficient to allow the children to feel some control over the situation and consequently react positively to your request "to go out and play in the park."

Translating the Essence of Leisure into Social Psychological Terms

A number of psychological theories and constructs have been developed to explain the importance of the processes of choice, control, and self-determination for human behavior and well-being. Central constructs include *perceived freedom* and *intrinsic motivation*. Today these two social psychological ideas are commonly used to characterize the essence of leisure. They have entered into popular, everyday language. However, these terms were invented and only began to be formally studied as social psychological concepts and theories during the last few decades—about the same time that the social psychological study of leisure itself began to develop. This is not to say that the ideas upon which the concepts of freedom and intrinsic motivation are based were not around before this time. The seeds of these ideas are found in the writings of philosophers, and social and political analysts dating back thousands of years. Attempts to define leisure and explain its importance to people also have a long history. The precursors of the psychological concepts of perceived freedom and intrinsic motivation can also be found in these discussions (see Goodale & Godbey, 1988; Kelly, 1972).

These ideas were "psychologized" and formally introduced into leisure theory with the development of several typologies (Neulinger, 1974, 1981; Kelly, 1972, 1978). This translation of the key characteristics of leisure into psychological terms has provided the basis for theory development, measurement, and research on leisure from a social psychological perspective (Mannell & Bradley, 1986; Tinsley & Tinsley, 1986).

A Typology for Describing Leisure

In his 1974 book, *The Psychology of Leisure*, John Neulinger developed a typology that he called a *leisure paradigm*. This model, resulting from the cross-classification of the perceived freedom and intrinsic motivation dimensions, was concerned with identifying and, in a sense, predicting when an activity or episode would be construed as some type of leisure or nonleisure by the individual participant (see Figure 5.1, p. 126). In the original model he incorporated a third dimension that he called "goal of the activity." He later removed this dimension from the typology because it overlapped substantially with the intrinsic motivation concept (Neulinger, 1981).

Neulinger identified the primary defining criterion of leisure as *perceived freedom*. A number of other theoretical models have also proposed

Perceived Freedom	Type of Motivation	
	Extrinsic	Intrinsic
Constrained	Pure Job	Pure Work
Free	Leisure-Job	Pure Leisure

Figure 5.1 Neulinger's "Leisure Paradigm"

Adapted from Neulinger (1981, p. 18)

perceived freedom (or similar notions) as a central defining element (e.g., Parker, 1971; Kelly, 1972; Gunter & Gunter, 1980). Neulinger defined perceived freedom as "a state in which the person feels that what she or he is doing is done by choice and because one wants to do it" (Neulinger, 1981, p. 15). While freedom is a complex phenomenon that includes political, social, and philosophical dimensions, one of its most important components is the subjective experience or perception of acting voluntarily. People in their daily lives perform thousands of acts. Each of these acts is experienced as being more or less compulsory, more or less voluntary (Csikszentmihalyi & Graef, 1980). Neulinger argued that everyone knows the difference between doing something because one "has to" and doing something because one "wants to." He pointed out that whether such a perception is true freedom or only the *illusion of freedom* is irrelevant based on the fact that in human behavior even illusions have real consequences (see Lefcourt, 1973). For example, the children in the hypothetical example at the beginning of the chapter would perceive that they had gained some freedom of choice and control when they lobbied to go to the park and were "successful." Consequently, they would likely feel that "going to the park" was self-determined behavior in this situation. However, from the adult's perspective, this choice and control would be an illusion.

Perceived freedom, as used by Neulinger and other authors, is equated with free choice which suggests the idea that to have leisure people must perceive that the social setting provides at least more than one opportunity for action. This type of perceived freedom has been called *decision freedom* (Steiner, 1970). Social psychologists have in general assumed that the experience of freedom is an attribution or construal people make about their behavior (see Steiner, 1970; Wortman, 1975; Brehm & Brehm, 1981). Perceived freedom is not an all-or-nothing condition. In fact, in most situations people are likely to be constrained in some way so that they typically feel only relatively free or free within certain limits. Though an individual may have the afternoon off to do as she or he wishes, in actual fact, choices for leisure are likely constrained to some extent by the time available (no time to take a long trip), finances, recreational skills, and the availability of friends.

The second dimension of Neulinger's typology is the *type of motivation* that underlies the decision to participate in an activity. Based on the emerging notions of intrinsic motivation (see Deci, 1971; Lepper, Greene & Nisbett, 1973), he distinguished between *intrinsic* and *extrinsic* motivation. For the purpose of his paradigm, Neulinger described motivation as being intrinsic when the rewards for participation are "seen as coming from engaging in the activity itself" (1974, p. 17). Motivation was labeled *extrinsic* when the activity is engaged in primarily because it leads to rewards external to the activity itself, such as money, grades, recognition, and awards.

The social psychological understanding of intrinsic motivation has continued to develop as Deci and Ryan (1985) have proposed *self-determination theory* to explain how it works. They identify four approaches that have been used to characterize intrinsic motivation (Deci & Ryan, 1991). First, intrinsically motivated behaviors can occur in the absence of any apparent external reward. Consequently, when people are in *free-choice* situations, that is, situations where they can freely choose among behavioral alternatives, it is assumed that what they choose to do is intrinsically motivated. Second, intrinsically motivated behaviors are engaged in out of *interest*. It is the experience of interest in an activity that impels people to become involved in it, and interest is frequently measured to indicate the presence of intrinsic motivation. Third, intrinsically motivated activities are *optimally challenging* and result in *flow experiences*. Consequently, "when people are intrinsically motivated they will seek out and attempt to conquer optimal challenges" (p. 242). Fourth, intrinsically motivated behaviors are based on "innate psychological needs" for *competence* and *self-determination*. Recently, Deci and Ryan (1991) have proposed a third innate need as the basis of intrinsic motivation—the need for *relatedness*. Relatedness refers to the need for people to feel that: (a) they are loved and connected to others; (b) those others understand them; and (c) they are meaningfully involved with the broader social world in which they live (p. 243). The idea of extrinsic motivation has also evolved. In addition to rewards, perceptions of extrinsic motivation can occur in situations where the reasons for participation are due to a wide range of factors including threats of punishment, evaluation, deadlines and obligations.

The cells in Neulinger's typology shown in Figure 5.1 (p. 126) represent four basic ways an activity can be experienced or perceived on the basis of how much freedom of choice and the type of motivation (intrinsic versus extrinsic) people perceive they had when becoming involved in an activity. For the sake of simplicity, the two dimensions have been dichotomized. Since Neulinger theorized that perceived freedom is the primary and critical determinant of what is perceived as leisure, the two cells that represent activities that are freely chosen are both seen as leisure and the other two cells as nonleisure. When an activity is perceived to be freely chosen and motivated for intrinsic reasons, Neulinger called it *pure leisure*. At the opposite extreme, there are activities that are experienced as least leisure-like or *pure job*. The individual has no choice about participating and is motivated by extrinsic reasons. The typology also provides a description of involvements which are neither pure leisure nor pure job. When people have little or no choice about participating but are intrinsically motivated, activities are experienced as *pure work*. Neulinger felt that activities engaged in for extrinsic reasons but that are freely chosen, what he called *leisure-job*, can be experienced as leisure. Later in the chapter we will examine recent developments in intrinsic motivation theory that help explain how activities that are extrinsically rewarded or regulated can still be perceived as freely chosen, self-determined and leisure.

The Experience of Work and Leisure Daily Life

Are perceived freedom and intrinsic motivation, in fact, important dimensions of a person's everyday experience? Do they distinguish leisure from nonleisure activities and settings? Their importance in a person's everyday experience is nicely demonstrated by several studies reported by Csikszentmihalyi and his associates. They studied a sample of 106 working men and women from the Chicago area with the Experiential Sampling Method over the course of a typical week in their lives (Csikszentmihalyi & Graef, 1980; Graef, Csikszentmihalyi & Gianinno, 1983). The respondents were asked to record the main activity they were engaged in when signaled, how free they felt to participate, and if they were intrinsically or extrinsically motivated. The percent of the time people perceived their actions to be freely chosen varied greatly between activities. As one might expect, work was rated as the least freely chosen activity. Only 15 percent of the time was it experienced as voluntary. Activities experienced as freely chosen most frequently were sports and games (90% of the time). As can be seen in Figure 5.2, leisure activities were experienced much more frequently as freely chosen, though there were interesting gender differences. Males rated most activities as more voluntary, especially cooking and childcare. The only activities for which this trend was reversed and women felt greater freedom of choice were in leisure settings outside the home (e.g., movies, restaurants), and during informal social gatherings. Idling, watching television, and reading were activities in which gender differences were least noticeable in terms of perceived freedom.

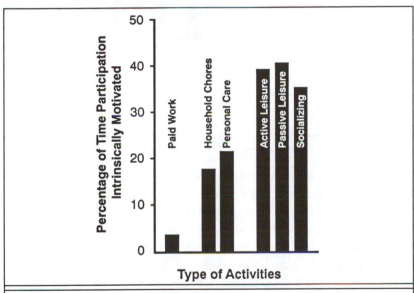

Figure 5.2 Frequency With Which Daily Activities Are Voluntarily Chosen

Adapted from Csikszentmihalyi and Graef (1980)

Work and obligatory activities were also seen to be extrinsically motivated much more frequently than leisure activities (see Figure 5.3, p. 130).

For instance, paid work (3.4%) and housework (17.5%) were rarely seen to be intrinsically motivated. This compares to over 40 percent for leisure activities in general.

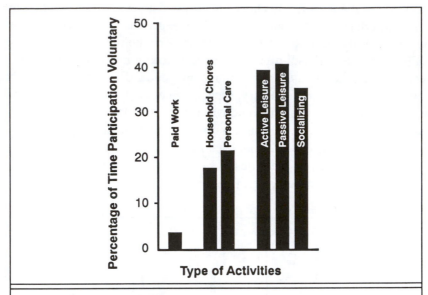

Figure 5.3 Frequency With Which Daily Activities Are Intrinsically Motivated

Adapted from Graef, Csikszentmihalyi and Gianinno (1983)

The researchers speculated that the gender differences seemed to indicate that the structure of daily activities is perceived as more voluntary by working men than by working women. This was true in both paid work, where the women in the study may have felt less free because it conflicted with their role as homemakers, and in activities like cooking and childcare which women likely felt compelled to do. Men, at least historically, have not felt as obligated to participate in cooking and childcare, and consequently, when they do participate they may be more likely to be intrinsically motivated.

These studies and others like them (e.g., Haworth & Millar, 1986; Mannell, Zuzanek & Larson, 1988; Stein, Kimiecik, Daniels & Jackson, 1995) suggest that perceived freedom of choice and intrinsic motivation are central dimensions in the experience of people's lives and are more likely to be found in leisure activities and contexts. Why is it that perceived freedom and intrinsic motivation are such potent forces in people's lives? In the following discussion, we will examine what social psychologists have had to say about the operation of these processes in human life and their role in an individual's leisure behavior.

Perceived Freedom and Control in Life and Leisure

The Importance of Perceived Freedom and Control

In the social psychological literature a variety of terms are used to identify the human desire for freedom and control. Theories have been proposed suggesting that a sense of freedom or control is a fundamental need and essential to health and well-being. (We will analyze the role of a sense of freedom and control for health in chapter ten).

For example, Adler (1964) suggested that to be human is to feel inferior which leads individuals to constantly compensate by *striving for superiority*. Consequently, a basic human response is to attempt to control one's life and surroundings in work, family, and leisure contexts. All humans have a need to understand their world and to exercise control over their environment, otherwise they would not survive. As Lefcourt (1973, p. 424) noted, "the sense of control, the illusion that one can exercise personal choice, has a definite and positive role in sustaining life."

White (1959) proposed a *competence* or *effectance* motive and suggested that individuals attempt to exercise control for its own sake. People engage in activities because the behavior "satisfies an intrinsic need to deal with the environment" and satisfies the need to see oneself as competent and masterful. Likewise, deCharms (1968) proposed that people are all motivated by the desire to be masters of their own fate, and that people strive to be *causal agents* or the *origins* of their behavior. In fact, exercising control is satisfying in itself.

Langer (1983) suggested that people have such a strong need for control that it leads them to perceive that they have control and freedom of choice even when they do not. In her *Illusion of Control Theory*, Langer suggests that people need to feel they can control the important events in their lives and that most people are unrealistically optimistic about the future and tend to exaggerate the amount of control they have over uncontrollable life events. She found that even bright, well-adjusted university students delude themselves by believing they can control the outcomes of games of chance. When the students she was studying played cards against a competitor, they bet more money when their competitor seemed nervous rather than confident even though they were aware that the winner was determined purely by chance. When the participants in her study played a lottery, they were more reluctant to sell their ticket after choosing the number themselves than after receiving an assigned number even though it did not improve their chances of winning (Langer, 1975). Langer also pointed out that it is not always good for people to feel that they have control because often they do not and they may set themselves up for feelings of failure.

Theories of Freedom and Control and Their Implications for Leisure

If perceived freedom and control are so important, it should come as no surprise that a threat to, or the elimination of, freedom can have negative psychological consequences. Brehm (1966) suggested that a threat to or loss of freedom generates a state of motivational arousal he called *psychological reactance* which results in attempts to regain the freedom. According to this theory, individuals have a set of specific behavioral freedoms—actions, thoughts, and feelings which they feel free to exercise. When a specific freedom is eliminated or threatened, the individual will evaluate that freedom more favorably and be motivated to reestablish it (Brehm, 1966; Brehm & Brehm, 1981). For example, an adolescent's parents have either threatened to restrict or forbidden him to go to the local video arcade. How strongly this individual will react depends on several factors according to reactance theory. First, the more this individual has learned to expect to have this particular freedom, the more psychological reactance will be experienced as a result of the threat to or elimination of that freedom. The adolescent will experience greater reactance if he has participated regularly rather than only occasionally. Second, his reaction to the threat, or to the actual elimination of this behavioral freedom is stronger if this freedom is perceived as important. The adolescent is likely to experience greater psychological reactance if video game playing is his favorite leisure activity and one from which he derives a great deal of recognition for his skill. Third, if his parents forbid any participation, he will experience greater reactance than if they only threaten to take it away. Finally, if the threat to this freedom is likely to negatively impact on the adolescent's other activities, then reactance will be greater than if there was no such impact. In other words, psychological reactance will be greater if the arcade is also a place were the adolescent meets friends and other leisure activities are planned rather than just a place to play a video game.

Brehm described several common consequences of experiencing psychological reactance. The threatened or eliminated behavioral freedom can become more attractive to the individual. In the previous example, forbidding or threatening the opportunity to play video games at the arcade may result in the adolescent wanting to pursue this activity even more than he currently does. Driscoll, Davis and Lipetz (1972) found that the more interference in a romantic relationship there was by parents, the more in love the couples were. On the other hand, if people are coerced into engaging in an activity it can reduce its attractiveness. For example, Wright, Wadely, Danner and Phillips (1992) found that matchmaking and arranging blind dates for friends can backfire. Motivated to preserve the freedom to make their own romantic choices, friends may become less attractive to each other than they would have without outside encouragement.

An individual can also react to psychological reactance by engaging in direct attempts to restore the threatened or eliminated option, or compensate for the loss by pursuing related behaviors. In the former case, the adolescent in the previous example may sneak out to play at the arcade or attempt to persuade his parents to restore this freedom. In the latter situation, the individual may choose to play at home more frequently or substitute an activity like billiards. Iso-Ahola (1980a, p. 199) suggested that a person with a wide variety of leisure skills is much better equipped to handle threats to or the elimination of "recreational freedom." More recently, Iso-Ahola has expanded this idea into a *Theory of Substitutability* and suggested that people will be less willing to replace one leisure activity for another when the external "pressure for substitution of leisure behaviors gives rise to psychological reactance or arousal that reduces one's willingness to substitute" (Iso-Ahola, 1986, p. 371).

In its application to leisure, psychological reactance theory would seem to allow researchers to "predict the arousal of negative affect when the individual has limited choice, which potentially could interfere with the individual's ability to enjoy and become involved in an activity" (Mannell & Backman, 1979, p. 301). Feeling that you had little choice in participating would also reduce the attractiveness of the activity. Some support for this hypothesis was provided by the study described in the last chapter which simulated a period of free time in the laboratory and manipulated the freedom of choice subjects had to play a game. As predicted, the participants were found to have less positive and psychologically involving experiences when they perceived they had less choice than other participants.

Learned helplessness is another important social psychological theory based on the belief that freedom and control are important for human functioning. Learned helplessness can be described as the phenomenon in which experience with uncontrollable events creates passive behavior toward subsequent threats to well-being (Seligman, 1975). In one study, dogs that received a series of electrical shocks over which they had no control later failed to escape from additional shocks by crossing a barrier into a compartment where no shocks were delivered (Maier & Seligman, 1976). Those that had not received uncontrollable shocks quickly learned to avoid the subsequent shocks. Similarly, human subjects exposed to inescapable bursts of noise failed to protect themselves in a later situation where noise could be easily avoided (Hiroto, 1974).

Seligman (1975) argues that these findings indicate that both animals and humans exposed to an uncontrollable event learn that control is not possible, and therefore, stop trying to exert control. Childhood or adult socialization experiences and social environments, where repeated failure occurs and which lead people to attribute these uncontrollable events to their own personal failings, are thought to be a source of low self-esteem and depression—that is, learned helplessness.

The theory of learned helplessness can be applied to understanding leisure behavior. For example, Iso-Ahola (1977, 1980a, 1980c) asked if participation in Little League Baseball can induce learned helplessness as a result of young players being exposed to failure and subsequent feelings of lack of controllability. He concluded that a team's repeated failure could under some conditions contribute to the development of learned helplessness. If players attribute their failure to a lack of personal ability or control, their persistence at and enjoyment of the activity is reduced and they are likely to withdraw. If the problem becomes compounded by repeated exposure to failures and uncontrollable events, such as striking out repeatedly, a state of generalized helplessness may be the consequence. This learned helplessness might influence involvement in other leisure or even nonleisure activities.

Today in many communities, leisure service providers have developed a variety of strategies to minimize these negative effects of children's organized sports. Noncompetitive recreational leagues that deemphasize winning and stress skill development and fun are common. Preseason practices followed by player drafts to allow the formation of better balanced teams have also been implemented. As Iso-Ahola (1980c) suggested, the most obvious solution would be to remove competition from leisure activities entirely. However, he points out that such solutions are unrealistic. While competition and winning can be deemphasized, elimination altogether is unlikely. In fact, even if society were to cease declaring people winners and losers, they would still continue to "compete" by using subjective criteria and standards. People, whether children or adults, seem to have a need and desire to evaluate their personal abilities relative to those of others (Festinger, 1954). Subtle and indirect social comparison can be as powerful as a direct failure in creating the illusion of incompetence or helplessness.

People learn to deal with failure by using a variety of psychological strategies, and consequently avoid developing feelings of learned helplessness. If one watches children who play on a losing team, it can be seen that they often are able to focus on their own personal successes and skill development, and attribute the failure to the team as a whole or other players. People also learn to place the importance of the outcomes of winning and losing into perspective when confronted with a failure. The importance of the leisure activity in which failures are experienced can be minimized and the importance of leisure activities in which the individual is proficient can be emphasized (Iso-Ahola & Mannell, 1985). Too much winning is not good either. People are not likely to develop strategies for coping with failure if they are not occasionally exposed to it (Iso-Ahola, 1980c, p. 199).

Learned helplessness theory also helps in understanding the psychological challenges that people with disabilities and institutionalized older adults may have in enjoying meaningful leisure (Dattilo & Kleiber, 1993; Iso-Ahola, 1980a; MacNeil & Teague, 1987). Both the disability itself and other people's reactions to it may lead persons with disabilities to perceive themselves to be helpless. This can reduce their efforts and thereby the possibility of achieving success in subsequent leisure engagements. In a study of older adults who were residents in a nursing home, Shary and Iso-Ahola (1989) demonstrated that these feelings of helplessness and lack of control can be reversed. They provided one group of residents with an orientation session that stressed the importance of the residents taking responsibility for making leisure choices that affected their daily lives at the facility. This group was given a choice over the type, scheduling, and length of a variety of leisure activities in which they could participate during the course of the study. A second group of residents, the control group, participated in similar activities but were not sensitized to the importance of taking responsibility and control of their lives in the facility, and they were given no opportunities to make choices or assume any responsibility over situations during the leisure activities. At the end of the study, the group that was encouraged to take control of their leisure perceived themselves to be much more competent, had higher levels of self-esteem, and enjoyed their leisure participation much more than did the control group; they had learned not to feel helpless.

Another social psychological theory based on the notions of control and freedom is Bandura's (1977, 1986) idea of *self-efficacy*. He defined self-efficacy as a person's belief that she or he is capable of the specific behavior required to produce a desired outcome in a given situation. This expectation of *personal control* underlies the motivation behind many behaviors. As people encounter a situation, they assess the abilities necessary for a successful experience and they assess their own capabilities of achieving success in the situation. Self-efficacy judgments influence the degree of effort people expend and their persistence in the face of obstacles or aversive experiences. Bandura also suggests that perceptions of efficacy developed within one domain of people's lives tend to generalize to other areas.

Arguing that some of the important benefits of therapeutic recreation interventions may result from enhancing people's sense of self-efficacy in leisure, Maughan and Ellis (1991) studied 32 clinically depressed adolescent inpatients at a private psychiatric hospital. These researchers examined the adolescents' efficacy judgments following participation in the recreational activity of video game playing. Half of the adolescents played in conditions predicted by Bandura to increase efficacy judgments. One at a time, half of the study participants watched a peer role model, who was actually a confederate of the experimenter's, successfully play at a skill level that corresponded to the participant's perceived skill level. The experimenter also gave each participant some control over the video game room environment by allowing them to adjust the lighting and type of music playing, and a recreation therapist provided verbal encouragement and praised the participants' performance while they were playing the game. The other half of the adolescents in the study (the control group) played the game without these conditions being present. Those adolescents who played in the setting designed to enhance self-efficacy came to feel that they were much more competent and had more control over the outcomes of the game than those who did not.

Generally, the need for a sense of freedom and control is thought to be important or common to all people. However, there are theories that suggest that the need for freedom and control varies in strength among people as a result of socialization experiences and personality. For example, Burger (1992) has proposed a *need for control* that he describes as a personality trait. In other words, some people have a high need for control, whereas for others this need is much less important. As we will discuss in chapter six, leisure researchers have examined these types of individual differences and their influence on the ability to experience leisure.

Intrinsic Motivation: The Need for Self-Determination, Competence, and Relatedness

As we presented in chapter four and consistent with Neulinger's (1974) leisure paradigm, researchers have found that intrinsic motivation is a major dimension or characteristic of leisure. As with the notions of freedom and control, social psychologists have developed theories and carried out a great deal of research to help explain this phenomenon. Intrinsic motivation has also been an important leisure research topic, and has been discussed in conjunction with children's play (Barnett, 1980; Barnett & Kane, 1985), tourism behavior (Iso-Ahola, 1983; McCullough, 1993), therapeutic recreation (Dattilo & Kleiber, 1993; Iso-Ahola & Crowley, 1991; Peterson & Gunn, 1984), serious leisure (Stebbins, 1992a), leisure and unemployment (Fryer & Payne, 1984; Haworth, 1986), sport involvement (Stein, Kimiecik, Daniels & Jackson, 1995), and leisure and well-being (Coleman, 1993; Weissinger & Iso-Ahola, 1984).

The Nature of Intrinsic and Extrinsic Motivation

Elements of the intrinsic motivation idea are related to the desire people have for freedom of choice and control. Deci's (1975) original ideas about intrinsic motivation were strongly influenced by White's (1959) notion of effectance motivation discussed earlier in the chapter. Deci theorized that people are often motivated to engage in activities because they want to demonstrate to themselves that they are capable of effectively exercising control over their environments. He makes a distinction between the notions of *control* and *sense of choice*. People do not always want control but they do wish to at least maintain a sense of choice over what happens to them. If a person chooses to ride a roller coaster, she or he essentially relinquishes control over what happens during the five or so minutes of the ride but maintain a sense of choice because she or he has done what she or he wanted. Deci and Ryan (1985) called this sense of choice *self-determination*. Self-determination theory proposes that people have an intrinsic desire to explore and understand their environment and that this desire is present in the very earliest stages of child development and continues to be important throughout life (Deci & Ryan, 1991).

Deci developed the theory of self-determination in response to earlier theories that suggested humans do everything for extrinsic rewards. The supremacy of extrinsic rewards for controlling behavior was challenged by research with humans and animals. Rats were found to learn to negotiate mazes out of apparent curiosity when no external rewards such as food were available (Montgomery, 1954), monkeys performed complex tasks for the opportunity to play with puzzles (Harlow, 1950), and children are known to play for the pure joy of it (Ellis, 1973).

The Danger of Rewards and Extrinsic Regulation in Leisure

It is common for people to strive for external rewards. In fact, rewards frequently are a part of leisure activities and contexts. Trophies and prizes are awarded for participation and good performance in children's and adult's leisure activities. Rewards are used by parents to encourage participation in those leisure activities that they feel are good for their children. But what happens to their intrinsic motivation once these rewards are no longer available? When people are rewarded for listening to music, playing games or volunteering, their behavior can become overjustified, that is, they may begin to attribute their participation to extrinsic motives. Research has suggested that such overjustification can be dangerous. The introduction of extrinsic rewards tends to undermine people's experience of self-determination and induce a shift in *perceived locus of causality* from internal to external (deCharms, 1968), and consequently their motivation from intrinsic to extrinsic. People come to construe their participation as due to receiving a reward which reduces their interest in the activity. This problem, the *overjustification effect,* has been demonstrated in numerous experiments (see Amabile & Hennessey, 1992; Deci & Ryan, 1985; Lepper & Greene, 1979).

Mark Lepper and his colleagues (Lepper, Greene & Nisbett, 1973), for example, gave children attending a preschool a chance to play with colorful felt-tipped markers—a chance most of them couldn't resist. By observing how much time the children spent on the activity, the researchers were able to measure their interest in the activity, that is, their intrinsic motivation. Two weeks later, the children were divided into three groups, all equal in their initial level of intrinsic motivation. One group of children was simply asked if they would draw some pictures with the markers. The second group was told that if they used the markers they would receive a "Good Player Award" (a certificate with a gold star and a red ribbon). In the third group, the children were not told they would receive the reward for drawing pictures but after they had completed drawing were given the same award as the children in the second group.

About a week later, the teachers placed the markers and paper on a table in the classroom while the experimenters observed through a one-way mirror. Since no rewards were offered, the amount of free time the children spent playing with the markers reflected their intrinsic motivation. The results were as predicted. Children who had previously expected and received a reward for their efforts were no longer as interested in the markers as they had been. Children who had not received a reward maintained their interest. Those who had unexpectedly received the reward, having played with the markers without the promise of reward, also remained intrinsically motivated (see Figure 5.4).

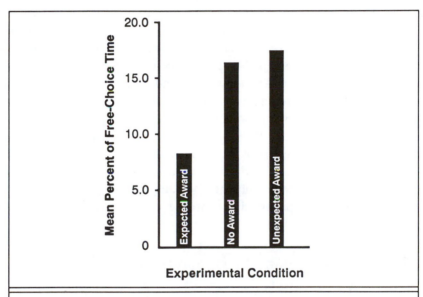

Figure 5.4   Time Spent Playing With Colored Markers

Adapted from Lepper, Greene and Nisbett (1983)

The paradox that rewards undermine, rather than enhance, intrinsic motivation has been observed in numerous settings with children and adults. If an individual accepts money for a hobby or leisure activity, before she or he knows it, what used to be "play" can come to feel like "work." In general, settings that are experienced as *autonomy supportive* (i.e., encouraging self-determination and choice) have been shown to maintain or enhance intrinsic motivation, whereas social situations that are *controlling* (i.e., experienced as pressure to perform in specific ways) have been found to undermine intrinsic motivation. In fact, it is not only material rewards and good player awards that create a controlling social setting. Situations where the motivation for participation is due to threats of punishment, obligations, evaluations, deadlines, and imposed goals can also undermine or reduce intrinsic motivation. This broad set of factors that can create controlling conditions is called *extrinsic regulation* (Deci & Ryan, 1991).

The overjustification effect can have serious implications for how classroom teachers use rewards and extrinsic regulation of various types to improve study habits, business managers use incentives to increase worker productivity, parents motivate their children, coaches encourage their players, and leisure service providers get the people with whom they work to become engaged and maintain their involvement in leisure activities. For example, most parents want their children to become involved in leisure activities that not only give them enjoyment but also provide a variety of benefits such as exercise, intellectual stimulation, physical skill development, and opportunities to develop friends and social skills. They would like their children to become intrinsically motivated to participate in these types of activities so that they do not have to coerce, bribe, or otherwise control them to participate. By fostering intrinsic motivation to participate, children are more likely to maintain their involvement in these types of activities as they develop and become independent of parents, teachers, and coaches. Consequently, they may be better prepared when on their own to seek and select personally rewarding and meaningful pursuits when they have free time available.

Self-Determination and Leisure in the Face of Extrinsic Regulation

Does this mean that all types of rewards and extrinsic regulation will undermine the development and maintenance of intrinsic motivation? Is there no role for rewards in developing intrinsic motivation for participation in a leisure activity where none previously existed? Should rewards always be avoided? No, not necessarily. If a person is not intrinsically motivated to start with, then a reward cannot hurt because the behavior could not become "overjustified." If receiving a reward does not depend on participating in an activity, then participation is likely to be seen as being under the individual's own control and the reward perceived as a *bonus*, rather than as a *bribe*. For example, as part of an experiment, university students were paid to play a laboratory game (Bradley & Mannell, 1984). Before deciding to play the game, students in one experimental condition were told that they would receive a monetary reward if they participated. The results of the experiment showed that they perceived the reward to be a bribe for playing. Students in a second group were offered the same reward after they had already decided to play the game. They were found to perceive the reward as a bonus for their participation. In a later phase of the experiment, when they had a free-choice period and could chose from among a variety of activities, this second group chose to play the original game more frequently and for longer periods of time than the first group who had perceived the reward to be a bribe. When the reward was seen as a bonus for participation, it had not interfered with the students' feelings of self-determination and their intrinsic interest in the activity. Research has demonstrated that intrinsic interest in an activity can often be maintained by fostering autonomy supportive conditions that allow people to feel their behavior is self-determined even in the face of extrinsic rewards and other forms of external control (e.g., Harackiewicz, 1979; Ryan, Mims & Koestner, 1983).

In Neulinger's paradigm (Figure 5.1, p. 126), it can be seen that his *leisure-job* condition (the perception that an activity is freely chosen and extrinsically motivated) fits the description of a self-determined, extrinsically motivated activity quite well; he saw this as a form of leisure, albeit not "pure leisure." Self-determination theory suggests that being able to experience intrinsic interest in externally controlled circumstances (i.e., extrinsic regulation) involves *internalization* and *integration*. This process allows people to expand their sense of freedom and control over their social environments even in the face of potentially controlling factors (Rigby, Deci, Patrick & Ryan, 1992). An activity that is engaged in because it is rewarded, an obligation or coerced can be experienced, under some circumstances, as self-determined. Consequently, the process of internalization and integration is the means by which extrinsically motivated activities can become self-determined and thus, like intrinsic motivation, provide the basis for highly satisfying leisure. This perspective helps in understanding how people can find leisure in their work, and how activities that involve rewards, obligations and commitments can at times be experienced as leisure.

Upon closer examination, Deci and Ryan (1991) have proposed that extrinsic regulation can take several different forms which vary in terms of how self-determined they allow people to feel when they participate. *External regulation* refers to behaviors that are controlled by factors clearly external to the individual, like the promise of a reward or the threat of punishment. Engaging in the activity of running to win awards and the praise of friends would be an example of external regulation. *Introjected regulation* refers to activities that are motivated by internal pressures and describes a form of motivation in which actions are controlled or coerced by internal needs other than competence, self-determination, or relatedness. In spite of the fact that these pressures are internal to the person, such behaviors are said to have an external perceived locus of causality because the source of their motivation is external to the person's sense of self or what is really important to them. It is introjected regulation that is operating when people participate because they feel they should or because they would feel guilty if they did not. For example, running during your free time can be motivated by a form of introjected regulation. People may run not out of a real and genuine interest (intrinsic motivation), but because they believe it is healthy to exercise. Consequently, they feel they should run, and they would feel guilty if they did not.

Integrated regulation is the most self-determined form of extrinsic motivation and results from the complete internalization and integration of the extrinsic regulation. The activity has become personally important and people are less likely to feel controlled by extrinsic rewards and regulation. With respect to running, such integrated regulation is different from that experienced by people who participate because they feel that they should exercise for health reasons (introjected regulation) or because their friends are pressuring them to do so (external regulation). They are well aware that there are health benefits and their friends would disapprove if they stopped. They may even occasionally receive awards for their participation in competitive races. However, they also feel that their participation is highly self-determined. This was the point Neulinger was making with his leisure paradigm and the "leisure-job" category (see Figure 5.1, p. 126), and what Iso-Ahola meant when he stated that perceived freedom is the "critical regulator" of something being perceived as leisure (Iso-Ahola, 1979a, p. 313). When integrated extrinsic regulation exists, people will likely continue to run even if friends turn to new activities and awards for participation are no longer available. They will likely continue to experience it as leisure.

Support for these ideas comes from several areas of research. For example, research in educational settings has shown that when people are more fully engaged in learning, whether through intrinsic motivation or integrated extrinsic regulation, they report greater interest in assigned material, higher levels of enjoyment of the material, more understanding, and greater flexibility in utilizing newly acquired information (Rigby, Deci, Patrick & Ryan, 1992). Stebbins' (1992a) notion of "serious leisure" is a good example of leisure behavior that is often motivated by integrated extrinsic regulation. He found that the amateur musicians and variety performers he studied often received payment for their performances and participated in their "leisure" in what could be seen as controlling conditions (e.g., required rehearsals, performances at required times and places). However, these activities were still experienced as leisure.

In a study of older adults using the experience sampling method (Mannell, Zuzanek & Larson, 1988), high intrinsic interest was often experienced in activities under the control of integrated extrinsic regulation. When signaled, the older adults rated the amount of choice they had perceived in selecting their current activity and whether they had been intrinsically or extrinsically motivated to participate. On the basis of these ratings, the researchers classified the activities reported during the study week into four types according to Neulinger's paradigm (refer back to Figure 5.1). Ratings were also completed that allowed the measurement of how intrinsically interesting the activities were experienced during participation. *In-*

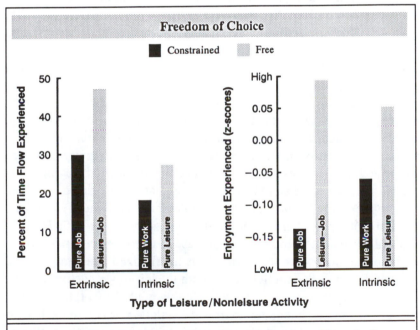

Figure 5.5 Percent of Time Flow Experienced, and Level of Enjoyment Experienced in Activities Classified According to Neulinger's Leisure Paradigm

Adapted from Mannell, Zuzanek and Larson (1988)

trinsic interest was defined as the extent to which the activity was optimally challenging or a "flow experience" and enjoyable (see Deci & Ryan, 1991, p. 242). An activity was considered optimally challenging or flow when the respondent rated it above average in challenge and their skills in the activity were also rated as above average (see Csikszentmihalyi & LeFevre, 1989). Enjoyment was assessed by having the older adults rate on seven-point Likert scales how "happy–sad" and "cheerful–irritable" they were feeling when participating in the activity.

The intrinsic interest experienced in the activities comprising each of the four leisure/nonleisure types is shown in Figure 5.5. The activities classified as leisure–job according the Neulinger's typology were experienced as the most intrinsically interesting, that is, they were experienced most frequently as flow and as the most enjoyable. These leisure–job activities appear to fit the definition of activities under "integrated extrinsic regulation." They were extrinsically motivated and yet freely chosen allowing a sense of self-determination.

A surprising finding of this study was that the older adults frequently experienced flow in activities that were extrinsically motivated (see Figure 5.5, p. 143). Pure-job activities produced as many flow experiences as pure leisure, and leisure-job activities were experienced as flow significantly more frequently than pure leisure activities. When the researchers examined the differences in the types of activities that were classified as extrinsically and intrinsically motivated, they found some interesting differences. The pure leisure of the older adults more frequently consisted of passive leisure activities, such as relaxing, reading, watching television and listening to music. In comparison, leisure-job activities were frequently more demanding activities such as hobbies, volunteering, caring and playing with grandchildren, and exercise. The extrinsic regulation associated with these latter activities included the obligation and commitment they felt either to others through their volunteer and family care activities or to their own health and personal development in the case of exercise activities and hobbies. It appears that when the older adults internalized and integrated extrinsic regulation of their activities, as with the leisure-job activities, they were more likely to experience flow and enjoyment. In fact, they seemed to "benefit" from this integrated extrinsic regulation. They felt self-determined (perceived freedom of choice) and yet their sense of obligation and commitment "pushed" them into activities that were more challenging and demanding of their skills than the ones they often chose for pure leisure. They also experienced as much enjoyment in the leisure-job activities as in the pure leisure activities (slight difference was not significant). In a follow-up analysis of this study, those older adults who had more of these experiences reported higher levels of life satisfaction (Mannell, 1993).

The older adults experienced flow as frequently in the pure-job activities as they did in the pure-leisure activities. These extrinsically motivated pure-job activities seemed to "push" the respondents to become involved in more demanding activities resulting in higher levels of flow. However, pure-job activities are not freely chosen. In this study, they were experienced as the least enjoyable of all the activities reported by the older adults, again demonstrating the importance of feeling one's behavior is self-determined even in the face of extrinsic regulation.

Fostering Freedom of Choice and Intrinsic Motivation in Leisure

Let's return for a moment to the hypothetical example discussed at the beginning of this chapter. Based on our discussion of freedom of choice and intrinsic motivation, certain guidelines can be suggested if parents and other caregivers want to maximize the likelihood of the children voluntarily going out and playing at the park and experiencing the activity as intrinsically interesting leisure. Generally, feelings of self-determination need to be fostered by providing opportunities for choice and control, using rewards with care to avoid perceptions of control and bribery, involving the children in the decision-making process, taking their perspective and showing care for them, not just their behavior, and encouraging the internalization and integration of extrinsic regulation when it is part of the setting. These factors all contribute to the creation of an *autonomy supportive environment*. As parents, teachers, coaches, and leisure service providers, caregivers can foster intrinsic interest in activities by providing people with such an environment (see Grolnick & Ryan, 1989). *Controlling environments* have the opposite effect. For example, Deci, Connell and Ryan (1989) found that when managers created autonomy supportive environments, trust and satisfaction in the workplace among their subordinates was high; dropping out of school has been found to be less common in educational environments that are more autonomy supportive (Vallerand & Bissonnette, 1992).

Leisure is an experience that is facilitated by autonomy supportive conditions that enhance the sense of self-determination, competence, and relatedness. Leisure can also be viewed as an autonomy supportive context itself. This is the essence of leisure's power and attraction.

Politics of Freedom and Control

The translation of the concept of leisure into the social psychological constructs of perceived freedom and intrinsic motivation has stimulated leisure research and provided a bridge to the extensive work in general social psychology on these constructs. The use of definitions, measures, research strategies and theories from these social psychological areas of inquiry has provided a basis for building an improved understanding of leisure, and provides useful ideas to help people experience more meaningful leisure. Given the importance of perceived freedom of choice and intrinsic motivation, it is no surprise that leisure, at its best, can provide a context that promotes extremely meaningful and psychologically powerful activities and experiences. It is also encouraging to see that leisure researchers are taking these ideas and applying them to understanding and improving the quality of people's activities and experiences in leisure contexts.

It should be noted that there have been criticisms in leisure studies of an overreliance on social psychological interpretations of important ideas such as *freedom*. For example, there are other ways of conceptualizing freedom than as "free choice" or "decision choice" as has typically been done in the leisure theory and research. Perceived freedom can be viewed an ongoing experience and even an outcome of the leisure experience (Harper, 1981, 1986; Kleiber, 1985). It might also be useful to distinguish between the different meanings of freedom suggested by the terms "freedom from" and "freedom to" (Bregha, 1980; Sylvester, 1985). It has been suggested that *freedom from* refers to the absence of duress, coercion and interference and *freedom to* involves willful choice and action on the part of the individual. These two types of freedom could have quite distinct implications for an individual's behavior and experience during leisure.

Other authors have suggested that the social psychological approach has tended to divert people from considering important *value-based* ethical issues such as the nature of their responsibilities when making leisure choices (Sylvester, 1985). Goodale (1990) has even suggested that by defining leisure as *perceived freedom* and emphasizing the importance of people's subjective impressions, researchers and leisure services practitioners have tended to ignore the sometimes negative *objective conditions* in people's lives that may limit their ability to experience meaningful and rewarding leisure. The result being that insufficient attention is being given to developing the strategies needed to correct these conditions. However, unless researchers develop an understanding of how people come to perceive and interpret the objective conditions of their lives as providing freedom, self-determination, and leisure, the impact of interventions on people for changing those objective conditions can not be understood or anticipated.

Personality and Leisure

Chapter SIX

Preview

What is personality? Does your leisure reflect your personality? Would the people who know you agree? Could they predict the leisure activities you would choose to participate in during your free time? How are your leisure interests different from those of others? Are they always different or only sometimes different? Do the things that you do during your leisure affect your personality and the way you see yourself? These are questions that make leisure a matter of personality.

In previous chapters, we have tried to make it clear that behavior generally, and leisure behavior in particular, comes about through the interaction of individual dispositions and situational influences. In this chapter, we will focus on the former, that is, those factors in individuals that cause them to behave consistently across a wide range of situations and react differently to the same situation than others do. Of course, age, gender, ethnic background and educational history are among the many factors that will also play a role in influencing behavior. The primary interest in this chapter, however, is in the set of personal characteristics that make people unique, that is, their personalities.

The Nature of Personality

Brenda Epperson is a 45-year-old divorcee who has the reputation of being "everywhere" in town. Her friends call her "the mayor" since she seems to know and be friendly with almost everyone she meets, and whether it's in the grocery store, a coffee house or a restaurant, she will have something engaging to say to those she encounters. Sheila Belichek is the same age as Brenda, is single, and has a similar educational background; but in contrast to Brenda, Sheila prefers to spend her free time reading mystery novels and developing some writing of her own. As has been established in previous chapters, there may be many factors that contribute to these differences in leisure behavior. To the extent that Brenda's and Sheila's patterns of behavior are consistent and distinctive, however, social psychologists are likely to regard these patterns as reflective of their *personalities*.

The term "personality" is used in everyday conversation. As with the cases of Brenda and Sheila above, when people make statements such as "John isn't really good-looking, but he has a nice personality," they typically use the term to denote the manner in which a person acts across a variety of situations. Psychologists use the term to describe not only an individual's "reputation"—the way the person acts and is known socially—but also the "internal processes" that create that reputation. Personality refers to the enduring patterns of thought, feeling, and behavior that are expressed in different circumstances (Hogan, 1987).

Theory and research on personality have been devoted to two separate aspects of those "enduring patterns." The first is what such patterns indicate about the "structure" of personality. Personality here refers to the *organization* of enduring patterns of thought, feeling, and behavior. Pervin (1990) characterizes this focus on intraindividual integration as follows:

> What is distinctive about personality is the focus on the person as a system, thereby involving the interplay between consistency and diversity, stability and change, and integration and conflict, as well as the study of people in a variety of contexts and over a long enough time period for patterns to emerge, in their private world of thought and feeling as well as in their public behaviors (p. 726).

The second task has been to study the way people resemble and differ from one another, that is, their *individual differences*. Thus, people are grouped as being higher or lower on various factors, many of which are reflected in leisure behavior as we shall explain shortly. Ideally, though, these two aims of personality research should be compatible as it is necessary to more fully understand how personalities are constructed to be able to make anything very meaningful out of the study of individual differences. Fortunately, there are a variety of perspectives on the nature of personality that are useful to this discussion.

Psychodynamic Theory

The psychoanalytic perspective, developed predominantly by Sigmund Freud (1933), is based to a great extent on the belief that much of behavior results from instincts and unconscious drives. The theory recognized that humans were not always rational in their motives and behavior and initially gave much credence to the power of libidinal (sexual) impulses. Neo-Freudians rejected psychoanalytic theory's emphasis on the central role of sexuality and focused on the role of culture, along with biology and childhood experience, in shaping psychodynamics and basic human motivation. For example, Fromm (1955) proposed that competitiveness, materialism and self-involvement are common personality traits in capitalist societies because of economic and social pressures people experience to compete, buy and focus on themselves. According to Horney (1937), the neurotic patterns that can be seen in society, such as endless striving for material goods or difficulty in committing to intimate relationships, are similarly shaped by cultural forces. Sullivan (1953) argued that the ways people relate to others, and their deepest views of themselves, are shaped by both cultural values and their interactions with caregivers during infancy and childhood. Among the major problems with the psychodynamic perspective has been the lack of scientifically sound support and the difficulty in generating testable hypotheses since so few of the relevant dynamics can be observed. It has also been criticized for overemphasizing sexual motivation and paying too much attention to childhood experiences and not enough to adult learning.

Cognitive-Social Theories

These theories portray people as more rational in their motives than psychodynamic theory. Learning rather than conflict, defense, or instinct is the basis of personality, and personality dispositions tend to be relatively specific and shaped by their consequences (Bandura, 1986). These theories focus on beliefs, expectations and information processing, and personality reflects the constant interplay between environmental demands and the way the individual processes information about the self and the world. People's actions reflect the schemata they use in understanding the world, their expectations of what will happen if they act in particular ways, and the degree to which they believe they can attain their goals. The limitation of this perspective, however, includes an overemphasis on the rational side of life and underemphasis on the emotional, motivational and irrational. This group of theories tends to assume that people consciously know what they want and hence can report it.

Humanistic Theories

These theories focus on the way people deal with fundamental human concerns such as mortality and meaning in life. Humanistic psychology asserts the importance of free will, abandons the view that environmental and genetic variables determine all behavior, and questions the applicability of scientific methods to all of human psychology (see, for example, Maslow, 1968). Humanistic approaches to personality hold that within each individual is an active, creative force or "self" that seeks expression, development and growth. (We will present an example of this type of theory in the next chapter on motivation when we discuss Maslow's hierarchy of needs). Thus, the aim of the humanistic psychologist is not to search for unconscious processes or environmental contingencies but to understand how individuals experience themselves, others, and the world to help them actualize their potentials (see also Rogers, 1961). These theories help social psychologists understand how and why people strive to make their lives meaningful. Also, these theories introduce the important distinction between the "true" and "false" self. They identified the feelings of unease that people may feel when they are essentially living their lives as others would have them live—going through the motions, but never really feeling as if they are themselves.

Trait Theories

These theories use everyday language to describe personality. Trait theories of personality have been largely derived from the words people use to classify themselves and others in their everyday lives—adjectives like shy, devious, manipulative, open or friendly. *Traits* are emotional, motivational, cognitive and behavior tendencies that constitute underlying dimensions of personality on which individuals vary. According to Allport (1955), who developed the trait approach to personality, the concept of trait has two separate but complementary meanings. On the one hand, a trait is an observed tendency to behave in a particular way. On the other, a trait is an inferred underlying personality disposition that generates this behavioral tendency. Presumably, a tendency to be cheerful (an observed trait) stems from an enduring pattern of internal processes, such as a tendency or need to experience positive affect, to think positive thoughts, or to wish to be perceived as happy (an inferred disposition). Trait theories provide the basis for most of the work on personality in leisure studies. Researchers have attempted to predict leisure behavior based on individual differences, as will be demonstrated shortly. Leisure behavior may also *contribute* to the development of some aspects of personality. We will present what evidence exists for this influence as well.

Among the more important dynamics of personality is the function of self-awareness. Being able to reflect on how consistently one is behaving or how one's behavior is changing is distinctly human and has a great deal of influence on other behaviors such as planning and self-regulation. This ability is in turn the source of information that allows people to form a general self-conception or picture of ourselves that includes internal consistencies and inconsistencies, differences from and similarities with others, and plans and goals for the future. This self-conception is also referred to as one's identity (see Schlenker, 1984; Stryker, 1987). In chapter ten, when we discuss social psychological costs and benefits of leisure, we will explore the manner in which choices made in the interest of enjoyment and self-expression during leisure influence the formation of personal identity and personal growth.

We are getting ahead of ourselves here though. Let's return to the subject of individual differences in personality and how such differences come to influence leisure behavior in the first place. We will consider which personality factors are correlated with leisure behavior, which ones are likely to influence leisure behavior, and finally, the characteristics of individuals that seem distinctly linked to certain patterns of leisure behavior.

Dimensions of Personality: Implications for Leisure

The most prominent and well-understood components of personality are those that define individuals as consistently different in some ways from other individuals. These components are traits. Traits become especially important in certain situations, especially those where environmental conditions are not very imposing, that is, where people feel "free to be themselves."

While we have already considered a number of different meanings of leisure, the special relevance of personality to leisure becomes most apparent when leisure is considered a context for self-expression, where an individual is most likely to feel like her or his "true self." Samdahl (1988, 1992) asked 18 young adults to carry a pager for a week to sample their experience of leisure and nonleisure. When they were "beeped" (according to a random schedule), they were to stop and indicate what they were doing at the time, with whom they were doing it, and what their subjective experience was on a variety of dimensions. They were asked to what extent they would regard a particular occasion as leisure and also whether they felt irritable, relaxed, comfortable, and so forth, and, perhaps most importantly, how much what they were doing was an expression of their "true self." She found that regarding a situation as leisure was highly associated with feeling like one's true self, especially in informal social situations. "The opportunity to be truly self-expressive and accepted for who you really are," she concluded, "may be one factor that makes informal social interaction an important leisure context" (1992, p. 28).

The point is that in leisure people generally feel free to be themselves; common feelings of being determined by others or situational demands are generally far less than in other social settings. Even if one interacts with others (and surely much if not most of leisure experience is social) and chooses to "go by the rules" (of a game, a dance, or an organizational meeting) the experience of leisure is sustained to the extent that the situation is relatively unimposing, thereby allowing individuals to "be themselves."

Personality traits are more likely to be influential in such casual situations in comparison to other situations where there are clear demands and expectations, such as is common in work settings. Traits become more important when the social situation is familiar, informal, or private (versus novel, formal, or public), when instructions are nonexistent or general (versus detailed and complete), and when choice is considerable (versus

little or none). The demands of the social situation become more important than traits when the opposite conditions (noted in parentheses) apply
(Buss, 1989). Support for this idea was demonstrated in an experimental
laboratory study of leisure and flow by Mannell and Bradley (1986). They
found that when the social setting was highly unstructured and there were
few guidelines and expectations for behavior, as in many leisure settings,
the participants' personalities (in this case, their locus of control) had a
greater influence on their behavior and experience in playing a game than
when they were in a more regulated setting. But whatever situational factors come into play, leisure choices and experiences are influenced at least
to some extent by stable individual differences. In this chapter, we are especially concerned with those individual difference characteristics or traits
that seem to lead people to behave in a certain way across a variety of situations or to change in predictable ways as the situation changes.

The "Big 5"

What describes you as a person? Are you kind? Anxious? Aggressive?
Exuberant? Extroverted? Conscientious? Do any of those characteristics
come into play in directing your leisure choices and experiences? Literally
hundreds of personality factors have been found to differentiate individuals
in a somewhat permanent way and across most if not all situations. But a
lot of these are somewhat interchangeable. Can a person who is "outgoing"
also be regarded as extroverted? Is nervousness the same thing as anx-
iousness? In recent years the study of personality has been able to reduce
the vast array of personality characteristics to five fundamental factors:
extroversion, agreeableness, conscientiousness, neuroticism, and openness
to experience (Costa & McCrae, 1985, 1988; Costa, McCrae & Dye, 1991;
Degman, 1990; McCrae & John 1992). While the names of these factors
vary somewhat among researchers, the five-factor model (FFM or "Big
Five") appears to be basic to all personality measures. Our goal here, then,
is to describe these higher order personality factors with an eye toward determining their relevance for leisure behavior and leisure experience.

Extroversion is the first such factor. This factor includes such traits as
assertiveness, gregariousness, excitement seeking, and positive emotionality.
An earlier word for it was "surgency," reflecting all those characteristics
that put one into action. People who are high on extroversion are "high
energy" people, to use a more common expression. It is easy to imagine
then that this dimension might be a prime predictor of those who do a lot
of different leisure activities or those who engage in the same activities

more intensely than others or those who engage in activities like whitewater rafting that can provide high levels of stimulation. Extroversion has been shown to have a physiological base. Eysenck (1967) first proposed that extroverts have "high cortical inhibition" and thus low baseline cortical arousal, thereby creating a "stimulus hunger" that leads them to seek out stimulation externally. In contrast, introverts have low thresholds of arousal and thus require less stimulation to stay at an optimal level of activation.

An element of risk in activities would be more appealing to those higher on this dimension as would contact sports. Athletes are typically higher on extroversion than nonathletes (e.g., Kane, 1972; Kirkcaldy & Furnham, 1991; Ogilvie, 1968; Schurr, Ashley & Joy, 1977), while those who spend a lot of time playing computer fantasy games (e.g., Dungeons and Dragons) have been found to be more introverted than others (Douse & McManus, 1983). Tourism patterns have also been associated with this cluster of characteristics. Plog (1972) contrasted the "allocentrics" who seek out unstructured and exotic travel from the "psychocentrics" who prefer familiar venues. Smith (1990a) found only partial support for Plog's allocentric/psychocentric model. But by combining measures of activation, introversion and locus of control, Nickerson and Ellis (1991) were able to elaborate the model for the purpose of predicting destination preferences, travel companions, interaction with local cultures, and degree of activity. Introversion, the opposite of extroversion in this study, proved to be a significant predictor of tourism styles.

A trait in the extroversion family is *sensation seeking*. Like extroversion, it is the tendency to pursue stimulation and take risks to bring about optimal experience (Zuckerman, 1979). According to Zuckerman, high sensation seekers tend to participate in more adventurous, intense activities and prefer a greater variety of activities. In contrast, individuals who are predisposed to avoid stimulation are likely to prefer more familiar leisure situations.

Agreeableness is another member of the "Big 5" and a "prosocial" factor. It includes such characteristics as trust, straightforwardness, and altruism and is contrasted with hostility, indifference, and self-centeredness. Those high on the components of this factor would be likely to welcome the social aspects of leisure and perhaps use the context of leisure to serve others as in volunteer work or coaching and teaching in youth recreation programs. And this may be a particularly important characteristic to have in staying socially integrated in later life (Reis & Gold, 1993). On the other hand, seeing leisure as an opportunity for self-indulgence and escape would likely be the orientation of those who are low on this factor. But there is little research in this area to support such speculation. In one study (Driver & Knopf, 1977), nature trail walkers were significantly lower than average on a measure of affiliation, but whether that is a reflection of an orientation toward escape and self-indulgence or merely a preference for solitude is not at all clear.

The third member of the "Big 5" is *conscientiousness.* According to McCrae and John (1992), the factor conscientiousness is defined with such components as order, dutifulness, achievement striving, self-discipline, and deliberation. Others (e.g., Goldberg, 1981) associate it with conventionality. A person high on these characteristics is organized, responsible and reliable, whereas one who is low on this factor is likely to be impulsive and oriented toward immediate gratification. Those high on this factor might be expected to embrace the goal-orientation and work ethic that characterize more serious leisure activities (Stebbins, 1992a), such as being a member of an amateur astronomers' club. On the other hand, those who are high on this factor may have some difficulty being spontaneous and giving in to the will of companions. Compulsiveness or orderliness may hinder a person from "letting go." Again, however, research on this subject is lacking.

Neuroticism, the fourth factor, represents the general tendency to experience distress. It is defined by such components as anxiety, hostility, depression, and self-consciousness. It is reasonable to assume that one high in this set of characteristics would have some difficulty achieving the depth of involvement necessary for fulfilling enjoyment. It may also be associated with the psychopathological condition of anhedonia, the inability to experience pleasure. In a study of 73 German adults (Kirkcaldy, 1989), neuroticism was associated with dislike of playful leisure activities. Athletes have been shown to be low in neuroticism (Kane, 1972; Schurr, Ashley & Joy, 1977), as have skiers, skydivers, and scuba divers (Martin & Myrick, 1976). Schill, Beyler and Sharp (1993) used ideas related to this dimension to develop a measure of what they called the "self-defeating personality." They found that people high on this measure reported less pleasure and enjoyment from individual and social activities than those who were low on the measure. According to the authors, this orientation is attributable to the tendency to discount the positives in one's life.

The fifth and final factor is the dimension of *openness to experience* and it has to do with aesthetic sensitivity, the need for variety, and unconventional values (McCrae & Costa, 1987). It is also called the "intellect" dimension, though it is independent of intelligence, because it tends to incorporate openness to new ideas, flexibility of thought, cultural interest, and educational aptitude. It would thus be likely that people high on this dimension would be disposed to reading, attending classes, and generally participating in high culture activities to a greater extent than others. But whether openness to experience is the same as intellectualism has been the subject of some debate. While it has been commonly associated with cultural orientation, it is also used to describe a particular attentional style associated with such things as absorption potential and hypnotizability (Swanson, 1978). The dimension of "sentience," the tendency to use one's senses, would seem to combine both aspects. In a study of various outdoor recreation activity groups, Driver and Knopf (1977) found nature walkers to be particularly high on this dimension. And the characteristic was regarded by Reis and Gold (1993) as being most likely to lead to developing more nonwork friendships in later life—a result that also enhances life satisfaction.

Where Do Personality Traits Come From?

The interactionist framework employed here recognizes stable individual difference, or "person," factors as interacting with situational, or "environment," factors in directing behavior. Thus, even though individuals must interpret what the environment affords them in terms of action possibilities or how those possibilities are constrained, one's personality provides a relatively permanent set of dispositions influencing both those interpretations and the choices and decisions for action one takes. How stable these dispositions are, is a matter of some controversy in the study of personality. To what extent has your personality changed in the last few years? Have your friends and relatives always been the same? What does growing older hold for you and them?

Part of the answer to those questions lies in where traits come from in the first place. If they are "learned," that is, the result of imitation, modeling, and response to the rewards and punishments of social life, they are more likely to change, as environmental conditions change, than if they are the expression of genetically-derived tendencies. But if a trait doesn't change much over the life course and is relatively resilient in the face of a variety of environmental conditions, how would researchers know if it was determined by one's genetic makeup or by some compelling experiences in early childhood?

One approach to that problem is to compare people with their "next of kin." The more similar they are to the ones who are "blood" relatives, the more likely it might appear that traits have been inherited. But be careful here! People who are genetically most similar are also most likely to have shared a similar "family" environment. If you are more like your mother than her sister (your aunt), it could be because you share more of your mother's genes or it could be because she raised you and "passed on" some of her characteristics to you in the process. One of the few ways to sort out the "heritability" of traits from their environmental sources is to compare people with the same genetic background who are reared together with those who are reared apart. Fortunately for research purposes—if not for the twins themselves—a substantial number of twins have been separated at birth and raised in different environments. If they are very similar despite this separation, it is an argument for the power of their genes (heritability) in determining that similarity.

Most twin studies have been conducted to address the nature versus nurture debate on the origins of intelligence. Relatively few psychologists have argued for the heritability of much of personality—except perhaps in activity level and aggressiveness. This has been due in part to the general abandonment of trait psychology in recent decades. But with the reemergence of attention to personality, there is renewed interest in the question of the heritability of traits. In a relatively recent study by Tellegen and his associates (1988), the personality characteristics of twins reared apart and together were examined. Using the Multidimensional Personality Questionnaire, eleven primary scales and three higher order factors were studied for monozygotic and dizygotic twins. Monozygotic (one egg) are "identical" twins and share more genetic makeup than dizygotic (two egg) or "fraternal" twins. The study addressed three higher order factors—positive emotionality, negative emotionality, and constraint—which compare closely to three of the "Big Five" traits described earlier: extroversion, neuroticism, and conscientiousness. Table 6.1 shows the average correlations for each group. The fact that the correlations for monozygotic twins reared apart are not much lower than monozygotic twins reared together and yet are much higher than dizygotic twins reared together reflects the heritability of those personality dimensions.

What becomes especially interesting for leisure studies is that the dimensions used in that study are made up of scales that have clear implications for leisure interests and behavior. Tellegen, Lykken, Bourchard, Wilcox, Segal and Rich (1988) note that high scores on the positive emotionality factor are found in those who are "engaged in active, pleasurable and efficacious transactions with the environment." Those low on this factor "report few of these pleasurable transactions...have a higher threshold for experiencing positive affect (meaning, it's more difficult for them), and

---

Table 6.1 Correlations on Three Personality Factors Between
Different Types of Twins (Reared Together and Apart)

	Types of Twins & Socialization Experience			
	MZA*	DZA	MZT	DZT
Positive emotionality	0.34	−0.07	0.63	0.18
Negative emotionality	0.61	0.29	0.54	0.41
Constraint	0.57	0.04	0.58	0.25

* MZA = monozygotic twins reared apart (n=44)
 DZA = dizygotic twins reared apart (n=27)
 MZT = monozygotic twins reared together (n=217)
 DZT = dizygotic twins reared together (n=114)

Adapted from Tellegen et al., 1988, p. 1,035

---

a tendency toward depressive, nonpleasurable disengagement" (Tellegen
et al., 1988, p. 1033).

Contrary to appearances, negative emotionality is not the opposite of
positive emotionality; one could be high or low on both dimensions at the
same time. High scorers on negative emotionality describe themselves as
"unpleasurably engaged, stressed and harassed and prone to experiencing
strong negative emotions such as anxiety and anger." Low scorers on this
dimension "convey….a tendency toward phlegmatic, nonunpleasurable
disengagement," that is, they are not likely to be anxious or otherwise dis-
tressed when they are uninvolved or have time to themselves. Finally,
constraint, like the conscientiousness factor referred to earlier, reflects the
tendency for "avoiding dangerous kinds of excitement and thrill" in favor
of caution, restraint and conventionality. In contrast, low scorers on the
scales associated with this factor "present a picture of impulsiveness, fear-
less sensation seeking, and rejection of conventional strictures on their behavior" (p. 1034).

Zuckerman (1979) also studied twins in his research on sensation-
seeking, finding similarly that identical twins are more alike with respect
to sensation seeking than fraternal twins even when reared apart.
Zuckerman concluded from this research that nearly one-half of the variability in the sensation-seeking trait was attributed to heredity, the same
figure arrived at by Tellegen and associates (1988) with respect to the personality characteristics they assessed.

In general, however, it is important to recognize that even if as much as 50 percent of the variability in some aspects of personality can be attributed to genetic differences, the rest of the variability is attributable to other sources. There have certainly been many social scientists who have asserted that environmental influences have had at least as much influence in determining personality, and, while the studies reviewed above emphasize the impact of genetics, environmental influences shape personality in a variety of ways.

Leisure Research on Personality: Approaches and Problems

Regardless of the origins of personality traits or their particular relationship to one another, they have been a popular subject for leisure researchers. This is partly due to their apparent ease of measurement. (In the discussion of leisure motives in the next chapter, we will explain that this "ease of measurement" is illusionary). Personality traits are typically assessed by having people fill out "paper-and-pencil tests" that require them to rate the extent to which a series of statements describe them (see Figure 6.1, pp. 164–5, for an example of a leisure-specific personality test developed by one of the authors). On the basis of these ratings, how strongly they exhibit a particular trait is determined. Personality trait research on leisure has also been popular because of the assumption that there are stable individual differences that explain leisure behavior and preferences. The differences have been seen as useful for predicting leisure interests and even in "target marketing" to potential program participants or resource users. For example, some early research on personality and leisure was driven in part by managers' desires to identify the reasons why recreationists chose their sites and activities. Escape, affiliation, achievement, exploration and social recognition were some of the personality-based needs identified that managers could use to distinguish between recreationists. It was hoped that this personality-based information might then be used to tailor leisure services and programs to give users what they wanted (Knopf, 1983).

Much of the early research on personality in relation to leisure behavior has focused on sports. For example, Ogilvie (1968) reviewed findings that indicated that athletes were more likely to be more extroverted and risk-taking than nonathletes, and higher in self-assertion, tough-mindedness, self-sufficiency, and forthrightness. Several other studies established athletes to be more extroverted than nonathletes (see also Browne & Mahoney,

1984). But Schurr, Ashley and Joy (1977) pointed out that individual sport participants may be different from team sport participants in that regard. In their study of 865 male athletes, individual sport participants were more self-sufficient and less dependent than team sport participants. They also suggested that sports that are more "directly" competitive, such as wrestling and basketball, are likely to involve participants who are different from those who prefer "parallel" competition such as baseball or tennis. Most of this early work was done on male athletes, and while comparisons on the basis of sex alone have not shown significant personality differences associated with *elite sport* involvement (Williams, 1978), it is clear that women face a very different socialization process with respect to sport, as will be discussed further in chapter eight. When it comes to more *casual sport* involvement, there is evidence that personality is predictive of sport involvement for females but not for males (e.g., Kleiber & Hemmer, 1981).

With a more general approach to personality-based leisure interests, Allen (1982) administered the *Personality Research Form* (Jackson, 1974), an instrument used to measure Murray's 20 personality "needs," and a leisure interest inventory to 212 undergraduates. Fifty-one leisure interests were then reduced to nine leisure interest factors through factor analysis, and seven of the nine factors were found to correlate with 12 of Murray's 20 personality needs. Of special interest was the relationship between athletic and outdoor interests and the need for dominance, and between an interest in mechanical activities and the need for autonomy. Driver and Knopf (1977) used this same measure of personality to find that while personality was only modestly related to the *choice* of outdoor recreation activity, it was a stronger predictor of the *extent* of participation. For example, regular male nature trail walkers and backcountry hikers had a higher than normal need for autonomy.

The use of another measure, the *Edwards Personal Preference Schedule*, in a study of participation in selected outdoor recreation activities, revealed a number of significant relationships (Moss & Lamphear, 1970). Hunters, for example, were found to be more dominant, traditional, and dogmatic than nonhunters (Moss & Lamphear, 1970); but again the correlations, though statistically significant, were only modest.

Part of the criticism of earlier research on personality and leisure is that personality measures have often been used as part of a "fishing expedition" to find anything at all that is related to activity participation. It has also become clear that participation alone is not likely to reveal much about personality; people participate in the same activity for a wide variety of reasons,

Self-As-Entertainment Scale

Most people have periods of free time ranging from a few moments during the course of their daily activities to large amounts of vacation time. The following statements reflect how different people feel about their free time and how they use it. Please respond as quickly and accurately as possible by indicating the extent to which each of the statements describes you.

	Doesn't Sound Like Me		Sounds A Little Like Me		Sounds A Lot Like Me
1. I have an active imagination.	1	2	3	4	5
2. I like to go places where there is lots to do.	1	2	3	4	5
3. I can make almost anything fun for myself.	1	2	3	4	5
4. I find at this stage of my life that there is not enough to occupy my free time.	1	2	3	4	5
5. When I have to wait for something, I usually get so engrossed in my thoughts that I fail to notice the time.	1	2	3	4	5
6. My most enjoyable vacations are those where I go some place new.	1	2	3	4	5
7. Filling my free time is a problem for me.	1	2	3	4	5
8. If something I have planned is canceled, I have difficulty finding an enjoyable substitute.	1	2	3	4	5
9. I am good at entertaining myself.	1	2	3	4	5
10. I like to go out a great deal.	1	2	3	4	5
11. I enjoy relaxing and letting my mind wander.	1	2	3	4	5
12. If I have a day free, I prefer to go somewhere away from home.	1	2	3	4	5
13. When I have time on my hands, I usually find someone to spend it with.	1	2	3	4	5
14. I am a person who likes to go to new places.	1	2	3	4	5
15. I am never at a loss for something to do.	1	2	3	4	5
16. I am good at thinking of things to do with my free time.	1	2	3	4	5
17. I often have a difficult time deciding what to do with my free time.	1	2	3	4	5

Figure 6.1 Self-As-Entertainment Scale

Adapted from Mannell (1984, 1985)

Self-As-Entertainment Scale

	Doesn't Sound Like Me		Sounds A Little Like Me		Sounds A Lot Like Me
18. I am good at thinking of fun things to do.	1	2	3	4	5
19. I remember my good times by the places I've been.	1	2	3	4	5
20. My life would be dull without my day-dreams.	1	2	3	4	5
21. I often use my imagination to entertain myself.	1	2	3	4	5
22. I have too much time on my hands.	1	2	3	4	5
23. I am good at making up games.	1	2	3	4	5
24. My favorite activities require me to use my knowledge and skills.	1	2	3	4	5
25. When I am bored, I go some place where there are things happening.	1	2	3	4	5
26. I like teaching myself to do new activities.	1	2	3	4	5
27. I often feel there is nothing to do.	1	2	3	4	5
28. It doesn't matter where I am, I enjoy myself.	1	2	3	4	5

Subscale Composition:

Self Mode refers to a person's physical and/or cognitive skills and ability to find or create challenging and interesting pursuits with which to fill their free time (includes items 3, 4, 7, 8, 9, 15, 16, 17, 18, 22, 23, 24, 26, 27 and 28— items 4, 7, 8, 17, 22 and 27 are reverse coded).

Environmental Mode refers to a person's capacity to fill their free time with interesting and enjoyable pursuits by actively seeking out places or environments and other people. These people or places in turn impose structure and determine the content of their free time for them (includes items 2, 6, 10, 12, 13, 14, 19 and 25).

Mind-Play Mode refers to person's capacity to fill their free time by turning inward and using imagination and fantasy (includes items 1, 5, 11, 20 and 21).

Figure 6.1 Self-As-Entertainment Scale *(continued)*

Adapted from Mannell (1984, 1985)

and the same people may participate for different reasons at different times. An example from a British researcher is as telling as it is unusual:

> the choice of leisure-time pursuits is a function of many variables. . . . Collecting birds' eggs has been given as an example of acquisitive or competitive needs, scientific or outdoor interests, or just an aesthetic interest in the shape or color of eggs. (Nias, 1977)

It is important to look beneath the behavior to personality-based needs. Backpacking, to pick a more common example, attracts some participants who characteristically seek high stimulation and others who search for escape and solitude (Knopf, 1983).

In some cases the causal direction has been turned around to see whether and how extensive activity involvement might influence personality. Sport research in particular has been directed by efforts to identify personality differences between athletes and nonathletes caused by participation in sport activities. However, this mostly correlational research usually fails to establish the dynamics of the relationships (see Stevenson, 1975 for a critical review), that is, evidence for how participation in sport activities actually causes personality differences to develop. Another problem has been the failure to include social setting factors when predicting behavior, a point which we will return to shortly. But first we will consider several personality characteristics that are relevant to leisure experience and behavior.

There are personality dimensions or traits that, in spite of the alleged inclusiveness of the Five Factor Model, seem to fall outside of it. Or perhaps they represent two or more factors in combination. Because they have been studied so frequently with respect to leisure however, we will consider them here. These are locus of control, attentional style, the Type-A behavior profile, playfulness, shyness, and the autotelic personality.

General Personality Traits Studied in Leisure Research

Locus of Control

As we discussed in chapter five, various theories assume that everyone has a need for freedom and control. However, a number of theories suggest that people differ in how important control and freedom are in their lives. For example, Burger (1992) proposes that some people have a high *desire for control* of events in their lives and others have a low desire for control, and that this characteristic is a personality trait that influences their behavior.

Rotter (1966) was one of the first researchers to suggest that people differ in the amount of control they feel they have over the positive and negative events they encounter in the course of their lives. He called this personality dimension *locus of control*. People with an *internal* locus of control believe they largely control these outcomes, and those with an *external* locus of control believe that luck, the environment or powerful others are responsible for these outcomes. deCharms (1968) describes this essential difference in personal orientation of control in terms of people who are *origins* and *pawns*. In 1966, Rotter developed the I-E Scale to measure locus of control. A great deal of social psychological research has been done with this scale and locus of control appears to be an important personality dimension along which people differ (Lefcourt, 1976).

With respect to leisure, Neulinger (1974, p. 16) suggested that perceptions of freedom, and consequently leisure, could be a function of stable personality differences such as locus of control. He argued that the more freedom of choice and control people characteristically feel they have in their lives, the more likely they are to experience leisure in a given situation. Using the locus of control scale (I-E Scale) developed by Rotter, several researchers have attempted to examine the relationship between locus of control and leisure behavior. If, in fact, leisure involvements are characterized by greater opportunities for freedom of choice, then people who believe that they have more control in their lives should prefer or feel more positive about these involvements.

In an attempt to examine whether internals and externals react differently to having choice in leisure settings, Mannell and Bradley (1986) conducted a laboratory experiment. Similar to the Mannell and Backman (1979) study described in chapter four, a free-time period was created in the laboratory. The 80 undergraduate students who participated in the experiment completed the I-E Scale and were classified as internals and externals. Of particular interest to the present discussion of personality and leisure is the behavior and experience of the study participants when they played a game in conditions that provided very few guidelines for how they played—a very open-ended unstructured "leisure setting." In this part of the experiment, conditions were created in the laboratory that led half of the internals and half of the externals to perceive that they had no choice in playing a laboratory game. The other half of the internals and externals were led to believe that they had a great deal of choice in the game they played, as well as whether they played at all during the "free time" period. The extent to which the participants had "flow experiences" while playing the game was measured using the "time duration" and "situational memory" measures discussed in chapter four. As predicted, the internals experienced higher levels of flow when they perceived they had greater freedom of choice, whereas the externals experienced slightly less flow while playing the game under conditions of greater freedom of choice (Figure 6.2).

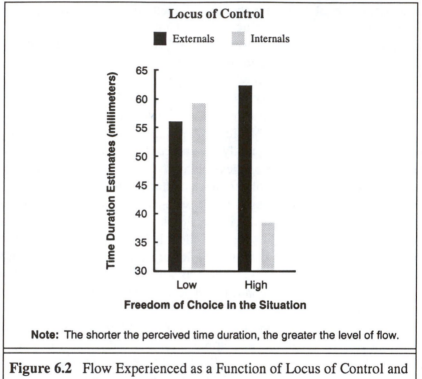

Figure 6.2   Flow Experienced as a Function of Locus of Control and Freedom of Choice in a Highly Unstructured Situation

Adapted from Mannell and Bradley (1986)

The results of this research suggest that to understand leisure behavior not only do the *actual opportunities for choice* available in the leisure setting need to be considered, but also *individual differences in how much control and freedom* people typically feel they have in their lives. These individual differences may influence how people perceive the actual choice available to them, and consequently, it may modify their leisure experience.

For example, if you generally feel that you have little control over the things that happen to you, then, it is unlikely that being in a situation where you have little or no choice will create much discomfort or psychological reactance to interfere with your experience. In fact, too much freedom of choice may be overwhelming or threatening. However, if you have an internal locus of control, you may desire much more choice.

In a study of sport participation among college students (Kleiber & Hemmer, 1981), the fact that females involved with sport were more internal in their locus of control than other females, and more internal than the males in the study regardless of their level of sport involvement, was interpreted as indicating that females in sport needed to feel especially internally directed to be able to forge their own way in a realm traditionally dominated by males. Those with an internal locus of control are also more likely to be adventurous in their style of travel and more likely to travel to exotic places than those with an external locus of control (Nickerson & Ellis, 1991).

Surprisingly though, internals seem to have a less positive attitude toward leisure than those with a more external locus of control. In a study of a group of college students (Kleiber, 1979), positive attitudes toward leisure were modestly correlated with an external rather than an internal locus of control. In spite of expectations to the contrary, internals were less likely to see leisure as "good" than externals and less likely to believe that living a life of leisure could be worthwhile.

The explanation that was entertained for these results was that students with a higher internal locus of control were more likely to be achievement-oriented and work-oriented, and more likely to see leisure as being the opposite (i.e., associating it with laziness and sloth). But a subsequent study of a different group of people, including both students and nonstudents (Kleiber & Crandall, 1981), wherein work ethic was measured and controlled for, yielded results that were not significantly different from the first study. Those with an internal locus of control, even if they were not very work oriented, were no more likely to embrace leisure than those with an external locus of control. In fact, among the female students in the sample, the opposite was true; those who were more external were more likely to value leisure. Perhaps, as the authors argued, those who feel a little less able to control their circumstances are more content to "give in" to the forces around them and when those conditions are benign, as in the circumstances of leisure, this type of person is especially appreciative. Obviously, more research is needed with this personality variable.

Attentional Style

The way that individuals typically process or deal with the information they receive from the physical and social environment may have a particularly significant impact on their leisure experience. People have been found to differ in how they process information and this is referred to as *attentional style*. Some of this was implied in our earlier discussions of extroversion and openness to experience. But the way in which attention is deployed or directed—independent of one's excitability or orientation to experience—may be implicated in leisure experience. This is particularly true with respect to the ability to get into "flow," the experience of being deeply absorbed in an activity that was discussed in chapter four. Getting into flow requires that limited attentional capacity be allocated to some sources of stimulation at the expense of others, and this capacity differs between individuals (Keele & Hawkins, 1982). Being able to "tune out" spectators and become absorbed while playing in a baseball game comes easier to some than others and makes flow-type experience more likely. The propensity for *absorption* is thought to be a stable personality characteristic (Tellegen & Atkinson, 1974). Using a measure called the *Tellegen Absorption Scale* (TAS), high-scoring and low-scoring subjects were found to have different electroencephalographical (EEG) patterns in response to competing secondary tasks (i.e., potential distractions) (Davidson, Schwartz & Rothman, 1976). Those with higher TAS scores were better able to ignore secondary stimulation. This ability has also been associated with hypnotic susceptibility (Davidson, Goleman & Schwartz, 1976) and with intrinsic motivation (Hamilton, 1981).

The fact that introverts score higher on tests of absorption than extroverts (Thackery, Jones & Touchstone, 1974)—presumably because the latter are more responsive to external stimuli—suggests some advantages for introverts in their leisure experiences. Though extroverts may be more responsive to a highly stimulating environment, introverts are likely to get more deeply involved in what they are doing. Also relevant to this discussion is Mehrabian's work on individual differences in *stimulus screening*. People who are better at screening out stimulation have a greater potential for becoming absorbed and are less likely to be distracted once activities have begun. Nonscreeners, on the other hand, may potentially get more out of simple activities in a less confusing environment, approaching such activities "with a passion" (Mehrabian, 1976, p. 31). The possibility that such attentional styles may be nurtured, rather than being genetically "hard wired" in the individual, is intriguing with respect to its implications for leisure skill development and education.

Type-A Behavior

In examining the life styles of people with a history of hypertension and other forms of coronary heart disease (CHD), physicians have come to the conclusion that there are other factors besides diet and smoking that are implicated in the course of the disease (Friedman & Rosenman, 1974). In fact, the "hurry sickness" found in many highly achievement-oriented people is a better predictor of heart ailments than those other factors. People with *Type-A behavior*, as it is called, show an incidence of CHD at least four times that of their opposite, *Type-B personalities*. Investigators have now compiled a large number of studies of Type-A people that consistently demonstrate several characteristic tendencies among these unleisurely people. These are hyperaggressiveness leading to competitiveness, insecurity leading to achievement striving, time urgency, the incessant struggle against time, and hostility leading to impatience with others (Friedman & Ulmer, 1984). Type-A people commonly do more than one thing at a time whereas Type-B people do not. Type-B people, who make up only about 10 percent of the population in contrast to a larger number of Type-As and combinations of the two, do things more patiently and in keeping with their own natural rhythms. The Type-B person does not feel challenged or threatened to the same extent as Type-A people do and thus does not experience the Type-A's typical insecurity and hostility. Type-Bs have, in fact, been found to be more responsive to relaxing stimuli (Strube, Turner, Patrick & Perrillo, 1983) than Type-As.

The relationship between Type A–B behavior and leisure has not been thoroughly investigated, but there have been a few important studies and many indications from other research. A study of married adults revealed a negative relationship between Type-A tendencies and involvement in relaxing activities (Becker & Byrne, 1984). Kircaldy, Shephard and Cooper (1993) found British police officers who were Type-As to be, in general, less likely than others to be involved in leisure activities. Among college students, on the other hand, Type-As have been found to attend more live concerts than Type-Bs (Tang, 1988), to take more competitive and aggressive approaches in experimental game situations (Van Egeren, Sniderman & Ruggelin, 1982), and to show a pattern of accumulating as much leisure activity experience as possible. Weissinger and Iso-Ahola (1987) studied college students and working adults to examine the relationship between Type-A tendencies and participation in 12 selected leisure activities. Using the Jenkins Activity Survey for Health Prediction (Jenkins, Zyzanski & Rosenman, 1979), these investigators found that Type-As reported significantly more overall participation than Type-Bs, especially in outdoor activities, competitive sports, fitness activities, and home-related, job-related and school-related activities.

An intriguing experimental study of Type-A and Type-B personality types reported by Tang (1986) points out that the influence of personality on leisure behavior and experience is often subtle due to its interaction with people's perceptions of the activity and social setting. Tang used a personality questionnaire to measure undergraduate students' Type-A–Type-B orientation. Then, one at a time, the participants in the study were taken into a laboratory room and randomly assigned to either a *work task* or a *leisure task* condition. The same anagram task (participant is given a set of letters and asked to make an English word) was used in both conditions. However, in the work condition, the task was described as similar to work (such as that done by an editor or librarian). In the leisure condition, the same anagrams were described as similar to leisure activities such as crossword puzzles and playing Scrabble. After performing the anagram task, the participants were given a choice of engaging in one of three tasks during a free-choice period. One of these tasks was an anagram-solving task similar to the one they had just completed. The participants were then left alone for 15 minutes and the amount of time they spent engaged in the tasks was recorded through a one-way mirror. As can be seen in Figure 6.3, Type-B people spent less time during the free-choice period engaging in the anagram activity when they perceived it to be "work" than did Type-A participants. When the task was labeled "leisure," there was a tendency for Type-Bs to spend more time on the task than Type-As. However, this difference was not statistically significant. Tang suggests that the results may be taken to mean that Type-As "tend to spill over their coronary behavior pattern to leisure activities" and that "there is no difference between work and leisure" (p. 8) for these people. On the other hand, Type-Bs appear to distinguish and "prefer leisure over work" (p. 8). Tang concludes that it is not clear if Type-As' participation in leisure activities is a blessing or a curse. Type As' leisure activity might either help them to relieve stress or might contribute to premature death due to coronary heart disease much sooner given their tendency to get highly involved in whatever they do.

In reviewing medical opinion on workaholism, Pietropinto (1986) likened it to Type-A behavior. "At the core of the workaholic's obsession with

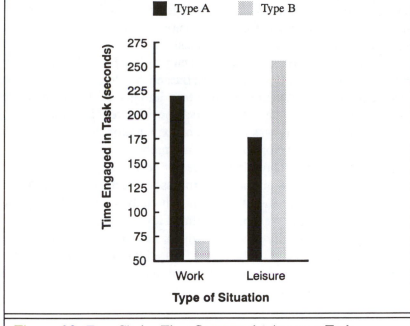

Figure 6.3 Free-Choice Time Spent on the Anagram Task

Adapted from Tang (1986)

performance is a neurotic need for love and acceptance" (p. 94). According to a survey of physicians, workaholics' typical approach to leisure is first to fill it with work (49%), second to follow a hectic schedule of varied leisure activities (33%), and third to engage in competitive sports or games.

Playfulness

Playfulness is a personality construct that has been measured reliably in studies of child development and that has implications for adult leisure behavior (Glynn & Webster, 1993; Liebermann, 1977). It includes components of cognitive, physical and social spontaneity, sense of humor, and manifest joy. Liebermann described the playful child as showing "bubbling effervescence" and "glint-in-the-eye" behavior and as demonstrating higher levels of creativity. What becomes of a person with an ample amount of this characteristic in later life is mostly a matter of speculation, but studies of adolescence suggest a greater emphasis on intellectual curiosity and humor as the playful child matures. A continuing emphasis on the physical spontaneity aspect of playfulness was shown to be maladaptive in some respects, being associated with restlessness in settings such as school where opportunities for overt physical self-expression are generally confined to periods of recess and locations such as the gymnasium.

Interestingly, the relationship between playfulness and creativity was found to be different for boys and girls (Barnett & Kleiber, 1982). Playful boys were no more likely to be creative than less playful boys when intelligence was controlled; whereas for girls, a positive relationship between playfulness and creativity was found. The explanation offered for the difference was that boys in North America are more generally expected to be playful, so their level of playfulness does not necessarily reflect the fluidity and independence of their thought processes—factors associated with creativity. On the other hand, when girls, who may not be encouraged to be playful, exhibit high levels of playfulness it is much more likely to reflect underlying personality processes which, in fact, are related to creativity. Such speculation needs to be tested further, but it suggests another way in which personality characteristics can interact with previous socialization and the demands of the social environment.

The Autotelic Personality

To the extent that people can be characterized as "types," as in Type-A and playful people, a type most intimately related to leisure is the *autotelic personality* discussed by Csikszentmihalyi (1975, 1990). Autotelic means that the purpose of an activity lies in the activity itself. Some activities—and many typical leisure activities—are rewarding enough in themselves to need no other justification or external reward. Thus, as was discussed in chapter five, they are intrinsically motivating. Usually such activities work that way when they provide an appropriate level of challenge that matches well with a person's skill level, thus allowing the experience of "flow." But some people are able to create such internal satisfaction with activities or situations that are not intrinsically motivating to most other people or to themselves initially. The *autotelic person* is one who is able to find intrinsic interest and enjoyment in almost everything he or she does. Such people are able to create leisure-like experience in unleisure-like circumstances. Consequently, boredom and anxiety are less common for them because they are able to find or create optimal levels of challenge in almost any activity or setting by reinterpreting the challenge to fit their interests and skills. This may mean finding something to manipulate or play with, cognitively or physically, in an otherwise boring situation (e.g., creating a mind game while waiting in line) or managing a more difficult situation by attending only to certain elements of it (e.g., focusing on a particular repetition in a complicated piece of music). It is likely that some of the characteristics discussed above, such as attentional style, are important to the autotelic personality.

Shyness

A final example of a personality trait that may influence leisure behavior and experience is *shyness*. Shyness has multiple properties, some of which may facilitate or interfere with certain leisure experiences (Lee & Halberg, 1989). In a study of 94 undergraduate students, the researchers found that people who were diagnosed as being chronically shy scored low in perceived freedom in leisure as measured by the Leisure Diagnostic Battery (Witt & Ellis, 1984). These individuals' perceptions of having little freedom and control in leisure suggests that they may have difficulty experiencing leisure and finding satisfaction in leisure. This interpretation is consistent with research on shyness that suggests that people who are shy may feel they lack control in their lives and have low social competence (e.g., Leary & Atherton, 1986).

Leisure-Specific Personality Dispositions

Leisure researchers have not always been satisfied with the personality traits derived from mainstream psychology as explanatory constructs. There has also been the suspicion that leisure is such a distinct and ubiquitous context that it brings out different characteristics than other situations. This has led some researchers to conceptualize leisure-specific dispositions that might prove to be more useful than general personality traits in describing and predicting leisure behavior (see Kleiber & Dirkin, 1985; Mannell, 1984b). These measures have been generated primarily for leisure research, and their application to other areas of human behavior has yet to be explored.

Leisure Boredom

Boredom is a general condition of mind that people experience to greater or lesser degrees depending on their circumstances and also their personality. As noted earlier, extroverts are more susceptible to boredom because they have a higher arousal threshold. But it has been proposed that boredom for some people is especially associated with leisure, that is, they find free time boring in and of itself, and/or the available alternatives unappealing. Iso-Ahola and Weissinger (1990) developed a personality test called the *Leisure Boredom Scale* to measure this leisure-specific trait by having people rate how well such items as the following describe them: "For me, leisure time just drags on and on" and "During my leisure time, I almost always have something to do" (second item is scored the reverse of the first item). Their research has shown that people who score higher on these types of items are less likely to perceive themselves as socially competent, are less likely to be able to entertain themselves, have lower self-esteem, are less positive toward leisure and less likely to be involved in a variety of leisure activities.

In a recent study (Iso-Ahola & Crowley, 1991), substance abusers were found to score higher on leisure boredom. Interestingly, though, they were also more likely to go to rock concerts and engage in physical recreation than nonabusers. The authors concluded that, "Because of their personality predisposition toward sensation seeking and low tolerance for constant ex-periences, substance abusers presumably prefer active leisure lifestyles. But if leisure activities fail to satisfy their need for optimal arousal, leisure boredom results and drug use may be the only alternative" (p. 260).

Self-As-Entertainment Capacity

The capacity or ability of people to fill their free or discretionary time with activity (i.e., mental, physical or social) that is personally satisfying and perceived as appropriate has been discussed as *self-as-entertainment* (SAE) or the ability to entertain oneself (Mannell, 1984b). Individuals high on this characteristic perceive a match between the time they have available and their capacity to use it. They do not experience time as "hanging heavily on their hands" and, as noted above, are less likely to regard leisure as boring. Nor are they likely to feel that they are wasting time in their leisure. Individuals low on this trait, on the other hand, perceive that they have too much free time and that there is frequently "nothing to do." A 28-item measure of this characteristic (introduced earlier in the chapter, see Figure 6.1, pp. 164–165) has been developed. Three "modes" of self-as-entertainment underlie the items: self, environmental, and mind-play. The central construct is measured by the "self" mode, that is, the extent to which people perceive they can successfully structure their own free time. The "environmental" mode reflects the extent to which people fill their free time by "going places" or by "seeking out other people." Finally, the "mind-play" mode refers to the extent to which people are able to use fantasy and imagination to fill their time. Several studies have been reported which support the scale's reliability and validity with undergraduate students and nonstudent adults (Ellis & Yessick, 1989; Mannell, 1984b, 1985; Iso-Ahola & Weissinger, 1990). Self-as-entertainment capacity would also seem to be consistent with the autotelic personality orientation and in fact may be the best measure of that construct since it has yet to be operationalized.

Intrinsic Leisure Motivation Personality Disposition

Weissinger and Iso-Ahola (1984) proposed that some people are more oriented to engage in and experience leisure as intrinsically motivated than other people. This notion is also similar to the idea of the autotelic personality discussed by Csikszentmihalyi (1975; also see Kleiber & Dirkin, 1985). Weissinger developed the *Intrinsic Leisure Motivation* scale to measure this individual difference and the research she has done with it so far suggests that it is reliable and potentially useful (see Weissinger & Bandalos, 1995). People with high scores on the scale are characterized as having a strong desire for self-determination, competence, deep involvement, and challenge while engaging in leisure pursuits. In one study, Iso-Ahola and Weissinger (1987) found that people who had a high score on the scale were much less likely to experience boredom during their leisure. She has suggested that the Intrinsic Leisure Motivation scale could be used to study how people come to see leisure as having the potential to be intrinsically rewarding. It also could be a useful tool in leisure education and counseling, and therapeutic recreation practice for identifying people who may have difficulty experiencing leisure.

Perceived Freedom in Leisure

Neulinger (1981, 1986) developed the *What Am I Doing Scale* (WAID) to measure the amount of perceived freedom people experience in leisure during a specific period of time in the course of their daily lives. This instrument has received only limited use (e.g., Ellis & Witt, 1984; Hultsman & Russell, 1988). A more widely used measure is the *Leisure Diagnostic Battery* (LDB) developed by Ellis and Witt (1984); of which a shorter version has also been developed (Witt & Ellis, 1985). The LDB assesses leisure functioning, that is, the extent to which people generally feel that their leisure is freely chosen. Perceiving freedom in leisure is felt to affect people's ability to use play and recreation to attain leisure and the benefits associated with it.

Several studies have been reported which suggest that the level of perceived freedom in leisure as assessed by the LDB is related to people's ability to experience meaningful and satisfying leisure. As we read earlier, Lee and Halberg (1989) found that people who were diagnosed as being chronically shy scored low in perceived freedom in leisure as assessed by the LDB. Adolescents scoring high in perceived freedom in leisure were found to participate more frequently, have more positive attitudes and be more satisfied with their leisure roles (Munson, 1993). They also participated more in volunteer and community service activities and found these activities more satisfying.

Interactionism and Other Issues of Personality and Leisure

In this chapter we have shown that one of the ways social psychologically-oriented researchers have attempted to understand leisure is by looking inside of people for the causes of their leisure behavior and experience. General personality dispositions that are useful in explaining a wide range of human behavior have also been found to have relevance to leisure behavior. Leisure-specific personality dispositions have been identified and they, too, show some promise. However, it is worth reminding ourselves that researchers cannot "see" personality dispositions and traits; they can only be inferred from what people do and say. Personality dispositions and traits are *hypothetical constructs*; that is, they are terms and ideas that represent the important interests, needs, and beliefs that are a part of an individual's motivational and thought processes. These interests, needs, and beliefs can be relatively stable characteristics and to some extent their importance and relevance varies from one person to another. As we have seen, these differences among people are related to how they use and experience their leisure. In the next chapter, we will focus more specifically on leisure needs and motives and their role in behavior.

As plausible and attractive as personality explanations of leisure are, it is important to note that personality does not act in a social vacuum. No matter how different they are from each other, people are influenced by the various social settings and social roles that they move in and out of during their daily lives. If a professor encounters the president of her university at a social reception, she may act differently than if she was in a bar or pub with longtime friends. A middle-aged man behaves differently with his children when he is the coach of their soccer team than when he is fishing with them during a family vacation. Sometimes the influence of the situation is so strong that one's personality appears to have little influence on one's behavior. On the other hand where there is little structure and few expectations in a situation, a person's behavior may be strongly influenced by her or his personality.

The importance of the interaction of personality and social situation was demonstrated in the experiments by Tang (1986) and Mannell and Bradley (1986) described earlier in this chapter. In the former case, the behavior and experience of the participants could only be understood when both social situation (work versus leisure context) and personality dispositions (Type A versus Type B) were taken into account. In the latter study, the influence of the amount of choice available in the social setting on game-playing behavior and flow experience was moderated by the locus of control of the participants.

Sometimes the interaction between personality and social situation is even more subtle as we saw in chapter two where several studies by Diener, Emmons and Larsen (1984, 1986) were discussed. They found that people's personalities were more likely to influence their choice of activities in leisure settings than work settings, and that engaging in activities that were consistent with personality dispositions (e.g., social activities are consistent with being extroverted) led to more enjoyment of the activities. However, this only occurred when people were in a leisure setting, not a work setting. This form of interaction is called *congruence*, and there appears to be an advantage in doing things where there is congruence between personality and the activity demands of the situation. In studies of teachers, engineers, physicians, and lawyers (Melamed & Meir, 1981; Melamed, Meir & Samson, 1995), personality factors did not cause these people to choose different activities, but those respondents whose leisure and work provided opportunities that were congruent with their personality-based psychological needs reported higher levels of well-being. In other words, if a person with an orientation to be investigative, social, or enterprising was regularly involved in activities judged to have similar characteristics, he or she was less likely to be anxious, sick, or depressed—a finding that we will return to in chapter eleven.

Ellis and Yessick (1989) have stressed the practical importance of taking the interactionist perspective into account when providing and assessing the effectiveness of therapeutic recreation interventions. For example, it would be useful to know if the effectiveness of a particular type of leisure counseling varied "according to the individual's status on such variables as perceived freedom, intrinsic motivation, and self as entertainment" (p. 33). Gramann and Bonifield (1995) have demonstrated the usefulness of considering both personality and situational factors in understanding recreationists' intentions to obey rules in outdoor recreation areas.

In concluding this chapter it should be noted that although it appears that personality "causes," or directs leisure behavior and experience (at least to some extent), the relationship implied is clearly more complicated. Personality dispositions and traits themselves are a function of social experience as well as innate predispositions. Leisure-specific personality dispositions, leisure motives and needs are strongly influenced by the socialization process and a variety of social factors. Also, it is likely that frequent and intense experiences with certain kinds of leisure activities have the effect of shaping personality characteristics that in turn determine behavior not only in leisure but in other settings as well. For example, a person who grows up hunting and fishing alone and comes to enjoy the incumbent solitude of that activity may learn to be somewhat introverted with respect to interacting with people in other areas of life. Such speculation, however, clearly needs the benefit of further research.

The social experience of being male or female and the gender-related differences that people experience while participating in leisure activities can also shape the way personality affects leisure. On the one hand, gender identity which is strongly influenced by socialization and social learning is sometimes treated as an aspect of personality and is seen to have an influence on leisure behavior. In a study of the perceptions of barriers to leisure among 500 female college students, Henderson, Stalnaker and Taylor (1988) discovered that those women with stereotypically masculine orientations were less likely to see "lack of awareness" of leisure opportunities and "difficulties in making decisions" as barriers to leisure involvement, while those women who were "feminine" in orientation were more likely to regard lack of self-confidence, fitness and physical skills as reasons for not participating. Women who were characterized as feminine were also more likely to be deterred from participation by a concern about their body image. On the other hand, the influence of personality differences have been shown to be different for men and women in some circumstances. For example, having an internal locus of control or a high-achievement orientation is apparently more important to females than males who choose to participate and who persist in what are considered masculine activities in Western society, such as some competitive sports. Locus of control and achievement orientation are not good predictors of participation in these same activities for males (Kirkcaldy & Cooper, 1992; Kleiber & Hemmer, 1981; Kleiber & Kane, 1984). The social environment is supportive of men becoming involved, whereas those women who become and stay involved do so in spite of activity stereotypes that make their involvement more difficult. Being a woman who values achievement and feels she has control in her life likely makes involvement in stereotypically masculine activities much more likely because she is highly motivated to overcome obstacles and achieve success, and she believes she can control many of the outcomes in her life. In any case, it is clear that personality does not operate alone in directing behavior or experience and that the social context must be taken into consideration.

Leisure Motivation
and Satisfaction

Chapter SEVEN

Outline

Preview

The issues examined in this chapter are closely linked to those discussed in previous chapters. In chapter four, the *immediate conscious* and *definitional* approaches to studying leisure as a subjective phenomenon were introduced. The *post-hoc satisfaction* approach is discussed in this chapter. With this approach, the subjective nature of leisure is assessed by examining the motives and satisfactions associated with participation. In chapter five, the need for freedom and control, and intrinsic motivation and satisfaction were found to be important processes underlying leisure behavior and experience. We will now discuss other needs, motives and satisfactions that affect people's leisure choices. In chapter six, leisure behavior and experience were described as being influenced by stable personality differences. As we will present in this chapter, people also differ from one another in terms of the needs and motives that are important to them. In fact, these motivational processes are often the basis of personality traits and dispositions.

Theory and research on leisure motivation and satisfaction have been stimulated by the attempts of practitioners to provide people with beneficial and satisfying leisure opportunities. Asking people what leisure activities and settings in which they would like to become involved is not necessarily the only or best approach. Lack of experience and/or skills may render people unaware of the leisure opportunities that would best meet their needs. To overcome this problem, researchers have attempted to identify the leisure needs people possess and the types of activities and settings that are best for satisfying these needs. Armed with this information, it is hoped that leisure programs and settings can be more effectively developed and managed.

Leisure motivation and *leisure satisfaction* have been popular constructs in leisure research and various terms including "preferences," "psychological outcomes and benefits" and "experience expectations" have been used to describe the social psychological processes they represent. The leisure motivation and satisfaction constructs continue to be used to explain a wide range of leisure behavior including activity loyalty (Backman & Crompton, 1991), sport participation among people with and without disabilities (Brasile, Kleiber & Harnisch, 1991), volunteering as recreation (Caldwell & Andereck, 1994), recreational running (Clough, Shepherd & Maughan, 1989), gambling as leisure (Coyle & Kinney, 1990), outdoor recreation (Ewert, 1993), participation in ecotourism (Eagles, 1992), and leisure travel (Fodness, 1994).

To help us make sense of the extensive literature on leisure motivation and satisfaction, consider the typology presented in Figure 7.1 (p. 186). The typology suggests four approaches that researchers have taken to defining and studying leisure motivation and satisfaction: component and global need-satisfaction, and component and global appraisal-satisfaction. Leisure satisfaction can be *motivation* or *evaluation* based (*basis of satisfaction* dimension). Researchers differ according to whether they conceptualize the leisure satisfaction construct to be closely tied to the idea of leisure motivation. If they do, leisure satisfaction is seen to result when people meet or "satisfy" corresponding leisure needs or motives through their participation. Leisure needs and satisfactions, then, are two sides of the same coin and are inextricably linked. This form of satisfaction is often called *need-satisfaction*. If leisure satisfaction is conceptualized as being unconnected to needs and motives, and is treated as an evaluation of the quality of leisure, we will call it *appraisal-satisfaction*.

Leisure motivation and satisfaction research can also be distinguished on the basis of *level of specificity*. Some leisure researchers have been interested in specific leisure motives, or satisfactions with specific recreational activities (molecular level), while others have focused on how well people meet all of their needs in leisure or how satisfied they are with their total leisure style (molar level). Consequently, the level of specificity being used in any particular study can be distinguished on the basis of the range or scope of the behavior being considered (specific activity versus large repertoire of leisure activities) or the need with which the satisfaction is associated (specific need versus large set of leisure needs). In the following discussion, we will examine leisure motivation and motivation-based views of leisure satisfaction. Most research has focused on specific needs and motives, and the need-satisfactions derived from specific activities.

Later in the chapter, we will present how leisure satisfaction as evaluation is used to describe and measure the quality of specific leisure activities as well as the overall quality of people's leisure.

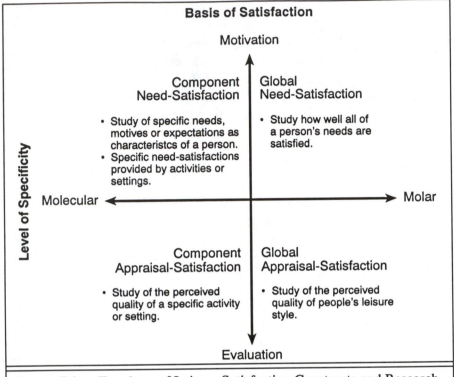

Figure 7.1   Typology of Leisure Satisfaction Constructs and Research

Adapted from Mannell (1989, p. 282)

The Nature of Motivational Explanations

Most people have had the experience of wondering "why" the people around them (or even why they themselves) engage in various leisure activities. The authors have also pondered these mysteries. Why do usually reasonable friends jog 10 kilometers (6.2 miles) every day during their lunch hour regardless of 100°F (38°C) summer heat waves or winter blizzards with wind chill effects falling below 0°F (–18°C)? Why is it that on many pleasant evenings during the summer months adolescent "vandals," under cover of darkness, "recreate" by throwing park benches into a nearby lake (where the next morning, parks and recreation personnel fish them out with the same unfailing regularity)? Why do people rock climb alone and unassisted, increasing the risk to their health and well-being? Why do the people in the next campsite in a tranquil wilderness area play their radio late into the night? Why does the 10-year-old kid on the baseball team who strikes out every at-bat come to each game with great enthusiasm, while one of the more highly skilled players acts like he wishes to be someplace else in spite of personal success?

Motivation theory and research attempt to provide answers to these "why-questions" by identifying the various needs, motives, and satisfactions that compel people to seek out specific leisure activities and experiences. At first glance, the focus of motivational explanations appears to be internal to the person. However, on closer scrutiny, the motivational answers to these "why-questions" have both *person* and *situational* components, and require an *interactionist perspective* to be understood. First, researchers using motivational explanations are primarily concerned with what arouses, energizes, or activates leisure behavior, that is, the forces within people that *push* them to engage in certain behaviors. Second, researchers are interested in the characteristics of leisure activities and settings that *pull* people to select certain activities rather than others. Different leisure activities, settings, and experiences are believed to have different *need-satisfying properties* that result in differences in the attractiveness of the activity and how well participation satisfies needs. Leisure researchers have been trying to identify differences in the *packages of satisfactions* that different types of leisure activities or settings can provide for participants.

For example, John has several needs that are currently aroused such as feeling connected and supported by other people (need for affiliation), feeling like he has accomplished something (need for achievement), and getting away from the stresses of his job (need for escape). Based on these needs, what would you recommend he do during his leisure this coming weekend? Where should he go and what should he do? Is there a single, specific leisure activity or experience that will best provide a "package of satisfactions" to meet his needs (i.e., affiliation, achievement, and escape rather than, say, relaxation and self-actualization) or are there a wide variety of activities available to him? Many people would be quite prepared to counsel John and make suggestions based on the belief that leisure activities and settings do differ in their ability to satisfy specific needs.

A General Model of Motivation

Before we examine if research supports this belief that leisure activities can satisfy needs, we will define the motivational process itself. The term "motivation" was originally derived from the Latin word *movēre*, which means "to move." In order to understand why people move or are active (e.g., running in all types of weather, recreating by committing vandalism, taking physical risks, creating noise in quiet recreation places, persisting in the face of apparent failure in sport), researchers have searched for a process within the individual that could be responsible. This something that impels people to action and gives direction to that action once it is aroused or activated is called a *motive*.

In addition to the term *motive*, a number of other terms have been used to label these internal activating factors, including drive, need, desire, and expectation. *Drives* are usually restricted to describing biologically-based physiological or what are often called survival needs. The term *need* has been used to refer to both physiological and socially learned motives. Though we will use the terms motives and needs, there are other theoretical perspectives on motivation. Instead of motives and needs, the motivational force underlying leisure behavior has been conceptualized as *expectations* (e.g., Driver & Brown, 1975; Manfredo, Driver & Brown, 1983). The assumption is that the recreationist is goal-directed, knowledgeable, thinks rationally and selects leisure activities that are suitable to fulfill expected and desired outcomes or goals. The source of these "desires" or "expectations" has not been a major issue for expectancy theorists (Vroom, 1964), though the types of expectancies found to be common and important to people are similar to the motives and needs identified by need theorists.

The basic components of a general model of motivation are: (1) needs or motives, (2) behavior or activity, (3) goals or satisfactions, and (4) feedback (see Figure 7.2). Basically, this model suggests that people possess a multitude of needs, motives, desires or expectations. For example, they may have a high need for affiliation, a strong desire for a vacation, or an expectation that skiing will make them a more attractive romantic partner. As suggested above, needs and motives are considered to "activate" behavior. This activation operates in two stages. First, the emergence of a need creates a state of disequilibrium within people (e.g., lack of something, desire for something, awareness of a potential satisfaction in a future situation) which they will try to reduce; hence, the energetic component of motivation. Second, the presence of such needs is generally associated with a belief or expectation that certain actions will lead to the reduction of this disequilibrium; hence, the goal-orientation or direction component of motivation. This model makes no distinction between conscious and unconscious needs.

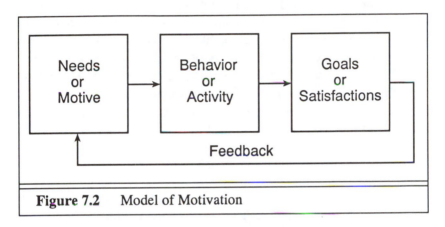

Figure 7.2   Model of Motivation

Theoretically, then, the following is assumed to be the chain of events. On the basis of some combination of this desire to reduce the internal state of disequilibrium and the belief that certain actions can serve this purpose, people act or behave in a manner that they believe will lead to the desired goal or satisfaction. If the behavior or participation in an activity results in the fulfillment of the need, the experience of satisfaction provides positive feedback that their behavior or activity is appropriate. If the behavior does not result in satisfaction of the need, this negative feedback may result in people modifying or stopping their behavior or activity.

This model is most clearly illustrated with reference to physiological needs. A need arises within the person when a biochemical imbalance occurs (e.g., blood-sugar level too low), resulting in a state of arousal or activation (e.g., feeling of hunger) in which the person is ready to engage in relevant behaviors, such as eating. The appropriate behaviors may be simple or complex (e.g., going to a fast-food restaurant when traveling by car versus making a fly rod, tying flies, going fishing, and catching, cleaning and cooking the fish on a solo wilderness trip). Either of these activities would presumably provide the desired satisfactions or rewards. Of course, understanding the motivation behind any activity is quite complex. Many needs and satisfactions usually underlie a behavior or participation in an activity. Catching and eating fish would likely also provide satisfaction of the needs for competence and self-determination.

The motivational process can also be applied to social needs. People who have a strong need or desire to be with others (motive) may attempt to engage in leisure activities, such as going to bars and drinking, that allow them to increase their interactions with other people (behavior) in the hope of developing more friendships (goal and potential satisfaction). The connection they believe to exist between their need, these behaviors and the satisfaction of their needs or desires is likely the result of social learning which may be reflected in their memory of past experiences where this has happened. The connection may also have come from observing or "modeling" other people's behavior in situations where they appeared to have derived satisfaction from having engaged in the activity or behavior (e.g., watching television commercials where people who frequent bars and drink beer make friends).

People may receive consistent negative feedback that informs them that their leisure behavior is not successful for goal attainment and need-satisfaction. Though they may have spent much time in bars recently, they may have made no new friends. They may decide to modify their behavior and, perhaps, join a tennis club as a way of meeting new people and making friends. Alternatively, going to bars may result in need-satisfaction and a point may be reached where enough social contact has been achieved (positive feedback). Generally, it is assumed that satisfying a need (e.g., need for affiliation by making friends) means that the need is no longer active in arousing, energizing and directing behavior. For example, people may no longer be preoccupied with making friends and shift their thinking and behavior toward other unmet needs (Franken, 1982; Heckhausen & Kuhl, 1985).

Motivational Dispositions and Aroused Motives

Implicit in the above description of the motivational process is a distinction between *motivational dispositions* and *aroused motives* (Hilgard, 1962). The motives that are generally important to people are called motivational dispositions and the assumption is that this set of motives differs from one person to another. In this case motives are essentially personality traits. For example, a person may be generally more achievement oriented and have a higher need for adventure than their best friend. However, not all of a person's important motives are likely to operate and influence her or his behavior at the same time. When a person's needs are active social psychologists call them *aroused motives* or *manifest needs* (Murray, 1938).

Though some people have a higher need for affiliation (motivational disposition) compared to others, they only pursue that need by associating with others when they "feel lonely" (internal state) and the environmental conditions are appropriate (other people present). Only then would the need be aroused or *manifest*. When the need is not aroused, it is said to be *latent*. When motives become manifest people are in a state of readiness for activity. For example, a student who has been working alone in a quiet library all day may be more "ready" to engage in some type of active social leisure pursuit than the student who has been on a day-long field trip with classmates. In addition to producing a state of readiness for behavior, an aroused motive tends to set off behavior in a particular direction. The gregarious person may be ready to party, the achievement-oriented one to play volleyball, and the one who is stressed with school work to escape by hiking with friends in a wilderness area.

There is evidence for the existence of leisure motivational dispositions. In a study of students in an outdoor leadership program, Williams, Ellis, Nickerson and Shafer (1988) found that motives for participation in outdoor pursuits (achievement, leadership, nature, escape from social pressure and escape from physical pressure) varied substantially among the students. Lounsbury and Hoopes (1988), in their study of 139 residents of a community, found that not only did their respondents differ in term of which leisure motives were important to them, but these differences persisted over a five-year period.

Hirschman (1984) measured motivational dispositions and demonstrated not only that these dispositions differed among individuals, but that they were related to other individual differences, in this case *gender identity*. The notion of gender identity is based on the idea that though people are born biologically male or female, they learn to become masculine or feminine through their socialization experiences. Consequently, people are seen to vary in how much they identify with and value the behaviors, attitudes and motives that society labels masculine and feminine. From this perspective, masculinity and femininity can be seen as independent characteristics that are free to vary from high to low within the same individual (see Figure 7.3, p. 192). Hirschman had the participants in her study complete a questionnaire which included a scale that measured their gender identities. Scores on this scale allowed both the female and male participants to be classified as having an *androgynous*—high on both gender identity characteristics or *undifferentiated* orientation—low on both gender identity characteristics. Those individuals scoring high on masculinity and low on femininity were classified as having a *masculine* orientation and those high on femininity and low on masculinity a *feminine* orientation.

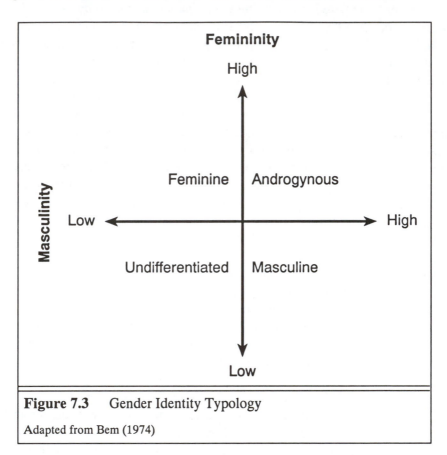

Figure 7.3   Gender Identity Typology

Adapted from Bem (1974)

Hirschman administered the questionnaire to 440 women and men. She also measured their leisure needs by having them rate how important it was for them to satisfy a variety of leisure needs in their three favorite leisure activities. The findings suggested that gender identity was a much better predictor of what leisure needs were most important to people than their biological sex. For example, psychologically masculine people were found to be most strongly motivated to seek out leisure activities that allowed for the satisfaction of the need for competitiveness whereas people who were classified as androgynous were most strongly motivated by needs for fun/pleasure, escaping reality, adventure and flow. Hirschman also found evidence to suggest that androgynous people were more likely to be looking for multiple and diverse satisfactions in their leisure behavior, and consequently, to seek satisfactions across a wide range of activities. Perhaps, people who "are in touch" with both their feminine and masculine sides have a capacity to satisfy a wider range of needs in leisure.

Leisure researchers have focused most of their attention on identifying and measuring motivational dispositions. They have shown only limited interest in studying the processes involved in the arousal and satisfaction of leisure needs and motives (Mannell, 1989; Lounsbury & Polik, 1992). An exception is a study reported by Iso-Ahola and Allen (1982) which suggests that this process can be quite complex. These researchers measured the leisure needs of 438 university students who were members of 60 randomly selected teams in an intramural basketball program that had both "competitive" and "recreational" leagues. The teams were randomly divided so that the members of some teams completed a questionnaire that measured their leisure needs before they played a game and the members of the other teams completed the questionnaire following the completion of their game. This procedure allowed the researchers to determine if and how the leisure needs of the students changed as a result of participation in this leisure activity.

The results supported the idea that the needs met through leisure are dynamic and change as a result of participation in leisure activities. The findings also suggested that this process is influenced by the nature of the experience in the activity (in this case, winning or losing the game), individual differences (such as gender), and the social setting in which the activity takes place (recreational or competitive league). For example, winning appeared to increase the need for affiliation and social interaction among women, whereas participation had little impact or slightly decreased this need among women who played on teams that lost their game. The opposite was found for men. Winning decreased the need for affiliation and social interaction among men and losing appeared to increase this need. These gender differences were likely due to social learning and the meaning of winning and losing may have been quite different for the men and women in this study. For example, it has been argued that women are socialized to value positive interpersonal relationships above winning over others, whereas the opposite may be true for men (Gilligan, 1982). Consequently, by winning the women may have felt guilty which intensified their need for affiliation and positive social interaction. Because of their socialization experiences, the men in this study may have experienced competition as an appropriate and satisfactory way to affiliate with other men, and winning may actually have enhanced this type interpersonal satisfaction, consequently, decreasing the postgame need for it.

Researchers have recently begun to show more interest in the dynamics of leisure needs and satisfactions. Stewart and Hull (1992) measured the satisfaction of day hikers several times during an actual hike in the White River National Forest in Colorado and compared on-site satisfaction with the post-hoc satisfaction experienced by the hikers when they recalled the event some time later. On-site and post-hoc differences in satisfaction were found and attributed to differences in the effects of the setting. For example, when on-site and involved in the leisure activity or setting, what is happening at the moment may dominate feelings of satisfaction. When rating satisfaction with the episode later (post-hoc satisfaction), memories of other past experiences are more likely to surface and become standards of comparison for better or for worse. Lounsbury and Polik (1992) measured the leisure needs of people prior to going on a vacation and the extent to which they had met these needs when it was over. Greater satisfaction with the vacation was reported by those people who more fully met their leisure needs.

Origin of Needs and Motives

Where do these needs and motives originate? Common practice has been to divide needs into those that have their basis in people's inherited biological nature (that is, the physiological drives and needs essential for survival) and those that they learn or acquire through their interactions with the social and physical environments. Agreement exists about the list of basic physiological needs, since these are founded upon "tissue deficits" or biochemical imbalances in the body (e.g., hunger, thirst, rest). Less agreement exists about learned needs. However, they appear to operate in similar ways. For example, the theory of "need achievement" suggests that people vary in how important it is for them to achieve and that this motive is learned (McClelland, Atkinson, Clark & Lowell, 1953). Deci and Ryan (1975) have suggested that through our interactions with the social environment as children, the basic needs for competence and self-determination can develop into specific needs, such as the need for achievement, self-actualization, or mental activity.

Even biologically-based physiological drives such as hunger and thirst are influenced by learning. People acquire different tastes for food and drink as a result of the culture in which they grow up, and in fact, these basic drives can become major "leisure needs." For example, some people learn to need or desire a "fine-dining experience" and to drink the "appropriate wine" with certain foods and occasions. People take courses in their leisure to learn about the preparation of special foods and winetasting.

There are also innate needs that are not based on tissue deficits. Foremost among these is the need for novelty, variety, and change that is based on the need to maintain an optimal level of arousal in the central nervous system. This *need for optimal arousal* is an important motive for a great deal of exploration and play (Ellis, 1973), as well as leisure (Iso-Ahola, 1980a). Each person has a level of arousal that is optimal, ideal, or psychologically comfortable and that person is in a continuous process of seeking and avoiding interactions with the environment to maintain this comfortable level (see Figure 7.4, p. 196). In other words, our choice of behavior and activity at any given moment is in part a function of the activity's ability to elicit different levels of arousal. If a person's current level of arousal is below her or his optimal level she or he is likely to seek out opportunities that will increase it toward the optimal level. If an individual's current level is above her or his optimal, she or he is likely to seek out activities that will decrease her or his arousal back toward her or his optimal level. Arousal below or above the optimal level is experienced as unpleasant, and increases or decreases of arousal toward the optimal level are experienced as pleasant. Consequently, the activities and settings that allow an individual to maintain or adjust her or his arousal level toward optimal will be experienced as satisfying. The more novel, incongruous, challenging, or uncertain the outcome of the involvement, the more arousing the activities are. For example, if a person is underaroused, she or he is more likely to seek out leisure activities that are new, challenging, or risky (e.g., hiking a new trail, playing at a higher level of difficulty in a video game, listening to new or more complex music). If a person is overaroused, she or he is more likely to seek out leisure activities or settings that are familiar, relaxing and predictable. For example, vacationers with a high need for arousal were found to be much more likely to seek out opportunities for adventure, risk, and novelty whereas those with a low need for arousal were interested in highly structured and predictable experiences (Wahlers & Etzel, 1985).

Researchers have also identified social and cognitive motives, such as the need for cognitive consistency (Festinger, 1957) and the need for

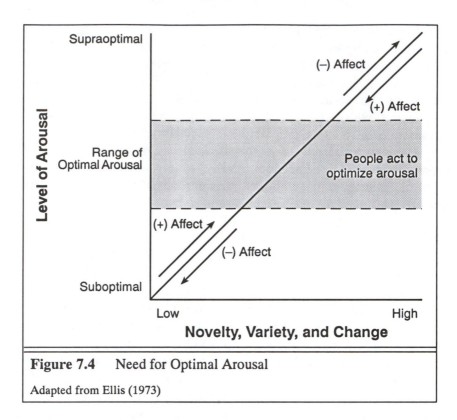

Figure 7.4   Need for Optimal Arousal

Adapted from Ellis (1973)

perceived freedom (Brehm, 1966) that are assumed to be present in all
people to some degree, and yet, have no obvious physiological basis in tissue deficits. As we discussed in chapter five, the need for competence
seems to be an essential feature of human nature (Deci, 1975; Deci & Ryan,
1991), as are so-called "ego-integrative" needs such as self-esteem and
self-actualization (Maslow, 1968). Even the desire to maintain contact
with other people, called the need for affiliation (that most social of social
needs), is seen as so nearly universal in human beings that some theorists
have considered it inborn (Skeels, 1973) or intrinsic (Deci & Ryan, 1991).
Recent approaches to motivation consider that most behavior is influenced,
to varying degrees, by biological, learned, and cognitively-based motives.

Expressed Leisure Needs: The Tip of the Iceberg

What are *leisure needs* then? Are they physiological, learned, cognitive-based, or some combination of these? Can you think of any needs that can only be satisfied in leisure? Is leisure, itself, a basic "human need?" In 1908, McDougall proposed that people are born with an instinct to play that motivates their behavior, and Ricci and Holland (1992) have suggested that the opportunity to engage in leisure (i.e., recreational travel), itself, can be a powerful motive among employees to work productively.

In fact, leisure research has not lead to the discovery of needs that can only be met through what a person does during leisure. The motivational forces operative in other areas of an individual's life also influence what she or he chooses to do in during her or his leisure. For example, Reid and Mannell (1993) asked a large group of working people to rate the extent to which they typically satisfied sixteen major needs in both their work and their leisure. Most of the respondents reported that all of these needs were satisfied to some extent in both work and leisure, though the needs for self-esteem and achievement were met to a greater degree in work and the needs for social interaction and escape were met to a greater degree in leisure.

If there are no unique leisure needs, what then, do researchers mean when they use the term "leisure needs?" Leisure needs are those identified by people when asked what needs they seek to satisfy through their leisure involvements. Researchers typically provide study participants with a list of reasons ("leisure needs") and ask them to rate the importance of each for their participation in various leisure activities. These reasons are sometimes called *expressed leisure needs.*

Do these expressed needs provide a clear picture of the actual needs and motives that operate to influence people's leisure behavior? Not necessarily, expressed leisure needs are just the tip of the motivational "iceberg" in more ways than one. When asked what satisfactions they receive from participation, people often give stereotypic responses that reflect the learned explanations that are typically used by those in their culture to explain their behavior. The real motives may be submerged—and unavailable to awareness (Iso-Ahola, 1980a) or consciousness (Franken, 1982).

Iso-Ahola (1980a) used the iceberg analogy (see Figure 7.5, p. 198) to illustrate the point that expressed leisure needs are only a small part of the motivational picture obtained when people report why they engage in leisure activities. Like the approximately 80 percent of an iceberg that is below water level, many of the motives for leisure that people report are based on physiological, learned and cognitive motives, and these, in turn, are influenced by the interaction of inherited characteristics and socialization experiences. People are often unaware of these motives when reporting the reasons why they engage in specific activities.

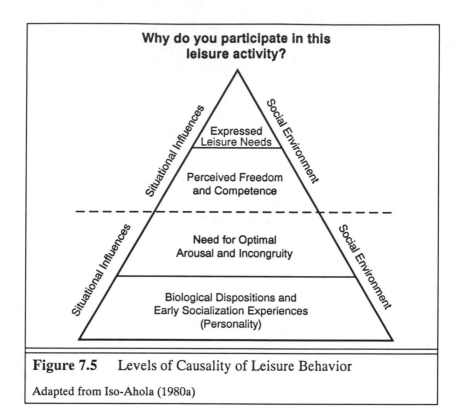

Figure 7.5   Levels of Causality of Leisure Behavior

Adapted from Iso-Ahola (1980a)

Leisure Motives and Need-Satisfactions: Measurement, Types, and Applications

Discovering and Measuring Motives and Satisfactions

To uncover leisure needs and the packages of satisfactions available in leisure activities and settings, researchers have had people complete paper-and-pencil scales or inventories, much like the personality test discussed in the last chapter. The respondents replied to questions about themselves and were typically asked to indicate on a Likert scale how important various reasons or "needs" are to them when they participated in leisure in general or specific leisure activities. These leisure-need inventories are often designed specifically for a particular study (e.g., Buchanan, Christensen & Burdge, 1981; Iso-Ahola & Allen, 1982; Pierce, 1980; Ulrich & Addoms, 1981). Efforts have also been made to develop standardized pencil-and-paper inventories (Beard & Ragheb, 1983; Lounsbury & Hoopes, 1988; Rosenthal, Waldman & Driver, 1982; Tinsley & Kass, 1979). These standardized inventories have the advantage of allowing easier comparison across studies and different populations. A few researchers have observed and interviewed participants during leisure activities, and have drawn conclusions about their leisure motives and satisfactions on the basis of their behavior and the meaning attributed to this behavior by the participants (e.g., Mitchell, 1983; Stebbins, 1992a).

Among the best-known and tested inventories are the *Recreation Experience Preference* (REP) scales developed by Driver and his colleagues, and the *Paragraphs About Leisure* (PAL) developed by Tinsley and his associates (see Driver, Tinsley & Manfredo, 1991). The "leisure needs" measured by these instruments were selected on the basis of the experience and observations of the researchers, leisure theory, and psychological need theories such as Murray's (1938). The REP scales were developed primarily to aid managers of parks and other natural areas in identifying the kinds of needs people visiting outdoor recreation sites are seeking to satisfy. Thousands of visitors to outdoor areas have completed these scales. The instrument measures the extent to which specific satisfactions are desired and expected from leisure activities/settings (e.g., enjoy nature, reduce tension, share similar values, independence, creativity, nostalgia, achievement). Each scale of the PAL consists of a single paragraph which describes the satisfaction of a particular psychological need. People are instructed to indicate

the extent to which each paragraph is an accurate statement about the satisfactions they receive from a specific leisure activity.

A need inventory developed by Beard and Ragheb (1983) has been
used frequently by researchers and inventories that focus on specific types
of leisure behavior have also been developed. For example, travel needs
were measured by Crompton (1979). These needs included escape, exploration, self-discovery, relaxation, prestige, regression, family bonding, and
social interaction.

How Many Leisure Needs Are There?

Some theorists have attempted to identify the full range of human needs.
Murray's (1938) well-known manifest need theory itemizes approximately
40 needs and motives. The two inventories developed by Driver and Tinsley
and their associates each measure a large number of motives and satisfactions. Other need theorists have proposed a much smaller number of basic
motives. For example, Maslow's (1954) theory identifies only five major
types of needs. Maslow theorized that everyone possesses this set of needs
and that they are arranged in a hierarchy of importance. At the lowest level
are physiological needs, followed in order by safety and security needs,
belongingness and love needs, ego and esteem needs, and self-actualization.
Once lower-level needs are satisfied, needs at the next highest level emerge
and influence behavior. The levels of the need hierarchy are not rigidly
separated but overlap to some extent. Thus, it is possible for a higher-level
need to emerge before a lower-level need is completely satisfied. In fact,
Maslow suggested that average adults in western societies have satisfied
about 85 percent of their physiological needs, 70 percent of their safety
needs, 50 percent of their social needs, 40 percent of their self-esteem needs,
and 10 percent of their self-actualization needs. Although Maslow never
collected data to support these estimates, research suggests that lower-level
needs are satisfied more than higher-level needs (Steers & Porter, 1991).

Although Maslow's theory has a great deal of appeal, it has proved to
be difficult to test (Wahba & Bridwell, 1976; Steers & Porter, 1991). There
is no clear evidence showing that human needs can be classified into five
distinct categories or that these needs are structured into any special hierarchy. Apparently, higher-level needs can influence behavior even when
lower-level needs are largely unfulfilled. However, the theory has been
widely adopted by theorists and planners who are interested in improving
social conditions. For example, the theory has provided a theoretical basis

for work organization improvement programs such as participative management, job enrichment, and quality of work-life projects (Cherrington, 1989). According to the theory, an organization must use a variety of factors to motivate behavior since people will be at different levels of the need hierarchy. Maslow's theory is also referred to frequently by leisure theorists and planners. It has provided a framework for specifying when and under what conditions leisure will become important to people. For example, leisure may be unimportant until at least physiological, safety and security needs are satisfied. Leisure is seen as ideal for providing appropriate settings and activity opportunities for the satisfaction of social, esteem, ego and particularly, self-actualization needs because involvement in leisure is typically self-determined (Csikszentmihalyi & Kleiber, 1991).

In spite of the large number and types of needs reported in various studies of leisure behavior and the different names used to label them, there is substantial agreement about the relatively small number of basic types that operate (Tinsley, 1984). Tinsley and Kass (1978) found that the 44 leisure needs that they measured could be reduced to eight types (i.e., self-expression, companionship, power, compensation, security, service, intellectual aestheticism and solitude). Driver's thirty-nine REP scales have been reduced to 19 categories, eight that research has shown are important to recreationists using natural and wilderness areas (Rosenthal, Waldman & Driver 1982). These include exploration, escape role overload, general nature experience, introspection, exercise, being with similar people, seeking exhilaration, and escaping physical stressors.

Iso-Ahola (1982, 1989) has suggested that the reasons people participate can be reduced to *two basic motivational dimensions* of leisure behavior—seeking and escaping (see Figure 7.6, p. 202). According to Iso-Ahola, these two motivational forces simultaneously influence people's leisure behavior. On the one hand, leisure activities are engaged in because they provide novelty or change from daily routine and stress. By *escaping* the everyday environment, a person can leave behind their *personal* and/or *interpersonal* worlds. The personal world refers to escape from personal problems, troubles, difficulties and failures, and the interpersonal world refers to other people such as co-workers, friends, and family members. A person can escape both worlds simultaneously. He suggests that escape is a powerful leisure motive due to the constraining nature of a person's life, particularly her or his work. Escape is also based on the need for optimal arousal; individuals are constantly trying to escape from underarousing and overarousing conditions.

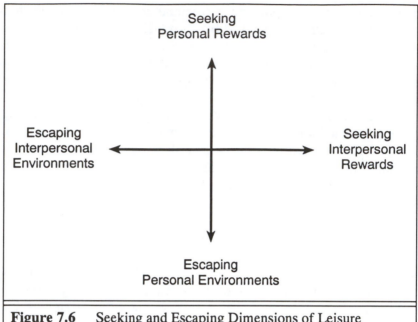

Figure 7.6   Seeking and Escaping Dimensions of Leisure
Motivation

Adapted from Iso-Ahola (1989)

   The other motivational dimension is the tendency to *seek* psychological satisfactions from participation in leisure activities. The satisfactions
that people may seek through leisure can also be divided into personal and
interpersonal types. Personal satisfactions consist mainly of self-determination, sense of competence, challenge, learning, exploration and relaxation. On the other hand, people often want to engage in leisure activities
for social contact and connectedness. Iso-Ahola (1989) suggests that both
the seeking and escaping motives are forms of intrinsic motivation (p. 259).
   In a recent study of the motives and satisfactions of a group of sightseeing tourists participating in a guided tour of Washington, DC, Dunn
Ross and Iso-Ahola (1991) found that the motives for participating in the
tour and subsequent satisfactions received from this participation could be
classified according to the seeking and escaping dimensions of Iso-Ahola's
model. Participants were primarily motivated by *knowledge seeking* and
opportunities for *social interaction*. However, there was evidence of an
escape dimension, in that, the tourists also wanted to escape their troubles,
work, and other responsibilities by participation in the tour. Though this
model is interesting, it remains to be seen how useful it is to reduce leisure

motives to two dimensions. Most applications of the leisure motive and satisfaction ideas are based on the belief that it is important and useful to identify in some detail the types of leisure needs people wish to meet in their leisure, on the one hand, and the types of need-satisfactions that are available through participation in leisure activities and contexts on the other.

Using Knowledge of Leisure Motives and Satisfactions

In addition to discovering the needs that *push* people to engage in particular leisure activities and settings, researchers have attempted to identify the need-satisfying properties of leisure activities and settings themselves (e.g., Tinsley & Kass, 1979; Pierce, 1980; Tinsley & Johnson, 1984) that *pull* people into action or participation. Tinsley and Johnson demonstrated that various types of activities produce unique packages of satisfactions. A taxonomy of nine activity types was suggested based on the activities' need-satisfying properties. For example, activities such as doing crossword puzzles, watching television, going to the movies, and reading fiction were found similar in providing satisfactions labeled "intellectual aestheticism" and "solitude," but contributed very little to the satisfactions of companionship, security, service, or self-expression. In contrast, respondents reported that activities such as picnicking and visiting friends and relatives provided high levels of satisfaction of the needs for companionship, service, and security, and little satisfaction of the needs for solitude or power.

Williams and Schreyer (1981) compared the motives of recreational visitors to two distinct wilderness settings, an alpine area and a desert/canyon area. Visitors to the latter environment saw it as providing higher satisfactions for tension release, competence, testing, escape and family togetherness. Stewart and Carpenter (1989) found that the greater the need for solitude among hikers in the Grand Canyon, the more likely they were to engage in their recreation in low-use zones. In another study by Manfredo, Driver, and Brown (1983), wilderness users were found to be seeking different packages of satisfactions which in turn were related to their preferences for activities and environmental settings. For example, users who were attempting to satisfy their needs for risk and achievement, showed a preference for areas with rough or undeveloped access, rugged terrain at destination sites, high naturalness and low probability of meeting other people. Wilderness users who were looking to satisfy the need for solitude, but were low on the needs for achievement, challenge, and risk preferred areas with moderate accessibility, little or no development, low probability of social encounters, and natural surroundings devoid of dangerous situations.

A third group preferred more accessible, secure and managed settings where the likelihood of meeting other people was higher.

These types of findings have been applied to the development and management of physical recreation resources and park areas. By surveying people in outdoor settings, researchers have developed various classification or zoning systems for natural recreation areas based on the leisure need-satisfactions (packages of satisfactions) typically experienced by users in these settings (Driver, Brown, Stankey & Gregoire, 1987). The U.S. Forest Service has been using the *Recreation Opportunity Spectrum*, or ROS (see Manning, 1985) and the Canada Parks Service has implemented the *Visitor Activity Management Process*, or VAMP (see Graham, Nilsen & Payne, 1988) to assist with decisions about the management and development of park areas. Potential park users are surveyed to determine what needs they are seeking to satisfy (packages of satisfactions). Managers inventory and catalog the various types of settings in their parks (e.g., primitive, semiprimitive motorized, rustic, modern urbanized). These different settings are thought to have distinct need-satisfying properties, and consequently, to provide different packages of satisfactions to visitors. For example, primitive areas can provide solitude, a feeling of oneness with nature, challenge and risk. Modern urbanized areas can provide affiliation with other people, relaxation, and a secure low-risk environment.

Management strategies can be based on this information and hopefully lead to a reasonable match between the *demand* for certain packages of satisfactions and the *supply* of opportunities available in the park or natural area. If the park lacks settings or support activities that could produce a particular package of satisfactions, the manager can decide to develop the necessary opportunities or to protect the resource from further development and advise potential visitors that they should go elsewhere.

Motivational Explanations in a Broader Context: The Case of Risk Recreation

When participation in a specific leisure activity is considered, it is clear that motives and satisfactions are only part of the social psychological explanation for participation. Nonmotivational factors, such as one's past experience, present leisure skills and repertoire, perceptions of the recreational opportunities available, and one's involvement in various social groups, play a role as well. Recent models of leisure participation among older adults (Losier, Bourque & Vallerand, 1993), leisure constraints (Jackson,

Crawford & Godbey, 1992), leisure travel (Mansfeld, 1992), and risk recreation (Robinson, 1992) illustrate how motives are only part of the explanation of leisure behavior. For example, motivational explanations have always dominated discussions of why people participate in *risk recreation* activities. Mountaineering, rock climbing, hang gliding, and whitewater kayaking are examples of risk recreation activities in which danger and sometimes hardship are faced. Involvement in these types of activities can be puzzling and appear irrational at times.

The motives proposed to explain why people engage in these types of activities have ranged from the abnormal and destructive to those that bring out the best in people. As an example of the former, psychoanalytic-based analyses have suggested that participants in risk recreation are motivated by a "death wish" or some other "unsavory" motive resulting from guilt related to unresolved problems with sex and aggression (Mitchell, 1983, p. 141). At the other end of the continuum, participation in risk recreation has been attributed to the search for self-actualization and ultimate self-knowledge as participants test their limits (Csikszentmihalyi, 1975; Iso-Ahola, Graefe & LaVerde, 1989). Others have indicated that participants are motivated by the opportunity for aesthetic experiences and self-expression (e.g., Mitchell, 1983; Ewert, 1994).

With the growing popularity and increasing number of participants in risk recreation in North America, a number of models have recently been developed by leisure researchers to account for participation in this type of activity (e.g., Csikszentmihalyi, 1975; Ewert & Hollenhorst, 1989; Robinson, 1992). These models suggest that though motivation is important, it is only part of the picture. For example, Robinson (1992) has suggested a *model of enduring risk recreation involvement.* Important factors identified by the model include motives, personality differences, cognitive processes, and social influences—that is, both motivational and nonmotivational conditions (see Figure 7.7, p. 206).

According to Robinson, two primary motivational dispositions are involved in determining if people are attracted to and stay involved in risk recreation activities. The first of these is the *need for stimulation* and the second is based on the *need for autonomy* (i.e., self-determination). These two sources of motivation were discussed earlier in the book. However, the model also proposes that these motives "serve only to provide a 'potential' for risk recreation involvement" (Robinson, 1992, p. 55). For example, other motives such as the "need for affiliation" and "need for recognition" contribute to the attractiveness of a risk recreation pursuit. In addition,

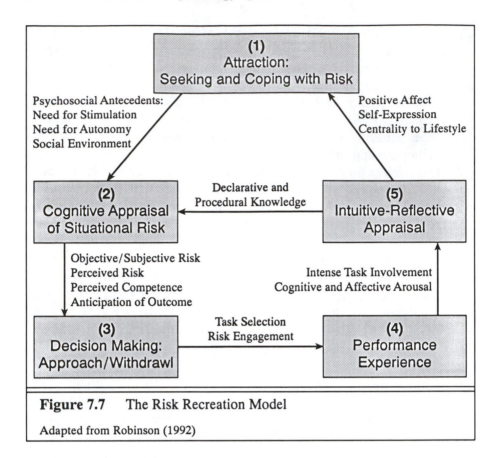

Figure 7.7 The Risk Recreation Model

Adapted from Robinson (1992)

conditions in people's social environment, such as the amount of *certainty* or predictability that exists in their daily life may affect their willingness to engage in risk recreation. The more predictable and unchanging their everyday lives, the more likely they are to seek out the unpredictable in risk recreation.

Robinson's model also suggests that whether the arousal of the motives of sensation seeking and autonomy lead a person to select risk recreation to satisfy these depends on several intervening cognitive processes—*cognitive appraisal* and *decision making*. Essentially, these processes refer to how people come to judge the actual level of risk involved in participation relative to their perceived competencies (that is, knowledge and skills in the activity). This decision, itself, is influenced by not only how risky the activity is perceived to be, but by the level of risk that is acceptable to them which is likely a personality characteristic, itself a result of socialization experiences.

If participation results in a successful experience then the needs for stimulation and autonomy will likely be satisfied according to this model. However, continued or repeat participation is thought to depend on whether success in the activity reinforces aspects of self-identity or personality, such as "I am adventurous" or "I am self-sufficient."

Whether or not this specific model is supported by future research, it does demonstrate the importance of incorporating motivational explanations into a larger social psychological framework if the complexity of leisure behavior is to be understood. However, leisure motivation and need-satisfaction theories have stimulated a great deal of research and thinking about the nature of leisure.

Leisure Satisfaction and the Quality of Leisure

Measures of *leisure satisfaction* are also used to assess the quality of people's leisure as they perceive it, and it is an alternative to measuring the frequency of leisure participation as an indicator of the quality of leisure style. As mentioned earlier in the chapter (see Figure 7.1, p. 186), this view of leisure satisfaction is based on an evaluation perspective called *appraisal-satisfaction*. Respondents are asked to rate their satisfaction with their total leisure style or some aspect of it on various types of rating scales.

Satisfaction as Appraisal and Evaluation

This evaluation approach to conceptualizing and measuring leisure satisfaction has emerged from the extensive research undertaken over the past several decades on the quality of life and subjective well-being of working-aged and elderly retired adults (see Mannell, 1989; Mannell & Dupuis, 1996). Initially, these types of studies focused on mental health problems and how well people coped with difficult life events (e.g., Gurin, Veroff & Feld, 1960), but later the issue became subjective well-being (Bradburn, 1969) or the quality of life as a whole (Campbell, Converse & Rodgers, 1976).

The appraisal-satisfaction approach reflects a concerted effort to assess the quality of contemporary life and its various domains other than with the use of objective measures. For example, economists have equated well-being with the gross national income, public health researchers with decreases in high-risk health behaviors, ecologists with the quality of the environment, and sociologists with levels of crime, suicide, public violence, and family disintegration. However, it has been argued that "we cannot understand the psychological quality of a person's life simply from a knowledge of the circumstances in which that person lives" (Campbell, 1980, p. 1) or gain more than a partial explanation of why some people find their lives enjoyable and satisfying and some do not. It is generally assumed that people "are able to describe the quality of their own lives, not as precisely as one might like, but with a kind of direct validity that more objective measures do not have" (Campbell, 1980, p.12).

A major task for researchers has been to achieve consensus on the definition and measurement of well-being or quality of life. Three psychological constructs—happiness, morale, and satisfaction—are frequently used to conceptualize well-being and quality. *Happiness* is considered to reflect a person's more temporary affective feelings of the present moment. *Morale* is considered to be a more future-oriented optimism or pessimism with people's lives. Different from happiness and morale, *satisfaction* "implies an act of judgment, a comparison of what people have to what they think they deserve, expect, or may reasonably aspire to. If the discrepancy is small, the result is satisfaction; if it is large, there is dissatisfaction" (Campbell, 1980, p. 22). The standards of comparison on which these judgments or appraisals are based are usually left unspecified. Satisfaction has a past orientation—an appraisal of how things have gone up until the present.

Sometimes overall measures of how satisfied people are with their lives are collected. A more detailed picture of quality of life has been obtained by examining satisfaction with the major divisions of life, often called "domains." Work or job satisfaction has been the focus of extensive research and theoretical interest (see Fincham & Rhodes, 1988; O'Brien, 1986). Of interest here is the attention researchers have given to satisfaction with the leisure domain, and their attempts to assess how satisfaction with leisure influences other areas of life as well as the whole of life. Measurements of appraisal-satisfaction have also been used to assess the quality of specific leisure activities and events with an eye to improving their quality. Some examples of this latter research follow.

Evaluating Leisure Activities and Settings

In the leisure research that has used the appraisal approach, leisure satisfaction has been measured at various levels of specificity. Researchers with more *molecular* concerns have examined satisfaction with particular components or subdomains of leisure behavior or experience. These subdomains have included satisfaction with provincial park campgrounds (Foster & Jackson, 1979), tourist destinations (Pearce, 1982), and outdoor recreation activity during a day trip (Vaske, Donnelly, Heberlein & Shelby, 1982).

Research that takes the level of specification even further has also been reported. Pizam, Neumann and Reichel (1978) found that satisfaction with eight subdomains (e.g., beach opportunities, cost, hospitality, commercialization) described tourist satisfaction with a well-known seaside destination. Graefe and Fedler (1986) examined satisfaction with a chartered recreation fishing outing. They not only measured overall satisfaction with the trip, but also satisfaction with various components or elements of the experience (e.g., enjoyment of the outdoors, types and number of fish caught, level of challenge). Noe (1987) surveyed spectators at a raft racing event. He measured overall satisfaction with the event as well as satisfaction with twenty-four specific aspects of the event (e.g., the rafters, food facilities, parking signs, music). A number of studies have examined a variety of factors that affect satisfaction with outdoor activities such as hunting (Hultsman, Hultsman & Black, 1989; Hazel, Langenau & Levine, 1990) and boating (e.g., Robertson & Regula, 1994). Standardized measurement scales have been developed to measure satisfaction with participation in specific recreation activities such as racquet sports (Aguilar & Petrakis, 1989).

This type of research with the leisure satisfaction construct is typically not theoretically driven. Researchers are interested in assessing the quality of a leisure event or activity and those aspects of it that contribute or detract from its quality. For example, Geva and Goldman (1991) used measures of satisfaction to assess the quality of 15 guided tours from Israel to Europe and the United States. By measuring the participants' satisfaction with various aspects of both the tour company's services (e.g., hotels, entertainment, scheduling) and the tour guide (e.g., conduct, expertise), they were able to suggest strategies to increase the likelihood that the tour company would get its fair share of the credit for a successful tour and that participants would choose the company in the future or recommend the company to other travelers. This use of the satisfaction construct has much in common with the notion of *service quality* used in understanding consumer behavior in leisure contexts (e.g., Crompton & Mackay, 1989; Colenutt & McCarville, 1994).

Antecedents and Consequences of Leisure Satisfaction

At the other end of the specificity continuum, a number of studies that have been concerned with satisfaction with the whole leisure domain of life. Single-item measures are frequently used and the domain of leisure behavior to be assessed has been identified in different ways by researchers. People have been asked to rate satisfaction with their "present level of leisure participation" (Guinn, 1980, p. 200), "amount of spare time" (Lounsbury, Gordon, Bergermaier & Francesco, 1982, p. 290), and "leisure in general" (Iso-Ahola & Weissinger, 1987, p. 360; Trafton & Tinsley, 1980, p. 37).

Other researchers, though also focusing on satisfaction with the whole leisure domain, measure satisfaction by asking the people they study how satisfied they are with different aspects of their leisure and summing or averaging across these components to arrive at a global satisfaction score. London, Crandall and Seals (1977) averaged Likert scale ratings based on their respondents' satisfaction with activities done with friends and/or family, other social activities, organizational involvements, recreational facilities used and various forms of entertainment. Ragheb (1980), and Francken and van Raaij (1981) had respondents rate their satisfaction with activities representing most types of leisure behavior, and computed an over-all leisure satisfaction score from these ratings. Backman and Mannell (1986) had the institutionalized older adults in their study recall during an interview the recreational activities that they had engaged in during the previous week. These older adults rated their satisfaction with each re-called activity and the researchers computed a global leisure satisfaction score based on these ratings.

The research reported using satisfaction as a global appraisal of the whole leisure domain has had several different goals. One of these has been to examine the factors that affect how satisfied or dissatisfied people are with their leisure style. To do this, researchers have examined the relationship between leisure satisfaction and other leisure phenomena such as leisure participation, attitudes, awareness and boredom. For example, Ragheb (1980) found that the higher people's leisure participation and the more positive their leisure attitudes, the higher their leisure satisfaction. Francken and van Raaij (1981) found leisure satisfaction to be higher for people who were older, had an optimistic outlook and perceived themselves as having the personal interests and capacity for leisure activity participation. Iso-Ahola and Weissinger (1987) discovered that the greater people's "boredom in leisure," the less their satisfaction with leisure. The impact on leisure satisfaction of other factors such as retirement (Dorfman, Heckert & Hill, 1988; Hatcher, 1988), stress (Cunningham & Bartuska, 1989), and the amount of freedom in leisure people experience (Ellis & Witt, 1994) has been examined.

Leisure satisfaction has also been used as an outcome measure to determine the impact of various kinds of counseling and therapeutic interventions used to improve the quality of people's leisure (Backman & Mannell, 1986; Caldwell, Adolph & Gilbert, 1989; Zoerink & Lauener, 1991). For example, in a field experiment, Backman and Mannell (1986) found that the leisure satisfaction of institutionalized older adults increased after participation in a leisure education and counseling program.

Little research has been reported examining the relationship between satisfaction with the leisure domain and other domains of life. One exception is a study by Lounsbury, Gordon, Bergermaier and Francesco (1982) that found that the more satisfaction workers had with their jobs, the higher was their level of leisure satisfaction, and the less likely was their intention to leave their jobs. The contribution of leisure as measured by leisure satisfaction to the overall quality of life will be discussed in chapter ten.

Usefulness and Limitations of the Leisure Motivation and Satisfaction Constructs

Researchers have found the leisure motivation and satisfaction constructs attractive for understanding leisure behavior and experience. Like other subjective approaches to understanding leisure, the leisure motivation and satisfaction constructs put researchers in the mind of the participant. They represent psychological processes that take researchers beyond what people do, and they provide a framework for understanding what leisure means to people. The *need-satisfaction* approach involves researchers examining the link and interaction between the psychological needs people have, that is, what they bring to leisure activities and situations and the nature of the leisure pursuits they choose. The *appraisal-satisfaction* approach has resulted from researchers attempting to assess the quality of leisure participation rather than just the quantity. The fact that leisure need-satisfaction and appraisal-satisfaction can be measured using the methods of the social sciences has facilitated a great deal of research.

Leisure service practitioners have found the leisure motivation and satisfaction constructs useful in helping them think about and plan the types of support, programs, and services that the people they work with want and need. The provision of quality services is seen to be dependent on identifying people's leisure needs, understanding the types of opportunities that can satisfy these needs, and developing the appropriate services (Howe &

Qui, 1988; Ragheb, 1988). For example, advocates of this approach have suggested that the provision of leisure counseling (Tinsley, 1984), the management of outdoor recreation resources (Driver, 1976), and the development of tourism products and opportunities (Mansfeld, 1992) benefit from this approach.

There are, however, limits to the constructs of leisure motivation and satisfaction. Though the motivational process model appears fairly simple and straightforward, and it is a useful tool for identifying individual differences in what people are seeking in leisure, in actual fact, motivational processes are dynamic and quite complex. Any individual at any given time usually has a host of needs, desires and expectations. Not only do these motives change but they may be in conflict with each other. A desire to improve one's golf game by playing more regularly out of a need for competence may be in direct conflict with a desire to spend more time with one's nongolfing friends (need for affiliation). Thus, given the changing nature of an individual's particular set of motives and given their often conflicting nature, it becomes exceedingly difficult to observe and measure them. Also, the need-satisfaction and reduction process does not describe all behavior. The intensity of certain motives (such as hunger, thirst, sex) is generally considerably reduced upon satisfaction. When this happens, other motives come to the forefront as primary motivating factors. However, the attainment of certain satisfactions may sometimes lead to an increase in the intensity of some motives. For example, winning at a music festival may not long "satisfy" the need for achievement. In fact, it may even heighten this need, causing a person to pursue other competitive activities. Thus, the satisfaction of certain needs may, at times, lead people to shift their focus of attention to different motives and, at other times, such satisfaction can serve to increase the strength of a motive.

One of the real challenges to leisure motivation explanations of leisure behavior concerns the fact that participation in any single leisure activity may express several motives, and conversely, similar motives may be expressed in different activities. Thus, when parents are observed taking children to the local swimming pool, it is unclear whether they are doing it because it is a family responsibility, they desire the feelings of connectedness that spending time with their children provides, they enjoy feelings of competence or relaxation in the activity, or if it is some complex combination of all of these. In other words, the need-satisfying properties of activities and settings exist to a large extent in the mind of the participant and not in the activity itself (Driver & Brown, 1984). The same activity can provide different satisfactions depending on the social and/or physical setting in which it occurs and some satisfactions can be achieved in a wide variety of activities and settings while other satisfactions are highly setting and activity specific (e.g., Yuan & McEwen, 1989; Virden & Knopf, 1989). Different levels of experience in a leisure activity or setting, personality differences, companions and success in the activity have been found to influence the links between the activity and setting and the satisfactions that people perceive to be available (e.g., Williams, Ellis, Nickerson & Shafer, 1988; Williams, Schreyer & Knopf, 1990; Ewert, 1993). London, Crandall and Fitzgibbons (1977) found that some of the individuals they studied perceived that they could satisfy their need for enjoyment and fun in sports activities, yet others saw sports activities as high in the ability to meet social needs. Yuan and McDonald (1990) found that though people from different cultures engaged in pleasure travel to satisfy similar needs, they preferred different destinations with different characteristics to do so.

Obviously, these activity-satisfaction links are strongly influenced by learning. Knopf (1983, p. 229) has suggested that researchers need to answer such questions as, "How do people get to know recreation environments?" and "How do they learn where to gratify their needs?" In other words, research is needed to better understand the socialization process by which people come to believe that participation in certain types of activities and settings will satisfy specific needs. The theories that are emerging and being tested to better understand gender, cultural and ethnic differences in leisure participation may eventually contribute to this knowledge (e.g., Clark, Harvey & Shaw, 1990; Falk, 1995; Floyd, McGuire, Shinew & Noe, 1994; Floyd, Gramann & Saenz, 1993; Frederick & Shaw, 1995; Henderson, 1990b; Jackson & Henderson, 1995).

The Social Context
of Leisure

Socialization and the Development of Leisure Orientations

Chapter EIGHT

Preview

This chapter addresses the subject of the *origins* of leisure orientations and interests. In so doing, it brings the subject of leisure into contact with one of its next of kin—children's play. Much of what leisure becomes for people, we will argue, is derived from the enjoyment of play and the departures from mundane reality that children find so captivating in play. But of course, leisure is more than play. The experiences of the freedom and intrinsic interest that individuals associate with leisure may be preconditions of play, and play may be a precursor to much of adult leisure whether it involves serious effort or peaceful reverie. In the course of childhood, there are many lessons to be learned about using time, wasting time, and alternating responsibility and effort with relaxation and diversion. This chapter will deal in part, then, with how these lessons are taught and learned. It will also focus on how the natural, biologically-directed tendencies of childhood change in some predictable ways with development and create changing interests that are also influenced by the responses of important "others" in a child's social environment. Most of the available research we will examine deals with factors that shape leisure interests and orientations. But we will also consider children as generators of their own socialization. Socialization is not only that which is done to children to bring them in line with the many demands placed on them by society, but it is also a process that is generated both by innate or intrinsic organismic tendencies and through interaction with the environment.

Emergent Interests and Self-Socialization

As with other orientations in life, the attitudes one develops toward leisure and the leisure interests that emerge are the result of developmental changes and social learning. When and how does a child come to see that there is time to be used at his or her discretion? Adults would be amused if a two-year-old responded to a request to talk to them with the words, "I don't have time." They might see it as "cute" since it is otherwise so adult-like. Leisure awareness has not been studied much in the periods before adolescence. Children are rarely heard to use the words leisure or recreation, though "fun," "play," "recess," "after school," "weekend," and "vacation" come to have meaning to most school-age children. Perhaps the start of school is a critical event in recognizing those times when one is constrained and those times when one isn't. "Playtime," however, is an idea that most children learn before starting school as they come to identify interactions around the rituals of eating, cleaning up, and bathing as within the control of parents or caregivers and that such impositions are sometimes suspended or at least softened through negotiation. But a concept of leisure comparable to that of adults would seem to require some adult-like experience with work or at least a clear sense of free and discretionary versus obligated time.

It might be suggested, however, that children have little to gain in developing a more "mature" perspective on free and obligated time. The youngest of children tend to live in the infinite present, able to commit themselves to the moment as if nothing else mattered. Arguably, babies and toddlers are the ultimate "leisure kind" (de Grazia, 1964) to the extent that they are led by their inclinations, wherever and whenever the spirit moves them. And this is not because they *play*, though that may be the quintessential leisure activity; it is that they are very likely to be *relaxed in the present*, unconcerned about the past or future.

Nevertheless, this may be an overly romanticized view of childhood. The youngest child is a likely victim of any number of upsetting events; playtime and relaxation periods eventually become distinguishable from those more stressful situations, but only as powers of discrimination are developed. The recognition of leisure is also, of course, the result of a kind of *cultivation* by significant others and society more generally. We will examine the social and cultural forces that shape various leisure orientations shortly, but first, there is more to be said about what children "bring to the table" as part of their basic nature.

The study of play and exploration offers a good starting place because these activities demonstrate the power of intrinsic interest in directing growth-producing interactions with the physical and social environments (see Barnett, 1990; Ellis, 1973). This power is due in large part to the survival values that accrue to species engaging in play and exploration. By forcing encounters with the environment, learning and adaptation are facilitated (Bruner, Jolly & Sylva, 1976, Christie & Johnson, 1983; Deci & Ryan, 1991). A child who drops a ball down an embankment and follows cautiously learns about the embankment, the properties of the ball and her or his own abilities. As discussed in chapter five, the sense of growing competence and mastery that such activities create is associated with positive affect. Enjoyment is increasingly recognized as not so much a matter of pleasure as the optimal experience resulting from a good fit between one's exerted skills and the demands of the environment (Csikszentmihalyi, 1990). Because skills improve through repeated encounters with the environment, there is a steadily increasing need for greater complexity in the environment. Thus, enjoyment becomes the psychic energy that fuels much of what social psychologists call *development*.

Play

Some time ago, the 17-year-old son of one of the authors acquired a two-month-old black Labrador retriever puppy who would respond to a water dish set in front of her by taking a few drinks, then putting her whole head in the water, then her paws, then knocking over the bowl, splashing in the puddle, carrying the bowl in her teeth, and knocking it all over the room. Initially, the annoyance of having to clean up the water was somewhat balanced by the amusement with the puppy's exuberant playfulness. Of course, this behavior got old rather quickly! It led to the question, though, of whether more mature dogs realize that the water is somehow to be treated more respectfully in the heat of a Georgia summer, or simply that spilling it is not in itself interesting anymore. Human babies play with their food on a regular basis, but, with the exception of the occasional cafeteria food fight among adolescents, such activities succumb to more "appropriate" behavior among adults.

Play is not the same as leisure, nor is it all that children do. It is different from exploration (Piaget, 1962; Hutt, 1971; Cohen, 1993) in that it is not so specifically oriented to revealing the true nature of things. Play is *nonliteral* behavior, a *transformation of reality* (Schwartzman, 1978). A doll represents a baby; a space under the stairs is a starship control room.

Play is *intrinsically motivated* (Huizinga, 1955; Ellis, 1973) and *freely chosen* or entered into (Huizinga, 1955). Hughes (1991) adds also that it is *actively engaging* (flow-like rather than relaxing). As was noted before, leisure may or may not be actively engaging. Play shares the qualities of intrinsic motivation and perceived freedom with leisure and, by being transformative, play represents the kind of action people sometimes seek in leisure to make it qualitatively different from what has been called the *paramount reality* of everyday life (see Kleiber, 1985, for further discussion of this point).

As the free exercise of personal dispositions, play is a clear reflection, at least in childhood, of the essential motivations and abilities that characterize a given age. The play of infants and toddlers is generally *practice play* and emerges during what Piaget (1962) has called the sensory-motor period of cognitive development. Children's interactions with the environment are restricted primarily to simple perceptual and motor responses and adjustments. They exercise various skills to create an effect on the environment and then change things to see what happens. Typically, infants begin exploring and playing by putting everything into their mouths to experience them, and they repeat actions and sounds seemingly ad infinitum. The world of play at this time is limited primarily to their own bodies or whatever they happen to have in their hands, what Erikson (1963) calls the *autosphere* (p. 220).

In the period lasting generally from the second to the fourth year of life, the child enters into the *microsphere* where, according to Erikson, attention is directed into the near environment, "the world of manageable toys" (p. 221), and where symbolic, pretend play emerges and is based on the child's development of representative intelligence (that is, the ability to pretend and imagine). This period coincides with a tremendous growth in language development.

During these first two periods of development play is largely solitary, but as children become aware of others their play expands from the microsphere to the *macrosphere*, the wider world of others beyond the family. Initially children relate to others by playing in *parallel*, that is, next to each other, without truly interacting or cooperating, but they eventually learn to play together in *associative play* (Parten, 1932). At this stage, they share to some extent, imitate each other and engage in what Piaget (1962) calls *symbolic* and *practice play*, pretending and exploring with new found physical and social skills. But children in this stage (4 to 7 years old) have not yet learned to fully take the perspective of others (seeing things as others do while maintaining their own perspectives). It is in the next period, from about seven to twelve years old, that children engage in truly *cooperative play,* and are able to participate in games with rules and organize themselves collectively for other play activities.

The connection of play with cognitive development is evident in the earliest stages. For example, toward the end of the first year, children develop what is called *object permanence* (Piaget, 1954). This is the understanding that people and things continue to exist somewhere even when they are out of the child's presence. (Prior to this change, the egocentrism of infants does not account for a world beyond themselves.) The difficulty with this development is that it also brings an awareness that parents actually leave and go somewhere else, and as a result, separation anxiety can emerge. Most infants and toddlers find "peek-a-boo" a delightful game—a game that would be impossible if a child had not achieved object permanence. Arousal is raised when a big sister hides behind the chair (disappears), and the tension is dissipated with great relief and laughter when she reappears with a resounding "peek-a-boo." Children also play a game Call (1970) refers to as "Gone." Knocking things off their high chairs, much to the chagrin of parents, they learn to look over the edge of the chair tray to see the result. These play patterns speak to the emotional value of play that gives it importance as a resource for children throughout childhood. Play is even used in therapy to enable children to deal with anxiety-producing and traumatic events (Axline, 1947; Erikson, 1963). Playing out anxieties, for example, pretending to be a doctor shortly after receiving medical care, gives a child a degree of mastery over the situation and allows her or him to assimilate the experience (Barnett, 1984; Singer, 1993).

Self-Socialization

Developing children are involved in *self-socialization.* They seek to become a greater part of the world around them. They are, in fact, "producers of their own development" (Lerner & Busch-Rossnagel, 1981), though not yet in the self-conscious sense of adolescents. The actions they take lead them progressively and constructively into their own futures (see Chickering, 1969). This involves leisure in three important ways. First, to the extent that leisure opportunities are made available for play, children are likely to benefit in the cognitive, social and emotional ways referred to above; second, activities that are enjoyable and personally expressive are likely to influence the development of interests in other socially- and age-appropriate roles (Csikszentmihalyi, 1981). And third, social integration and involvement are facilitated when social experience is both voluntary and enjoyable as epitomized in scouting, clubs, and youth sports (McLeod, 1983), and in festivals and cultural rituals of various kinds (Pieper, 1952).

Play activities allow children to express themselves in enjoyable ways, and *enjoyment*, itself, is inherently developmental as was noted earlier. Expressive activities are "ontogenetically" prior to instrumental ones (Csikszentmihalyi, 1981). In other words, enjoyment can motivate children to try challenging activities in which they must "work hard" at acquiring new skills. These types of activities can be socially integrative by providing useful models or strategies that will allow them in the future to make the "transition" to the adult world (Kleiber, Larson & Csikszentmihalyi, 1986). For example, a friend's sixteen-year-old son developed a collection of baseball cards that he brought as trading material to baseball card and hobby fairs. He studied the value of them and engaged others, mostly adults, in the activity of trading. While having fun, he learned some useful lessons—negotiating and communication skills, long-term planning, and financial management.

Social integration is also dictated, of course, by social interests and the desire to be more involved with others. Initially, children seek out others in self-directed activities—such as "to come out to play," "to sleep over"—and then join more formally organized activities either with friends to create some shared involvement or actually to make new friendships. Learning to be with others is a developmental task of later childhood (Havighurst, 1972) and is reinforcing to social interest in general. Elkind (1981) speaks of the importance of children's self-directed games for the development of social and moral competence:

> I believe that children learn the other side of contracts with other children and with siblings. Here the relationship is one of mutuality; it is not unilateral. In playing and working with other children, young people can begin to expect such behaviors in return for certain favors. In childhood, the rewards for obeying contracts are most often personal acceptance. For example, a child that shows he or she is willing to abide by the rules of the game is permitted to play. It is with peers that children learn the reciprocal nature of contracts and how to be on the giving as well as the receiving end" (p. 133).

Of course, the benefits of leisure for self-socialization just described do not always result. Indeed, there are leisure patterns that are personally destructive, socially alienating, and developmentally retrogressive. These directions and their causes will be addressed shortly as well. Suffice to say here, however, that given a supportive environment, leisure will be useful to those who are "producers of their own development."

Changing Patterns Through Childhood

A state of relaxed wakefulness and a trusting attitude may be part of the openness to experience that is important to the capacity to enjoy leisure (Neulinger, 1974). When do children learn to relax? And what are the conditions of relaxed wakefulness? Erikson's (1963) stage model of development would suggest that this feeling is the best result of the first real developmental issue in life, that of *trust versus mistrust*. When babies become confident that their primary caregivers will return and tend to them in a predictable and continuous fashion, they show visible signs of relaxation. This condition in turn affords them the emotional security necessary for exploration, experimentation and play. To call such a primitive emotional condition "leisure" may be a stretch, but the ability to cultivate a peacefulness about oneself throughout life may well depend on the earliest parent-child interactions.

In the next of Erikson's stages the one to three-year-old child is faced with the problem of establishing *autonomy*. Gaining control of vital functions, being able to say "no" and to move independently of parents, provides children with an initial experience of freedom. As such it is a critically important antecedent to the realization of freedom in leisure later on. According to Erikson (1963, p. 251–153), failure to achieve autonomy results in a state of doubt about one's ability to be independent and self-directed that may undermine further development.

Typically by three or four years of age, according to Erikson, children who have successfully resolved the previous two issues begin to exercise a sense of *initiative*. Depending on the response received when venturing out and attempting some new activity, they are more likely to be predisposed to such risk-taking in the future. As we will explain in the next section, parents can stifle such initiative, and according to Erikson, guilt may be that prevailing feeling of "overstepping one's bounds." Here again though, the ability to optimize leisure, to be one's own source of entertainment (Mannell, 1984b) would seem to rest on successfully traversing this period.

The latter years of childhood are devoted in large part to establishing competence, to achieving a sense that one has and can develop skills that are well regarded by others. Being able to "produce" in one way or another results in a sense of *industry* (Erikson, 1963, p. 252). Failure to do so is likely to result in a prevailing sense of inferiority. It should come as no surprise, then, that in this "age of instruction" children are most likely to take on group learning activities where they can develop skills that compare favorably with those of others. It is during this time that children enter into the Boy Scouts and Girl Scouts, and join youth sport teams. With respect to activities that serve as the basis for adult and lifelong leisure pursuits, it is when they begin to take their expressive and creative abilities seriously. It is, in fact, the most likely starting place for the "serious leisure" discussed in previous chapters.

Even in the games children organize themselves they are exercising certain skills that will continue to be useful. In fact, Elkind (1981), Piaget (1962) and others (e.g., Devereux, 1976; Lever, 1976) have suggested that games and sports are the primary context for children to learn organizational skills such as the ability to manage and cope with a diversity of perspectives, adjudicate disputes, and work for collective goals. But Lever notes that such experiences are much more common to boys during this period. Their games show greater role differentiation, interdependence, group size, explicitness of goals, number of rules and team formation, and coordination processes than do those of girls, thus conferring on boys an advantage in this kind of "training." The factors that create such differential opportunities are certainly worthy of further consideration. For example, Frydenberg and Lewis (1993) found that in coping with stress boys tend to get involved in physical recreation and girls typically turn to others for social support.

Critical Influences on Leisure Orientations in Childhood

Socialization "Into" and "Through" Leisure

As we described in the discussion of personality and leisure in chapter six, interests emerge at least partly out of biological predispositions and the forces of maturation. Consequently, some of the variability with which particular leisure orientations and interests take shape can be traced to inherent personality and gender differences. But most of the variability in leisure behavior is attributable to how such inclinations are responded to and reinforced by the society in which children live. This process, by which children acquire motives, attitudes, values, and skills that affect their leisure choices, behavior and experiences throughout their lives, is referred to as *socialization into leisure*. There are many agents of socialization that we will consider in more depth shortly. Parents, siblings, teachers, and coaches all have an impact, though to varying degrees. There is a "climate," beyond the weather, that is more or less favorable to the development and continuation of various activity patterns and interests. Included are the facilities at children's disposal, the programs in the community, the natural resources (e.g., lakes, mountains) that are accessible and the prevailing norms of behavior that allow them to be playful, expressive, mischievous, restful, alone or musical.

In some cases the climate is discouraging of innovation, of rest, and of unauthorized congregation or of socializing with peers. Leisure itself elicits a great deal of ambivalence in many contemporary societies. It is often regarded as the enemy of productivity. Relaxation and enjoyment are distrusted, whereas delay of gratification is seen as necessary for achievement, future success, and security (Fine, 1987). From this perspective, "leisure socialization" is an oxymoron. It is as if "leisure," in this case defined as idleness and self-indulgence, is the result of faulty or improper socialization. At best, some see leisure as a vehicle for preparing children for their future social roles and responsibilities. However, to put a more positive spin on this view of leisure socialization, leisure is recognized by many as a valuable resource for cultural innovation, social solidarity and personal development. This is *socialization through leisure*.

Socialization *into* leisure occurs in large part because of an appreciation of the potential for socialization *through* leisure. In earlier work, these two approaches to leisure socialization have been treated somewhat independently (Kleiber & Kelly, 1980), but no one would support leisure socially if it was not perceived to have benefits for the child and society. Play is encouraged, for example, because it is viewed as a source of creativity (Liebermann, 1977) and social and cognitive development (see Barnett, 1990) which are highly valued. Sport is encouraged because it is thought to contribute to the ability to work with others in the achievement of shared goals. Structured leisure activities, such as music, sports and creative activities have been hypothesized to provide an important developmental context for growth of the capacity to direct, control and focus attention. Larson and Kleiber (1993) point out that this latter ability is seen as one of the most important achievements of child development. It allows individuals to formulate and act upon personal goals, and, in adulthood, it is associated with creative achievement and self-actualization.

The fact that many structured and challenging leisure activities are found enjoyable and intrinsically interesting motivates children to participate; consequently, they have the opportunity to receive these benefits. For example, in a study of 483 fifth through ninth graders, using the experiential sampling method, Larson and Kleiber (1993) examined the children's experience of "paying attention" in a wide variety of contexts. They found that "paying attention" was more frequently experienced in self-controlled leisure contexts than other contexts, including school work, and provided opportunities for the development of voluntary control of attention.

Such benefits may depend on how children learn to construe time itself. Children's experience of time and leisure is the result of many different factors. Being in a family of six or seven will probably give a different feeling about control over one's time than being the only child of a single mother. Being in a culture where punctuality is stressed would be different from one in which everything happens "in due time." Institutional life in school teaches children that there is clearly time to be "on task" and time which is "free," as in recess.

Beyond the structure of a child's circumstances, society provides *agents* of influence. Parents, peers, teachers, television, and community programs are the usual sources of influence in childhood. We will return shortly to each of these. But what is actually communicated to children by these various sources about what is appropriate use of time and leisure is extremely variable. What were the injunctions of your childhood? "Idleness is the devil's workbench." In other words, stay busy and avoid temptation. "If you are not helping yourself, you should be helping others." "Service to God and humankind should take preference over individual pleasures." Or perhaps it was recognized that, "All work and no play makes Jack a dull boy."

Some activities and patterns of enjoyment, such as the frequenting of video game parlors discussed in the book's opening illustration, are largely discouraged by adults, while others may be seized upon and promoted by parents and the community to such an extent that the qualities of play and leisure are largely lost through everyone's overinvestment (Fine, 1987). The "fun" of a sport may come primarily in the joy of the activity itself, in being with friends, or in the prospect of being victorious. But this latter orientation can, in fact, be the undoing of leisure if the experience of playing ceases to be enjoyable in its own right. Early research on children's orientations toward game playing (Maloney & Petrie, 1972; Webb, 1969) found that children's reasons for participating in organized games and sports change with age and grade in school. Webb asked a group of children of different ages the question, "What do you think is most important in a game?" and had them rank "to play as well as you are able," "to beat your opponent," and "to play fairly." Figure 8.1 shows the various combinations reflecting a continuum from a *play orientation* to a *professional orientation*. This research indicates that as children get older and become more involved in organized sports, they are more likely to value beating an opponent than playing well or fairly. In a sense, it is argued, children become "professionalized" in such games. The outcome becomes so important that the leisure involvement is more like work than play.

This process underlying "professionalization" can be applied to many areas of children's leisure and provides people who deal with children a useful lesson. An activity that has been intrinsically enjoyable, such as playing a musical instrument, can lose that quality if too many payoffs and other external contingencies, such as parental approval, are present. This

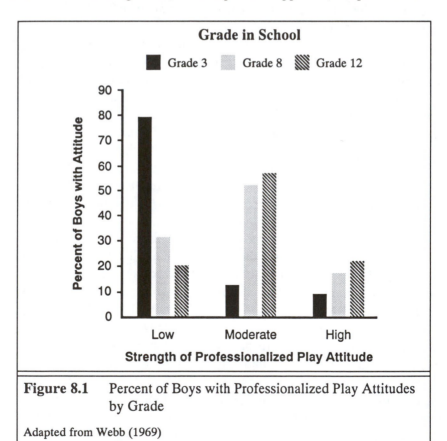

Figure 8.1   Percent of Boys with Professionalized Play Attitudes by Grade

Adapted from Webb (1969)

is another example of the "overjustification effect," of turning play into work, that was discussed in chapter five.

Finally, the assumption that leisure is intrinsically interesting may not always apply in some societies and subcultures. Leisure may be dedicated intentionally to other purposes and activities such as devotion to God, service to others, or self-development. To call such activities leisure may be stretching its meaning somewhat, but these activities may be seen as the most appropriate for the use of discretionary time in some groups. Again, as we discussed in chapter five, if the extrinsic regulations governing participation in these activities are integrated and internalized, intrinsic interest can still result.

The Influence of the Family on Leisure

Parenting styles have direct implications for leisure in childhood and likely influence lifelong habits and patterns. The three most commonly cited parenting styles are authoritarian, laissez faire, and democratic/authoritative (Baumrind, 1971). Children whose parents are very *authoritarian* are allowed little opportunity for decision-making and are required to be obedient to the parents' wishes. Though this may result in apparently well-behaved children, independent initiative may be stifled along with the capacity for self-directed leisure activity. In contrast, *laissez-faire* parenting leaves children pretty much to their own devices as children are given a great deal of freedom. But such parents often overestimate their children's ability to act independently. The total absence of structure may have the effect of stressing children (Elkind, 1981), ultimately undermining the more positive experiences and benefits of leisure. *Democratic/authoritative* parents treat children as if they are capable of decision making, but establish limits and guidelines and provide some direction. This combination is thought to encourage independence while providing children with the security necessary to build confidence. It may also be the best combination to allow children to realize the full potential of leisure as we will see shortly.

Child-rearing practices have changed considerably over time, with important implications for leisure. A comparison of primary family values of the parents studied sixty years ago by Lynd and Lynd (1929, 1937) with those of today indicates a sharp decline in the importance of obedience and a comparable increase in the importance of independence. Again, this might auger well for the emergence of an earlier appreciation of leisure were it not for the fact that some of this emphasis on independence is the result of needing children to fend for themselves because many parents work outside the home. One result of this trend in Elkind's (1981) view is that contemporary children are "hurried" into growing up, and in fact, miss some of the ease and leisure of childhood. Too much is expected of them too soon. According to Elkind, such children experience "responsibility overload," "change overload," and "emotional overload." He further indicates that the "hurrying" of children results in large part because parents hurry themselves. The need to create a "higher" standard of living often takes precedence over leisure and relaxation, and keeps even the most affluent families operating at a feverish pitch. Recently researchers have begun to examine this issue and the "time crunch" faced by families as family and work roles compete for time and energy (e.g., Higgins, Duxbury & Lee, 1994; Kirchmeyer, 1993; Pittman, 1994). Though this sense of hurry is often described as a phenomenon of the 1990s, Linder (1971) in his book the *Harried Leisure Class* anticipated it 25 years ago.

In early childhood, playfulness has been associated with parents having a flexible cognitive and parenting style. Parents with this style seem to be more likely to provide an enriched play environment (Bishop & Chace, 1971) and to encourage exploration and experimentation (Liebermann, 1977). In their widely cited study of a group of preschool children and their parents, Bishop and Chace (1971) examined the relationship between the cognitive style of the parents (how flexible and open-minded they were), their attitudes toward play and how well the home environment promoted play. The researchers measured parents' cognitive style with a personality scale designed for this purpose and attitudes toward play with a specially developed questionnaire. They also visited the children's homes to observe how the parents interacted with their children, the rules they imposed and the availability of play space and materials. The more open, flexible, and less authoritarian parents' personalities, the more they valued fantasy and independence in the play of their children and the more the home environment seemed to foster play. In a separate phase of this study, the children were administered a creativity task in a laboratory setting. Those children with parents having a more flexible cognitive style and who encouraged play were found to score higher on the creativity task (see Table 8.1).

Such flexibility may continue to be important as children move into adolescence, but *structure* is an additional ingredient that enables children to use leisure constructively and creatively. Rathunde (1988) found that the ability of adolescents to find optimal experience ("flow") in any situation was most common among those from homes where five conditions existed: (1) a feeling of choice and control; (2) clarity of rules and structures; (3) a recognition of the value of centering or focusing attention; (4) encouragement

Table 8.1   Parenting Style, Play and Creativity Study Results

	Cognitive Style*	
	Concrete	Abstract
Cognitive Style and Play Attitude (percent of parents)		
Toys should be kept and used in separate places (No)	46.0	59.0
Few rules for watching television (Yes)	38.5	59.0
Children should be heard and not seen (No)	7.7	59.0
Allow or encourage play with opposite sex toys (Yes)	15.4	70.0
Play Environment and Cognitive Style (percent of homes)		
Child allowed to play anywhere in the home	7.7	29.5
Parent helped make toys	23.1	53.1
Child plays with noncommercial toys	53.9	88.5
Creative Productivity and Cognitive Style (higher scores indicate greater creativity)		
Sequential variation	7.3	13.2
Variation choice and color	0.9	1.3
Inflection points	6.7	8.2

* Abstract: Open and flexible, less authoritarian
Concrete: Less open and flexible, more authoritarian

Adapted from Bishop and Chace (1971)

of commitment to tasks; and (5) the creation of meaningful challenges. Taken all together, according to Rathunde, these conditions make up the *autotelic family context,* or in other words, a context where children learn to engage in activity for its own sake. Rathunde found that the resulting orientation to achieving optimal experience and enjoyment generalized from home to school settings as well.

Child rearing emphases also differ by culture, again with resulting implications for patterns of self-expression. In a classic study of 56 different native cultures, Roberts and Sutton-Smith (1962) found that there was a relationship between a culture's particular emphasis in child rearing and the games that were preferred by the children in that culture. In cultures where there was a great emphasis on *obedience*, children were likely to prefer *games of strategy.* Where *achievement* was stressed, the *games of skill* were practiced. And where child rearing was *unpredictable*, that is, parents' rewards and punishments were somewhat arbitrary, *games of chance* were preferred. More complex societies combined these patterns in various ways. However, Roberts and Sutton-Smith proposed that two processes are involved in these differences in child rearing and children's game-play. First, it appears that the content of games has some value in helping children deal with the conflict and stresses created by the demands of the adults in their respective societies and their own natural inclinations for control and independence. If adults are highly controlling, stress is released in games related to strategy, and where high expectations for success create pressure, games of skill are preferred. If parents are relatively unpredictable in their dealings with their children, the stress of not knowing is relieved in games of chance. Second, game patterns may represent the workings of the larger culture and serve thereby to enculturate or socialize those who play them. Roberts and Sutton-Smith referred to both in the *conflict-enculturation hypothesis*: games and expressive activities both prepare children for their life in their culture and enable them to adjust and cope with the conflict and stress resulting from child-rearing practices that essentially attempt to control and shape their behavior.

Before leaving this discussion of parental influences on the development of children's play and leisure orientations, it should be made clear that the process of socialization is quite complex and there is a great deal that researchers don't know as yet. Parents' influence on children's leisure behavior and interests is not necessarily direct and unequivocal, and may be complicated by socially acquired gender roles. For example, Barnett and Chick (1986) found that the social play of female and male children was related to their parents' satisfaction with their social leisure experiences. However, young boys' play styles were more affected by their parents' leisure than was true of young girls, and both girls' and boys' play was more strongly related to their mother's leisure participation than their father's. Barnett and Kleiber (1984) also found these types of complex relationships including evidence that later born children are more playful than those born earlier. Leisure socialization research is in its infancy and is in need of more attention by researchers.

Influence of Peers on Leisure

As noted earlier, the play of very young children is essentially solitary and doesn't move beyond a kind of parallel participation with others until the third or fourth year. But association with others ultimately becomes a very powerful motivation for shared play and may even be biologically directed. In a classic study of rhesus monkeys, Harlow and Harlow (1962) found that infant monkeys who were deprived of peer play were more retarded in social and sexual development than those who were not. As we discussed in earlier chapters, the recognition that human beings seem to have similar needs recently led Deci and Ryan (1991) to revise their view of intrinsic motivation to recognize *relatedness* as an intrinsic need comparable to competence and autonomy.

In later childhood, though adults often direct the form and content of play and leisure activities, age-mates provide the social context for the experience. This becomes increasingly true as children grow older. Research on sport suggests that peers are more influential for boys' interest in sports while the family is more influential in getting girls started (McPherson, 1983). But sustained interest for girls seems to be dependent on an actively participating cohort of friends. We will return to the issue of the influence of peers on leisure when we examine the transition from adolescence into adulthood.

Opportunity Structures and Leisure

An awareness of the value of play referred to earlier has led to an integration of play in the preschool curriculum and sometimes beyond. In some cases *play training* has been used to develop children's ability to play (Smilansky, 1968). In these activities, often targeted at disadvantaged children, teachers and play leaders teach children to engage in sociodramatic play (especially role-playing) in the interest of cultivating cognitive abilities, social skills and creativity. Some of the results have been encouraging (e.g., Curry, 1988; Dinwiddie, 1993; Galda & Pellegrini, 1982), but whether the structure imposed in such training situations is truly conducive to real play is an issue. As noted earlier, children have a way of socializing themselves. In fact, in spite of all the criticism of daycare settings where children are largely on their own, there is evidence that children who have been in daycare longer typically play at a more sophisticated level (Howes, 1988).

The influence of attending school on the development of leisure interests and orientations is paradoxical. The knowledge developed through formal education as well as the cognitive skills associated with learning to read and write provide a strong foundation for learning activities outside of the school, but children all too often leave such interests at the schoolroom door. Most schools use an elaborate system of extrinsic motivation in the form of grades to ensure that the skills necessary for participation in the work force and those needed to contribute to society are developed. In so doing, however, the intrinsic interest that children bring to learning is often undermined in the same way that external rewards can turn other forms of play into work (see Boggiano & Pittman, 1992). Nevertheless, schools, at least in North America, provide an introduction to sports and other activities in the context of extracurricular activities.

Municipal recreation departments, youth sport agencies, community theater, and other youth-serving agencies also provide opportunities for an enormous number of young people in many countries. As with school extracurricular activities, much of the initial attraction is to join in with friends and to learn activities that have carry over value for the rest of life. It is also the case that children in later childhood seek opportunities to develop respected skills that can be tested against and compared with those of their age-mates. Instruction in sport is, at least initially, readily accepted in most cases. It is a context for establishing a sense of competence and for learning some important achievement patterns such as goal setting and persistence in the face of failure. Though there are critics who argue otherwise (e.g., Ogilvie & Tutko, 1985), some degree of sportsmanship may also be shaped under the right circumstances.

Given the possibility of such outcomes, the popularity of structured activities among parents is understandable, and if children show some talent, they are often pushed into more advanced training. But as was noted before, though this can have a positive influence on skill-building, it can be a kind of *premature structuring* that can make children performers before they are ready (Elkind, 1981).

It is also true that opportunities are not distributed evenly across all segments of society. For whatever problems overstructuring might create, there are many children who have relatively little access to structured programs. In a California study, Medrich and his associates (1982) found that children from lower socioeconomic groups, especially urban children, rarely had access to community leisure services in terms of the people, places and physical resources that middle and upper socioeconomic status children did. Also, opportunities in sports for girls and for children with disabilities still lag far behind despite significant gains in recent years.

Media Influences

It is certainly true that children get an enormous number of ideas about leisure opportunities and possibilities—and even the idea that it is good to
enjoy oneself—from watching television. Nevertheless, the amount of time
given to watching television in childhood, estimated to be as much as 30
hours per week by some accounts (e.g., Creasey & Meyers, 1986; Van Evra,
1990), can preempt more active involvement in play and other leisure activities (Provenzo, 1991). In one study reported some years ago (Barnes,
1970), it was found that the play behavior of a group of preschool children
was significantly less social when compared with play norms collected more
than 40 years before that time, and greater exposure to television was considered the most likely explanation. Studies with adults suggest that television viewing is associated with lower levels of participation in physically
active leisure (Tucker, 1993). Higher levels of television watching have
also been found to be associated with play styles that are less imaginative
(Singer, 1973), though television can, under some conditions, stimulate the
child's imagination (Singer & Singer, 1986). Using the experience sampling
method, Kubey and Csikszentmihalyi (1990) found that children experienced lower affect, lower motivation, and higher boredom when they were
watching television than in other activities. Television can also promote
aggressive play behavior (e.g., Van Evra, 1990). For example, children
are fond of imitating the martial art fighting of cartoon and movie charac-
ters such as the "Teenage Mutant Ninja Turtles" (Gronlund, 1992), and
teachers and childcare workers have had to develop strategies to curb such
aggressive play (see Voojs & vanderVoort, 1993). Such impacts notwith-
standing, television is tremendously influential in shaping leisure styles,
including dress, language, sexuality, and in the case of music television,
musical interests.

Of course, involvement with the media need not be passive as our initial encounter with video game playing suggests, nor is this involvement
necessarily negative (Sakamoto, 1994). Indeed, technologically-enhanced
fantasy game playing is a multimillion dollar industry whether the money
is spent in game parlors or in the purchase of interactive video equipment
(Provenzo, 1991). Unlike the case with passive television viewing, video
game playing can be intensely absorbing and motivating (Creasey & Meyers,
1986; Egli & Meyers, 1984; Ellis, 1984). However, some researchers and
many parents have been concerned about those video games that promote
gender stereotypes and aggressive behavior (see Braun & Giroux, 1989;
Provenzo, 1991; Sneed & Runco, 1992).

Leisure in Adolescence and the Transition to Adulthood

Leisure and the Developmental Tasks of Adolescence

Research on the antecedents of adult leisure interests has demonstrated that less than 50 percent of adult leisure activities are begun in childhood (Kelly, 1977). Clearly leisure socialization continues beyond childhood in different ways. This will be the subject of chapter nine. But it is also apparent that a great deal of change in leisure interests occurs during adolescence; the period when the leisure of childhood—much of it play—gives way to the leisure of adulthood.

The way in which adolescents utilize free time reflects the psychological changes that they are experiencing. Their decisions reflect a sense of leisure that is neither fully childlike nor fully adultlike. Adolescents are more actively producers of their own development than younger children. They are likely to be literally creating themselves with whatever opportunities they have. According to Csikszentmihalyi and Larson (1984), the primary task of adolescence is "learning to allocate attention to various activities in a manner acceptable to adults" (p. 4). However, as they argue, this is only half of it. It is at least as important that adolescents learn to enjoy what they are doing and come to feel "that their actions are worthwhile and that the goals that society sets make sense" (p. 4).

According to Piaget (1954), adolescents become preoccupied with themselves and who they are. The source of this preoccupation with the "self" coincides with the onset of the ability to engage in abstract reasoning which brings with it the ability to consider hypothetical possibilities for themselves as well as such ideas as beauty, truth and ultimately even leisure. The child's ability to be unself-consciously immersed in the present moment is limited by this change in self-awareness which is a significant challenge to any emerging sense of leisure. Erikson (1963) sees the principle developmental issue of adolescence to be one of establishing a sense of *identity*. It comes about in the course of both identification with others and *individuation*. Individuation is the process of adolescents defining themselves as unique and different from others. Leisure plays a prominent role in these apparently competing processes (Kleiber & Rickards, 1985).

In the course of expressing their preferences in music, dress, and other indicators of style, including recreational activities, adolescents make a symbolic statement about who they are like, their peers and role models, and from whom they differ, often their parents. In many cases the experience of the moment is less important than the message conveyed to themselves and to others about who they are. Frequently, who adolescents are with is far more important than what they are doing (Bibby & Posterski, 1985; Hendry, Shucksmith, Love & Glendinning, 1993). It is for this reason that Noe (1969) regarded most of adolescent leisure as "instrumental" in nature, rather than truly expressive and intrinsically motivated as is true of leisure more generally. Though somewhat dependent on the opportunities and resources available, the choices adolescents make frequently their efforts to deal with this developmental issue of identity and the stretch toward maturity (Silbereisen, Noack & Eyferth, 1986). The leisure choices made during adolescence reflect the desire to become producers of their own life, while the quality of the experience is secondary.

On the other hand, when activities are entered into seriously—for their intrinsic value—they contribute to individuation and self-development. The natural course of enjoyment of any moderately complex activity, from playing a musical instrument to raising golden retrievers, leads to the refinement of judgments and the development of skills (Csikszentmihalyi, 1990), and this in turn, helps to clarify one's specialness. The most common means of identity formation discussed in the literature include the development of vocational interests, political and religious ideology, and gender identification; but Erikson (1959) noted that "favored capacities" also play a role in the evolving configuration of identity (p. 116). Sports, music and other arts are often embraced as play, shaped into competencies through instruction and self-discipline and emerge as clearly defined vocational alternatives. Choices can be digressive or even regressive, but to the extent that they reflect on the continuity of the self from one time to the next, they may be important in the course of identity formation. The critical factor that determines whether this expressive individuation is incorporated into the identity formation process is whether such activities are taken seriously. The investment of time and effort in such activities to the point that there is perseverance, a sense of future possibilities (a "career" in the activity), a recognition of effort, knowledge and training required, and an identification with others makes them "serious" (Kleiber & Kirshnit, 1991; Stebbins, 1992a).

The same characteristics of perseverance and focused attention are sometimes found in part-time jobs. In fact, most discussions of adolescent identity formation place great importance on developing a work ethic or ideology. But most of the work opportunities adolescents have are not very demanding of their abilities or very significant for them psychologically

(Greenberger & Steinberg, 1986) whereas many serious leisure activities are. Additionally serious leisure activities can present a more optimistic view of the future for they suggest that activities requiring "hard work" can be enjoyed and self-directed. As noted earlier, this feature is what led Csikszentmihalyi and Larson (1984) to discuss such leisure activities as "transitional." Involvement in them can make adolescents aware that the patterns of enjoyment and intrinsic interest experienced in childhood play can be found in the structured and required activities of adult society.

As important as such serious leisure activities may be to development, however, they are in fact relatively uncommon for many children during adolescence. Effort and perseverance are not associated particularly strongly with the concept of leisure. In one of the few studies of leisure meanings among adolescents, Mobily (1989) noted that, compared with the term "recreation," leisure was associated far more often with passivity, though both leisure and recreation were equally as likely to be associated with the word "fun." More recently, in an experience sampling study of high school juniors and seniors in the southeastern U.S., Kleiber, Caldwell and Shaw (1993) found that while the experience of leisure was most often associated with social interaction, it was usually in very low challenge situations. In other words, when they were paged, if they regarded their experience as leisure, the adolescents studied were likely to be involved with others but not in activities they regarded as challenging.

What was also interesting in this study was that maintenance and extracurricular activities were perceived as being leisure-like for females but not for males. The gender difference in the perception of maintenance activities may relate to the time and effort that the adolescent girls devoted to clothes and cosmetics because of their concern with their appearance and the desire to present the "right image" (see Kotash, 1987). Much of this maintenance time was spent with friends and so it had a strong social component as well. The different perceptions of extracurricular activities by the females and males in the study may also have been due to the types of activities included in this category, namely band, drama, photography, shop-crafts, other clubs and field trips.

In the same study, when the respondents were asked directly to indicate what leisure meant to them, "relaxation," "free choice" and "free time" were the most frequently used terms. Females, in particular, tended to place more emphasis on leisure as relaxation. In general, the findings indicated that leisure is not generally associated with self-development. In fact, for these adolescents, especially for the females, leisure seemed to be understood as a condition of easy, relaxed enjoyment, with little emphasis on action and challenge-seeking.

The available research also indicates that adolescents are more likely to link leisure with *social interaction* than with being alone. When alone, adolescents generally experience loneliness, little intrinsic interest, and low affect (Csikszentmihalyi & Larson, 1984). Nevertheless, the experience of solitude has advantages for the development of the adolescent. Being alone affords time for personal reflection (Larson, 1990). Relaxation, rest, contemplation and peace all become more likely when alone. Though such experiences are far less attractive in adolescence than they typically become in adulthood, the discomfort some feel in being alone is often offset by the mental balancing such experiences provide. Certainly choice in the matter is likely to determine the desirability and leisureliness of being alone, but evidence indicates that whatever the reason for being alone, adolescents' moods *after* being alone and their cognitive efficiency are better than if they are continuously with others (Larson, 1990).

Intensity of experience is also an important part of adolescence. Loud music, bright lights and other extreme forms of stimulation are more characteristic of adolescence than of any other age group. To a large extent this is a function of group identification and affiliation. Exhibiting extremes in behavior with others confers a sense of belonging. This leads to what Csikszentmihalyi and Larson (1984) refer to as the *deviation amplifying* effects of adolescents on each other. Behavior and activities that are departures from the norms of society by adolescents' closest friends are less likely to be reproached than they are encouraged, especially when done in the interest of enjoyment. Experimentation with alcohol and other drugs is consistent with this tendency, although many other factors are involved. Alcohol use combined with aggressive and boisterous acts are part of masculine socialization in many societies (Burns, 1980), while the use of psychoactive drugs is attractive as a means to enhance awareness and alter perceptions in other societies. Whatever the particular experience, sharing it with friends and peers, apart from others (frequently adults), is often part of the process of establishing identity.

Certain leisure activities and expressive patterns are also important because of the status they confer. In Eckert's (1989) ethnographic study, the labels used by high school students to identify groups of their peers differing in status were based on the extent of their involvement in extracurricular school activities. Those students who were involved in extracurricular activities, not necessarily just sports, were called *jocks*; those who were uninvolved or not identified with any extracurricular activities were called *burnouts*. In Coleman's classic study of adolescent life (1961), being involved in sports was the most important factor contributing to the social status of high school boys. Popularity for girls was less dependent on extracurricular activities at that time. This gender difference may be changing particularly with respect to involvement in sport (Holland & Andre, 1994) as many girls and women are becoming more involved in physical leisure pursuits (Archer & McDonald, 1990). This conclusion should be treated with caution, however. A recent U.S. survey found the participation gap for physically active leisure and exercise between men and women, particularly younger women, to be increasing (Robinson & Godbey, 1993).

The Transition to Adulthood

So, what leisure orientations and interests do adolescents carry with them into adulthood? Some activities may be easier than others to continue and enjoy in some fashion throughout the life course. Outdoor activities in particular show continuity through the life course. Estimates are that, of those who actively enjoy outdoor recreation in adulthood, about 80 percent participated in these activities during childhood and adolescence (Bradshaw & Jackson, 1979). Some activities become leisure "careers" in that they develop into lifelong interests and commitments (Stebbins, 1992a). However, other researchers have pointed to the vast discontinuity between adolescent and adult leisure activities, with many adult leisure activities—over 50 percent by some estimates—having no childhood antecedents (Kelly, 1977; Yoesting & Christensen, 1978). A continued need for change and the emergence of new leisure orientations as a result of changing life circumstances characterizes much of adulthood (Iso-Ahola, 1980a)—an issue we will consider further in the next chapter.

Many activities are also abandoned during adolescence itself. In the case of sports, though youth participation is a strong predictor of adult participation (Spreitzer & Snyder, 1976), there is an enormous drop-off in sport participation during adolescence. The reasons for the decline in participation have been the subject of a significant amount of research (e.g., Curtis & White, 1984). An overemphasis on winning, a lack of fun, and growing preferences for other activities are common reasons associated with giving up sport involvement. Organized adolescent sports typically become more competitive and demand higher levels of skill with age. The perceived lack of ability to be competitive at these higher levels has also been consistently implicated in the decrease in participation.

High ability is not necessarily required to enjoy most activities, but those that are continued through adolescence and into adulthood are most likely to be complex enough to provide ever-increasing levels of challenge commensurate with growing skills and to include peers with similar interests. This describes many activities that people continue to take "seriously" through their lives, those that are likely to be intrinsically enjoyable and "flow-producing" (Iso-Ahola, 1980; Spreitzer and Snyder, 1976) and that are adaptable and relevant to changing life circumstances. Though little research has been reported examining the role of leisure in the transition from adolescence to adulthood, a few studies have recently appeared. For example, a British study by Bynner and Ashford (1992) begins to document the emerging and diverging lifestyles of older adolescents and the different types of leisure involvements that accompany these lifestyles. As we will see in the next chapter, there has been a general lack of research on the changes in leisure behavior and the role of leisure in making transitions from one stage of life to another.

Leisure Socialization: An Interactive Process

Families, peers, schools, the media, and sport and recreation programs are among the many sources of leisure interests and orientations. They represent the "E," or environment, in the $B=f(P, E)$ interactionist equation (with "B" as behavior and "P" as the person). As we have discussed, behavior doesn't occur in a social vacuum; people are social beings from the time they are born and each person develops her or his leisure interests and activity patterns largely in response to the influences of others as she or he grows toward adulthood. Nevertheless, it is important to acknowledge those impulses toward play, exploration, self-expression and social interaction that emerge rather naturally for healthy children in accommodating and supportive circumstances. Where conditions are supportive, it seems clear that children will use play and leisure to socialize themselves and invite and embrace contact with others.

Leisure Behavior Over the Life Span

Outline

Chapter NINE

Preview

An old saying: "You can't teach an old dog new tricks."

Contemporary bumper sticker: "We're spending our children's inheritance."

There are many contrasting ideas about what it means to grow older. Some of them involve clear misconceptions; others are stereotypes that may have some truth but are clearly overgeneralizations. However, age does have its behavioral and attitudinal correlates: most people have children before the age of 40; most people retire sometime after age 60; and most older people are more conservative than most younger people. There are many other consistencies associated with aging as well. The models of development introduced in the last chapter have in some cases been elaborated beyond the childhood period to suggest that people pass through a series of stages that comprise the life course or life span and presumably apply to everyone. What should become clear in this chapter is that aging is not only a biological process. Age may also be regarded as another social context affecting leisure. In other words, being a certain age brings about certain experiences just as, for example, being at work in a corporation brings about specific experiences. In this chapter we will examine this issue of age as a social context and its influence on leisure behavior.

There is another important aspect to the leisure and aging question. As mentioned above, leisure behavior may be viewed as being inexorably tied to certain predictable changes associated with aging—changes that are a function of biological changes and the changing social context. However, rather than just being affected by aging, it can also be asked if leisure influences how people age. Does leisure contribute to stability and continuity in people's lives as they grow older? We will touch on this issue from time to time in this chapter and in the next two chapters.

Leisure and Life Span Development

Imagine you have kept a record of your leisure behavior during the past year, the types of activities and the frequency of participation, and you put this record in a time capsule, or better yet, you travel to your future in a time machine and observe yourself five, ten and 20 years from now. If you are a young adult, you could even go 50 or 60 years into your future. What would your future leisure style look like as compared to the past year? Would you be doing the same types of things with the same frequency? Would you have dropped some activities and added new ones? As you look "back from the future," do you think that you would have been able to predict your leisure style based on what you did in the "present?" Would there be a pattern to the changes that occurred in your leisure style as you aged? Would this pattern be similar to that of your parents or your friends? What is it about growing older that leads to these changes? Would you find that your leisure helped you deal with these changes?

Development is not completed when one leaves adolescence. For most it is a process that occurs over the entire life span and applies to nearly all areas of human behavior. Development is not simply the accumulation of interests, abilities and experiences; it is *systematic and predictable change* by which people become qualitatively different in some way from what they were before, even as they maintain other aspects of themselves.

Development involves three types of influences: (1) normative age-graded influences; (2) normative history-graded influences; and (3) nonnormative life events (Baltes, Cornelius & Nesselroade, 1980). Stage theories such as those of Erikson and Piaget referred to in chapter eight address the first type, normative age-graded influences. These theories describe *ontogenetic changes*, changes that are "species-specific" and biological in origin; that is, they apply to everyone, even if there are variations in how they influence people's behavior. The emergence of "object permanence" in infants and "self-consciousness" in adolescence that we noted in the last chapter are examples. Presumably, such changes should be found across cultures and historical periods. Other age-graded influences include predictable life events such as graduation from high school at age 17 or 18, taking a first full-time job sometime in the twenties and retiring somewhere around age 65; these changes are more dependent on social expectations and norms, and apply to most but not all members of a given society (in this case, most industrialized western societies). These changes are both expected and accepted by others, thus making them "the thing to do at the time."

The second type of developmental influence, normative history-graded, involves a form of evolutionary change associated with significant histori- cal events, such as the worldwide depression in the 1920s and 30s and, for Americans, the Vietnam War in the 1960s, or secular trends such as changes in attitudes toward women. Often, what appear to be inevitable, stage-related changes, such as retirement from work in the late 50s or early 60s, are more the result of living at a particular time in a particular culture than being attributable to any universal human ontogenetic pattern. Leisure behavior patterns may be susceptible to normative history-graded influences as well. For example, McPherson (1990) points out that a fondness for dancing characterizes people who grew up in the 1920s to a greater extent than other cohorts (groups of people of similar age and who have had simi- lar "historical" experience), while those going through their formative years in the 1970s and 80s are more likely to be a part of the "fitness boom." Persons who grew up during the economic depression of the 1930s have been shown to place less value on leisure than those of other cohorts (Elder, 1974). Ekerdt (1986) points to the emergence of a "busy ethic" among this group, an action orientation that "legitimates the leisure of retirement, de- fends retired people against judgments of senescence, and gives definition to the retirement role" (p. 243). In other words, leisure is all right for this cohort group only if it is used "productively."

Finally, development is influenced by nonnormative life events, such as a divorce, disability or a new job, where the changes experienced by people are precipitated more by unexpected life circumstances than by bio- logical, social or large scale cultural changes. In this case, it is certainly more difficult to predict the impact of such changes, but leisure activities are often altered as a result. Hormuth (1984) found that being transferred to a new location because of a job is likely to be seen as an opportunity to reinvent oneself to some extent, to try on new hats and establish some new relationships and activity patterns.

During adulthood, life events (both normative and nonnormative), so- cial expectations and role responsibilities such as being a parent, worker, or volunteer have more influence on adult behavior, including leisure behav- ior, than ontogenetic changes. Nevertheless, there are some changes that are consistent enough across people, cultures, and historical periods to suggest some inevitability. It takes a critical perspective on development and an appreciation of longitudinal research to begin to understand the nature of changes over the life course and to sort out their causes. In this chapter we will examine how leisure behavior changes over the life course and how the above influences come into play in bringing about such changes.

Changes in Leisure Participation

One of the most widely cited studies of variations in leisure activity across the life span was done with a survey in the 1970s of 1,441 people between the ages of 20 and 94, and stratified according to gender, ethnicity and two occupational groups (Gordon, Gaitz & Scott, 1976). This investigation showed that overall leisure activity level decreased with age (see Figure 9.1) and that with very few exceptions (e.g., solitary activities and cooking among men) most individual activities showed this same pattern (see Table 9.1, p. 248). In other words, the older adults are, the less likely they will be found on the ski slopes and other such places. Activities done outside of the home and those requiring physical exertion and a high intensity of involvement showed the highest negative correlation with age. Would the same

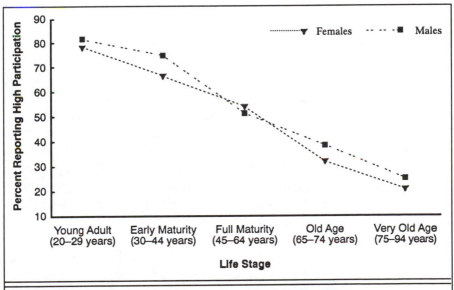

Figure 9.1   Leisure Participation Over the Life Span

Adapted from Gordon, Gaitz and Scott (1976)

Table 9.1   Relationship Between Age and Level of Participation in Various Leisure Activities

Activity	Males	Females
Dancing and Drinking	–0.77*	–0.75*
Movies	–0.67*	–0.69*
Sports and Exercise	–0.56*	–0.54*
Outdoor Activities	–0.43*	–0.53*
Travel	–0.38*	–0.37*
Reading	–0.36*	–0.36*
Cultural Production	–0.34*	–0.25*
Television Viewing	–0.17*	–0.19*
Discussion	–0.16*	–0.17*
Spectator Sports	–0.14*	–0.19*
Cultural Consumption	–0.17*	–0.08
Entertaining	–0.17*	–0.06
Number of Clubs	–0.02	–0.07
Home Embellishment	0.03	–0.01
Cooking	0.59*	–0.25*
Solitary Activities	0.26*	0.40*

*Gamma values statistically significant at the 0.05 level or better.

Adapted from Gordon, Gaitz and Scott (1976)

pattern of participation over the life span be found if this study were repeated today? Will your leisure style follow the same pattern over the course of your life? In fact, this negative relationship between activity and aging has been found in many other studies (see Kelly, 1987a; Unkel, 1981).

If the entire life span is used as a frame of reference, the relationship would not show such a precipitous decline. Children and adolescents must develop skills and establish some degree of independence from parents en route to broadening their leisure horizons. Iso-Ahola (1980a) suggested a curvilinear relationship, with the size of people's *leisure repertoires* reaching a peak in early to middle adulthood and declining thereafter (see Figure 9.2). It should be noted that this model represents just what people can do rather than what they actually do, as we will explain shortly. Still, it is Iso-Ahola's view that for most of people's adult lives there is a decline in the number of personal leisure resources (e.g., skills, physical energy) available corresponding to the apparent decline in number of leisure activities engaged in and the intensity of involvement noted above.

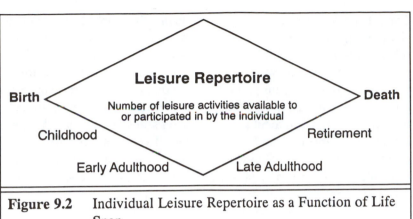

Figure 9.2 Individual Leisure Repertoire as a Function of Life Span

Adapted from Iso-Ahola (1980, p. 174)

More recent research has provided additional data in support of this general finding. In a study of 3,927 households in Alberta, Canada, Iso-Ahola, Jackson and Dunn (1994) found that the number of people who indicated they had started *new* activities within the last year decreased steadily over three periods of adulthood until retirement age and then leveled off. The number *replacing* activities (dropping one but starting another) also declined over the life course. Thus it could be concluded that, in general, as people get older their level of leisure activity declines. But is this a justifiable interpretation in all cases?

The Cross-Sectional Data Interpretation Problem

Studies like that of Gordon, Gaitz and Scott (1976), which compare different age groups on their frequency of leisure participation, are called *cross-sectional* studies because they assess types and rates of participation across different segments of society, age being just one criterion used to classify people (gender, race, social class, geographic location are examples of others). With respect to developmental studies, age group differences, especially if they show a linear progression, make it tempting to assume that getting older leads to the difference or "change" observed, whether positive or negative. But age differences may be associated with all those influences referred to earlier; that is, though it may be that getting older brings certain inevitable changes, it is possible that older people differ from younger people not because they are older but because they have lived through a different historical period. Younger people may be more like other members of their young age cohort than they are members of older cohorts not so much because they are younger but because they share a certain set of experiences. For example, will you and your friends engage in leisure activities similar to those of your parents when you are their current age? Will you be as active or inactive? Younger people have had electronic media and entertainment equipment such as video games, televisions, VCRs, and computers available to them for most of their lives. Children are now growing up with the Internet. Do the different opportunities and constraints that people experience early in life cause them to exhibit consistently different leisure behaviors and orientations as they grow older?

Consider the survey data collected by Gordon, Gaitz and Scott (1976) and in particular the activity of reading. The data could be interpreted to suggest that reading declines as people get older; there is a negative relationship of −0.36 (see Table 9.1, p. 248). But it may well be that the members of the older cohorts surveyed never did read as much as those who were members of younger cohorts at the time of the survey. This explanation seems plausible when one considers the great improvements in access to education experienced by younger cohorts compared to those born 60 or more years ago. So it is important to be critical when interpreting findings from cross-sectional studies.

Studying the Life Course More Rigorously

The only way to be completely confident that the behavior and attitudes of people actually change over the life course is to study them over time. This approach is called *longitudinal* research. If researchers had data on the reading patterns of a cohort of older adults from twenty years ago and they studied it again today, they could determine if there had actually been any decrements over that time. Longitudinal studies of the leisure patterns of older people in fact give a rather different picture than do most cross-sectional studies. The prevailing evidence suggests continuity of interests rather than decline (Culter, 1977; Lounsbury & Hoopes, 1988; Palmore, 1981; Schmitz-Scherzer, 1976; Scott & Willits, 1989). One longitudinal study even showed an increase in activity involvement from early adulthood to middle age (Freysinger & Ray, 1994).

Caution should be taken in interpreting these findings as well, however. If scientific observers follow people for less than their whole lives (and even five-year longitudinal studies are exceedingly difficult, cumbersome and costly), they cannot conclude much about increases or decreases in

behavior or attitudes across the life span. Furthermore, they cannot generalize beyond the age group studied because, again, they have a different
history than other age-cohort groups. Even if they have changed in a consistent way, the changes may not apply to a cohort that has had a dramatically different life history. Consider wars and economic depressions; if a
group of adults experienced the loss of economic resources when living
through a depression, it is likely that their activity patterns will be affected
accordingly. They may be less willing to abandon themselves to immediate gratification and self-indulgence than those who grew up with relative
economic security (again, for more on this point see Elder, 1974). This
argument can be applied to explaining differences between the cohort of
"Baby Boomers" born after World War II in more prosperous times and
their parents who lived during the "Great Depression" of the 1930s.

Social scientists rely heavily on cross-sectional data to "suggest" developmental changes because they can better cover the entire life span. But,
if a researcher has the time and money, there are ways to have the best of
both worlds and control for interpretation problems. A *cohort sequential
research* design allows the researcher to take into account two important
measurement factors: year of birth (which tells the researcher about the
time in which the cohort lived) and age when studied. By repeating measurements on multiple cohorts over time it is possible to sort out the sources
of group differences and if there are changes associated with aging (Baltes,
Cornelius & Nesselroade, 1980). To stay with the previous example, by
following multiple cohorts, or age group panels, over a period of time, say
20 years, it would be possible to sort out the change in reading behavior
attributable more generally to the aging process, (i.e., happening to all cohorts) from that which is cohort specific.

Ideally, researchers would carry out cohort-sequential studies to more
clearly determine if there are predictable patterns of change in leisure behavior and orientations over the life span. But as with all longitudinal research, such studies are extremely costly and difficult, and they still do not
guarantee that all the information needed will be acquired. Even if it were
determined that a change in participation, attitudes or satisfaction occurred
at a predictable point in the life course for almost everyone in a cohort-
sequential study, researchers would still be unable to conclude that the
change is a universal effect (ontogenetic) and an inevitable consequence of
aging. Unfortunately, people from cohorts of the past or those yet to come
cannot be studied, and, even more lamentable, researchers rarely consider
members of other cultures than their own. Hence, generalization should
always be limited to the populations sampled; and when changes that are

associated with age are discovered, the temptation to conclude that the changes are the inevitable consequence of aging should be resisted.

Researchers must start somewhere however, and the data on leisure behavior that social psychologists possess—mostly cross-sectional with a few longitudinal and retrospective studies (people are asked to describe their behavior during the course of their lives as they remember it)—can begin to help in understanding changes in leisure over the life course. More detailed qualitative and quantitative studies of specific age groups would also be useful. They could help in more fully elaborating the circumstances and experiences of a given age cohort and contribute to the understanding of age-related changes in leisure behavior and experience.

Patterns of Change and Continuity in Leisure

A Changing Preference for Change Itself

One of the leisure behaviors that seems to change substantially over the life course is "interest in change" itself. *Experimentalism* seems much more common among youth than their elders. Indeed, experimentalism and an orientation to change seems to describe younger age groups. An evolutionary perspective on this age-related difference is that younger cohorts need to be flexible and adapt to whatever changes the social environment demands of them, while older generations are responsible for providing stability and security in a constantly changing environment so that the young can experiment and change, and hopefully survive and prosper (Brendt, 1978). One reaction to this different orientation is the "generation gap" that seems to arise between the existing social order which parents usually represent, on the one hand, and children and youth, on the other. These age-related differences in experimentalism and the desire for change versus stability seem to be reflected in patterns of leisure activity over the life course as well.

Iso-Ahola (1980a) offers a hypothetical profile of the relative strength of preferences for novel versus familiar leisure pursuits over the life course (see Figure 9.3). It is noteworthy that, if the suggestion is valid, older people are more like young children than adolescents and young adults in their greater preference for familiarity. Though there are few studies that cover the entire life course, the Canadian study referred to earlier (Iso-Ahola, Jackson & Dunn, 1994) found that over the four stages of adulthood studied, those who chose to continue with the same activities increased in number while those who started new activities decreased. The authors concluded that the "tendency to seek novelty through new leisure activities declines with advancing life stages, whereas the tendency to maintain stability through old and familiar activities increases with life stages" (p. 243). They hasten to add, however, that this does not support an image of older people as disengaging from life and becoming inactive, but rather as being more selective and discriminating in what they do.

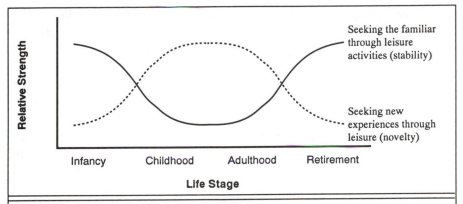

Figure 9.3   Change in Tendencies to Seek Familiar and New Forms of Leisure Over the Life Span

Adapted from Iso-Ahola (1980, p. 176)

As people age they still have a need for stimulation and challenge for which leisure becomes, in many cases, ever more important. As Iso-Ahola and his colleagues (1994) point out, in later life the "need for novelty may be satisfied within a narrower scope of activities" rather than by expanding the repertoire and replacing discontinued activities with new ones. "Need for arousal manifests itself differently at different life stages" (p. 245). Change in leisure can occur not just by taking on new activities and/or dropping old ones (*between activity* change). Change can occur in the style or way that people engage in long-time favorite leisure activities—that is, change can occur *within activities* (see Iso-Ahola, 1980a). For example, people who enjoy playing competitive tennis may change from singles to doubles play in their older years; parents who no longer have time for individual pursuits such as dance or sports may stay involved as volunteer teachers or coaches of their own and other's children.

One of the problems with research on changes in leisure activity participation over the life course is that researchers have been preoccupied with counting activities and have not given enough attention to how they are adapted to meet the changing circumstances that people encounter as they grow older. We will discuss some of the factors that affect the willingness to substitute new forms of leisure activity for old ones in chapter twelve.

Individual Differences in Patterns of Continuity and Change

Some activities are more likely to be given up in the older-age periods than others, and women are generally different from men in some of the established patterns of continuity and change. For example, though involvement in sports and other physically demanding forms of recreation shows decrements with successive age cohorts (e.g., Gordon, Gaitz & Scott, 1976; Kelly, 1987a; Unkel, 1981), the pattern applies mostly to men; there is some evidence that women in older cohorts are more likely to begin participation in physically active leisure, such as exercise, than women in younger adult cohorts (Iso-Ahola, Jackson & Dunn, 1994). However, when these researchers examined leisure activities other than physically active leisure, men in the latter stages of life were more likely to begin new activities than women. Are men inherently more experimental in later life then? A better explanation is that retirement typically affords men more freedom than it does women. The investigators (Iso-Ahola, Jackson & Dunn, 1994) suggested that there may be no such thing as retirement for some women. Unlike the situation for most men, the role responsibilities of women, particularly those related to care of the home and family obligations, often do not change significantly after age 65.

The overall decrease or decline in leisure participation that appears to occur with aging has sometimes been attributed to a decline in leisure opportunities. This loss of opportunity can result from a variety of personal constraints (e.g., decreases in skill, illness, injury), social constraints (e.g., demands of caregiving, social expectations that certain activities are inappropriate, loss of friends) and economic constraints (e.g., reduced income) (McGuire, 1985). However, consistency of leisure interests and behavior over the life course may be less a matter of limited opportunities for change than it is a preference for maintaining old and familiar patterns. A favorite activity may be as important to hold onto as an old friend. Accordingly, a considerable amount of attention in leisure research has been devoted to the question of the predictability of adult leisure patterns from those of childhood. The question is of special interest to managers who plan for recreation resource use, marketers who want to know to whom their promotions should be targeted and caregivers who seek clues for stimulating leisure interests in older and disabled individuals.

Depending on the rules researchers use to decide if leisure behaviors engaged in at different stages in life are the same activity (e.g., "traversing rugged terrain in a wilderness area on foot during early adulthood" and "walking the well-tended trails of a bird sanctuary during retirement" could be both classified as hiking or they could be defined as different activities), it is estimated that 40 to 80 percent of adult leisure activities have a close equivalent in childhood activities (e.g., McGuire, Dottavio & O'Leary, 1987; Sofranko & Nolan, 1972; Yoesting & Christensen, 1978). These figures suggest that new patterns of participation are indeed established throughout adulthood. But it is clear that people differ considerably in the extent to which they maintain activity interests over the life course, give them up or replace them with new interests.

These individual differences were demonstrated with data from the 1982–1983 Nationwide Recreation Survey (NRS) based on a survey of 6,000 individuals 12 years of age or older. McGuire, Dottavio, and O'Leary (1987) attempted to determine whether late life differences in outdoor leisure activity participation could be explained as due to early life participation patterns. They found that those respondents aged 65 and over could be categorized as either "expanders" or "contractors" based on their patterns of leisure involvement. *Expanders* altered their leisure patterns by the addition of new activities throughout the life course, consequently showing less continuity, whereas *contractors* had learned and become committed to most of their outdoor recreation activities before age 21, thereby showing evidence of continuity.

To better understand changes in leisure behavior and the issue of continuity over the life course, researchers have begun to examine the factors that lead people in different age groups to quit, replace, add or continue leisure activities (see Jackson & Dunn, 1988; McGuire, O'Leary, Yeh & Dottavio, 1989). In another analysis using data from the NRS cross-sectional study discussed above, McGuire and Dottavio (1987) looked for evidence of *abandonment, continuity* or *liberation* in outdoor recreation participation among respondents in different age categories that spanned the adolescent to adult portion of the life course. The investigators found that though the continuity pattern was the most dominant, the abandonment pattern (where activities are consistently given up), and the liberation pattern (where people freely chose new activities) also existed at each life course stage.

Searle, Mactavish and Brayley (1993) confirmed these patterns in a Canadian study of 1,209 residents of the province of Manitoba ranging in age from 16 to over 65 years. They found that about 20 percent of the people surveyed could be classified as *replacers* (during the previous year they had quit doing an activity they had been participating in for several years and had begun a new one), 25 percent were *quitters* (quit an activity and did not begin a new one), 16 percent were *adders* (did not quit an activity but added an activity), and about 40 percent were *continuers* (neither added nor quit activities). The researchers also found that the number of people who were continuers increased with the age of the cohort group (see Figure 9.4).

These results led Searle and his associates (1993) to suggest that other factors besides age need to be examined to help explain these patterns. Clearly the biological and normative social context factors associated with aging are not the only factors that affect the frequency of leisure participa-

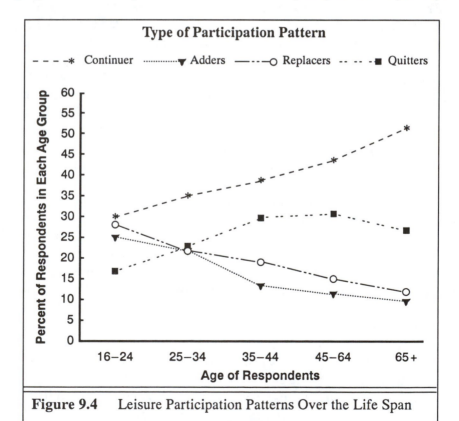

Figure 9.4   Leisure Participation Patterns Over the Life Span

Adapted from Searle, Mactavish and Brayley (1993)

tion over the life course. Researchers need to develop a better idea of the factors that lead some people to quit an activity and not seek a replacement or add to their repertoire of leisure activities while others do quit one activity and start another. For example, do people continue with an activity because of a strong attachment to the activity, as a source of personal identity? If an activity is maintained primarily as a familiar pattern, is it a buffer against stress, or is it a reflection of resistance to change? Alternatively, does a change in a person's activities reflect a response to other developmental changes, or is it a failure to find activities that are sufficiently meaningful to support a commitment? Recent models and theories of leisure constraints (see Jackson, 1988; Crawford, Jackson & Godbey, 1991) have been developed to help answer some of these questions. We will return to these issues in chapter twelve where we will discuss constraints that affect leisure participation and satisfaction, and strategies used to encourage leisure involvement.

Stability or Change—Which Is Best?

The notion of change often seems to be associated with growth and development, adaptation and well-being; but in the context of aging it may be the extent to which a person maintains her or his sense of self in the face of change that marks successful adjustment; resisting change in some respects may mean keeping a sense of integrity. However, it has often been noted (Buss, 1979; Freysinger, 1995; Iso-Ahola, 1980a; Iso-Ahola, Jackson & Dunn, 1994; Kelly, 1987b; Kleiber, 1985; Kleiber & Kelly, 1980) that the process of development and aging is a *dialectical* one, and stability and change define an important component of that dialectic. In other words, one's personal development relies on experiencing both stability and change in one's life; these processes are in tension and stimulate each other. Too much change is unsettling, and stabilization is needed to continue to grow and cope. Too much consistency and stability are stultifying, and variation, novelty and change become necessary for personal growth and development. It is necessary to consider these forces and their effects on leisure before reaching conclusions about how leisure is best used to facilitate development and optimal aging.

Theories of Change in Adulthood and Aging

Now that we have discussed basic age-related changes in leisure behavior, we now turn to theories of adulthood and aging that help social psychologists interpret these changes. As we will show, these theories can be criticized for oversimplifying the nature of human development over the life span and for failing to adequately represent the pluralism or diversity of paths that people take as they age. Also, these types of theories have not been formulated to explicitly account for the changes in leisure behavior that occur, or the contributions that leisure may make to development and adjustment throughout life. However, they are useful to consider because they alert researchers and service providers to what it means to grow older by breaking up the life span into identifiable *stages* based on the major issues and challenges faced by many people as they age and take on new roles and responsibilities. On the one hand, these issues and challenges may affect behavior, including leisure. On the other, the things that people choose to do in their leisure help them or hinder them in dealing with these issues and successfully moving on to the next stage. Though no comprehensive life span and leisure theories have been proposed, examples of the application of the general life span theories of Erikson (1963) and Levinson, Darrow, Klein, Levinson and McKee (1978) to leisure have been provided by Kleiber and Kelly (1980), and Iso-Ahola (1980a), respectively.

Models that distinguish between stages based on the psychological issues or challenges faced by individuals are referred to as *life span* models while those that emphasize role-related changes that occur in contemporary society are referred to as *life course* models. The latter are more sociological in nature and focus more on the cultural and historical relativity of changes while the former give credence to the idea of some biologically-based inevitability to the changes.

Life Span Models

As noted at the beginning of the chapter, influences on aging include those that are biologically programmed into human beings (ontogenetically determined), those that are predictable and normative in a particular culture at a particular point in time, and those that are unpredictable life events but nonetheless seem to affect behavior in predictable ways. Stage theories of child development like Piaget's (1954, 1962) that were discussed in the previous chapter are based on the assumption that the sequence of development is to some extent biologically programmed. Such theories have been useful in explaining child development, particularly the physical and cognitive changes that occur with age. In spite of the fact that there are individual differences between children in the onset and duration of these stages, children of a particular age tend to think and act more alike than children or adults in other age groups.

Changes and development in adulthood, however, appear to have much more to do with differences in normative and "unpredictable" social influences. These vary from culture to culture and also depend on immediate social circumstances that vary from individual to individual. Thus, stage theories that link change and development to specific ages would seem to be considerably less relevant in explaining adult behavior than children's behavior. Nevertheless, there are stage theories that continue to be regarded as useful in representing adult development and aging. Though the changes these theories describe may be driven as much by social as by ontogenetic forces, they nonetheless appear to reflect consistency in human experience and behavior across a number of cultures and subcultures.

As noted, two life span models have been quite popular. Erikson's model provides a useful perspective for thinking about leisure behavior and its role in development over the life course (see Kleiber & Kelly, 1980). The early stages of Erikson's (1963) model were considered in the previous chapter, but Erikson argued that predictable changes do not end with the transition from adolescence to adulthood. He identified three subsequent issues, or developmental crises, that occur in sequence in the lives of many people and that are useful for understanding behavior. These issues correspond roughly to crises of early adulthood, middle age, and later life.

The first is the issue of *intimacy versus isolation.* Those people who have been able to resolve the identity crisis of adolescence are faced with the next challenge of having to establish intimacy with another person or other people, particularly once they have left their childhood home. The resolution of this issue often takes the form of marriage and having children, but it can also be characterized by the development of other types of strong, lasting relationships. Accordingly, it would be expected that leisure during this period is associated with the cultivation of intimate interpersonal relationships. And indeed, the priority for people in their twenties is to spend whatever free time is available to them with a significant other (Brehm, 1992). Often, the activity is irrelevant as long as "you are with the one you love." We will discuss the relevance of leisure for interpersonal relationships in chapter eleven.

The next crisis is identified as *generativity versus stagnation.* Erikson argues that generativity becomes an issue as a person approaches middle adulthood, and at this time productivity and contributions to society become priorities. For many, this productivity is not only a matter of having children and successfully raising them; becoming a productive member of society, successful at work or being creative in some other demonstrable way also resolves the issue in favor of generativity rather than its opposite—stagnation. Stagnation is associated with self-absorption and personal impoverishment. To some extent a concern with the next generation and what contributions people are making to their future leads many to begin taking life "seriously" for the first time and relinquishing many forms of self-indulgence. Caring for others is not always compatible with leisure activities done only for personal satisfaction. Devotion to children or a work career often comes with a loss of free time (Witt & Goodale, 1981). But in the caregiving that characterizes family leisure or through the volunteer leadership of youth activities, for example, generativity can be served in ways that enhance the enjoyment and self-expression normally associated with leisure (Kleiber & Ray, 1993). Still, it may be because of the imperative of generativity that many adults seem to defer the personal and immediate gratification of certain types of leisure activities, or to temper it significantly, during early and middle adulthood.

The final crisis is *integrity versus despair.* In later life if a person does not come to terms with their past and present in a way that provides a sense of wholeness and continuity, despair is the likely result. Understanding and accepting ourselves is an important part of the process. Thus, there is a greater tendency in later life to reminisce about the past as time permits. Reminiscence can be done alone—as a kind of life review—or more casually with others, but in either case it can reinforce continuity and contribute to a sense of integrity (Parker, 1995). Nor do activities need to be passive and reflective to contribute to a sense of integrity. Hobbies and expressive patterns of various kinds that connect one to the past and provide a sense of continuity are typically preferred over new activities, as was reflected in the research reported earlier.

Though Erikson's stages provide some interesting insights, they have been regarded as too general and broad to provide a basis for understanding age-related differences in behavior. A life span model that is more specific and detailed is that of Levinson et al. (1978). This model was first applied to thinking about changes in leisure behavior by Iso-Ahola (1980a). Levinson and his colleagues interviewed adult males of different ages and from various walks of life, and on the basis of the information gathered proposed more specific age periods, or *seasons of life*, during which certain developmental issues are predictably faced (see Figure 9.5). Levinson et al. suggested that these "seasons" involved alternating periods of structure building and structure changing throughout the adult life course. These processes are similar to the ideas of stability and change discussed earlier. Midlife, in particular, drew the attention of Levinson et al. as a time of significant change. They found evidence of what they called "deillusionment" where the goals of earlier adulthood were likely to be reconsidered in light of current realities.

In contrast to the emphasis on generativity that Erikson associated with middle adulthood, the research by Levinson et al. suggested that for many, midlife brings a growing unwillingness to keep up appearances and

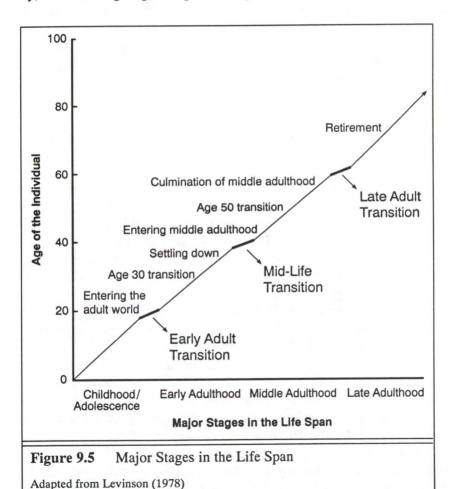

Figure 9.5   Major Stages in the Life Span

Adapted from Levinson (1978)

associate with people merely out of a sense of obligation and responsibility, a reaction driven by the need to establish a distinct identity. He referred to this process as "detribalization," or breaking with convention. Presumably, this response creates a sense of considerable freedom for experimentation, and leisure provides opportunities for this. But in an interview study of people who were in their midlives and who were presumably changing and building life structures, in Levinson and his colleagues' terms, Carpenter (1988) found that the builders perceived more freedom than the changers. Apparently, the loss of structure and the relinquishing of some commitments can also create a kind of confusion that requires a considerable amount of energy and attention. Nevertheless, the "midlife crisis" that many people report—80 percent of the Levinson et al. middle-aged subjects demonstrated "tumultuous struggles within the self and with the external world" (p. 199)—is based on a growing awareness of their mortality that would naturally predispose them to make the most of the time left to live.

With respect to later life for males, Levinson and his colleagues noted that a man who traverses the life event of retirement:

> ….has earned the right to be and do what is most important to himself. He is beyond distinctions between work and play. He can devote himself in a serious playful way to the interests that flow most directly from the depths of the self. (p. 36)

The work of both Erikson and Levinson et al. has been criticized as being *androcentric*, that is, as applying only to males and perhaps being *ethnocentric* as well since little has been done to establish the validity of the theories in other cultures. For example, girls and women are likely to be more consistently involved in issues and matters of intimacy and nurturing throughout their lives than simply in early and middle adulthood. Intimacy and caregiving are also likely to be more directly related to identity formation in women (see Gilligan, 1982). Furthermore, a large number of people's jobs change very little during their working lives, while another sizable group goes from job to job without having anything resembling a "career." Thus there is good reason to see the Levinson et al. model as only a prototype of male life in middle-class, white, North American culture. The extent to which models such as these can be generalized and to which the psychological issues faced are characteristic of people in other life circumstances is still to be determined.

In fact, it is clear that the tremendous diversity in lifestyles that exists today is also accompanied by diversity in the developmental paths that people take over the life span. People who are single or divorced, single parents, partners in childless or same-sex couples, and people with different ethnic and cultural backgrounds likely follow different routes and face different issues as they age. For example, Zuzanek and Smale (1992) studied the amount of time a group of 25-year-old to 44-year-old people devoted to leisure and work during a typical week. Even in this restricted age group, they were able to classify the people that they studied into five major life span or life cycle groups on the basis gender, marital status, presence of children, and employment status. The time devoted to leisure differed significantly among these groups.

Life Course Models

If there is any consistency across gender, social class and culture with respect to changes over the life span it may be the change in *time orientation* that takes place at midlife. Neugarten (1977) noted that as people are "growing up," they think of their age as time since birth, accumulating maturity as they accumulate years. But when people begin the process of "growing older," they begin to see their lives in terms of "time left to live." This changing orientation to time, with the sense of a limited future, would help to explain the selectivity and discrimination that takes place in later life where, as we discussed earlier, people begin new activities less frequently. However, other than this one dramatic change, Neugarten's research with adults led her to see change as occurring mostly in response to a *social clock* that may vary according to culture. Cultures have a clear set of "sign posts"—that is, norms—that tell people what is supposed to happen when, and that govern life accordingly.

The figures listed in Table 9.2 (p. 264) were based on a study carried out by Neugarten and her colleagues (Neugarten, Moore & Lowe, 1968) almost 30 years ago. How, if at all, have things changed? Is it still common, that is, "normative," to finish high school at around age 18, to get a first job, to get married and have a first child before the age of 30, to complete child rearing during the 40s, to expect children to follow a similar pattern and to retire at 65? Certainly this pattern is changing in western cultures to the extent that nuclear families and single-job career patterns are no longer normative; but to the extent that one deviates in school, work or family matters, there is still a sense of being out of sequence or "off-time" (Neugarten, 1977), the consequences of which can be discomfort, disorientation and lack of social support. In her work, Neugarten was fond of asking, "What does it mean to be an adult? What are the markers?" And leisure researchers can ask, "What are the implications for leisure?" In a study of newly married young adults, Kelly and Masar (1970) found that marriage brought an increased interest in some activities such as gardening, and a decreased interest in others including going out socializing and drinking. Is it marriage alone that leads to such effects or is it a matter of what people think they ought and ought not to do once they are married?

Many of the changes that occur over the life course, then, are predictable but not inevitable. There is considerable variance across cultures and among various segments of society. For example, there is evidence that in

Table 9.2   Consensus in a Middle Class, Middle-Aged Sample Regarding Various Age-Related Characteristics

Characteristic	Age Range*	Percent Who Concur	
		Men (n = 50)	Women (n = 45)
Best age for a man to marry	20–25	80	90
Best age for a woman to marry	19–24	85	90
When most people should become grandparents	45–50	84	79
Best age for most people to finish school and go to work	20–22	86	82
When most men should be settled in a career	24–26	74	64
When most men hold their top jobs	45–50	71	58
When most people should be ready to retire	60–65	33	86
A young man	18–22	84	88
A middle-aged man	40–50	86	75
An old man	65–75	75	57
A young woman	18–24	89	88
A middle-aged woman	40–50	87	77
An old woman	60–75	83	87
When a man has the most responsibilities	35–50	79	75
When a man accomplishes the most	40–50	82	71
The prime of life for a man	35–50	86	80
When a woman has the most responsibilities	25–40	93	91
When a woman accomplishes most	30–45	94	92
A good-looking woman	20–35	92	82

* Age range designated as appropriate or expected.

Adapted from Neugarten, Moore and Lowe (1968)

working class communities, the experience of distinct stages and transitions is less common than in segments of the population with more education (Giele, 1980). The rates of participation in leisure activities discussed earlier are likely to have as much to do with the expectations of others as with the inevitable course of aging (Cutler & Hendricks, 1990; Lawton, 1993). Older people may be inclined to feel uncomfortable in certain recreational contexts, such as an outdoor concert, where everyone else is younger and where youth is the "target market." Miller (1965) once wrote of the "portent of embarrassment" in describing what keeps older people disengaged from active involvement. Trying new activities or even drawing on old skills often evokes the self-consciousness that comes with declining competence and the appearance of "being old." The prevailing evidence is that older people can learn new activities about as well (albeit perhaps more slowly) as younger people (Schaie & Geiwitz, 1982); but the expectation that "you can't teach an old dog new tricks" often keeps an older person from trying and may lead leisure service providers to prefer other clients.

Family and work role changes are also likely to dictate changes in behavior and experience, including those related to leisure. Graduation and the transition from school leaves young adults with a newfound independence but also typically with a somewhat narrower set of recreational activities and opportunities (Kelly & Masar, 1970). This pattern of constriction continues with marriage and especially with having children (Witt & Goodale, 1981).

Many writers and researchers have spoken of the compromises in lifestyle that having a family brings. Gutmann (1975) referred to it as the "chronic emergency of parenthood." In the study referred to earlier, Gordon, Gaitz and Scott (1976) noted "Nothing changes life like the marriage-parenthood package." There is often precious little time left after children are satisfied and/or asleep, and when it comes to leisure, children influence the leisure of parents and caregivers as much as the children are influenced by parents, though this is more typically true of women than men (Horna, 1989, Shaw, 1992). Nevertheless, there are important changes that occur even in the course of the family life cycle. When children are young and "portable," or teenagers are off on their own, it is possible for parents to choose activities that are of special interest to themselves, but in the middle years of childhood, children's interests typically dictate much of what parents do. Research on the constraints to leisure experienced by parents indicates that these years are accompanied by an increasing scarcity of time (Witt & Goodale, 1985). When children have grown up and are off on their own, adults often have the experience of not knowing how to get back to their interests. But the leisure of parenting has a special quality of its own and is thus part of the elaboration of leisure interests and abilities and, as we noted before, can contribute to a sense of generativity. Modeling, teaching, providing opportunities are all part of family-oriented leisure. It is also true, however, that relationships may suffer to the extent that attention to children keeps couples from relating to each other. In one study (Orthner, 1976), it was found that in only the first and last phases of the family life cycle did shared leisure enhance marital satisfaction, and those are the phases when children are the least demanding.

Changes in work roles are also significant in dictating leisure activities and interests. To the extent that young adults find themselves heavily involved in establishing work careers, they may not want to stray too far from those tasks that will insure progression toward getting established and are thus likely to choose recreation and leisure activities that complement work roles or compensate in some useful way. By middle age there may be some reduction in the pressures to become established, but the desire to contribute to the well-being of others may be equally as demanding on time and energy. Furthermore, midlife is often a time when women return to the work force after completing childrearing, thus reintroducing all the pressures of becoming established. Retirement from paid work, of course, brings an end to most work-related role constraints, but dramatic increases in free time are often offset by dwindling resources and a decline in physical health. But it is quality rather than quantity of leisure that is most important to continuing development and well-being in any case.

The Value of Leisure in the Course of Aging

Though researchers have been able to theorize about leisure in relationship to predictable changes in priorities and role requirements over the life span or life course, the question of what value leisure has in the course of aging remains to be more fully addressed. Again there is no comprehensive theory available to act as a guide in understanding this relationship. In chapter eleven, we will examine research that focuses on the influence of leisure on several specific types of life course changes and transitions (e.g., retirement, becoming unemployed, developing intimate relationships). We have already considered the idea that leisure might help in addressing such developmental tasks as establishing intimacy, being generative, and breaking with convention in early and middle adulthood. The greatest attention has been given, however, to how leisure may contribute to ego integration and the other needs of later life; three theories of what constitutes successful aging have been developed.

Activity theory asserts that people will be happiest and most fulfilled in direct proportion to how much activity they are able to maintain (Hooyman & Kiyak, 1996). Indeed there is some evidence that older people who are happier are more active (see Bengtson, 1969; Kelly, Steinkamp & Kelly, 1987). But the correlations found have never been large, and in some cases they have been negative. Furthermore, health tends to be a confounding variable that is seldom taken into account. But even when health is controlled, the question remains, are people happier because they are active or more active because they are happier?

Another theory that has been considered is *disengagement theory* (Cumming & Henry, 1961). Disengagement theory suggests that as the end of life draws near, people will voluntarily disengage from others and from their former activity patterns, and society's withdrawal from them will in turn leave them in peace and happiness. But the evidence does not support the idea that people with reduced activities are happier, and the theory has drawn criticism because it is perceived as legitimizing the neglect of older adults. Nevertheless, to the extent that voluntary withdrawal from some activities is necessary to preserve one's integrity and afford more time for the kind of reminiscence that integration requires, it is worth considering further.

The theory that enjoys the most support, however, is *continuity theory* (Atchley, 1988). This theory of successful aging is most consistent with a recognition of the need to establish ego integrity that we discussed earlier. It also has the most empirical support. As we have suggested throughout this chapter, it is not the activity per se that is important, it is what the activity and its social context mean to people (see chapter seven). It stands to reason that those activities and relationships that have been cultivated and maintained over a long period in people's lives are the most likely to contribute to well-being and a sense of integrity.

So whether an activity is useful in the course of development through adulthood cannot be judged from the activity alone. Leisure involvements must be considered in terms of their relationship to developmental tasks and the needs for social integration and adaptation to social change. Clearly, it is more important to look at the quality rather than the quantity of leisure activity in any case. It is also important to recognize that though continuity of leisure preserves identity and may contribute to a sense of integrity, the possibility of new leisure opportunities is an important source of self-renewal. High-investment activities in particular offer new directions for the development of competence and social integration, and these have been found to be particularly important to life satisfaction (Kelly, Steinkamp & Kelly, 1987; Mannell, 1993).

Aging as a Context for Leisure;
Leisure as a Context for Aging

The idea of aging clearly suffers from a bad image, at least in Western cultures. Perhaps, as has been argued, industrialization has stripped age of its status as a fountain of wisdom and tradition (McPherson, 1990). Though people recognize the refinement that aging brings to some wines, society seems far less likely to acknowledge similar advantages for people. Maybe this follows from the view that aging takes people, albeit against their will, "into that dark night." The inevitability of death makes society see aging only as decline, and if development unfolds according to some genetically-coded set of instructions, the lack of control seems even more depressing.

It should be kept in mind that, on the one hand, people begin to "age" as soon as they are born; there are patterns of deterioration from the first day. On the other hand, people are also capable of developing throughout life, and it is largely social conditions that define what is expected of an individual at a given age. Age, then, can be considered a social context that influences a person's leisure behavior and experience. Individual inclinations and interests based on needs, attitudes and personality dispositions interact with the social context associated with a given age to direct behavior, leisure activities included.

Leisure shows some important relationships with age. Knowing how old people are, especially if researchers have some clues as to the history that they share with other members of their age cohort, may allow the prediction of leisure interests and leisure activities. However, it should also be clear by now that leisure behavior is in many cases resistant to the influences of age; it is as if leisure is the one context in which people have permission to not "act your age." The control that leisure affords may give it special significance as a source of meaning in the personal life narrative that people write for themselves as they grow older.

Cultivating Leisure and Well-Being

Psychological Benefits of Leisure: Concepts, Theories and Evidence

C
h
a
p
t
e
r

T
E
N

Outline

Preview

Many benefits have been claimed for leisure. However, leisure has also been associated with a variety of personal and societal costs. In this and the next chapter, we will discuss these benefits and costs of leisure. A major thrust of social psychological research on leisure for the foreseeable future will be to understand the role of leisure in fostering the psychological benefits of mental health and well-being. Of course, these psychological "benefits of leisure" are likely to impact both on people's physical health and indirectly on the vitality of their interpersonal relationships, the organizations of which they are a part, their communities and society-at-large. To set the stage for this discussion, a general model of leisure benefits will be presented. On one hand, this model will help in understanding the nature of leisure benefits and the challenges involved in establishing links between leisure behavior and experience, and on the other, various psychological and social outcomes. Various ideas and theories are then examined that give the reader some idea of the psychological mechanisms that may link leisure with its benefits; evidence for the existence of these mechanisms is also reviewed. In the next chapter, we will look at some examples of how leisure can benefit people's behavior and interactions in other areas of their lives, such as their work, family and interpersonal relationships.

Knowledge of leisure benefits is important if public and private service providers are to create high-quality leisure opportunities and help people experience meaningful leisure. This knowledge is also of relevance to every individual if she or he is to make wise choices for the use of her or his free time. As you read about theory and research on various types of leisure benefits in this chapter and the next, ask yourself if enough is known about leisure and its benefits to develop a *Consumers' Guide to "Wholesome" Leisure* that could be used by individuals and service providers to better plan for leisure.

The Concept of Leisure Benefits

The study of people's behavior during their free time and the factors that influence it are interesting in their own right, yet an important reason for the considerable social psychological interest in leisure is the belief that it is important, or at least has the potential to contribute, to individual well-being and quality of life. This belief is reflected in a statement that was published by the World Leisure and Recreation Association in 1975:

> People cannot grow on the basis of physical sustenance alone; they need a cultural identity, a sense of social fulfillment, a regeneration of body and spirit which comes from various forms of recreation and leisure and makes their role one of growing importance on the world agenda.

Though this statement is noble sounding, what is really known about the benefits of leisure, particularly leisure's contribution to individual health and well-being? If you were asked to make a list of the social and psychological benefits that people can derive from leisure, what would you include? Could you explain why or how leisure produced these outcomes? Finally, why would you consider the outcomes of leisure you identified to be "benefits;" would everyone agree that they are benefits, or might some people see these as negative outcomes or personal and social costs?

Consider the questions raised by the following brief scenarios. Identify the *benefits* that could result from the behavior described. Do you agree that these benefits would result from leisure? Think of some reasons or *theories* that would explain why these benefits might result from the leisure portrayed. Would everyone agree that the various outcomes described in these leisure scenarios are, in fact, "benefits?"

Scenario 1

> Alison feels alive and on the edge! Lately school's been a drag and so have her old friends. But for the past few weeks she and her new friends have been having a blast. Though her parents and the police might not agree, she feels that she and her recent acquaintances are not really hurting anyone— just having fun. They don't take much or do any damage, but breaking into people's homes to "liberate" a few of the homeowner's possessions on the weekends is exhilarating.

Can illegal and antisocial activities be leisure? What is it about breaking social conventions that can make leisure exciting? What leisure benefits is Alison experiencing? What are the potential costs?

Scenario 2

Consider Matthew and Christopher who are in their first semester of study at a large urban university. They are both from small rural towns where they were part of a small and well-known high school graduating class. Neither student knew anyone upon his arrival. Their programs of study are very demanding and just finding the location of classrooms and labs has been a major undertaking. Of the two, Matthew seems to be coping better. He appears to be less anxious, has maintained his sense of humor, and has been sick less often during the semester than Christopher.

Could Matthew's more effective coping ability be due to his leisure style? What types of leisure interests and involvements might be useful in helping Christopher cope with the stress he is experiencing? Are some activities better than others?

Scenario 3

Sheila is one of 12 adolescents and two instructors clinging to a large sailboat slowly fighting its way up a lake as it tacks into a stiff wind. Like the other adolescents on the boat, she doesn't really want to be there. She's cold, wet and stiff, and she's never been good at this "outdoor stuff." However, participation in this two-week outdoor adventure program was a condition of Sheila's court sentence; its successful completion will keep her out of a juvenile detention center.

What are the benefits of this leisure activity for Sheila? Beyond surviving the experience and some stiff muscles, will the experience result in Sheila feeling better about herself and help keep her out of trouble with the law when she returns home?

*   *   *   *   *

What benefits did you identify? The ability of leisure involvements, even illegal ones, to provide fun and excitement in the company of friends as described in the first scenario will come as no surprise. Leisure has typically been seen as a source of fun, enjoyment and excitement. Coping with stressful life events, such as a stressful work environment as described in the second scenario, seems to be an essential survival skill in today's society. Many people feel that their leisure helps them, but can the things they do in their leisure actually enhance effective coping, and if so, how? For the third scenario, did you identify benefits such as improved self-esteem and reduced delinquent behavior. A variety of leisure programs have been based on the belief that certain types of leisure activities and experiences can bolster people's identity and self-esteem which will allow them to function more effectively as individuals and avoid destructive behavior. In this chapter, we will explore the types of questions raised in the above scenarios and the social psychological explanations that are available for why these and other benefits might be expected. First, we will examine the idea of leisure benefits. Next, we will discuss and assess the assumptions and "theories" that underlie contemporary ideas about the contributions of leisure to individual health and well-being.

The Demand for Research on Leisure Benefits

The idea that leisure is beneficial or "good" for people has been around for a long time, as has research which attempts to link leisure with various health and well-being outcomes—*outcomes* that most people would agree are *benefits* rather than *costs*. For example, would anyone question that good mental health and successful retirement are benefits. However, efforts to formally define the nature of a *leisure benefit* are relatively recent. There has been an increase in interest among researchers in identifying and studying the benefits of leisure as reflected in the publication of the book, *Benefits of Leisure* (Driver, Brown & Peterson, 1991a), in which a group of leisure researchers reviewed what is known about a whole range of psychological and social leisure benefits.

In part, these developments have been driven by the increased need of leisure policymakers and planners to justify public support for leisure services ranging from national parks to community recreation programs for youth. Leisure researchers have been called on to provide evidence of these benefits. Large public budget deficits and competition with other social services for scarce tax dollars have made it necessary for leisure service providers to demonstrate that their services contribute to important community goals which include *psychological, social, economic* and *environmental* benefits (Driver, Brown & Peterson, 1991b; Schreyer & Driver, 1989). As a sign of the times, a consortium of organizations representing leisure service practitioners in Canada recently commissioned the compilation and publication of a *catalog* of leisure benefits believed to result from leisure and leisure services (*The Benefits of Parks and Recreation: A Catalogue*; The Parks and Recreation Federation of Ontario, 1992). A similar project is underway in the United States.

There has also been growing interest among leisure practitioners in *benefit-based planning*. Rather than automatically offering traditional recreation programs, practitioners would help the people they serve identify the "benefits" they are looking for, and then develop programs and services that provide these benefits. The hope is that this strategy will lead to new approaches and innovative planning. To do this planning effectively, a practitioner needs to have a good idea of the outcomes and benefits of various types of leisure involvements.

Defining a Leisure Benefit

A benefit resulting from leisure refers to "a *change* that is viewed to be advantageous—an improvement in condition, or a gain to an individual, a group, to society, or to another entity" (Driver, Brown & Peterson, 1991b, p. 4). This definition identifies two very important aspects of a leisure benefit. First, it must be demonstrated that involvement in some form of leisure is responsible for, or causes, a *change*. Additionally, a benefit can also be the *maintenance* of a desired condition or state of affairs. Second, this change or maintenance must be seen as an *improvement* over what would have otherwise occurred.

Well-designed social science research can be used to establish the consequences or outcomes of leisure involvements. For example, research can be designed to determine whether people's leisure can, under some conditions, enhance their enjoyment with their work or allow them to work more efficiently. However, whether these outcomes are seen as benefits is largely a question of *values*, and individuals and groups may differ as to what they see as a benefit. For example, say that certain kinds of leisure styles do cause people to feel more satisfied with their jobs, even if the working conditions are poor. Employers would likely see this outcome as a *benefit* of leisure. However, union groups might feel that this outcome of leisure is a *cost* since workers may be less likely to organize and demand improved working conditions.

Consequently, though the focus of this chapter and the next is on the benefits of leisure, do not overlook the fact that there are also potentially negative leisure outcomes or costs. A number of antisocial and illegal behaviors can be leisure as was suggested by the first scenario. Activities such as vandalism and excessive drinking are usually pursued during free time or in conjunction with leisure activities. For example, it has been found that under some conditions adolescents who are more actively involved in some leisure activities are also more likely to use drugs (Iso-Ahola & Crowley, 1991) and alcohol (Caldwell, Smith & Weissinger, 1992). Alcohol consumption was found to be higher among adults who more frequently engaged in sports and exercise (Watten, 1995) and community, social and outdoor activities (Carruthers & Busser, 1995). Adult drinkers often expect that drinking will enhance their recreation and social leisure experiences (Carruthers, 1993). Are these outcomes costs or benefits? Often, it depends on who is making the judgment. Illegal and antisocial activities may have outcomes that are seen as benefits by those who participate in them, and costs by outsiders or society-at-large. Clearly, researchers and practitioners must be alert to the possibility that leisure is not automatically beneficial to individuals or society and may result in negative outcomes.

Studying Leisure Benefits

To clarify the meaning of the leisure-benefit concept and promote the study of leisure benefits, Driver and his associates (Driver, Brown & Peterson, 1991b; Schreyer & Driver, 1989) have described the steps that are involved in establishing if and how leisure leads to specific benefits. These steps and the difficulties of studying leisure benefits are represented in a model suggested by Mannell and Stynes (1991) and shown in Figure 10.1 (p. 278).

As can be seen from the model, there are three major sets of factors (inputs, outcomes and benefits) linked by two types of processes (production and valuation).

Leisure as an Input or Cause

In leisure-benefits research, leisure is treated as a major *input* or cause. As we discussed in chapters three and four, leisure can take a variety of forms and be defined subjectively or objectively in terms of activity, time, setting, or experience. Researchers have examined the impact on psychological well-being of leisure *settings*, such as natural and built environments (e.g., Ulrich & Addoms, 1981; Ulrich, 1984; Ulrich, Dimberg & Driver, 1991), frequency of participation in leisure *activity* (e.g., Cutler Riddick, 1985), proportion of leisure *time* spent in joint activities with a spouse (e.g., Orthner, 1975), and quality of leisure *experience* during daily life (e.g., Graef, Csikszentmihalyi & Giannino, 1983).

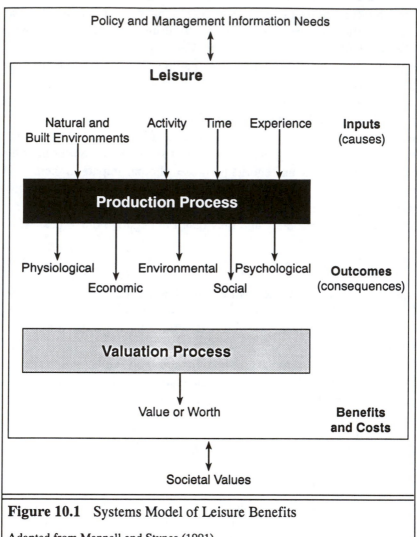

Figure 10.1 Systems Model of Leisure Benefits

Adapted from Mannell and Stynes (1991)

Outcomes and Consequences of Leisure

Though in this chapter and the next we are largely concerned with psychological and social psychological *outcomes*, the model shown in Figure 10.1 reminds us that leisure may also produce physiological, economic and environmental outcomes. Researchers have identified a large number of potential consequences of leisure involvements ranging from the thoroughly researched to the highly speculative (see Driver et al., 1991). On the well-researched end of the continuum, an outcome such as *physical fitness* has been well-established. A considerable body of biomedical research finds that physical exercise causes cardiovascular changes associated with lower rates of heart disease and increased life span (see Froehlicher & Froehlicher, 1991; Paffenbarger, Hyde & Dow, 1991). However, research examining the impact of nonexercise forms of leisure on physiological outcomes associated with *stress, illness, and so-called lifestyle diseases* is lacking (Coleman & Iso-Ahola, 1993). Outcomes of leisure that have received only a small amount of research attention include the role that leisure services play in fostering *community satisfaction* (Allen, 1991) and the role of leisure in facilitating *self-actualization* (Csikszentmihalyi & Kleiber, 1991). At the speculative end of the continuum, some authors have suggested that there are *spiritual* outcomes of leisure (e.g., McDonald & Schreyer, 1991). These types of consequences truly challenge the social scientist's ability to measure all leisure outcomes (Mannell, 1996).

The *economic* outcomes of leisure, particularly outdoor recreation, have received substantial attention (see Johnson & Brown, 1991). It has also been argued that there are *environmental* outcomes, both cost and benefits, of human leisure. On the one hand, people can damage the environment with their recreational pursuits, for example, snowmobiling in sensitive natural areas. On the other, leisure gives people time to enjoy and appreciate the natural environment and consequently encourages them to preserve and protect it (Rolston, 1991). *Social* outcomes of leisure have been discussed and include those that may accrue to friendships, intimate relationships and family. For example, Orthner and Mancini (1991) have examined the impact of leisure on family bonding. Leisure has also been seen to have an impact on larger groups such as work, leisure and community organizations, as well as society as a whole. The impact of organizational wellness or industrial recreation programs in the workplace on worker productivity and company loyalty has been studied (Ellis & Richardson, 1991). The influence of leisure services on people's satisfaction with the quality of life in their communities (Allen, 1991), and in enhancing the attractiveness of a community to businesses looking to relocate (Decker & Crompton, 1990) has also been examined. Little research has been directed at assessing the impact of leisure on society as a whole or its large institutions (Burch & Hamilton-Smith, 1991; Cohen, 1991).

Psychological Well-Being as an Outcome

A variety of terms, concepts and measures have been used by researchers to characterize the psychological well-being and mental health outcomes that individuals may receive from leisure. Frequently used are concepts and measures of *subjective well-being* such as happiness (e.g., Bradburn, 1969), life satisfaction (e.g., Neugarten, Havighurst & Tobin, 1961; Diener, Emmons, Larsen & Griffin, 1985) and morale (Lawton, 1975). Less common is research that uses *mental illness* or its absence (e.g., Sharp & Mannell, 1996) as an outcome by measuring psychopathological symptoms or psychological distress (e.g., depression, anxiety, obsessive-compulsiveness, hostility, psychotism). How positively people see themselves, that is, their *identity* (e.g., Haggard & Williams, 1991), *self-concept* and *self-esteem* (Dattilo, Dattilo, Samdahl & Kleiber, 1994) have also been thought to be important psychological well-being outcomes of leisure.

Researchers have generally been concerned with groups of people who are "at-risk," and for whom leisure is seen to have some potential for reducing or eliminating a variety of problems. For example, the role of leisure participation and satisfaction in the lives of older, retired adults has been given major attention. The problems of concern include adjusting to loss of work and loss of childrearing roles in addition to the physical changes associated with aging (see Kelly, 1993). Similar research is beginning to emerge that examines the influence leisure can have on the quality of life and psychological health of people who lose their jobs (e.g., Winefield, Tiggemann, Winefield & Goldney, 1993). Also being studied is the role of leisure in helping people deal with various kinds of physical and psychological disabilities (e.g., Harlan & Hawkins, 1992), as well as problems related to juvenile delinquency (e.g., Munson, 1991), eating disorders (e.g., Kaufman, McBride, Hultsman & Black, 1988) and the difficulty of coping with stressful life events (Coleman, 1993). Researchers are also examining the impact of leisure on the quality of people's experiences in and satisfaction with specific areas of life, such as interpersonal relationships, family life, and work. We will explore some of these latter issues in the next chapter.

The Production Process: Linking Leisure to Outcomes

It is not enough to say or demonstrate that some type of leisure involvement is responsible for a particular outcome. The processes or social psychological mechanisms that underlie these links need to be understood. The model in Figure 10.1 (p. 278) includes a box designating the *production process*. When it comes to understanding the relationship between leisure and its outcomes this box is often a "black box," meaning researchers and practitioners have little or no understanding of the social and psychological processes that may link leisure to specific well-being outcomes in the production process. Part of the problem has been the lack of explicit theories that identify the conditions and processes by which leisure may impact on psychological well-being. There are a number of ideas about how leisure influences well-being but until recently, few attempts have been made to develop explicit theories.

The difficulty of identifying the processes by which leisure outcomes are "produced" should not be underestimated. The relationship between leisure and well-being is not a simple one. Not only is leisure just one of a number of factors that affect well-being, but leisure behavior, itself, is also likely influenced by well-being. Little discussion has been given to these types of *feedback effects* (Mannell & Stynes, 1991). Feedback effects are likely to be important in the analysis of many leisure outcomes. For example, feedback effects may play a role in the relationship between leisure activity choice and identify affirmation as discussed by Haggard and Williams (1991). Not only does participation in an activity provide opportunities for identity development and consolidation, but conversely, the choice of an activity itself is likely influenced by the nature of an individual's identity at any point in time. Similarly, the flow experience may not only contribute to self-actualization as suggested by Csikszentmihalyi and Kleiber (1991), but as we discussed in earlier chapters, individuals who are more self-actualized may be better able to experience flow in a wider variety of situations (Csikszentmihalyi & Csikszentmihalyi, 1988; Kleiber & Dirkin, 1985).

The Valuation Process: When Outcomes Are Benefits

Earlier in this chapter, we suggested that not everyone would necessarily agree that certain leisure outcomes are benefits. We used the example of the possible contribution of leisure to job satisfaction—employers might see this outcome as a *benefit* and union groups as a *cost*. The process by which leisure outcomes come to be valued and defined as benefits is called the *valuation process* in the model in Figure 10.1 (p. 278). For the most part, leisure researchers have ignored this process. As members of the societies in which they carry out their research, researchers frequently share the same beliefs and values as the people they study, including what constitutes leisure benefits. In the case of psychological well-being, most people would not question the belief that increases to self-esteem and life satisfaction, or reductions in stress are benefits. However, more attention needs to be given to these assumptions about what outcomes are benefits, and researchers need to study how individuals, social groups and societies weigh the relative importance of different leisure benefits (Cohen, 1991; Ajzen, 1991). In Figure 10.1, inputs, outcomes and benefits and the production and valuation processes linking them are shown to be bounded and influenced by the broader values and norms of society. These social values and the needs of leisure managers, policymakers and planners for information about leisure benefits influence researchers' efforts to study, understand and apply their knowledge about leisure behavior and experience.

Leisure and Psychological Benefit "Theories"

It has long been claimed that leisure contributes to well-being (e.g., Caldwell & Smith, 1988; Chalip, Thomas & Voyle, 1992; Iso-Ahola, 1988; Kleiber, 1985; Tinsley & Tinsley, 1986). Various links between *leisure and well-being* have been suggested throughout the previous chapters. For example, in chapters five and seven leisure was seen to have the potential to provide opportunities for the satisfaction of needs such as competence, self-determination, and a host of other biological and social needs which appear to be important for human health and well-being. In chapter six, we mentioned that personality development may be fostered through leisure, and in chapters eight and nine, that some types of leisure participation may help people successfully navigate various life span transitions.

However, when reviewing the leisure literature, the social psychological benefits claimed for leisure appear to be based on a number of assumptions that are for the most part untested. In fact, there are very few clearly stated theories about the nature and dynamics of the links between leisure and well-being. To help better understand the various leisure and well-being links that may operate, we have classified the various ideas and assumptions available into several types of *explanations* or *theories*. We use the term "theories" loosely. Most of these ideas have not been stated formally and would not meet the requirements of full-fledged scientific theories.

It should be recognized that these explanations are not necessarily competing hypotheses nor are they mutually exclusive explanations. Some of these leisure-psychological benefit theories propose social psychological links that have certain ideas in common. More than one of the different links suggested by these various explanations may operate at any one time. Also, most theories about the relationship between leisure and well-being are based on the assumption that the freedom of choice available in leisure allows people to select for participation those activities and experiences that are good or beneficial for them—that is, if unconstrained people will choose what is good for their well-being and health. Some of these hypotheses assume that the actual exercise of freedom of choice through leisure itself fosters and strengthens the sense of self-determination and control that social psychologists see as critical to all forms of well-being.

"Keeping Idle Hands Busy" Theory

One explanation of how leisure may be beneficial to people is what we will call the *keeping idle hands busy* theory. It is probably the most basic explanation of all. People are thought to be happiest or at least mentally healthy when they are busy. From this perspective, leisure is important because it keeps people with too much free time on their hands (idle hands) occupied. Having unoccupied time available is assumed to be psychologically and behaviorally risky for some people resulting in a state of boredom and/or participation in destructive activities. This view of idleness has a long history with strong roots in Christian thinking—most notably the Protestant Work Ethic. "Idleness was considered an enemy of the soul" (Goodale & Godbey, 1988, p. 34) and work a religious obligation because it prevented idleness. Play, recreation and leisure only become acceptable when they are constructive, more worklike and thus prevent the evils of idleness.

Whether true or not, older retired adults (e.g., Belanger & Delisle, 1979) and adolescents (e.g., Iso-Ahola & Crowley, 1991) have sometimes been identified as groups of people who are at risk of idleness. For example, juvenile delinquency is often seen to be a result of adolescents having too much free time available with no socially acceptable leisure alternatives available; this leads to boredom and consequently engagement in harmful activities such as drug use (see Iso-Ahola & Crowley, 1991; Crompton, 1993). There is also some evidence that the experience of boredom during free time is associated with health compromising behaviors (Caldwell & Smith, 1994; Smith & Caldwell, 1989). In a study of 2,756 high school students in the southeastern United States, Caldwell and Smith (1995) found that adolescents who were bored in their leisure or whose leisure was chosen to reject adult values and structure were more likely to engage in risky health behaviors (e.g., smoking, alcohol abuse, bulimia, attempting suicide). University students who experience their leisure as boring have reported lower mental and physical health (Weissinger, 1995).

Leisure activities and programs to keep people busy are considered to be constructive behavioral alternatives (e.g., Grubb, 1975; McKay, 1993; Munson, 1991). Little or no research has been carried out to actually test this theory. It is also doubtful that simply keeping people busy without fostering other changes (e.g., leisure skill development, positive leisure attitudes, intrinsic leisure interest) would do anything more than temporarily delay the occurrence of whatever problems are of concern. As we will explain, other theories do suggest that it is not enough to just keep people busy with leisure activities. It appears that activities with certain types of characteristics may be necessary to produce benefits.

Leisure has also been described as a way of keeping the mind busy, and consequently, diverting or distracting people from distressing thoughts that may be triggered by stressful life events, such as the death of a spouse or the excessive demands of a job. By keeping the mind busy, people may temporarily avoid or escape the stress of these events. This "break" may allow them to psychologically "regroup" and when they "return" they may be better able to deal with their problems (e.g., Harvey & Bahr, 1980; Lopata, 1967; Parkes, 1972). Monat and Lazarus (1977) have identified two forms of coping, including *direct action strategies*, where specific behaviors are used to alleviate or eliminate a problem, and *palliative methods*, which refer to the use of thoughts or behaviors that, though not altering the problem itself, will divert the person's attention for a time. A direct action strategy to deal with job-related stress, for example, could involve changing jobs or talking to management about eliminating those aspects of the job that are causing the stress. There has been some speculation in the leisure literature about the role of leisure participation in dealing with stress that is consistent with the notion of palliative coping (Hogan & Santomier, 1982; Kleiber, 1985). This hypothesis is based upon the assumption that while people are involved in a leisure activity, their attention shifts away from the source of their stress. This idea is comparable to what Csikszentmihalyi (1975) has referred to as "flow," the process through which a shift of attention from thoughts to actions occurs. Leisure participation may serve as an adaptive form of palliative coping.

A few studies have found evidence that when people in stressful conditions are actively involved in leisure, the impact of the stress on health and well-being is reduced. In an early experimental study, Heywood (1978) demonstrated that the stress of performing a challenging task was relieved to a greater extent by passive activities such as music, reading and television viewing when they were perceived as leisure. Physically active leisure was found to help patients reduce hypertension resulting from stress (Pierce, Madden, Siegel & Blumenthal, 1993) and older adults decrease anxiety and the symptoms of depression (King, Barr Taylor & Haskell, 1993). Patterson and Carpenter (1994) found that greater participation in leisure activities was associated with higher levels of morale among widowed men and women. Caltabiano (1995) found that people who participated more frequently in passive cultural and hobby activities reported fewer illness symptoms when they were under greater stress. Unfortunately, none of these studies examined the actual psychological process or nature of the link between leisure participation and coping with stress. Palliative coping could be involved or some other psychological mechanism as we will explain when we cover the "buffer and coping" theory later in this chapter.

In a test of the "keeping busy" or palliative leisure coping hypothesis, Sharp and Mannell (1996) studied 62 recently widowed older women and a comparison group of 19 married women. They found that those widowed women who were more active in their leisure experienced less guilt and sadness, and greater happiness during their daily lives. Also, the higher their overall leisure participation and level of enjoyment of their three most frequent leisure activities, the lower the emotional distress (e.g., depression) reported (see Figure 10.2). The widowed women reported that they attempted to keep busy with leisure activities to temporarily escape or distract themselves from emotional distress (palliative coping). Among the married women in the study, only a small proportion kept busy for these types of reasons. A much higher proportion of the married women kept busy to enjoy themselves and for personal development than did the widowed women (see Figure 10.3).

Psychological Hedonism: Pleasure-Relaxation-Fun Theories

Another outcome of leisure involvements is the experience of *pleasure*, *relaxation* or *fun* they can provide. In fact, as we mentioned in our earlier discussion of the defining characteristics of leisure in chapter four, people frequently identify pleasure, relaxation and fun as important criteria of their leisure experiences (e.g., Shaw, 1985a).

Hedonism as a psychological theory refers to the fact that people act in such a way as to seek pleasure and avoid pain (Chaplin, 1985). Many

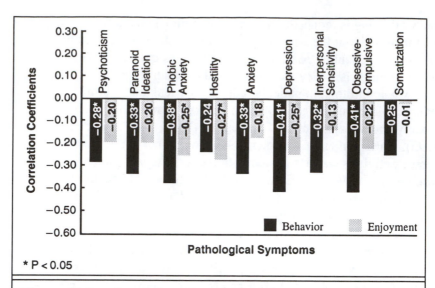

Figure 10.2   Correlations Between Leisure Behavior and Enjoyment and Symptoms of Emotional Distress

Adapted from Sharp and Mannell (1996)

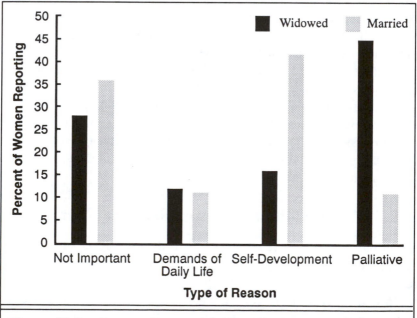

Figure 10.3   Reasons Reported for Keeping Busy

Adapted from Sharp and Mannell (1996)

psychological theories are in part based on the idea that pleasure seeking and its kin are important elements in understanding people's behavior. For example, psychoanalytic theory proposes that the "pleasure principle" is a primary process in mental functioning. The power of psychological needs (see Murray, 1938) is thought to be in the pleasure that is experienced when they are fulfilled or satisfied (see chapter seven).

Pleasure-relaxation-fun theories suggest that people seek fun or pleasurable experiences in their leisure and that these relatively brief and transient experiences not only enhance the quality of the present moment, but that cumulatively, they can "spice up" and enhance long-term psychological well-being. In fact, Larsen, Diener and Cropanzano (1987) have proposed that to maintain well-being people have a need for many small moments of enjoyment, rather than less frequent great peaks of pleasure. Consequently leisure activities may influence health and well-being by promoting positive moods (Hull, 1991). A great deal of the leisure that people engage in during their daily lives is, in fact, characterized by fun and pleasure seeking. People spend substantial amounts of time, energy and money to be entertained, to be amused, and to have fun. There are television sitcoms, amusement parks, stand-up comedy, and so forth. The entertainment (Chapman & Foot, 1976; Fry & Allen, 1975) and tourism (Pearce, 1982) industries know how important it is to make people laugh and provide opportunities for fun and pleasure. The notions of fun and pleasure have been recognized by some writers as being an important leisure construct (Smith, 1990b). Even authors who have advocated the importance of serious leisure for well-being (e.g., Stebbins, 1992a) have recognized that entertainment and diversionary activities are also an important part of leisure.

Leisure pursuits that become personally meaningful and important to people and that provide psychological benefits are inevitably structured or organized in ways that provide opportunities for "fun" and "pleasure" as part of the ongoing experience (Fine, 1989; Podilchak, 1991a, 1991b; Wankel, 1985, 1993; Wankel & Berger, 1991; Wankel & Kreisel, 1985; Wankel & Sefton, 1989a, 1989b). It has been suggested that the ability to experience fun and pleasure in leisure, particularly serious leisure activities, is important to acquire during adolescence (Hamilton, 1983a, 1983b; Kleiber, Larson & Csikszentmihalyi, 1986; Kleiber & Rickards, 1985) and that adults clearly differ in this ability (e.g., Schill, Beyler & Sharp, 1993).

Distinctions have also been made among the notions of "fun," "pleasure" and "enjoyment" (e.g., Csikszentmihalyi, 1990; Podilchak, 1991a, 1991b). For example, Csikszentmihalyi (1990) suggests that *pleasure* is a feeling of contentment that results when one's various needs are satisfied and one's expectations met. In comparison, *enjoyment* involves experiences that are not only pleasurable, but that are accompanied by a feeling of increased competence and growth—by a sense of "forward movement: by a sense of novelty, of accomplishment" (Csikszentmihalyi, 1990, p. 46). We will discuss this notion of leisure, competence and well-being as a separate hypothesis later.

Though people tell researchers that feelings of pleasure, relaxation and fun are an important part of their leisure, there is only limited evidence that a greater number of pleasurable moments experienced in daily life leads to higher levels of psychological well-being. Lewinsohn and Graf (1973) reported that the number of pleasant activities the people they studied experienced was positively related to their mood states. In particular, people who were depressed engaged in a smaller number of pleasant activities. Mannell and McMahon (1982) had a group of students keep diaries of all the humorous and pleasurable events that they encountered in the course of a day. They also assessed their mood states. These humorous events resulted primarily during their unstructured interactions with other people; a small percentage were triggered by watching television or listening to the radio. Those respondents who reported more of these pleasurable events felt more relaxed and happy, and less anxious and hostile at the end of the day. Tarrant (1996) found that when the students he studied in a laboratory experiment recalled past outdoor recreation experiences, they reported greater positive moods and fewer physical health problems. However, Larson, Mannell and Zuzanek (1986) found that a higher frequency of pleasurable experiences with friends and family members was unrelated to more stable, long-term measures of life satisfaction.

Need-Compensation Theory

Another type of explanation of how and why leisure contributes to psychological well-being is provided by the *need-compensation* theory. As we saw in our discussion of leisure motivation and satisfaction in chapter seven, human beings are thought to have a variety of physiological, cognitive and social needs that they must regularly satisfy if they are to lead happy and fulfilled lives. These needs can be met through a wide range of activities and experiences. However, due to the particular lifestyle circumstances in which people find themselves, they are often unable to satisfy specific needs as fully as they would like. Given that leisure is typically the least constrained domain of people's lives and provides greater freedom of choice, leisure activities can be selected to "compensate" or satisfy these unmet needs.

This need-compensation idea has its roots in theories about the relationship between work and leisure, particularly the impact of work on leisure (see Kabanoff, 1980; Iso-Ahola & Mannell, 1985). One of these theories suggests that people can compensate for the negative aspects of their jobs in their leisure. For example, if their jobs are constraining and socially isolating, they will participate in leisure activities which allow them to exercise control over their lives and socialize. Most of the research on work-leisure relationships has focused on determining if the activities or tasks that comprise people's work influence the activities in which they engage during their leisure. At the behavioral level, only limited support has been found for the compensation notion. Little research has been reported that examines whether needs that go unmet on the job actually influence people to choose leisure activities on the basis of their need-satisfying properties and ability to compensate. Several studies have suggested that working people do feel that their leisure compensates for needs that go unmet in other areas of their lives (e.g., Kelly, 1975; Hildebrand & Mannell, 1996). In a study of vacation preferences, Wahlers and Etzel (1985) found that if work was stressful, relaxing leisure activities were preferred and if work was not stimulating people would look for stimulation and excitement in their leisure. It has also been suggested that leisure can compensate for needs that go unmet due to loss of a job because of unemployment or retirement (e.g., Haworth, 1984; Shamir, 1988; Stebbins, 1992a). We will examine this issue of leisure, unemployment and retirement in the next chapter.

Personal Growth Theories

The most popular explanation of the way in which leisure is linked to psychological well-being is *personal growth theories*. From this perspective, leisure provides an opportunity for people to develop a clear idea of their strengths and weaknesses, continually develop their skills and abilities, become the kind of people they would like to be and feel good about who they are. Terms used to describe these types of personal growth outcomes include self-esteem and self-actualization.

This idea of personal growth is captured best by the notion of self-actualization. Maslow (1968) described self-actualization as the process of developing one's true potential as individuals to the fullest extent, and expressing one's skills, talents, and emotions in a personally fulfilling manner. According to this theory, people possess an innate potential that serves as a blueprint to describe what they are uniquely capable of becoming; they are continually in the process of moving toward that goal, and it may or may not be realized. For one individual the process of self-actualization might take the form of becoming an ideal parent, while other people could express this same need athletically, musically, artistically or administratively. According to Maslow, self-actualization does not demand that individuals excel as the best in the world, but only as the best they can possibly be. For example, people expressing their self-actualization through music do not have to be world-class musicians to develop and enjoy their musical talents. Fulfillment can be derived from achieving their personal best performances.

A number of versions of this theory can be found in the literature. Most prevalent are explanations based in part on the idea of human needs and motivation. As we discussed in chapter five, the needs for self-determination and competence are considered central motivating forces in human life. If people are to experience psychological well-being, they must develop relatively enduring feelings of competence, self-efficacy and control—in fact, according to some theories people are innately and intrinsically motivated to do so. Leisure, because it is based on freedom of choice, allows people to structure social settings and participate in activities that foster the development of these feelings. Feelings of competence and control are viewed to be the basis of a positive self-concept, as well as high self-esteem which, in turn, have been described as essential components of self-actualization and personal growth. From this perspective, then, if leisure is to provide psychological benefits, it must be challenging and require some effort.

This growing belief among researchers that leisure must be more than simply a pleasant, diversionary, escape-oriented experience if it is to contribute substantially to psychological well-being has lead to substantial interest in the constructs of *commitment* (Haworth, 1986), *serious leisure* (Stebbins, 1982, 1992a) and *flow* (Csikszentmihalyi, 1975). The idea is that people who experience higher levels of well-being and life satisfaction are more involved in freely chosen activities that challenge their knowledge and skills, and require an investment of effort. Kelly and his associates have coined the term *high-investment activities* and suggest that they are leisure activities that have been learned over time, require a great deal of effort, the acquisition of skill, and are most likely to yield outcomes of an enhanced sense of competence and worth (Kelly, Steinkamp & Kelly, 1987, p. 194; Kelly & Ross, 1989, p. 57). To put it simply, it could be said that *the more a person invests in the activities in which they choose to participate, the more they get out of these activities.* Of course, this is not a new idea. It is an adage that many people have frequently heard from parents, teachers and coaches.

According to Csikszentmihalyi (1975; 1990; Csikszentmihalyi & Kleiber, 1991), leisure involvements that result in flow experiences may contribute to self-actualization and personal growth. Flow experiences are based on people's constant striving to match their skills with challenges provided by the environment (see chapters four and eight). The freedom of leisure provides a marvelous opportunity to choose activities that provide this match. As skills improve, people can seek out greater challenges and thereby constantly push themselves to new levels of accomplishment. This process of constantly seeking to be in a state of flow is consistent with intrinsic motivation theory where the competence and self-determination motives push people toward growth and development (Deci & Ryan, 1991). As people successfully take on more challenges, that is, continue to achieve a state of flow, their behavior and skills continue to become more complex and rewarding. This ongoing experience of flow and the accumulation of these experiences is believed to contribute to personal growth.

Tinsley and Tinsley (1986) have proposed a similar theory in part based on the flow idea. According to this theory, leisure experiences that are challenging, intense and to which people are committed are likely to satisfy a variety of needs not met in other areas of life. The satisfaction of these needs can contribute to physical and mental health, and consequently, life satisfaction. Similar to Maslow's theory, Tinsley and Tinsley argue that people must meet most of their needs and be reasonably satisfied with their lives before they can experience personal growth. People who are relatively dissatisfied with their lives must attend to the satisfaction of their physiological, safety and "belongingness" needs. Consequently, they have little energy available to direct toward personal growth. However, if these needs are met, psychological resources are freed up allowing people the time to focus on those aspects of themselves that they would like to change and develop through their leisure.

Haworth (1984, 1986) has focused on the role that *commitment* to a leisure activity plays in the quality of life. He has argued that participation in leisure activities that require substantial commitment can counter the detrimental effects on psychological well-being (e.g., increased susceptibility to mental illness and lowered self-esteem) of being unemployed, retired, or employed in an unsatisfying or alienating job. In the studies reviewed by Haworth, committed leisure activities included home improvements, gardening, hobbies, learning new activities, active leisure, games and sports, and voluntary activities. The mechanism linking commitment and subjective well-being, according to Haworth, is the opportunity provided for status recognition and self-development.

Commitment is also at the core of Stebbins' theory of *serious leisure*. In fact, the construct provides a clear picture of what being committed to a leisure activity entails. As we have noted, he proposed the idea following his studies of amateurs and hobbyists (see chapter three). Serious leisure demands perseverance, personal effort in the development of specially acquired knowledge and skill, the development of a career in the activity, and strong attachment to or identification with the activity.

Stebbins believes that serious leisure can make a significant contribution to the quality of life of the individual and in the short-term, this type of leisure may be no fun. However, the hard work and perseverance by amateurs, hobbyists and volunteers to meet the challenges of their leisure is predicted to engender feelings of accomplishment and provide psychological benefits that include self-enrichment, self-gratification, self-actualization, self-expression, positive social identity, re-creation and escape from personal problems, social belonging and a feeling of contributing to a group (Stebbins, 1992a, p. 17).

Research is only now being conducted to directly test these types of hypotheses. For example, in the study of nursing home residents discussed in chapter five, Shary and Iso-Ahola (1989) found that not only did feelings of competency result from enhancing nursing home residents' choice and control over their lives through leisure participation, but that these feelings of competence were accompanied by increases in *self-esteem*. Dattilo, Dattilo, Samdahl and Kleiber (1994) examined the relationship between self-esteem and the leisure orientations of 222 women who were predominantly African American. Those women with higher self-esteem also reported greater active participation in recreation activities. In an experiential sampling method study, Mannell (1993) examined the relationship between the frequency with which a group of older adults experienced flow in their daily activities and their *life satisfaction*. He found that those older adults who were significantly more satisfied with their lives experienced flow significantly more frequently in freely chosen daily activities than older adults who reported low levels of life satisfaction. Though some evidence has been found that positive attitudes toward wilderness activity are associated with higher levels of self-actualization, little research has been reported examining the validity of the theory with respect to leisure and personal development (Shin, 1993; Young & Crandall, 1984).

Identity Formation and Affirmation Theory

A related leisure and personal growth theory is *identity* theory. Human beings have self-awareness and people create images of themselves in response to their own behaviors and the reactions of others to them. For example, based on the success and failures of an individual's efforts, and the feedback she or he receives from those around her or him, that person may come to see herself or himself as good at fixing things, a lousy golfer, concerned about the environment or fun-loving. To the extent these images form a somewhat consistent and stable picture, an identity is formed (*identify formation*). Though this identity can change, and indeed must change to allow for growth and development, its stability, however temporary, derives from the consistency of the messages people receive about themselves. Taking action, expressing ourselves and assuming social roles provide that information.

For the most part, research and writing on the factors that influence identity formation have emphasized work, religion, sex roles and political ideology. It is around these matters that important values and beliefs are typically developed. Yet the process of identity formation is an active one requiring self-expression and interaction with other people; leisure is considered significant for its ability to provide both types of opportunities. It is in the liberating context of leisure that identity alternatives are often initially considered through the expression of personal interests. In leisure, people "feel free" not only to be themselves but also to try out new possibilities (see Kelly, 1983). Leisure can provide an opportunity to play and experiment with the kind of person someone might want to be. Leisure involvements may not result in feedback that contributes in any substantial way to a person's sense of self or identity, but as particular actions, however experimental, are recognized as being self-determined and one's own, as being rewarding, and as offering direction for the development of one's talents and abilities, identity can take shape. Furthermore, some leisure activities may be taken *seriously* enough to offer levels of commitment comparable to those in other domains such as work and family.

Stryker (1987) has proposed an identity theory that is based on the assumption that people's self-concepts are composed of different identities (e.g., caring parent, skilled worker, knowledgeable winemaker), and that these identities are organized according to a hierarchy of salience or importance. The more salient, the more influence a particular identity component will have on a person's self-concept, and the more likely she or he will be to seek out opportunities to perform in terms of that identity. Based on this theory, Shamir (1992) has proposed that *leisure identities* can become highly salient to the self-concept of people for three reasons:

(1) these identities express and affirm individual talents and capacities;

(2) they provide some degree of social recognition; and

(3) they affirm central values and interests.

In a series of studies with university students, some of whom were involved in serious leisure activities (e.g., art, voluntary activities, amateur archaeology, politics), he found that the leisure activities most likely to meet these criteria required a social commitment from the participants, higher levels of effort and skill in the activity, time investment, and a willingness to maintain or increase their involvement in the activity in the future (Shamir, 1992).

These findings suggest the development of skills is important in identity formation. Learning to ride a bicycle extends one's range of competence and makes other bike riders part of an accessible reference group (Kleiber & Kirshnit, 1991). Iso-Ahola, Graefe and LaVerde (1989) studied participants in risk recreation and sports. Increases in self-esteem as a consequence of participation were found to be linked to increases in perceived competence in these activities. In other words, it is not enough just to do an activity to feel good about yourself, some expression of skill is necessary to create that effect. A study of girls' participation in female adolescents' jazz bands in Scotland demonstrated that such an experience could contribute to identity formation and be socially integrative. It provided a sense of friendship and identification, and an opportunity to practice self-discipline and develop a sense of pride and commitment (Grieves, 1989).

The idea that leisure participation can provide *identity affirmation* is also important. It is based on the idea that people choose to participate in leisure activities partially on the basis of the identity images associated with them. Schlenker (1984) proposed that people are motivated to develop and maintain a consistent and positive self-concept or identity, and consequently, they engage in behavior that allows them to affirm or validate "desired identity images," that is, images they have or would like to have of themselves. Participation in certain types of leisure activities may provide a way of doing this (Haggard & Williams, 1991; Neulinger, 1981). This theory has two components. First, according to this view, different leisure activities embody distinct and measurable *identity images*, that is, people in a particular society share beliefs or stereotypes about the characteristics of people (e.g., physical appearance, personality, attitudes, skills and abilities) who participate in different activities. For example, people may perceive those who rock climb to be competent, strong and adventurous. Second, people may want to be "competent, strong and adventurous" themselves. By participating in activities that embody this set of identity images (that is, by climbing rocks), people are able to *validate or affirm* that they are (or aspire to be) this kind of person. Wearing certain types of clothing and using the "right" equipment can also signify and reinforce one's identification with a particular leisure activity (Kelly, 1983; Mitchell, 1983). This view of identity images is similar to the concept of "sign value" found in the consumer behavior literature (Dimanche, Havitz & Howard, 1991; Dimanche & Samdahl, 1994). People often purchase leisure products and services for their symbolic value, that is, to identify with a social group, to express something about themselves to others or to affirm something meaningful about their personal identity.

As a result of this identification, a person may develop the desired identity and develop a positive self-concept as well. Involvement in these activities may also challenge an individual, and over time lead to the development of new skills and psychological resources so that she or he can "live up" to that new identity. Of course, some leisure pursuits may have identity images that are negative from society's perspective. The identity affirmation that participation in illegal or antisocial activities might encourage, as in the case of the teenager in Scenario 1 described at the beginning of the chapter, is not likely to be seen as a positive outcome or benefit of leisure.

Most of the evidence for identity affirmation through leisure participation is indirect and addresses the first component of the theory—that certain activities have identity images associated with them. In a survey study, Paluba and Neulinger (1976) had their respondents rate golfers, bowlers and tennis players on a variety of personality traits. A distinct personality profile was found to characterize people who participated in each of these activities. Golfers, for example, were perceived to be higher in extroversion and ego organization than bowlers and tennis players. Spreitzer and Snyder (1983) found that the runners, racquetball players and nonparticipants they studied also systematically differed according to the identity images they associated with these activities. Interestingly, highly involved runners and racquetball players felt that their preferred leisure activities said more about what kind of person they were than did the type of job they had.

Haggard and Williams (1992) conducted two studies to test this identity affirmation theory. In the first study they mailed a survey to students registered in eight different university recreation classes (volleyball, weight training, racquetball, backpacking, kayaking, outdoor cooking, folk guitar and chess) and asked them to define the characteristics of people who participate in "their" activity. Distinct images or stereotypes were found for different types of leisure activities (see Table 10.1 for examples) confirming the earlier studies of Paluba and Neulinger (1976), and Sprietzer and Snyder (1983).

Table 10.1 Leisure Identity Images of Participants in Four Leisure Activities

Volleyball Player	**Kayaker**
Athletic	Adventurous
Energetic	Fun loving
Health conscious	Likes scenic beauty
Physically fit	Loves fresh air
Sports minded	Naturalist
Team player	Outdoorsy
Guitarist	**Chess Player**
At peace with themselves	Analytical
Creative	Good problem solver
Introspective	Logical
Intelligent	Math minded
Patient	Quiet
Quiet	Strategic

Adapted from Haggard and Williams (1992)

In the second study, Haggard and Williams (1992) attempted to test the idea that people "desire the identity images associated with their respective leisure activity" and "the leisure activities they select should symbolize identity images that are highly desirable to that individual, representing greater identity affirmation potential" (p. 10). Using different students but ones who regularly participated in one of the four leisure activities examined in Study 1 (those activities shown in Table 10.1), the researchers administered a questionnaire to measure their desire to acquire the different identity images that had been found to be associated with these activities (also in Study 1). They were asked to rate on seven-point Likert scales how important these identity images were to them, that is, to indicate which of the characteristics they most wanted to acquire. No reference was made during the study to the leisure activities in which they were presently active participants. The findings indicated that the students rated as most important those identity images associated with the leisure activities in which they were currently heavily involved. These findings provide some support for the identity affirmation theory of leisure behavior. The greater freedom afforded by leisure likely allows people the flexibility to choose activities with identity images that are consistent with the kind of person they are or would like to be.

Buffer and Coping Theory

Another psychological leisure benefit explanation is based on the idea that leisure indirectly influences health and well-being through its ability to facilitate coping behavior in response to stressful life events and transitions (e.g., Iso-Ahola, 1980a; Kleiber & Kelly, 1980; Kleiber, 1985; Kelly, Steinkamp & Kelly, 1986; Carpenter, 1989; Coleman, 1993; Coleman & Iso-Ahola, 1993). Coleman and Iso-Ahola (1993) have elaborated this theory based on the findings of social psychological research on coping with stressful life events. It differs substantially from the palliative coping version of the "keeping idle hands busy" theory discussed earlier. In the *buffer and coping theory*, well-being and health are more narrowly defined as the absence of physical and/or mental illness. Well-being and health are at risk when people experience negative life events and *life stress*. Various life events, especially negative events such as losing a job and financial debt, have been shown to lead to a higher incidence of mental and physical illness (see Coleman & Iso-Ahola, 1993). Life stress refers to how serious and traumatic people perceive various events to be that occur to them in the course of their lives.

Coleman and Iso-Ahola argue that leisure participation facilitates coping with stressful life events in two ways (see Figure 10.4). First, it has been found that an effective source of relief from life stress is people's perception that social support is available to them. Therefore, leisure that is highly social in nature can facilitate the development of companionship and friendship, and consequently, *social support*. Second, enduring beliefs of *self-determination* have been found to contribute to people's coping capacity and health. When people feel that they generally have some ability to control the good and bad things that happen to them, they experience less mental and physical illness or ill health. The central characteristics of leisure, perceptions of freedom and control, allow the development and maintenance of stable self-determination dispositions, that is, feelings of being in control of one's life. These perceptions of social support and self-determination are described as *buffers* against life stress, and when life stress is high leisure's contribution to health is expected to be greater. The leisure buffer and coping theory postulates that:

> leisure impacts health by providing buffering mechanisms
> that come into play when life presents significant problems.
> On the other hand, when life stress is relatively low leisure's
> contribution to health is expected to be less substantial on
> the short-term basis. In the long run, however, leisure is
> hypothesized to contribute to health by building health-
> promoting dispositions, such as self-determination.
> (Coleman & Iso-Ahola, 1993, p. 113)

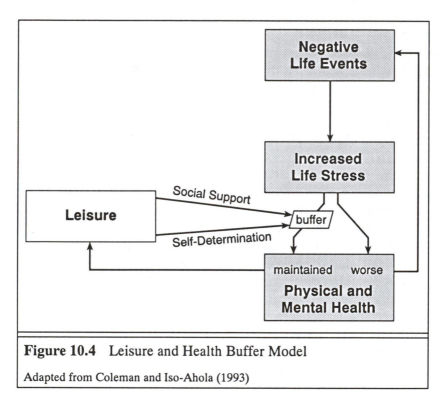

Figure 10.4   Leisure and Health Buffer Model

Adapted from Coleman and Iso-Ahola (1993)

Little research has yet to be conducted that directly tests this theory that people whose leisure fosters feelings of social support and self-deter-mination are able to cope with life stress more effectively. We explained in our earlier discussion on palliative coping that leisure participation has been found to be associated with more effective coping, and the findings of a few studies have been consistent with the buffer and coping theory. Reich and Zautra (1981), in an experimental study, failed to find any benefit to mental health for students who faced lower levels of life stress, but those students under higher levels of stress did benefit from engaging in leisure activities. Wheeler and Frank (1988) found that people whose leisure participation was high or who were satisfied with their leisure were less vulnerable to the adverse effects of life stress than those who were less active and satisfied with their leisure. A similar buffering effect was found by Brown (1991) for exercise and stress, and the buffering effect did not appear to be due solely to the increased physical fitness benefits of physical recreation. Brown speculated that the increased feelings of competency that the exercise provided might have contributed to its buffering effects. Caltabiano (1995) examined the buffering effects of participation in several types of leisure activities and found partial support for the leisure buffer and coping theory, though she did not directly examine whether participation fostered feelings of social support and self-determination. A recent study reported by Coleman (1993) attempted to more directly test the linking mechanisms. He found that among people who experienced higher levels of life stress, those who perceived a high degree of freedom and control in their leisure reported significantly lower levels of illness than those people who perceived low levels of freedom and control (see Figure 10.5). However, he found no evidence that leisure-based social support acted as a buffer. Clearly more research is needed on these and other possible buffering mechanisms.

Activity and Substitution Theory of Aging

As presented in the last chapter, activity theory was developed to explain successful aging in the later years of life. *Activity and substitution theory*, the idea that keeping active will help people adjust successfully to aging, was first put forward by Havighurst and Albrecht (1953). The theory suggests that as people age they should maintain active lifestyles by replacing or substituting lost roles and social activities with new ones in order to maintain their self-concept and a sense of well-being or life satisfaction. Leisure is seen as crucial in allowing the maintenance of this active lifestyle. Recent reviews of the activity theory of aging conclude that there is substantial support for the hypothesis that the more active people are in their later years, the greater will be their subjective well-being (Kelly, Steinkamp & Kelly, 1987; Kelly & Ross, 1989; Steinkemp & Kelly, 1986). As with much of the research on leisure and well-being, the process by which

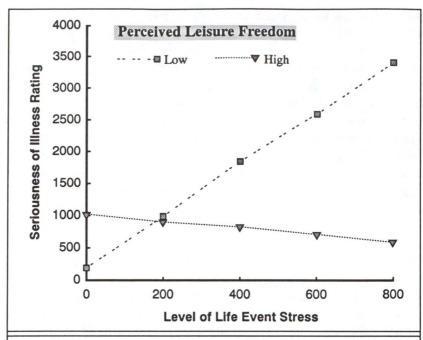

Figure 10.5 Relationship Between Illness and Life Event Stress
for Low and High Levels of Perceived Leisure
Freedom

Adapted from Coleman (1993)

leisure activities contribute to life satisfaction and successful aging has
been left unspecified and has not been examined empirically (Dupuis &
Smale, 1995; Kelly & Ross, 1989). However, if older adults are able to
remain active by continuing to engage in life-long leisure involvements or
by substituting new activities to replace those they have lost, then it is reasonable to believe that the psychological mechanisms that link leisure participation and successful aging include many of those suggested by the
theories we have presented in this chapter.

Progress in Understanding Psychological Leisure Benefits

There is no shortage of ideas about how and why leisure provides psychological benefits. Some of these ideas that we have called *leisure and psychological benefit theories* have been formally discussed in the literature and others, at best, represent groups of "loose" ideas or assumptions that are in need of further development. If you return to the scenarios that opened this chapter, you will find that these theories provide a wide range of "answers" to the questions they raised—often competing answers. In recent years, the *personal growth, identity and coping theories* have been given greater attention. These types of theories can help in understanding the role that leisure may play in personal development, life satisfaction and coping with the difficult times that inevitably come along. However, caution should be adopted in applying these theories because as this chapter has shown, they all need more study and testing.

It should also be clear that there is a substantial amount of overlap among these theories in the types of psychological processes that are described as linking leisure and well-being; more than one of these processes may operate at any time. For example, involvement in a leisure activity may act as a buffer against life stress, and at the same time, provide opportunities for identity affirmation and self-actualization. In fact, it is likely that self-actualized people are better able to deal with life stress.

Finally, it is important to note that the psychological benefits of leisure are not an automatic result of leisure involvements. Some theories suggest that only certain types of activities or experiences are beneficial. Personal growth theories recognize that activities that challenge people and that require effort are more likely to produce self-actualization benefits. Identity theories share this assumption and, in addition, suggest that identity affirmation is more likely to occur when the characteristics of a chosen leisure activity match those personal characteristics that an individual values and either already has or would like to have. Also, leisure participation may only contribute to well-being under some conditions. For example, the influence of leisure participation on the ability to cope is only likely to enhance psychological well-being when people are exposed to stressful life events and not when things are going well.

There is much theorizing and research yet to be done. However, as we have shown, these ideas and theories have stimulated some fascinating leisure research, and work in these areas continues.

The Benefits of Leisure in Other Domains of Life

Outline

Chapter

ELEVEN

Preview

We continue our examination of the psychological benefits and costs of leisure for the individual. Our focus changes, however. We will now consider the effects of leisure on behavior and the quality of experience in other life domains. Can one's leisure enhance and contribute to satisfaction with nonleisure activities and involvements, and changes or transitions in lifestyle? Are there conditions in which the things people do during their leisure have a negative effect on their behavior and experience in areas such as work, family and interpersonal relationships?

We address these questions by first taking a brief look at what is known about the contributions of leisure to *satisfaction with life as a whole.* The discussion then shifts to focus on examples of leisure research on several central life domains and important lifestyle transitions. These include the impact of leisure on behavior and experience in the specific life domains of *paid work* and *family and interpersonal relationships.* Additionally, research on the role of leisure in the normative and nonnormative lifestyle transitions involved in job loss through *retirement* and *unemployment,* respectively, is discussed. Again, as you read this chapter, ask yourself if enough is known about leisure and its benefits to develop a *Consumers' Guide to "Wholesome" Leisure* that could be used to better plan for leisure.

Leisure and the Rest of Life

Leisure as a Life Force

Can the things that people do during their leisure help them enjoy and deal with the challenges and demands that they often face in other areas or domains of their lives? Can leisure contribute to how positively or negatively people feel about their lives as a whole? Read the following scenarios as you think about these questions.

Scenario 1

> Sally and John had spent many years as effective senior administrators in hospitals in different cities. They were both forced to take early retirement during the preceding year. Sally had a large number of leisure interests and was very active in her free time prior to retirement. John had few leisure interests and most of his friends and acquaintances were associates from work.

Will Sally likely be more satisfied with her life in retirement than John? If yes, why? What other types of information would help in making this prediction?

Scenario 2

> Consider Jack and Harry who hold similar positions in the design department of a successful company that is downsizing its work force to remain competitive. However, fear of further job cuts and the increased workloads for those remaining have created a stressful work environment. Of the two, Jack seems to have better maintained his enthusiasm for his work. He appears to be less anxious, has maintained his sense of humor and has taken fewer sick days during the previous year than Harry. He has also created several new product designs that show some commercial promise.

Could Jack's higher job satisfaction be due to his leisure style? What types of leisure interests and involvements might be useful in helping Harry deal with the job-related pressures these men are experiencing?

Scenario 3

> Ron, who is a single father with two children ages 13 and 15
> years old, has taken the children on a two-week family camp-
> ing trip in each of the previous five years. At home they don't
> get to spend much time together because of involvements with
> friends, school and work. Though they seem to have some
> fun on the camping trips, it is becoming more difficult to
> convince the children to leave their friends. Also, the three
> of them seem to argue more during the trip than when they
> are at home.

*Does the "family that plays together, stay together?" Does family leisure
increase the stability and cohesion of the family and enhance satisfaction
with family life or does it detract?*

*   *   *   *   *

There is certainly good reason to believe that people's leisure can contribute to their satisfaction with the "rest of life." As we discussed in the
last chapter, leisure can provide opportunities that foster various forms of
psychological well-being. It seems reasonable, then, to assume that people
with higher levels of psychological well-being may have more personal
resources to deal with, and even enjoy the demands and challenges they
experience in other areas of daily life, whether it be on the job or in the
context of family or other interpersonal relationships. In both the first and
second scenarios, one might expect that Sally would be able to make the
best of forced early retirement and Jack would make the best of an unsettling work environment in the design department, if their identities are just
not based on their work activities but meaningful leisure interests. Regardless of what might happen with respect to their work, they still have opportunities to meet important needs (compensation) and engage in pursuits
that foster positive feelings about themselves. Also, their leisure may act
as a buffer providing them with the psychological resources needed to cope
with the life stress they are currently undergoing.

There are, however, ways in which leisure may contribute to people's
experiences in other life domains that are relatively independent of its influence on psychological well-being. In Jack's case where he is continuing
to work, there may also be additional leisure benefits for his work. It would
be interesting to know if some of his leisure involvements contribute directly to his work performance and job satisfaction, perhaps, by stimulating

creative design ideas. The third scenario suggests that leisure involvements may influence the quality of interaction with other people. Ron, the single father, is concerned that the type of leisure he has planned is having a negative effect on the relationships among his children and himself, and on their sense of being a family—exactly the opposite outcome than the one he intended.

As interesting as these types of leisure benefits and costs are, researchers studying the relationship between the leisure and nonleisure domains of life have frequently treated leisure behavior as the *dependent variable*; that is, as the area of life that is the least constrained, and consequently, most susceptible to the demands of the other domains such as work, school, home, family, and interpersonal relationships and obligations. In other words, researchers often assume that leisure is more likely to be influenced by experiences in other areas of life than it is to influence what goes on in those other domains. For example, in chapter three, we noted that the social role of parent, particularly the working mother substantially reduced the amount of leisure time available to those women who worked and had young children (Zuzanek & Smale, 1992; Shaw, 1985b). The demands and obligations in the work and family domains combined to strongly influence behavior in the leisure domain. Family, work and gender roles have a powerful effect on leisure (e.g., Bella, 1989; Horna, 1989a; Horna & Lupri, 1987). However, it is also important to consider the ways in which leisure participation might positively and negatively influence experiences of work and family. For example, leisure involvements can be a form of resistance against role constraints that may lead to changes in other areas of life—a benefit. This idea of leisure as resistance has been applied primarily to understanding the role that leisure can play in helping women resist and challenge gender stereotypes that limit what is seen as appropriate behavior (Wearing, 1990; Freysinger & Flannery, 1992). For example, participation by women in certain types of physical recreation (Bialeschki, 1990) and highly competitive sports (Kleiber & Kane, 1984; Griffiths, 1988) challenges and hopefully changes dominant views in society about what women can and should do. The phenomenon of leisure as resistance is based on the idea that leisure is a domain of life where people, in this case women, are relatively free to step out of constraining social roles and define and express who they are. The effects of leisure on other areas of life can also be negative. For example, leisure involvements can constrain women and men's behavior in a variety of life domains if they reinforce traditional views of "femininity" and "masculinity" (Shaw, 1994)—a cost.

The Whole of Life: Leisure and Life Satisfaction

When researchers have been interested in the impact of leisure on other domains of life, they have often focused on satisfaction with the whole of life—that is, what is called *life satisfaction*. Life satisfaction is a popular measure of quality of life. People are typically asked to rate their satisfaction with life as a whole or some aspect of it. Satisfaction is seen to have a past "time orientation" and life satisfaction scales measure relatively enduring and stable *beliefs* or *cognitions*. Various measures used, differ in terms of whether they assess global satisfaction or satisfaction with specific domains of life (e.g., work, family, leisure and neighborhood). By examining satisfaction with each of these domains, some researchers believe that a more accurate picture of overall quality of life can be obtained (see Mannell & Dupuis, 1996).

Numerous studies have attempted to establish that a positive relationship exists between what people do during their leisure time and their general feelings of well-being and life satisfaction. In this research, rarely have specific hypotheses about the nature of the links been examined. A general assumption has been that the more leisure activity in which people are involved and/or the higher their satisfaction with what they do in their leisure, the higher the level of satisfaction with life as a whole. In a sense, any or all of the leisure and well-being theories discussed in chapter ten could be responsible for this relationship.

Generally, small but significant relationships have been found between frequency of *leisure participation* and *life satisfaction*. For example, positive relationships have been found for a number of different age groups including adults over the age of 18 years (Herzog & Rodgers, 1981), individuals 55 years and older (Ragheb & Griffith, 1982; Romsa, Bondy & Blenman, 1985), and those aged 65 and over (Ray, 1979; Kelly, Steinkamp & Kelly, 1987; Kelly & Steinkamp, 1987; Brown, Frankel & Fennell, 1991; Ragheb, 1993).

The best support for the link between leisure participation and life satisfaction comes from research on successful aging and life satisfaction. Positive relationships between leisure activity patterns and the life satisfaction of older adults have frequently been found. In fact, some research has suggested that leisure activity levels may be better predictors of life satisfaction than health and income (see Mannell & Dupuis, 1996). Though a few studies have found that social and psychologically involving pursuits such as hobbies, sports and outdoor recreation may be more strongly related to life satisfaction than participation in passive pursuits (e.g., Kelly,

Steinkamp & Kelly, 1987; Ragheb, 1993; Evans & Haworth, 1991), these relationships appear to differ according to gender, age and stage in the life course (e.g., Brown, Frankel & Fennell, 1991).

Additionally, there is growing evidence that the strength of the influence of leisure participation on well-being varies substantially depending not only on age and gender, but on socioeconomic status, ethnicity and race (Brown, Frankel & Fennell, 1991; Brown & Frankel, 1993; Evans & Haworth, 1991; Cutler Riddick & Gonder Stewart, 1994). It is too early to identify any clear patterns. More research is needed to improve our understanding of the meaning of the differences that have been found. This understanding would be aided if researchers would design their studies to examine and test the various social psychological links that have been suggested to exist between leisure and well-being outcomes.

Measures of *leisure satisfaction* have been found to be better predictors of life satisfaction than have leisure participation measures—the higher leisure satisfaction, the higher life satisfaction (e.g., Ragheb & Griffith, 1982; Russell, 1987; Brown, Frankel & Fennell, 1991; Ragheb, 1993). However, the relationship between leisure satisfaction and life satisfaction is moderated by occupation (Willmott, 1971; Trafton & Tinsley, 1980), gender (Allison & Duncan, 1987; Brown & Frankel, 1993), age and ethnicity (Allison, 1991; Allison & Smith, 1990), and marital and employment status (Haavio-Mannila, 1971). In a widely cited study, London, Crandall and Seals (1977) found that job satisfaction and leisure satisfaction contributed independently to the quality of life, and that leisure satisfaction was the better predictor. However, they found the pattern to be more pronounced for some people than others. For example, neither leisure nor work satisfaction was important to the quality of life of relatively disadvantaged groups, and leisure satisfaction was more important for individuals with lifestyles not dominated by work activity. This latter finding was supported by Guinn (1980), who reported that, among retired recreational vehicle tourists, leisure satisfaction was strongly associated with life satisfaction. This latter finding points out an important issue. Regardless of how satisfying people experience their leisure or how frequently they participate, their leisure may not strongly influence life satisfaction if they are at a stage in their lives where leisure is overshadowed in importance by other concerns. On the other hand, there are likely times in people's lives leisure participation and satisfaction are highly salient and important to them.

In summary, evidence has been found that what goes on in the leisure domain can influence how people feel about their lives as a whole. There is also a clear indication that life satisfaction is less dependent on what people do during their leisure (leisure participation) and is influenced more by how people feel about what they do (leisure satisfaction). However, no simple relationship or links have been found. In fact, the picture is quite complex. The leisure–life-satisfaction link has been found to vary as a function of a wide range of social experiences as reflected by differences in age, ethnicity, gender, occupation and social status. Again, research is needed that examines and tests theories about the nature of the links between leisure and life satisfaction.

Leisure and Other Domains of Life

The Domain of Paid Employment: The Case of Job Satisfaction

In an effort to improve worker productivity, reduce absenteeism and labor turnover, social and organizational psychologists have devoted considerable attention to understanding the factors that affect job satisfaction (Argyle, 1990; Steers & Porter, 1991). Unfortunately, though workers' leisure is sometimes assumed to contribute to satisfaction with the job, research has primarily concentrated on how job-related variables affect job satisfaction. In fact, when the relationship between work and leisure has been studied, the leisure domain is typically seen to be dominated by the "long arm of the job" (Meissner, 1971) rather than vice versa. For example, this research has primarily focused on how work influences people's leisure activity preferences (e.g., Bacon, 1975; Banner, 1985; Spreitzer & Snyder, 1987) and how the job affects leisure satisfaction (e.g., Chambers, 1986). The rationale for this research focus is rooted in the assumption that the job dictates activity selection, participation times and the people with whom an individual has frequent contact. On the other hand, leisure which occurs during free time is relatively unconstrained, and consequently, it is free to vary in response to paid work demands and arrangements (Iso-Ahola & Mannell, 1985).

Two theories have dominated thinking regarding the nature of work's influence on leisure (Wilensky, 1960; Kando & Summers, 1971; Parker, 1971). The *spillover* and *compensation* theories suggest that the nature of people's work directly influences their choice of leisure activities. Based on the former theory, workers are thought to participate in leisure activities that have characteristics similar to their job-related activities and tasks. Conversely, compensation theory, which we briefly mentioned in the last chapter, suggests that deprivations experienced at work are made up for during leisure, or that people participate in activities which satisfy needs that they cannot satisfy at work. Research testing these theories has provided findings that are generally contradictory and inconclusive, though there has been more support for spillover than compensation (see Kabanoff, 1980; Iso-Ahola & Mannell, 1985; Staines, 1980; Zuzanek & Mannell, 1983).

In studies of job satisfaction, the influence of job-related factors such as working conditions, pay and promotions, and adequacy of workplace resources have typically been examined (Argyle, 1990; Steers & Porter, 1991). Little attention has been paid to leisure variables. However, a social psychological understanding of job satisfaction could profit from a broader perspective and there have been suggestions that workers' involvement in a variety of activities external to the job can influence satisfaction with paid work (Near, Rice & Hunt, 1978). Leisure may be one such nonwork variable that can contribute to job satisfaction. Though few tests of this proposition have been reported, the belief that leisure has some affect on work has been with us since the beginning of the industrial revolution. Early classical theories of play and recreation (e.g., Patrick, 1916) suggest that leisure is an important element in determining satisfaction at work. The recreation and relaxation theories of play were based on the belief that most work was boring and monotonous and that engagement in play and sports had restorative qualities (see Ellis, 1973). Play and leisure, in this respect, were seen to enhance the quality of work by revitalizing people, so that they would be able to return to the job to work hard day after day.

Ideas like these have provided the rationale for work organizations' to support recreation programs for employees. In partial response to the demands of the labor movement and concern about poor working conditions for employees, work organizations began to provide leisure activities to promote employee loyalty, fellowship, physical and intellectual development, all in an attempt to make the employee work harder for the company (e.g., Toleman, 1909). The emerging recognition that employee health and well-being are important for company success led to the beginning of the wellness movement in the 1970s with the implementation of leisure and wellness programs to help deal with employee psychological and physical health on the job.

Unfortunately, research into the effectiveness of organizational recreation programs is lacking and the research that has been reported is weak (Ellis & Richardson, 1991). Based on the psychological leisure benefit theories discussed in the last chapter, a number of *leisure and job satisfaction hypotheses* could be proposed and tested. Researchers have not attempted to determine if leisure might influence work by providing a buffer against the stresses that occur on the job. This "leisure buffer and coping" hypothesis makes some sense in light of Coleman and Iso-Ahola's (1993) recent theorizing. Also, Kelly (1983) and Shamir (1988) have suggested that when work-setting rules and expectations impede the satisfaction of important needs, leisure can provide opportunities for people to more readily meet these needs and affirm who they are. In other words, it could be postulated that leisure provides the opportunity to "compensate for psychological needs" not met by work, help workers achieve a better balance in their lives, and consequently feel better about their work.

This is not to suggest that compensation will occur automatically. If it did, all workers should have high levels of psychological well-being and job satisfaction. Constraints, such as a lack of skill or time, may prevent people from engaging in the appropriate leisure activities to achieve compensation. Though the research evidence for compensation is rather weak and there is greater evidence for spillover (Zuzanek & Mannell, 1983), some empirical evidence suggests that people at least perceive that their leisure can compensate for needs not met on the job. For example, Lounsbury and Hoopes (1985) found that one of the main reasons the workers they studied gave for taking vacations was to escape the routines of work.

Some evidence has been found to suggest that enhanced job satisfaction may, in fact, be a benefit of leisure. The more satisfied workers (265 support staff at a university in the United States) were with the amount of leisure time they had available, the less likely they were to leave their jobs and search for another one (Loundbury, Gordon, Bergermaier & Francesco, 1982). The reason for this link was not examined. In a study of Israeli female elementary school teachers (Meir & Melamed, 1986) and engineers, physicians and lawyers (Melamed, Meir & Samson 1995), researchers looked at the degree of correspondence between the workers' personality-based needs and the opportunities available to satisfy these needs in both their work and their leisure. They found that the opportunity to meet important needs in both work and leisure contributed to job satisfaction. In fact, when participants were unable to meet their needs at work, engaging in leisure appeared to *compensate* these unmet needs and contribute to job satisfaction. However, in a second study of teachers (Meir, Melamed & Abu-Freha, 1990), no support for the leisure involvement-job satisfaction relationship was found.

Recently, Kirchmeyer (1993) studied a sample of 221 experienced managers and assessed their perceptions of the impact of their nonwork involvements on their work. Both the men and women in her study perceived nonwork involvements, including what they did during their leisure, as supporting and enhancing the quality of their work experiences. Hildebrand and Mannell (1996) found that the 103 school teachers they studied perceived that their leisure contributed to their job satisfaction by providing for relaxation, relieving stress, recharging, providing a positive frame of mind, maintaining self-esteem, and influencing teaching ideas. They also found that a greater frequency of participation in leisure activities by the teachers was associated with higher levels of need satisfaction in leisure, and higher levels of leisure satisfaction contributed to higher levels of job satisfaction.

Surprisingly, one type of leisure influence on satisfaction with work that has been neglected is that of vacations (Lounsbury & Hoopes, 1986). Paid vacations are the subject of organizational policies, and are considered to be very important benefits by workers and unions. Generally, vacations are viewed as a time for such positive outcomes as escape, tension release, personal improvements and an expanded opportunity to engage in satisfying activities which should increase life satisfaction and have carryover effects into the job setting (Klausner, 1968; Rubenstein, 1980a, 1980b). Klausner (1968) surveyed 361 steel workers and found that 25 percent of the respondents felt that their "work efficiency" had increased and 16 percent felt that their jobs were "more interesting" after their vacations.

In a study that directly examined the impact of taking a vacation on job satisfaction, Lounsbury and Hoopes (1986) measured the job satisfaction of 128 working men and women in a number of occupations from a variety of work organizations. The researchers measured job satisfaction one week before and one week after a vacation. The influence of taking the vacation on job satisfaction differed depending on how satisfying the vacation was judged to be by the individual worker. For those workers who experienced their vacations as highly satisfying, their level of job satisfaction was higher after their vacations than before (see Figure 11.1, p. 314). Job satisfaction actually decreased for those workers who experienced their vacations as less satisfactory. Once again this study reinforces the need for researchers to study the social psychological links between leisure involvements and outcomes to better understand the conditions under which leisure can produce benefits.

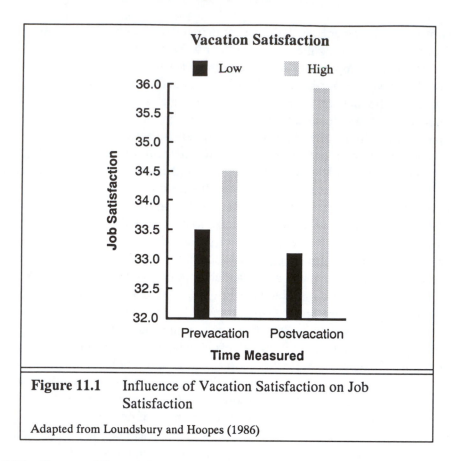

Figure 11.1   Influence of Vacation Satisfaction on Job
Satisfaction

Adapted from Loundsbury and Hoopes (1986)

Life Course Transitions:
Job Loss Through Retirement and Unemployment

In chapter nine, we examined how leisure changes across the life course.
A number of the *transitions* (normative and nonnormative) that are commonly experienced by most people were identified (e.g., departure from the
family home, birth of a first child, retirement). As we described, on the
one hand, leisure participation often changes as a result of these life events,
and on the other, the right type of leisure may help people maintain their
well-being and cope or grow with these transitions. In this section, we will
look closely at the potential benefits of leisure in assisting with lifestyle
transitions involving job loss, in particular, retirement and unemployment.

    The loss of a job whether through retirement or unemployment can
involve the same types of problems—loss of income, social isolation (e.g.,
contact with friends and coworkers) and psychological losses (e.g., feelings

of contributing to society, opportunity to develop and exercise skills and abilities). Of course, loss of a job and the resulting unemployment before the age of retirement is likely to be a more traumatic change due to the lack of a "retirement" income, lack of opportunity to plan for the change and the social stigma associated with it. Retirement is socially accepted today and is usually seen as a reward after many years of work. Many factors have been proposed to affect successful coping with both retirement and unemployment. Leisure is one of these factors and its impact on psychological well-being when people are dealing with job loss has been of interest to researchers.

The study of reactions to *retirement* has generated a large body of literature (see McPherson, 1983, 1991; Calasanti, 1993; Theriault, 1994). Much of this work has been based on the assumption that being retired is a traumatic event, and that many elderly people, particularly men, do not adjust well. Recently, researchers have begun to show more interest in gender differences (e.g., Dorfman, Heckert & Hill, 1988; Szinovacz & Washo, 1992) and the problems of the synchronization of retirement for couples (e.g., Henretta, Orand & Chan, 1993). The retirement literature has been further expanded by the long-standing interest of researchers, as we have noted, in accounting for the life satisfaction and well-being of older adults (Larson, 1978; Reis & Gold, 1993; Madden, Pierce & Allen, 1993, Mannell & Dupuis, 1996).

The onset of retirement represents a major transition point that has the potential to alter lifestyle. However, accumulated evidence shows that a large portion of retired men have few problems in adjusting to retirement, though there is still substantial variation in the degree of adjustment and the subsequent quality of life experienced (see McPherson, 1983; Jensenscott, 1993). Research suggests that the retirement transition is less traumatic and more satisfying among people with higher perceived levels of health and economic status; who have harmonious marriages and social support from their spouses and families. Consistent with activity and continuity theories, research has also shown that those people who use their free time to continue to participate in similar types of social activity at about the same level as they did prior to retirement, and who have positive attitudes toward leisure, adjust better and are more satisfied with their lives (e.g., Goudy & Meyers, 1985; Long, 1987; Russell, 1987).

However, consistent with the personal growth theories of leisure, it has been argued that some types of activity and involvement are better than others. Stebbins (1992a) suggests that serious leisure can be important to the quality of older retired adults' lives by providing work-like activity, offering a link with former work associates, current friends and relatives, expanding one's social circle, fostering responsibility, and creating the opportunity to feel needed by other people (p. 127).

A recent study reported by Chiriboga and Pierce (1993) demonstrates how leisure behavior may play a role in successful retirement and psychological well-being. They examined 44 older adults who were part of a larger longitudinal life span study and who had retired at least five years before the end of the study. The respondents' participation in solitary activities, sports, social activities and contemplative activities was measured early in retirement and about five years later. Measures of the stressful life events they had experienced during the previous year, psychological distress symptoms, happiness and self-reported health were also collected.

Participation levels in the various leisure activities were not related to self-concept at or soon after retirement. After five years, however, the situation had changed. Activity involvement was significantly related to self-concept. Specifically, those retired individuals who were more positive about themselves were also more likely to be engaged in outdoor and social activities, and tended to participate less in contemplative activities which were characterized as solitary and passive.

Recently there has been increased attention given to the role that leisure can play in helping people contend with unplanned and unwanted *job loss* and *unemployment* (e.g., Pesavento Raymond, 1984; Pesavento Raymond & Kelly, 1991; Reid & Smit, 1986; Spigner & Havitz, 1992–93). As suggested earlier, unemployment prior to planned retirement would appear to be a much more traumatic event with even greater negative impact on psychological well-being than retirement. A number of theories have been proposed to explain the significance of employment and unemployment, and why unemployment would be expected to result in threats to psychological well-being. Based on a review of the research, Warr (1983) identified nine potentially negative features of unemployment—financial anxiety, less variety in life due to reduced income and more time spent at home, fewer goals or aims in life, reduced opportunity for making important decisions, reduced opportunities to exercise skills or expertise, increase in psychologically threatening activities such as unsuccessful job searches, insecurity about the future, fewer social contacts, and reduced social status.

However, in spite of all these potentially negative consequences of unemployment, not all unemployed people report being worse off in terms of psychological health. In a study of nearly 1,000 unemployed men, Warr and Jackson (1984) found that although 20 percent reported a decline in health, eight percent actually reported an improvement. Consequently, researchers have been interested in discovering the possible moderating factors that may explain the considerable individual variation in response to unemployment. In a review of the literature, Winefield, Tiggemann, Winefield & Goldney (1993) found important factors to include attitudes toward paid employment (the more positive, the more psychological distress experienced), age (middle-aged men compared to younger and older men experienced more stress because of greater family responsibilities), length of unemployment (decline in psychological health particularly in middle-aged men during the first few months before it stabilizes), availability of social support (more support, less stress), local unemployment levels (higher levels, less stress because people are more likely to see their unemployment as due to economic and social conditions beyond their control rather than as a failing on their part), and *access to constructive and stimulating leisure activity.*

Researchers have found that though leisure participation and satisfaction often decrease with unemployment (e.g., Pesavento Raymond, 1984; Pesavento Raymond & Kelly, 1991; Reid & Smit, 1986), the way in which unemployed people use their free time and leisure can reduce the negative effects to some extent. In a study of unemployed university graduates, Feather and Bond (1983) found that the structured and purposeful use of free time was positively correlated with self-esteem and negatively correlated with depressive symptoms. Other studies have also shown that unemployed people who cope best are engaged in purposeful activity and maintain regular contact with people outside the nuclear family (McKenna & Fryer, 1984; Warr & Jackson, 1985). Much of this "purposeful" activity is what Stebbins would call serious leisure.

Haworth and Ducker (1991) found that young unemployed adults who were engaged in more work-like and active leisure pursuits also had higher levels of psychological well-being. In a study of 228 unemployed African-American and Hispanic youth in the United States, Pesavento Raymond and Kelly (1991) concluded that leisure appeared to help reduce the negative effects of unemployment. Kilpatrick and Trew (1985) showed that mental health in a group of 121 unemployed men was affected by how they spent their "free" time. They identified four groups among the people they studied. The *passive* group spent most of their time watching television or doing nothing. They showed the poorest psychological well-being. The *domestic* group also spent most of their time at home, but unlike the first, assisted with household tasks. They showed only slightly better mental health than the first group. A third *social* group spent much of their time with people outside their immediate family. They exhibited superior mental health to the first two groups. Finally, a fourth group, the *active* group, not only spent more time on work-related activities, but also engaged more frequently in active leisure pursuits outside the home. They were psychologically affected least by unemployment.

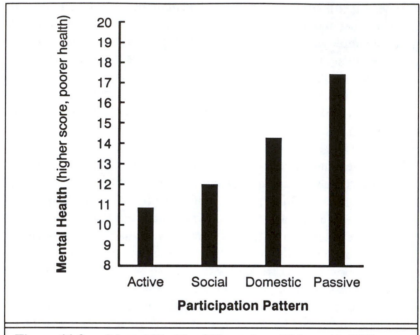

Figure 11.2   Mental Health of Unemployed Men with Different Participation Patterns

Adapted from Kilpatrick and Trew (1985)

Active involvement in leisure did not completely prevent the unemployed participants in a British study reported by Roberts, Lamb, Dench and Brodie (1989) from experiencing some health problems. However, among people who were unemployed, those who participated frequently in a wide range of leisure activities were physically healthier (measured as optimal weight, number of visits to a doctor, use of prescribed drugs, quality of sleep, self-assessed health and fitness).

Winefield, Tiggemann, Winefield and Goldney (1993) have recently reported the results of a longitudinal study of employment among a group of young people in Australia. Not only did they study people who were unemployed, but they also followed employed individuals who differed in how satisfying they found their jobs. They assessed the study participants' psychological well-being by measuring their self-esteem, level of depression, moods and leisure activity levels at various points in time—for the unemployed young adults this meant early in the period of their unemployment and approximately four years later. The main factors that were found to moderate the affects of unemployment were age, length of unemployment, financial security, social support and *leisure*. Interestingly, the dissatisfied employed group was more similar to the unemployed group than they were to the satisfied employed group. With respect to leisure, unemployed people whose leisure was characterized as "doing nothing" and "watching television" developed lower self-esteem during the period of unemployment. Those who were engaged in more challenging activities, both social (e.g., sport, dancing) and solitary (e.g., hobbies, reading, cooking) had higher levels of self-esteem. These relationships became much stronger as time went on and were also found among those people who were employed but unhappy with their jobs.

The Domain of Close Interpersonal Relationships: Family, Friends and Significant Others

Leisure has been described as "the central social space for the development and expression of primary relationships" (Kelly, 1993, p. 6). The family is a focal point for many of these important interpersonal relationships. Some types of leisure are generally assumed to have positive outcomes for families. Studies by Kelly (1983) and Horna (1989b) suggest that parents see family leisure activities as more important than they do their own individual activities. In a review of the literature, Orthner and Mancini (1991) found that research studies have been relatively consistent in demonstrating the positive impact of shared leisure experiences on the quality of family relationships. However, this positive view of family leisure has recently been challenged (Shaw, 1992). Family leisure may lead to conflict and some family members may feel obligated to participate (Orthner, 1985; Shaw, 1992).

The benefits for families claimed for leisure can be divided into three major types: family stability, family interaction, and family satisfaction (Orthner & Mancini, 1991, p. 290). The idea of *family stability* is reflected in the common phrase used to promote family recreation, *"The family that plays together stays together."* Stability implies a continuity of interpersonal relationships in the family and a reduction in the probabilities of marital separation and divorce. Few studies have directly examined the leisure and family stability hypothesis. However, in a recent study, Hill (1988) directly tested the relationship suggested by this hypothesis. Using the United States 1975–1981 Time Use Longitudinal Panel Study, she found that the more shared leisure reported by married couples at the beginning of the study, the greater was their marital satisfaction and stability over the next five years, even when controlling for the presence and age of children in the household.

Family interaction refers to communication, conflict, and the distribution of household tasks and roles among family members (Orthner & Mancini, 1991). A few studies have supported the hypothesis that family leisure can enhance communication, reduce conflict, and lead to greater equity in the distribution of household tasks and roles (e.g., Orthner, 1976). Several studies have found that leisure participation can increase conflict between family members (e.g., Strauss, Gelles & Steinmetz, 1980; see Orthner & Mancini, 1991). The more frequently couples did things together, the more likely they were to communicate and as part of that communication, to argue. However, verbal disagreements have been viewed as indicators of strategies being used for reducing family tension and disagreements (Orthner & Mancini, 1980).

Most of the research that has focused on family leisure behavior has examined its consequences for *family satisfaction*, and most often, *marital satisfaction*. The consistent finding is that husbands and wives who share leisure time together in joint activities tend to be much more satisfied with their marriages than those who do not (see Orthner & Mancini, 1980, 1991; Holman & Epperson, 1984). Another consistent finding is the negative impact on marital satisfaction of frequent independent, individual activities by family members. If there are too many "girls' or boys' nights out," marital satisfaction appears to be lower. This pattern seems to be stronger for women than men, suggesting that women may be more likely to interpret the time spent in individual activities without their spouse as a lack of concern about the relationship by their marital partner. Parallel leisure activity (Orthner, 1975), which involves sharing time but without substantial amounts of interaction (e.g., watching television, going to the movies), was found to have a moderate impact on the marital satisfaction of husbands and wives. More recently, Holman and Jacquart (1988) found that parallel activities were actually negatively associated with marital satisfaction for both husbands and wives. They concluded that leisure activities that involve little or no communication provide little benefit to families and may actually harm relationships.

Though there is some research that suggests that joint wife-husband leisure activities do lead to greater marital stability (e.g., Orthner, 1975; Hill, 1988), there is a lack of research on the outcomes of family leisure when *children* are also involved (Shaw, 1992). The influence of gender relations on family leisure has also been largely ignored (Bella, 1992). The greater responsibility of mothers for family leisure identified by some authors (e.g., Bella, 1992; Hunter & Whitson, 1991) may interfere with the ability of family leisure to foster more positive experiences of family life and relationships among women (Shaw, 1992).

Freysinger (1994) found that satisfaction with being a parent was best predicted by marital satisfaction and frequency of leisure with children. However, the relationship between leisure with children and parental satisfaction was only significant for the men in her study. Mannell and Zuzanek (1995) found that family leisure was experienced as the most satisfying type of activity during the course of daily life by both the female and male parents in their study. However, joint participation by family members in social and active leisure activities were related to satisfaction with family life only for the men in the study. Active leisure activities such as sports, games and hobbies were particularly important. Men participated in twice as many of these types of family activities as women. These gender differences provide some support for the suggestion that gender-role differences may result in leisure having different meanings for women and men. The heavier responsibilities for planning and managing family leisure experienced by women may prohibit them from experiencing the benefits in spite of the fact that they enjoy it as much as men at the time of occurrence. For men, family leisure may be the primary context for establishing and maintaining family relationships, whereas women, particularly because of their heavier role in childcare, may be less reliant on family leisure for this. They may develop family relationships in all types of family contexts.

There has been little research or discussion about leisure and its impact on *friendships and intimate relationships.* However, a few researchers have explored the impact of disability on leisure and friendships (Lyons, 1985; Lyons, Sullivan & Ritvo, 1995). Also, as already discussed, marital satisfaction in the context of family leisure has received a great deal of attention. Leisure is a major social space for the development and maintenance of relationships (Kelly, 1983, 1993). The need and desire for social interaction is also a powerful motive for a great deal of leisure behavior (Crandall, Nolan & Morgan, 1980; Iso-Ahola, 1980a). There is some evidence that certain kinds of leisure can spice up or enhance both friendships and marital relationships by making the social interaction more exciting and enjoyable (Larson, Mannell & Zuzanek, 1986), as well as by contributing to the participants' personal growth through the enhancement of their social relationships (Reissman, Aron & Bergen, 1993).

In a study using the experience sampling method, Larson, Mannell and Zuzanek (1986) examined the influence of leisure on the quality of interpersonal relationships with friends and family members in leisure and non-leisure settings. When the quality of the respondents' experiences in these relationships was examined, it was found that interactions with a spouse were experienced as the least positive and exciting; interactions with friends were experienced as much more positive and exciting.

However, before one gets too cynical about long-term intimate relationships, it should be noted that the researchers found that the most positive and exciting experiences occurred when individuals were interacting with friends *plus* their spouse (see Figure 11.3). Further analysis suggested that the power of friends to generate positive feelings and excitement was tied to the more frequent participation in active leisure pursuits that typically occurred when with them. Most interaction with family members, particularly spouses, was done in the context of maintenance and passive leisure activities—housework and watching television. In contrast, when the people in the study were with friends, or friends and spouses, socializing was engaged in more than a third of the time, and active pursuits, such as religious and cultural activities, hobbies and sport were more frequent. Watching television and doing housework were well down the list in frequency.

Surveys of married couples suggest that spending time together is considered to be an important relationship maintenance strategy by couples themselves (Dindia & Baxter, 1987; Baxter & Dindia, 1990). Consequently, some marital therapists have encouraged couples experiencing marital problems to spend more time together as an intervention strategy (e.g., Stuart, 1980). However, it is not likely that simply spending more time with a spouse or partner will enhance satisfaction with the relationship. As previously noted, participation in joint activities, that is, activities that require reciprocal interaction that are enjoyable and exciting, may be a further requirement. Aron and Aron (1986) have developed a theory which is based on this idea. They propose that if leisure time spent together is to enhance marital satisfaction, the partners need to engage in joint activities which are "expanding," that is, activities which are exciting and stimulating because they provide new experiences. This notion of "expansion" assumes that people are motivated to expand and grow as we described in the discussion of personal growth theories. The theory further suggests that one

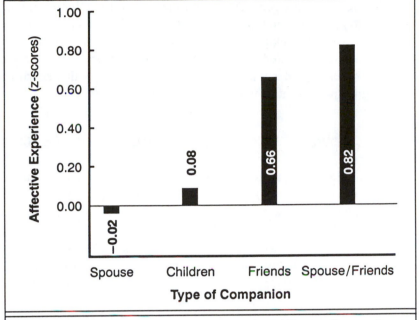

Figure 11.3   Affective Experiences with Different Companions

Adapted from Larson, Mannell and Zuzanek (1986)

way in which people seek to expand or grow is through social relationships, since interacting with other people can open up new perspectives and opportunities for people to learn about themselves. Aron and Aron (1986) go on to theorize that this opportunity is enhanced with participation in new and exciting activities.

Consequently, some shared activities with a long-term partner might even intensify boredom with the partner by forcing the individual to spend time with her or him in ways that do not expand the self. Reissman, Aron and Bergen (1993) carried out a field experiment to determine if spending time with one's partner was a good strategy for maintaining a marital relationship, and if leisure activities that provided opportunities for "expansion" were critical to this process.

Fifty-three married couples were randomly assigned to one of three study groups and each couple was asked to engage in leisure activities together for 1.5 hours each week for 10-weeks. One group was asked to choose what they thought were "*exciting*" activities. The second group were asked to choose "*pleasant*" activities and the third *control* group were given no special instructions other than to make sure that they spent an additional

1.5 hours together each week. The couples recorded the activities in which they chose to participate together. Marital satisfaction was measured before and after the 10-week period. Only the group that engaged in "exciting" activities demonstrated a significant increase in marital satisfaction over the 10-week period, supporting *self-expansion theory* that sharing stimulating leisure activities will enhance marital satisfaction.

A Consumer's Guide to "Wholesome" Leisure

At the beginning of chapter ten, we suggested that as you read about the research on the social psychological benefits of leisure, you think about whether or not enough is known about these benefits to develop a *Consumers' Guide to Wholesome Leisure*. The need for a consumers' guide suggests that, when it comes to leisure, people can make choices and get involved in activities that will have good or bad outcomes for them. The development of a consumers' guide also assumes that guidelines can be developed to help people make these better choices. Were you surprised about how much or how little is known; how many or how few of the claims made for leisure can be supported with research evidence? Is enough known to develop such a guide?

Clearly, there is evidence that what people do in their leisure *can* have a significant impact on a wide range of psychological outcomes that most of us would see as beneficial. However, the operative word is "can." Leisure is not automatically beneficial. The nature of people's leisure behavior and experience; the skills, attitudes and needs people possess; and the social circumstances of their lives—not only leisure contexts but interaction with family, interpersonal and work contexts—all interact to affect whether their leisure is a benefit or a cost. Researchers have found evidence that the right kind of leisure can make people feel better temporarily during the present moment, facilitate long-term personal growth, affirm their identities, provide a buffer against stress, enhance their satisfaction with their work and personal relationships, and support their efforts to deal with transitions in their lives. However, researchers also saw that leisure may have no affect or in some cases negative affects on a person's well-being and satisfaction with different domains of her or his life.

If this chapter and the previous one have created the impression that the psychological benefits of leisure are thoroughly studied and well-documented, it should be noted that in all but a few of the areas we examined, the research is very limited. Also, theories of leisure–and–well-being links need to be more fully developed and tested. The research examined, however, does suggest that it is possible to explore and study leisure and psychological well-being. Many interesting research questions were encountered in our review and there are many opportunities for researchers to improve existing theories and develop new ones. Perhaps some of you will eventually become involved in this enterprise. It would seem that the development of a *Consumers' Guide to Wholesome Leisure* may be a bit premature, but if current research trends continue, researchers will have a great deal more to say on this topic in the near future.

Negotiating Leisure Constraint and Creating Leisure Affordance

Outline

Chapter TWELVE

Preview

Practitioners and volunteers active in providing leisure services have a long tradition of making a difference in the quality of people's lives. Leisure studies is largely an *applied field* that has evolved to provide knowledge for the development of effective leisure services. Consequently, in this final chapter, we bring the discussion of the social psychology of leisure to a close by highlighting its potential for application. Of particular interest is how knowledge based on the social psychology of leisure can be used to help people lead more satisfying and involving leisure styles. In this book we have attempted to demonstrate that the social psychology of leisure can help people with this applied enterprise by contributing to a better understanding of leisure behavior and experience. By becoming more sensitive to the *person* and *social situational* factors that influence leisure and its costs and benefits, people are better able to assert positive control over their own leisure and help others realize the benefits of leisure. First, we will examine theory and research efforts that have specifically focused on identifying the *barriers* and *constraints* that prevent or inhibit people from fully participating in and benefiting from leisure, as well as the strategies that they use to overcome these. These ideas provide a framework for those people who are interested in ameliorating these constraining conditions and creating leisure *affordance*, that is, conditions that foster satisfying and rewarding leisure. Second, examples of social psychological theories and leisure research findings encountered throughout the book will be identified that can be applied in the design of services and interventions for working with individuals to enhance their involvement in satisfying leisure.

The Nature of Leisure Constraints

Bill Markowitz was an avid snow skier and amateur nature photographer. One sunny summer day, he dove off a rock ledge just outside a designated swimming area. His dive was interrupted by a rock that was hidden just below the surface of the water and, though he lived, he ended up paralyzed from the waist down. Initially, he felt as if his life as an independent person was over and that he would no longer be able to tend to his own basic needs, let alone engage in his favorite leisure activities—activities that were an important part of his identity. Even after he learned to master his wheelchair, there was still the awareness of having to survive an inhospitable environment with few ramps, inadequate bathroom facilities, and doors too difficult to open. But Bill learned that new technologies were available to him to enhance his mobility; a return to the ski slopes might even be part of the foreseeable future. With time and effort, he came to regard the wheelchair itself differently—as specialized equipment necessary for participating in a new and challenging leisure pursuit—wheelchair basketball. One of the more difficult barriers to overcome, however, was the way others continued to regard him as helpless and dependent. Though he gained a large measure of respect from some people for his renewed investment in a challenging leisure activity, the attitudes of many of the other people he encountered made normal human interaction and casual socializing at times awkward. These people seemed to regard him as an object, with the stigma of being a "victim," and not as a unique person.

* * * * *

Bill's case demonstrates the *constraints* of physical limitations (paralysis), environmental limitations (lack of accessibility) and social limitations (the attitudes of others) to leisure participation and enjoyment. But conversely, technology (a wheelchair), education (e.g., learning the skills and knowledge required to use the wheelchair, media campaigns designed to change other people's attitudes about disability) and institutional change (e.g., laws requiring buildings be designed and built to be more accessible) can be *affordances* that provide new opportunities that allow constraints to be managed, reduced or eliminated. It should be clear from this scenario, however, that the process of both understanding and responding to such circumstances can be exceedingly complex. Even when people face less serious problems, sensitivity to the social psychological factors operating are important in maintaining or enhancing active and satisfying leisure styles.

For many people, leisure seems either unavailable or unfulfilling. Sometimes the "problem" of getting involved or participating is "out there." All the tennis courts are being used for instruction, or the concert costs 30 dollars and you're on a budget. At other times, the problem lies within oneself; feeling uncomfortable because you can't sing as well as others or seeing nobody your own age at a party can inhibit getting involved or enjoyment. The first type of problem is generally regarded as an *external constraint* while the latter type is an *internal constraint*. But the line between them is sometimes fuzzy. The apparent external constraint of a 30 dollar concert ticket cost may be the result of a previous decision to spend the money on another leisure activity which may reflect an internal constraint (i.e., lack of interest in the concert relative to other possible leisure involvements). The older people at the party may have shown by their body language that younger people were not welcome thus creating an external constraint that contributes to the internal constraint of discomfort. Nevertheless, leisure researchers have found it useful to classify constraints into broad categories for purposes of understanding and application.

History of the Idea of Constraints

Interest in the subject of constraints in leisure studies emerged initially from a national study of outdoor recreation done in the United States in the early 1960s by the Outdoor Recreation Resources Review Commission (ORRRC). This group was concerned primarily with the factors that influenced the demand for recreation activities, and its questions focused almost exclusively on external barriers to participation such as the proximity of parks and services and whether respondents had the time and money to pay for activities. In the 1970s and 80s, research on the subject became more sophisticated and it was recognized that social psychological factors are also important (e.g., Wade, 1985). It was acknowledged that there are many types of participants and nonparticipants who are constrained in different ways by a variety of circumstances. For example, Figure 12.1 shows the many different types of people in whom constraints researchers have taken an interest. Though *participants* are typically given the most attention by leisure practitioners and researchers, it is clear that there are different types of *nonparticipants* about whom they need to know if they are to understand the leisure constraints that keep people from getting involved.

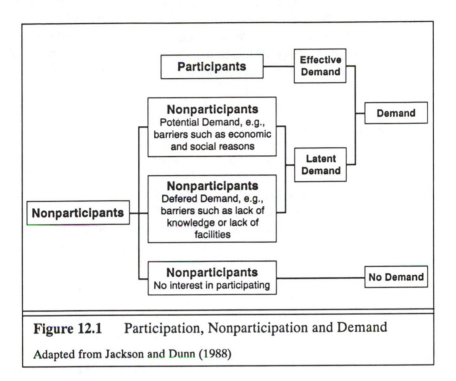

Figure 12.1   Participation, Nonparticipation and Demand

Adapted from Jackson and Dunn (1988)

In some cases people want to increase their frequency and/or intensity of participation but cannot; others have completely stopped or reduced their participation; and still others participate but cannot achieve the level of satisfaction they desire (Jackson & Searle, 1985). A distinction is sometimes made between conditions that are *barriers*, which presuppose that people have an interest in participating (e.g., sailing) but are blocked from doing so (e.g., lack of financial resources, living too far from a large body of water), and those that are *constraints* which may act to limit interest in the activity itself (e.g., a fear of water may suppress any interest in sailing). Constraint is the more frequently used term and is more inclusive since it refers to psychological factors within the individual as well as factors in the external social and physical environment.

Ideas similar to those of constraints and barriers have also been found useful in other human service areas where practitioners are concerned with the lack of participation in behavior that may contribute to health and well-being. For example, in the area of health promotion, the health belief model (see Kaplin, Sallis & Patterson, 1993) has been developed to explain the factors that inhibit preventive health behaviors such as check-ups and immunizations, sick-role behavior, adherence to medical regimens and avoidance of high-risk health behavior such as smoking. In the exercise promotion area, nonadherence models (see Dishman, 1988, 1994) use the concept of barriers to explain why people do not begin or sometimes drop out of exercise programs.

Models and Types of Leisure Constraints

Three major types of constraints have been identified by leisure researchers: intrapersonal, interpersonal, and structural (see Crawford & Godbey, 1987; Crawford, Jackson & Godbey, 1991). *Intrapersonal constraints* refer to those psychological conditions that arise internal to the individual such as personality factors, attitudes, or more temporary psychological states such as moods. For example, Bill, the person in the opening scenario, may have initially been quite depressed by his accident and have had little interest in any type of leisure involvement, or perhaps he had always had a negative attitude toward team sports which would constrain his interest in wheelchair basketball. For someone else, being a Type-A person might make having a relaxing and enjoyable vacation difficult (see chapter six). *Interpersonal constraints* are those that arise out of interaction with others such as family members, friends, coworkers and neighbors (e.g., having to keep the volume of your favorite music low to avoid disturbing members of your family). In Bill's case, he may feel he lacks friends with whom to share new leisure interests that are more suited to his changed circumstances. *Structural constraints* include such factors as the lack of opportunities or the cost of activities that result from external conditions in the environment. Sailing is impossible if there is no wind. Attending an expensive major sporting event is unlikely for an inner-city teenager whose only income is provided by his single mother who works part-time. Bill's disability, itself, could be considered a structural constraint, or the lack of accessible pathways in a local bird sanctuary would be a structural constraint to his desire to continue his involvement in nature photography.

Intrapersonal and interpersonal constraints are of particular interest in this chapter. Structural constraints, such as unequal access to opportunities for people who are impoverished or physical barriers that limit accessibility for those with physical disabilities, demand social action to create environments that provide better opportunities. Overcoming or removing structural constraints requires socially and politically based analysis and action more than it does a social psychological approach with its focus on the individual. However, it is important to remember that when people continuously encounter physical, social, and cultural restrictions on their behavior, such as those experienced by Bill as described in the scenario, these structural constraints can eventually be internalized to become intrapersonal constraints. People begin to believe it is they who are "limited" and not the environment (e.g., Hutchison & McGill, 1992; McGuire, 1985; Pedlar, Gilbert & Gove, 1994).

Some of those constraints normally regarded as intrapersonal are also outside the purview of this chapter. Trait-like personality characteristics, such as extroversion, which were discussed in chapter six are largely resistant to change and intervention. However, intrapersonal constraints like learned attitudes, such as negative feelings toward leisure in general or specific leisure activities, can be influenced and changed. Low perceived competence and learned helplessness are also intrapersonal constraints that are amenable to intervention, and as we have described in earlier chapters, they have been the focus of a considerable amount of research. Nevertheless, even in the case of relatively permanent limiting characteristics, be they physical limitations or personality characteristics, an enlightened approach to intervention would take these factors into account. For example, even if people's personalities cannot be changed, they can be counseled and advised about the types of leisure settings and activities that might best enhance the quality of their leisure experiences.

The relationship between intrapersonal, interpersonal, and structural constraints has been the subject of some analysis. The *hierarchical constraints model* developed by Crawford, Jackson and Godbey (1991) is summarized in Figure 12.2 (p. 334). The model suggests that one's experience of leisure constraints is a linear and sequential process. Accordingly, to understand why Bill does not participate in a particular leisure activity (e.g., why he may not continue to engage in nature photography), first look for intrapersonal constraints; if these constraints (e.g., his belief that he now lacks the competence to pursue the activity) suppress an interest or preference for the activity, there is no need to look much further, since other types of constraints are irrelevant to understanding his nonparticipation. In other words, those people with intrapersonal constraints such as negative attitudes toward a leisure activity or low expectations for their ability to successfully participate (i.e., self-efficacy) are unlikely to have a preference for the activity or a desire to participate. If an interest in participating is present, however, participation and enjoyment may be prevented by the lack of appropriate partners or coparticipants, that is, by interpersonal constraints. Finally, if intrapersonal and interpersonal constraints are not operating, structural constraints such as a lack of time, money, or activity accessibility will determine participation.

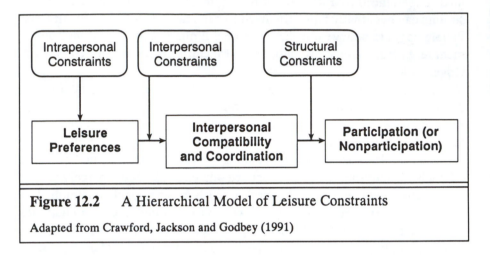

Figure 12.2   A Hierarchical Model of Leisure Constraints

Adapted from Crawford, Jackson and Godbey (1991)

However, it seems that this order, or sequence, of constraints only applies in the most general sense (see also Henderson & Bialeschki, 1993). In reality, the different types of constraints often act simultaneously and they likely influence each other in a reciprocal manner. For example, the reoccurring difficulty of finding someone with whom to share a leisure activity (i.e., interpersonal constraint) or the social expectation that people in wheelchairs do not engage in nature photography (i.e., structural constraint) may act to create negative attitudes toward these activities (i.e., intrapersonal constraint), and consequently, inhibit interest in the activities (see Floyd, McGuire, Shinew & Noe, 1994). In a study of contract bridge players, Scott (1991) discovered these types of reciprocal links. He found that:

> . . . . intrapersonal constraints on the part of young people (i.e., an aversion to playing bridge) create structural constraints for others by limiting opportunities (not enough players to keep the groups going). Similarly, time commitments (a structural constraint) experienced by the individual may result in scheduling problems for group members as a whole (an interpersonal constraint). (p. 334)

A study of people suffering from alcoholism presents another example of the interaction of different types of constraints (McCormick, 1991). In the interest of keeping their identities as alcoholics private and avoiding the stigma of being seen as alcoholics, the study participants avoided contact with others and tended not to participate in leisure activities. It appeared that the fear of the stigma of alcoholism (an intrapersonal constraint) was enough to deter them from participation, leading to an actual waning of interest in leisure participation. This lack of interest also led other people in their social environment to stop asking them to participate (an interpersonal constraint).

Jackson, Crawford and Godbey (1992) point out that even the *anticipation* of interpersonal and structural constraints may reduce the desire to participate and create an intrapersonal constraint. These authors use the example of an avid snow skier who moves to Florida. Though she still thinks of herself as a skier, her awareness of the conditions in Florida that await her causes that interest to fade into the background of her consciousness.

The constraint process can be even more complex. For example, people often use the other people with whom they participate to judge how well they themselves are doing. Festinger (1954) has called this process "social comparison." According to Frederick, Havitz and Shaw (1994), who studied participation in aerobics classes, the presence of people (interpersonal factor) can either constrain or facilitate the quality of the experience depending on the participants' level of self-esteem and their reasons for participation (intrapersonal factors). For those participants more interested in psychological self-enhancement (ego-building) than in physical self-improvement, the presence of others who look better or move more gracefully can be inhibiting and may even be threatening to self-esteem. For those with an orientation to improving themselves, such coparticipants are an asset in providing opportunities for social comparison and standards for achievement.

Researchers studying constraints have also made use of the distinction between *antecedent* constraints that determine interest in participating and *intervening* constraints that prevent people from following up their interests with participation in the desired activity (Henderson, Stalnaker & Taylor, 1988). Though this distinction is a simpler one than that suggested by the hierarchical model just referred to, it offers a useful distinction (see Jackson, 1990). Using this approach, Shaw, Bonen and McCabe (1991) challenged one of the more central assumptions underlying constraint ideas—that there is a direct link between participation levels and the level of constraint perceived by people. In an analysis of intervening constraints on participation in physical activity, where the respondents were clearly interested in participating, the investigators found that lack of time and money, and greater distance from exercise facilities were not associated with less participation in physical activities. In fact, in some cases, participation was higher among those who identified these factors as constraints. With respect to time as a constraint, these authors suggest that participation itself creates the time scarcity that is felt as a constraint to further involvement. Active people are likely to be busy people and to feel that time is more precious (see also Jackson, 1993; Mannell, 1994). To look at it another way, perception of lack of time may be a reflection of being "over scheduled" or unwilling to sacrifice some activities to have more participation in others (Jackson, 1988). In this sense, time-allocation problems are as much a matter of *attitude* toward leisure and activity as they are a reflection of any uncontrollable scarcity in available time.

Psychological Dispositions as Intrapersonal Leisure Constraints: The Case of Attitudes

Throughout this book we have examined psychological dispositions that can be considered "intrapersonal constraints" in the sense that they affect people's interest in participating in certain leisure activities and their ability to derive enjoyment and various benefits from this participation. For example, feelings of freedom, self-determination and self-efficacy (chapter five), individual differences in playfulness, orientation to intrinsic motivation and Type-A behavior (chapter six), the arousal of needs and motives (chapter seven) and identity (chapter ten) can all act as intrapersonal constraints. One type of psychological disposition that we have not discussed thus far is attitude. A negative *leisure attitude* can be seen as a constraint on behavior. Only a limited amount of research has been done on leisure attitudes, but research has shown that they are amenable to influence and change, and thus the constraint they provide to participation and enjoyment can be overcome. In fact, attitudes have been seen as so important that attitude change theories and strategies have been developed and applied to overcoming constraints to a wide range of lifestyle behaviors including health and exercise behavior.

Is idleness the devil's workshop? Should the length of the work week be reduced? Are people on welfare entitled to leisure? Should cultural activities such as the ballet or public television be supported with tax dollars? Is participation in organized sports a good way for children to spend their leisure? Is bungee jumping a safe and worthwhile leisure pursuit? Is downhill skiing an appropriate leisure activity for people without the use of their legs? Your answers to these questions reflect your attitudes toward various aspects of leisure which may also impact on your own leisure behavior and experience. Leisure itself may be unappealing to some. A strong Protestant work ethic may be associated with a view that leisure is frivolous, trivial, and even decadent. To the extent that what people do is judged entirely in terms of that which is produced, much of leisure is likely to be regarded as relatively worthless. Such an ethic may stand in the way of participation and enjoyment. There is also the question of who, if anyone, is "entitled" to leisure. Those who work at home, but do not earn a wage—as with many mothers, for example—may be less likely to see leisure as something that they deserve (Henderson, 1991b; Henderson & Bialeschki, 1993). Similarly, those who are retired or unemployed may have some difficulty if they have come to regard enjoyment as something that must be "earned" by socially sanctioned productive work. Such attitudes, which incorporate both self-perceptions and social norms, may be very potent intrapersonal leisure constraints.

Although there are various approaches to attitudes, social psychologists generally agree that attitudes vary in level of intensity from mild to extreme (Petty & Cacioppo, 1986; Zanna & Rempel, 1988). "Like," "dislike," "love," "hate," "admire" and "detest" are the kinds of words people use to describe their attitudes. And attitudes can be measured. The easiest and most often used method to assess a person's attitude about something is to ask. For example, a researcher could ask someone how positive or negative they feel about the role leisure plays in people's lives today, about people who retire early, or about a specific activity like opera. Although self-report is straightforward, attitudes are sometimes too complex to be measured with a single question. Responses can be influenced by wording, the context, and other extraneous factors. Consequently, researchers often use multi-item questionnaires called attitude scales which come in various forms. The most popular is the Likert scale named after its inventor, Rensis Likert (1932). In this technique, people are presented with a list of statements on an attitude object and are asked to indicate on a multiple-point scale how strongly they agree or disagree with each statement. Their total attitude score is calculated by summing their responses to all the items. Researchers often create their own attitude scales to meet the needs of their specific research study, however, there are many standardized attitude scales that have been developed. Several such scales have been developed to measure attitudes toward leisure in general. For example, the frequently used *Leisure Ethic Scale* (Crandall & Slivken, 1980) is comprised of ten items (see Figure 12.3). Ragheb and Beard's (1982) 24-item *Leisure Attitude Scale* has also been used.

It should not be assumed that negative leisure attitudes always constrain behavior. In fact, research has demonstrated that the link between attitudes and behavior is far from automatic (see Eagly & Chaiken, 1993). Someone having a negative attitude toward television viewing, does not mean that she or he does not watch television. Conversely, holding positive attitudes toward spending more leisure time with family, exercising regularly, or traveling to exotic places does not necessarily mean that a person does those things. However, researchers have identified conditions under

---

This scale measures your attitudes toward leisure. By this we mean how you feel about your leisure, your recreation, or the things you do in your free time. Please answer as quickly and accurately as possible by indicating whether you agree or disagree with each of the following statements.

	Completely Disagree	Moderately Disagree	Moderately Agree	Completely Agree
1. My leisure time is my most enjoyable time.	1	2	3	4
2. I admire a person who knows how to relax.	1	2	3	4
3. I like to do things on the spur of the moment.	1	2	3	4
4. I would like to lead a life of complete leisure.	1	2	3	4
5. Most people spend too much time enjoying themselves.	1	2	3	4
6. I don't feel guilty about enjoying myself.	1	2	3	4
7. People should seek as much leisure as possible in their lives.	1	2	3	4
8. I'd like to have at least two months vacation a year.	1	2	3	4
9. Leisure is great.	1	2	3	4
10. It is good for adults to be playful.	1	2	3	4

Note: All items are scored 4 points for "completely agree" to 1 point for "completely disagree," except for item five which is reversed.

Figure 12.3   Leisure Attitude Scale

Adapted from Crandall and Slivken (1980)

which attitudes are linked to behavior. One key factor is the *level of generality and specificity* of the attitude and behavior of interest. Attitudes affect behavior only when attitude measures closely match the behavior in question. Research on a wide range of issues has supported this principle (Ajzen, 1991). To illustrate, assume that researchers are trying to use attitudes to predict whether people will visit a museum sometime within the next two years. Attitudes might be measured in a series of questions ranging from very *general,* such as "How do you feel about museums?" to very *specific,* such as "How do you feel about visiting a museum during the next two years?" Because the latter type of question is more specific, it would be more likely to predict actual museum visiting behavior.

The link between one's attitudes and one's actions must also be placed within a broader context. Attitudes are only one determinant of behavior. This limitation formed the basis of Fishbein's (1980) *theory of reasoned action* which Ajzen (1991) then expanded and called the *theory of planned behavior.* This latter theory states that attitudes influence behavior through a process of deliberate decision making and that their impact is limited in four respects (see Figure 12.4).

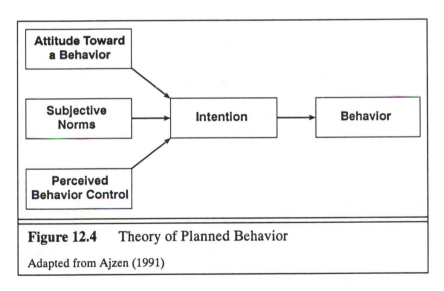

Figure 12.4 Theory of Planned Behavior

Adapted from Ajzen (1991)

First, as we have just described, behavior is influenced less by general attitudes than by *attitudes toward a specific behavior.* Second, behavior is influenced not only by attitudes but by *subjective norms*—one's beliefs about what others think she or he should do. Social pressures toward conformity, compliance, and obedience often constrain one's behavior in ways that are at odds with her or his inner convictions. In the introductory scenario, if everyone Bill encounters feels and expects that he can no longer be an active sports person, he is less likely to engage in this type of activity during his leisure. Third, attitudes give rise to behavior only when an individual *perceives the behavior to be within her or his control.* To the extent that people lack confidence in their ability to engage in some behavior, they are unlikely to form an intention to do so. If Bill does not feel confident in his athletic ability, he is less likely to plan to try adapted downhill skiing during his leisure, even though he feels quite positive about it. Fourth, although attitudes—along with subjective norms and perceived control—contribute to an intention to behave in a particular manner, people often do not or *cannot follow through on their intentions.* Bill may have intentions to resume photography during his leisure, but it may turn out that he has little time to do so because of family or work obligations. This factor is similar to the idea of "structural constraints."

There is good research support for the theory of planned action (Ajzen & Madden, 1986; Madden, Ellen & Ajzen, 1992). This general approach—that is, placing the link between attitudes and behavior into a broader context—has been successfully used to predict a wide range of behaviors such as losing weight, donating blood, exercising, smoking, attending church, shoplifting, voting, and choosing an occupation (Sheppard, Hartwick & Warshaw, 1988). Within leisure studies most of the research has addressed attitudes toward leisure in general (e.g., Ragheb, 1980; Ragheb & Tate, 1993; Cutler Riddick, 1986) and has not examined the links between attitudes, intentions and behavior. Typically, a small but positive relationship has been found between leisure attitudes, on the one hand, and overall leisure participation and satisfaction, on the other. Leisure researchers are also becoming more interested in the attitude-behavior link (e.g., Young & Kent, 1985). Ajzen and Driver (1991, 1992) recently demonstrated the theory of planned behavior's ability to predict leisure intentions and behavior. Consistent with the theory, intentions to perform five different activities (i.e., spending time at the beach, outdoor jogging, mountain climbing, boating, and biking), together with perceptions of behavior control, were shown to predict the extent to which respondents engaged in these activities over a 12-month period.

To summarize, attitudes toward a person, object or behavior do not always influence people's actions because other factors must be taken into account. However, when attitudes are strong and specific to a particular behavior, they can constrain or motivate leisure behavior. The question then becomes, "How are leisure attitudes changed so that they are not intrapersonal constraints to leisure participation?" We will deal with this question in the next section.

Overcoming Leisure Constraints

In spite of encountering constraints, individuals often do manage to stay active in their leisure, they continue to participate in and enjoy favorite activities, and they even begin new pursuits. How they manage to do this has been of interest to researchers. An understanding of the strategies used by individuals to overcome and cope with constraints, as well as the psychological and social factors that influence their success at using these strategies, would be very useful in efforts to help people engage in beneficial leisure. Two "leisure-related" mechanisms that have been proposed are "constraint negotiation" and "recreation substitutability." *Constraint negotiation* refers to the strategies people use to avoid or reduce the impact of the constraints and barriers to leisure participation and enjoyment that were discussed earlier. The theory of *recreation substitutability* explains a narrower range of constraint coping behavior. It deals with how people stay active and continue to meet their leisure needs by choosing a new leisure activity or setting when a preferred leisure behavior is no longer possible.

Negotiating Constraint

Constraints on leisure vary in intensity and impact according to Jackson, Crawford and Godbey (1992). Many constraints can be overcome rather easily (e.g., finding someone to go to the movies with when alone), though others, such as a spinal cord injury, can be permanent and severe in their negative impact on leisure behavior and experience. But even in the most extreme cases, people often find ways to manage constraining conditions and to find or create circumstances that afford new possibilities (see also Henderson, Bedini & Schuler, 1995; Whyte & Shaw, 1994).

People engage in constraints negotiation when they are interested in participating and have difficulty doing so because of intervening interpersonal and structural constraints. In some cases an activity is abandoned in the face of constraints; in other circumstances the constraints result in less participation and/or enjoyment than desired; and still in others, people find a way to work through or around constraints. Jackson, Crawford and Godbey (1992) have discussed a variety of strategies for negotiating constraints.

Though there is certainly thought and action associated with all of them they distinguish between "cognitive" and "behavioral" strategies.

Cognitive strategies include such processes as cognitive dissonance reduction, where unchosen or constrained activity alternatives are devalued and no longer seen as interesting. Not having the money to attend a concert, for example, might lead to less interest in the music or performer featured. Emphasizing the benefits of the activity that was chosen and the costs of an activity not chosen is a related approach. This type of cognitive strategy can be both positive and negative. On the plus side, it allows people to enjoy and feel good about the leisure choices they make and experience a reduction in interest for activities that may be unavailable to them. On the negative side, people can be so adaptable that they "lose interest" in potentially worthwhile and satisfying activities when, in fact, there are strategies that might allow them to become involved. If Bill was to devalue and lose interest in physically active leisure because of his injury, he would be unlikely to be motivated to expend the effort to get involved and become successful at wheelchair basketball.

Behavioral strategies include modifying aspects of leisure (e.g., giving up "happy hour" with co-workers to go ice skating with a niece, making an effort to learn about other leisure opportunities, altering the timing and frequency of participation, learning new recreation skills) and changing other aspects of lifestyle (e.g., spending less time at work).

In a study of 425 junior-high and high-school students, Jackson and Rucks (1995) asked the students if they participated "even though [they] have problems in doing so." The 23 percent who indicated that they often did so, reported encountering a variety of constraints in their daily lives: other commitments (e.g., school, family); activity inaccessible; ill health; and lack of necessary skills, partners, self-confidence, transportation, and/or approval of parents. Of the strategies used to overcome these problems, most frequently mentioned by the students were better time management and the acquisition of necessary skills, but the strategies used varied according to activity. For example, skill-related constraints were more common with competitive activities and were addressed by lowering aspirations (a cognitive strategy) as well as raising competence levels (a behavioral strategy).

Time management is a major behavioral negotiation strategy that is apparently common throughout adulthood. Contrary to the popular opinion that older people have an abundance of time, Mannell and Zuzanak (1991) found that a lack of time was even a significant leisure constraint experienced by a group of older retired adults, just as it often is with adolescents and younger adults. In interviews with 88 adults ages 30–65, Samdahl and

Jekubovitch (1993) identified several common time management strategies for dealing with constraints. First, daily routines were controlled to guarantee that opportunities for desired activities were available, despite being very busy in other respects. Second, with family helpmates, chores were effectively divided up to accommodate leisure interests. Third, alternative activities were chosen that were less time intensive. Finally, many of the adult respondents simply accepted that life changes make continuing participation in the same activities irrelevant in some cases.

To the extent that time continues to be in limited supply, some people cope by simply recognizing that they cannot do everything and indeed must make some sacrifices and set priorities. Goodale and Witt (1989) point out that "increased participation in various activities may not be a panacea, or even an improvement, in a culture where pace, stress and overload seem already to have exceeded the limits of well-being for many" (p. 444). Success in negotiating a constraint, especially when that constraint is a shortage of time, often lies in people recognizing their priorities and resisting the temptation to do more than is possible, prudent, or in keeping with personal and social commitments.

Recreation Substitutability

To stay active in his leisure, Bill has to negotiate the constraints created by his permanent physical injury. One way he can negotiate these constraints is by substituting entirely new or adapted preinjury activities for the old activities in which he can no longer participate. What approach is he likely to take? What type of activity substitution is likely to be most successful and lead to the greatest amount of satisfaction? *Recreation substitutability theory* attempts to answer these types of questions.

Introduced in the mid-1970s (Hendee & Burdge, 1974), the theory has primarily been of interest to researchers concerned with understanding what happens to outdoor recreation users when they are displaced from an activity that they are committed to and enjoy because of changes in social, physical environmental, or managerial conditions (Brunson & Shelby, 1993). For example, what would you do if the friend with whom you annually took a canoe trip moved and could no longer participate? What if pollution barred you from swimming at a favorite beach, or you could not get a permit for the river you had fished on most of your life due to the implementation of new wildlife conservation policies? Recreation substitutability theory suggests that people will choose as substitutes those activities that provide similar psychological experiences, satisfactions, and benefits as the original activity. For example, if risk and challenge were the primary motives for participation, activities that meet these needs would be chosen and substituted.

The theory has also been applied to leisure behavior in general whenever an "originally intended activity is no longer possible and therefore must be replaced by another behavior if leisure involvement is to be initiated or continued" (Iso-Ahola, 1986, p. 369). Iso-Ahola (1986) has proposed that *psychological reactance* (Brehm, 1972; see chapter five in this book) is a key process underlying people's willingness to substitute. Essentially, he has argued that the greater a person's feeling of choice or freedom in selecting a new activity, the greater his or her willingness to substitute. In other words, if people perceive that there is a great deal of external pressure for them to substitute, if the reasons for substitution are perceived to be unjustified or unfair, if the number of substitute alternatives is small, and if the need for substitution is unexpected, then psychological reactance will set in and the willingness to substitute will be lower. Iso-Ahola also contends that the more similar the substitute activity is perceived to be to the original, the greater the willingness to substitute. This similarity consists of the motives and rewards available, attractiveness, and costs of participation. To return to the scenario, because Bill's injury forces him to make changes in his leisure style, he is unlikely to feel a great deal of choice. Initially, he may even feel that the need for substitution is unfair, that his injury restricts his options and that those assisting him in becoming independent again are pressuring him to participate (of course, for his own good). However, the greater number of options he has, the more willing he will be to substitute and become involved during his leisure again. Also, the less adaptation required for him to continue to participate in activities that he enjoyed before his accident, the more likely he is to successfully substitute. For example, rather than substituting a completely new activity for nature photography, he might begin to pursue portrait photography which he may perceive as more similar.

The task of identifying the ways in which original and new substitute activities are similar remains a major challenge for recreation substitutability theory. As Brunson and Shelby (1993) note, some people may require substitutes that provide the same set of motives, needs and preferences as the original activity. Some may require only that substitutes promise as enjoyable an experience as the original, even if an entirely different set of motives, needs, or preferences is associated with the substitute activity. And yet, others may not require that the substitute be enjoyable at all, as long as other recreation benefits (e.g., physical fitness) can be derived. More recently, a broader definition of recreation substitutability has been proposed. "The term recreation substitutability refers to the interchangeability of recreation experiences such that acceptably equivalent outcomes can be achieved by varying one or more of the following: the time of the experience, the means of gaining access, the setting, and the activity" (Brunson & Shelby, 1993). This view of substitution is based on Shelby and Vaske's (1991) identification of substitution strategies other than the "replacement of one activity with another." These other forms of substitution include *temporal* (i.e., participating in the original activity at a different time), *resource* (i.e., finding a new setting to participate in the original activity) and *strategic* (i.e., finding a different way to participate in the original activity in the same setting at the same time).

Helping Ourselves and Others to Create Leisure Affordance

Now that we have presented the idea of leisure constraints and what leisure researchers know about how people overcome them, we will briefly discuss some of the social psychological ideas that have been encountered in this book that can be used to create leisure affordance, that is, conditions that will promote and support satisfying leisure styles. Not surprisingly, these factors involve influencing and managing both person and social situational factors. Just as there are personality characteristics and psychological dispositions that facilitate leisure behavior and experience, so there are social and physical environmental conditions that are conducive to leisure behavior. Perception psychologist J. J. Gibson suggested an environmental model of behavior that identifies characteristics in the environment that, once perceived, *afford* certain behaviors (Greeno, 1994). To use a couple of simple examples, a mailbox affords the delivery of mail and a fishing rod affords catching fish. Technology creates a wealth of *affordances*; but so do forests and rivers. Even a crowd can be an affordance. A concert might lose its appeal if a person were one of only a few people in attendance. The standard of living in most of North America affords the time for leisure, and the abundance of resources affords a wide variety of leisure opportunities. Nevertheless, affordance is not equally distributed among all people and even as some conditions afford, other conditions constrain. Managing these conditions is something that people do, for the most part, themselves, using strategies involving constraints negotiation and recreation substitutability. However, sometimes people may need help in doing so. Creating leisure affordance is often a matter of helping people to see the possibilities that are available to them, or in fact arranging such possibilities. Recognizing and creating leisure affordance is almost always a partner to managing and negotiating leisure constraints.

The potential for facilitating leisure participation and enhancing leisure experience lies in understanding both the nature of the constraints and affordances that are present or can be created in the immediate environment and the psychological factors within individuals that influence perceptions of these constraints and affordances. There are a variety of strategies that individuals, themselves, and others, including parents, friends, caregivers, instructors, coaches, and service providers, can use to help people overcome leisure constraint and create affordance. These strategies involve both managing leisure settings and activities and dealing with the psychological state of the individual.

Setting and Activity Management for Participation and Leisure Satisfaction

One of the major tools available to help someone become more involved in leisure is an intimate familiarity with leisure activities and settings. Recreation practitioners are traditionally very knowledgeable in this area of leisure services. Whether trying to get a child involved in painting, running a summer arts festival sponsored by the local community or operating a commercial whitewater rafting business on a stretch of wilderness river, leisure service providers must be able to manage the setting and activity in such a way as to optimize interest and the experience and benefits participants are seeking. Consider the following scenario involving a service provided by a commercial recreation company:

> Christine took a three-hour trip in an inflatable raft down a section of a wild river which has a series of huge rapids and churning falls. During this rough trip, she got wet, cold, and bounced around in the raft. After she returned home, she told friends that she had had a great deal of fun that made the substantial travel time to the site and the cost very worthwhile. Her "fun" experience included fear, extreme excitement, a sense of adventure, relief at surviving, a sense of accomplishment, and wonder at the power of nature.

The leisure behavior described in this scenario requires an extremely high level of *setting and activity management* to produce the successful rafting experience. It is somewhat like a theatrical production whereby the company carefully "orchestrates" the sequence of events to ensure that their customers get down the river safely, but in such a way that the event is experienced as exciting and risky, and not too safe! This balance between safety and risk is the most critical management task for the company. First, there is arrival at the site, hearing, and then seeing the roaring river. Next, Christine puts on the protective clothing and equipment with the other apprehensive yet excited adventurers. Then she receives directions on how to behave while in the raft, followed by boarding the heaving raft itself. All this activity is designed to set the "stage" and create the appropriate expectations. Once on the river, the comments of the company guides who steer the raft down the river are calculated to raise tension and excitement levels. At the completion of the trip, opportunities are provided to share stories of the experience with fellow adventurers over a meal, and finally there are photographs of the participants, in their rafting gear, to remind them of the experience after returning home.

Of course, not all leisure opportunities and services are this "managed" and most people seem to desire a variety of leisure involvements that range from the completely spontaneous to the well-orchestrated. Also, successfully managing leisure settings and activities would be impossible without a good knowledge of the psychological state of the participants. For example, this raft trip would likely only work well with whitewater rafting novices who come to the event with certain kinds of needs and expectations. As we noted in chapter seven, researchers have devoted a great deal of attention to understanding both the needs and motives that shape leisure interests and preferences and the characteristics of settings and activities that can allow people to meet these. During our discussion of leisure and personality in chapter six, we discovered that high quality leisure experiences are more likely to occur when *personality-environment congruency* is created. In the study of aerobic participants referred to earlier (Frederick, Havitz & Shaw, 1994), there were substantial differences in participant responses to the social environment of the aerobics class. There were those whose experience would not be positive if they worked out with people with greater skills, and those for whom participation with slightly superior coparticipants would actually enhance the experience.

Providing *optimal challenge* is another way of enhancing leisure experiences through setting and activity management (see chapters four and eight). Promoting optimal experience, or "flow" by offering challenges that are reasonably well-matched with participant skills was found to be an important characteristic of rewarding and beneficial leisure. If the challenges are too low for a person, boredom is the result; if they are too great, anxiety can be expected (Csikszentmihalyi, 1975; 1990). It is important, as facilitators of leisure and enjoyment, that providers consider this match (Voelkl, 1990). As we have discussed previously, some activities such as electronic video games are almost self-managing when it comes to automatically adjusting challenges to the skill level of the participant. Also, as people become more proficient at an activity they develop the ability to manage optimal challenge themselves. For example, Mitchell (1983) describes how rock climbers can intentionally make a particular climb more or less difficult by their choice of equipment, how much they party the night before a climb, and the route they take up the mountain.

Providing *appropriate feedback* is another important aspect of setting and activity management. The setting can afford involvement and enjoyment if it allows feedback about learning and mastery, whether that feedback is offered by instructors, coparticipants, or comes from interaction with objects, playthings or other materials. Generally speaking, anything that takes a person away from her or his focus on the task at hand can be regarded as disruptive and potentially constraining. With respect to children, Ellis, Witt and Aguilar (1983) point out that parents, coaches, and teachers can be disruptive to leisure experience when they are so invested in their children's activities that they praise or correct them to the point that the children lose track of why they are there.

Optimization of a setting for leisure also involves attending to how it is socially defined and who is seen to "belong" there. People may feel uncomfortable or uninterested in leisure participation in certain settings and activities. For example, some ethnic, cultural, and racial groups have been traditionally underrepresented among park users (Floyd & Gramann, 1995; Karlis, 1990). *Promoting inclusiveness* is a setting management strategy that involves making it clear that activities are open to everyone regardless of race, age, gender, social status, sexual preference or level of ability. However, participant diversity in programs, particularly with respect to the level of experience and knowledge, may not facilitate the interests of those committed to a certain level of involvement, activity specialization or style of performance.

Technology can also be either constraining or affording. With respect to leisure, the development of assistive devices for people with disabilities has had an extremely positive impact on participation. People without the use of their legs, for example, are able to swim, ski, and do auto mechanics while people with sensory impairments and communication disorders have devices to enhance nearly all of the senses. Nevertheless, though technology is intended to make life easier, if not more leisurely, it may have quite the opposite effect at times. It is entirely possible for the fax machine, the VCR, and the computer to all be operating at the same time and vying for people's attention. This observation is not entirely new. Linder spoke of the problem over two decades ago in *The Harried Leisure Class* (1971). In fact, communication technology has made it difficult for many people to get away from their work. Computers, telephones, and fax machines can easily be taken on holidays and seem to have fostered the expectation that people are always on call. The fusion or interpenetration of work and leisure seems to be benefiting work but not leisure.

The "toys" of leisure represent an endless list of possibilities for capturing people's attention, distracting them or enhancing their leisure experience. The linkage of the mundane telephone with computers to allow access to the Internet has allowed this technology to achieve a distinction that was once claimed by Citizens Band radios (CBs)—"the world's fastest growing communication sport." Technology is not always or inevitably affordant, but it has great potential.

Changing and Fostering Psychological Dispositions Conducive to Leisure

Although affordance refers to setting and activity opportunities, enabling someone to take advantage of these alternatives requires more than just managing the environment. It means getting into the mind of prospective participants to understand their needs, the constraints they feel and how their leisure orientations differ. As we have shown, there are a variety of psychological dispositions (e.g., needs, motives, interests, attitudes, personality traits, self-esteem, competence, self-efficacy, identity) that influence how people construe the social situation and setting and, consequently, leisure behavior and experience.

The most difficult intrapersonal "constraint" or psychological disposition to deal with when helping people with their leisure is *lack of interest* in participating. Knowing what is causing the lack of interest in a particular activity and whether it is due to a constraint can be tricky (see Mannell & Zuzanek, 1991). Sometimes what is expressed as a lack of interest is a reflection of an intrapersonal constraint, for example, a lack of confidence in one's ability to successfully engage in an activity or a negative attitude toward the activity. Interventions that lead to skill improvements, the development of feelings of self-efficacy for an activity or the promotion of positive attitudes toward it may be required.

Lack of interest may also result from continued lack of success in overcoming interpersonal (e.g., finding other people with whom to participate) or structural constraints (lack of facilities); people finally give up and "lose interest." In some cases a lack of interest in an activity is the result of the successful negotiation of constraints to other activities. For example, by finding the time and money to commit to regularly going to live theater, one may have little time and money, and consequently, little interest in attending professional sports events. It cannot be assumed therefore that lack of interest necessarily reflects a constraint. Nonparticipation in a particular activity may be largely a matter of having previously established priorities and choosing those leisure involvements that are the most important. Here lack of interest may reflect a low priority.

However, it is possible to intervene and "remedy" a lack of interest in a leisure activity as we found in the discussion of intrinsic motivation in chapter five, though it does raise an ethical dilemma (Goodale, 1990; Sylvester, 1985). If practitioners, parents or outsiders decide to intervene and interest someone in participating in an activity, they may be implying that they know "what is best for the individual concerned." As we discussed in chapter five, parents often make the decision that they know what is best for their children and attempt to foster intrinsic interest in what they feel are "beneficial" leisure activities. The same perspective is often taken by practitioners in promoting certain activities, for example, fitness activities to improve physical health or social activities to combat loneliness and depression in institutionalized older adults.

Influencing attitudes held toward a specific leisure activity can also create an interest and motivation to participate. Attitudes may be a type of intrapersonal constraint, and negative attitudes toward leisure may reduce or completely suppress interest in participation. For example, a middle-aged man who might enjoy attending an exhibit on aerial photography does not even consider it because he regards museum- and gallery-going as too "highbrow." Practitioners in a variety of fields have given considerable attention to attitude change as a way to promote behavior that is viewed as beneficial by people in their fields. Leisure researchers and service providers have only recently begun to formally explore and assess attitude change as a way to overcome constraints and create affordance.

Typically, leisure service providers have attempted to create positive attitudes toward activities by exposing people to activities in recreation programs where skills and knowledge in the activity are taught. Leisure counseling and education programs are also used to change attitudes towards leisure activities (e.g., Backman & Mannell, 1986; Aguilar, 1987; Searle & Mahon, 1991). Backman and Mannell (1986) found that just the opportunity to think about and discuss their attitudes and values toward leisure with other people, and to have it affirmed that leisure is appropriate behavior, was sufficient to change leisure attitudes and encourage greater participation among a group of institutionalized older adults. However, they also found that those participants who were involved in both a leisure counseling program and a recreation activity program designed to expose them to new activities showed the greatest increase in leisure behavior— an increase that was maintained after the program was over.

Another approach to changing attitudes is to engage in *persuasive communication*. Personal, face-to-face communication, signs and billboards, brochures and pamphlets, and television and radio advertisements can be used. Petty and Cacioppo (1986) have proposed a dual-process model of persuasion and attitude change, the *Elaboration-Likelihood Model* (ELM). This model is based on the assumption that individuals do not always process communications the same way. The term "elaboration likelihood" refers to the probability that people will either think about and analyze the information contained in a communication or attend instead to peripheral cues accompanying the message's delivery (e.g., use of an attractive or celebrity spokesperson to deliver the message). Elaboration differences determine both the extent to which a message affects attitude change and the persistence of the change. When people think carefully about the contents of a message, they take a *central route to persuasion* and are influenced by the strength and quality of the arguments. When people do not think carefully about the contents of a message but focus instead on other cues (e.g., the handsome face or athletic prowess of the spokesperson), they take a *peripheral route to persuasion.*

Although both routes to persuasion can result in change, the persistence of change differs as a consequence of elaboration. Attitudes changed by way of the peripheral route usually revert to their original position when the peripheral cue is no longer present. This is because the attitude change that occurs as a result of peripheral processing is not based on information contained in the message itself. When an attitude is changed by way of the central route, the change is based on the recipient's elaboration of the information contained in the message. The material is considered carefully and it is this information that is remembered.

The ELM social-persuasion approach has received support using a variety of nonleisure issues (Petty, McMichael & Brannon, 1992). Also, there is preliminary evidence for the usefulness of this approach in overcoming barriers to health and exercise behavior (see Kaplin, Sallis & Patterson, 1993; Brawley & Rodgers, 1993). Recently, there have been applications to leisure-related issues. For example, the influence of persuasive messages on the purchase of recreation services from public or commercial providers (Havitz & Crompton, 1990), on the willingness to pay fees for recreational services (Kerr & Manfredo, 1991; McCarville, Driver & Crompton, 1992), and on attitudes toward management decisions in parks (Bright, Fishbein, Manfredo & Bath, 1993) have been examined.

Full participation in and enjoyment of leisure activities are often constrained by a perception of oneself as incompetent or inadequate with respect to a particular activity (see chapter five). The challenge in such cases is to create enough change to allow the individual to experience some success as a function of effort and learning and thereby to gain a sense of *self-efficacy* in that activity. There is also the potential that this sense of efficacy (i.e., sense of competence or self-confidence) will generalize to other activities, thus encouraging increased participation. Though the evidence for self-efficacy as it relates to changing health behavior (see Strecher, DeVillis, Becker & Rosenstock, 1986) and exercise behavior (see Brawley & Rodgers, 1993) is fairly well-established, the importance of self-efficacy in leisure behavior has only recently been addressed. In general, individuals who are highly efficacious about their abilities to engage in a particular leisure behavior will tend to actively participate. They will persist with or initiate the activity even in the face of obstacles to do so. Less leisure-efficacious individuals would not be likely to initiate activity or to maintain their activity patterns. Dropout or irregular activity would be more characteristic of their behavior. It is also important that they believe that these behaviors lead to desired or beneficial outcomes.

The results of several investigations of exercise behavior support the development of self-efficacy as a function of experience with an activity. For example, in a study of 98 sedentary male and female university students who were starting a structured aerobics class, McAuley and Rowney (1990) found that perceived exercise performance during the class predicted efficacy after the program was over. The research findings clearly suggest that social-learning experiences based on participation in activities are an important determinant of feelings of efficacy for specific behaviors. Research on the efficacy enhancement of leisure behavior has also been reported. As we mentioned in chapter five, Ellis and his colleagues (Ellis, Maughan-

Pritchett & Ruddell, 1993; Maughan & Ellis, 1991) have demonstrated that adolescent psychiatric patients playing video games come to see themselves as more effective players if they have appropriate role models who are successful at the game, are given some control over the leisure setting, and are given feedback that focuses on their performance.

There are many more social psychological ideas that we have discussed throughout the pages of this book that could be applied to the development of effective interventions to help people get more out of their leisure. When researchers theorize and study these ideas, they tend to isolate and treat them as distinct to more easily understand the social psychological processes they represent. However, one should keep in mind that any effective intervention to help people with their leisure usually involves a number of these social psychological processes. Being aware of them and sensitive to their operation can help us better design methods of assistance and intervention.

A Final Note

In this book, we have tried to convey our enthusiasm for studying leisure. Simply put, it is fascinating to examine why people do what they do in their free time. We have also attempted to demonstrate that the social psychological perspective, with its focus on both the person and the social situation, provides an ideal framework to study people at leisure and satisfy this curiosity. On the practical side, hopefully this social psychological analysis of leisure will prove useful by sensitizing you to the cues to look for and the issues to be aware of when managing your own leisure as well as assisting others. Goodale and Witt (1989) have pointed out that "among the tasks of education and other socialization processes is teaching each generation how to find contentment and happiness in a world of constraints and barriers" (p. 444). As we presented in chapter eight, people acquire most of their leisure orientations and attitudes through the informal processes of socialization. This process of socialization involves the spontaneous experimentation facilitated by childhood leisure, influences by various socialization agents (e.g., parents, peers, coaches, media) and involvement in formal leisure activity programs in the community and at school. Most people find leisure and make of it what they will based on their own personal and social resources. In fact, to the extent that others arrange activities and experiences for people, there is a real potential that the perceived freedom and intrinsic motivation which are the preconditions or foundations of leisure will be undermined. Where independence is desired, people find ways to negotiate the constraints that they face to enable continuing participation at some level. However, it is sometimes necessary to intervene directly and "educate" for leisure, and for some people leadership, therapy, counseling and environmental management will be necessary to create affordances to make the most of leisure. Given that the most common leisure activity is television watching and that it offers so little in terms of satisfying experience (Kubey & Csikszentmihalyi, 1990), finding ways to move people into satisfying leisure action patterns would seem to be a reasonable goal for intervention and the application of the social psychology of leisure.

Adler, A. (1964). *Superiority and social interest: A collection of later writings*. Evanston, IL: Northwestern University Press.

Aguilar, T. E. (1987). Effects of a leisure education program on expressed attitudes of delinquent adolescents. *Therapeutic Recreation Journal, 21*, 43–51.

Aguilar, T. E. and Petrakis, E. (1989). Development and initial validation of perceived competence and satisfaction measures for racquet sports. *Journal of Leisure Research, 21*, 77–91.

Ajzen, I. (1991a). Benefits of leisure: A social psychological perspective. In B. L. Driver, P. J. Brown and G. L. Peterson (Eds.), *Benefits of leisure* (pp. 411–417). State College, PA: Venture Publishing, Inc.

Ajzen, I. (1991b). The theory of planned action. *Organizational Behavior and Human Decision Processes, 50*, 179–211.

Ajzen, I. and Driver, B. L. (1991). Prediction of leisure participation from behavioral, normative and control beliefs: An application of the theory of planned behavior. *Leisure Sciences, 13*, 185–204.

Ajzen, I. and Driver, B. L. (1992). Application of the theory of planned behavior to leisure choice. *Journal of Leisure Research, 24*, 207–224.

Ajzen, I. and Madden, T. J. (1986). Prediction of goal directed behavior: Attitudes, intentions, and perceived behavioral control. *Journal of Experimental Social Psychology, 22*, 453–474.

Allen, L. R. (1982). The relationship between Murray's personality needs and leisure interests. *Journal of Leisure Research, 14*, 63–76.

Allen, L. R. (1988). Management and evaluation of leisure programs and services: Past, present, and future research. In L. A. Barnett (Ed.), *Research about leisure: Past, present, and future* (pp. 95–107). Champaign, IL: Sagamore Publishing.

Allen, L. R. (1991). Benefits of leisure services to community satisfaction. In B. L. Driver, P. J. Brown and G. L. Peterson (Eds.), *Benefits of leisure* (pp. 331–350). State College, PA: Venture Publishing, Inc.

REFERENCES

Allison, M. T. (1988). Breaking boundaries and barriers: Future directions in cross-cultural research. *Leisure Sciences, 10*, 247–259.

Allison, M. T. (1991). Leisure, sport and quality of life: Those on the fringes. In *Sport for all* (pp. 45–55). New York, NY: Elsevier Science Publishers.

Allison, M. T. and Duncan, M. C. (1987). Women, work and leisure: The days of our lives. *Leisure Sciences, 9*, 143–161.

Allison, M. T. and Smith, S. (1990). Leisure and the quality of life: Issues facing racial and ethnic minority elderly. *Therapeutic Recreation Journal, 24*, 50–63.

Allport, F. H. (1924). *Social psychology*. Boston, MA: Houghton Mifflin.

Allport, G. W. (1954). *The nature of prejudice*. Reading, MA: Addison-Wesley.

Allport, G. W. (1955). *Becoming*. New Haven, CT: Yale University Press.

Allport, G. W. (1985). The historical background of social psychology. In G. Lindzey and E. Aronson (Eds.), *Handbook of social psychology* (3rd ed., Vol. 1, pp. 1–46). New York, NY: Random House.

Altergott, K. (Ed.) (1988). *Daily life in later life*. Newbury Park, CA: Sage Publications.

Amabile, T. M. and Hennessey, B. A. (1992). The motivation for creativity in children. In A. K. Boggiano and T. S. Pittman (Eds.), *Achievement and motivation* (pp. 54–74). New York, NY: Cambridge University Press.

Ammassari, E. K.-W. (1991). A framework for the quantitative study of leisure styles. *Loisir et Société/Society and Leisure, 14*, 411–432.

Archer, J. and McDonald, M. (1990). Gender roles and sports in adolescent girls. *Leisure Studies, 9*, 225–240.

Argyle, M. (1990). *The social psychology of work*. London, UK: Penguin Books.

Aron, A. and Aron, E. N. (1986). *Love and the expansion of self: Understanding attraction and satisfaction*. New York, NY: Hemisphere.

Asch, S. E. (1956). Studies in independence and conformity: A minority of one against a unanimous majority. *Psychological Monographs, 70*, 416.

Atchley, R. (1988). A continuity theory of normal aging. *The Gerontologist, 29*, 183–190.

Axline, V. (1947). *Play therapy*. New York, NY: Ballantine Books.

Babbie, E. (1992). *The practice of social research* (6th ed.). Belmont, CA: Wadsworth Publishing Company.

Backman, S. J. and Crompton, J. L. (1991). The usefulness of selected variables for predicting activity loyalty. *Leisure Sciences, 13,* 205–220.

Backman, S. J. and Mannell, R. C. (1986). Removing attitudinal barriers to leisure behavior and satisfaction: A field experiment among the institutionalized elderly. *Therapeutic Recreation Journal, 20,* 46–53.

Bacon, A. W. (1975). Leisure and the alienated worker: A critical reassessment of three radical theories of work and leisure. *Journal of Leisure Research, 7,* 179–190.

Baltes, P. B., Cornelius, S. W. and Nesselroade, J. R. (1980). Cohort effects in developmental psychology. In J. R. Nesselroade and P. B. Baltes (Eds.), *Longitudinal research in the study of behavior and development* (pp. 61–87). New York, NY: Academic Press.

Bandura, A. (1973). *Aggression: A social learning analysis.* Englewood Cliffs, NJ: Prentice-Hall.

Bandura, A. (1977). Self-efficacy: Toward a unifying theory of behavioral change. *Psychological Review, 8,* 191–215.

Bandura, A. (1986). *Social foundations of thought and action: A social cognitive theory.* Englewood Cliffs, NJ: Prentice-Hall.

Banner, D. K. (1985). Towards a theoretical clarification of the 'spillover' and 'compensatory' work/leisure hypotheses. *OMEGA: The International Journal of Management Science, 13,* 13–18.

Barnes, K. (1970). Preschool play norms: A replication. *Developmental Psychology, 1,* 99–103.

Barnett, L. A. (1980). The social psychology of children's play: Effects of extrinsic rewards on free play and intrinsic motivation. In S. E. Iso-Ahola (Ed.), *Social psychological perspectives on leisure and recreation* (pp. 138–170). Springfield, IL: Charles C. Thomas, Publisher.

Barnett, L. A. (1984). Young children's resolution of distress through play. *Journal of Child Psychology and Psychiatry, 25,* 477–483.

Barnett, L. A. (1988). *Research about leisure: Past, present, and future.* Champaign, IL: Sagamore Publishing.

Barnett, L. A. (1990). Developmental benefits of play for children. *Journal of Leisure Research, 22,* 138–153.

Barnett, L. A. (1991). Developmental benefits of play for children. In B. L. Driver, P. J. Brown and G. L. Peterson (Eds.), *Benefits of leisure* (pp. 215–247). State College, PA: Venture Publishing, Inc.

Barnett, L. A. (1995). *Research about leisure: Past, present, and future* (2nd ed.). Champaign, IL: Sagamore Publishing.

Barnett, L. A. and Chick, G. E. (1986). Chips off the ol' block: Parents' leisure and their children's play. *Journal of Leisure Research, 18*, 266–283.

Barnett, L. A. and Kane, M. J. (1985). Individual constraints on children's play. In M. G. Wade (Ed.), *Constraints on leisure* (pp. 43–82). Springfield, IL: Charles C. Thomas, Publisher.

Barnett, L. A. and Kleiber, D. A. (1982). Concomitants of playfulness in early childhood: Cognitive abilities and gender. *The Journal of Genetic Psychology, 141*, 115–127.

Barnett, L. A. and Kleiber, D. A. (1984). Playfulness and the early play environment. *The Journal of Genetic Psychology, 144* , 153–164.

Barnett, L. A. and Wade, M. G. (1988). In celebration of leisure research: A reflective look back. In L. A. Barnett (Ed.), *Research about leisure: Past, present, and future* (pp. 1–16). Champaign, IL: Sagamore Publishing.

Baumrind, D. (1971). Current patterns of parental authority. *Developmental Psychology Monographs, 4*, No. 1, Pt. 2.

Baumrind, D. (1985). Research using intentional deception: Ethical issues revisited. *American Psychologist, 40*, 165–174.

Baxter, L. A. and Dindia, K. (1990). 'Marital partners' perceptions of marital maintenance strategies. *Journal of Social and Personal Relationships, 7*, 187–208.

Beard, J. G. and Ragheb, M. G. (1983). Measuring leisure motivation. *Journal of Leisure Research, 15*, 219–228.

Becker, M. A. and Byrne, D. (1984). Type-A behavior and daily activities of young married couples. *Journal of Applied Social Psychology, 14*, 82–88.

Belanger, L. and Delisle, M. (1979). Relationships between compulsory activities, leisure, life satisfaction and boredom in a group of aged people. *Loisir et Société/Society and Leisure, 2*, 427–447.

Bella, L. (1989). Women and leisure: Beyond androcentrism. In E. L. Jackson and T. L. Burton (Eds.), *Understanding leisure and recreation: Mapping the past, charting the future* (pp. 151–179). State College, PA: Venture Publishing, Inc.

Bella, L. (1992). *The Christmas imperative.* Halifax, NS: Fernwood Publishing.

Bem, S. L. (1974). The measurement of psychological androgyny. *Journal of Consulting and Clinical Psychology, 42*, 155–162.

Bengtson, V. (1969). Cultural and occupational differences in level of present role activity in retirement. In R. Havighurst, J. Munnichs and H. Thomae (Eds.), *Adjustment to retirement: A cross-national study* (pp. 35–53). Assen, The Netherlands: Van Gorcum.

Benjamin, L. T., Jr. (1986). Why don't they understand us? A history of psychology's public image. *American Psychologist, 41*, 941–946.

Berkowitz, L. and Devine, P. G. (1989). Research traditions, analysis, and synthesis in social psychological theories: The case of dissonance theory. *Personality and Social Psychology Bulletin, 15*, 493–507.

Berscheid, E. (1992). A glance back at a 1/4 century of social psychology. *Journal of Personality and Social Psychology, 63*, 525–533.

Berscheid, E. and Walster, E. (1974). Physical attractiveness. In L. Berkowitz (Ed.), *Advances in experimental social psychology* (Vol. 7, pp. 157–215). New York, NY: Academic Press.

Best, F. (1988). *Reducing work weeks to prevent layoffs: The economic and social impacts of unemployment insurance.* Philadelphia, PA: Temple University Press.

Bialeschki, M. D. (1990). The feminist movement and women's participation in physical recreation. *Journal of Physical Education, Recreation and Dance, 61*, 44–47.

Bibby, R. W. and Posterski, D. C. (1985). *The emerging generation: An inside look at Canada's teenagers.* Toronto, ON: Irwin.

Bishop, D. W. (1970). Stability of the factor structure of leisure behavior: Analyses of four communities. *Journal of Leisure Research, 2*, 160–170.

Bishop, D. W. and Chace, C. A. (1971). Parental conceptual systems, home play environments, and potential creativity in children. *Journal of Experimental Child Psychology, 12*, 318–338.

Bishop, D. W., Jeanrenaud, C. and Lawson, K. (1975). Comparison of a time diary and recall questionnaire for surveying leisure activities. *Journal of Leisure Research, 7*, 73–80.

Bishop, D. W. and Witt, P. A. (1970). Sources of behavioral variance during leisure time. *Journal of Personality and Social Psychology, 16*, 352–360.

Boggiano, A. K. and Pittman, T. S. (1992). *Achievement and motivation.* New York, NY: Cambridge University Press.

Bowers, K. S. (1973). Situationalism in psychology: An analysis and critique. *Psychological Review, 80*, 307–336.

Bradburn, N. M. (1969). *The structure of psychological well-being.* Chicago, IL: Aldine Publishing.

Bradley, W. and Mannell, R. C. (1984). Sensitivity of intrinsic motivation to reward procedure instructions. *Personality and Social Psychology Bulletin, 10*, 426–431.

Bradshaw, R. and Jackson, J. (1979). Socialization for leisure. In H. Ibrahim and R. Crandall (Eds.), *Leisure: A psychological approach* (pp. 93–121). Los Alamitos, CA: Hwong.

Brandmeyer, G. A. and Alexander, L. K. (1986). "I caught the dream:" The adult baseball camp as fantasy leisure. *Journal of Leisure Research, 18*, 26–39.

Brasile, F. M., Kleiber, D. A. and Harnisch, D. (1991). Analysis of participation incentives among athletes with and without disabilities. *Therapeutic Recreation Journal, 25*, 18–33.

Braun, C. M. J. and Giroux, J. (1989). Arcade video games: Proxemic, cognitive and content analyses. *Journal of Leisure Research, 21*, 92–105.

Brawley, L. R. and Rodgers, W. M. (1993). Social-psychological aspects of fitness promotion. In P. Seraganian (Ed.), *Exercise psychology: The influence of physical exercise on psychological processes,* (pp. 254–298). New York, NY: John Wiley & Sons.

Bregha, F. J. (1980). Leisure and freedom re-examined. In T. L. Goodale and P. A. Witt (Eds.), *Recreation and leisure: Issues in an era of change* (pp. 30–37). State College, PA: Venture Publishing, Inc.

Brehm, J. W. (1966). *A theory of psychological reactance.* New York, NY: Academic Press.

Brehm, J. W. (1972). *Responses to loss of freedom: A theory of psychological reactance.* Morristown, NJ: General Learning Press.

Brehm, S. (1992). *Intimate relationships.* New York, NY: McGraw-Hill.

Brehm, S. S. and Brehm, J. W. (1981). *Psychological reactance: A theory of freedom and control.* New York, NY: Academic Press.

Brent, S. (1978). Individual specialization, collective adaptation and rate of environmental change. *Human Development, 21*, 21–33.

Bright, A. D., Fishbein, M., Manfredo, M. J. and Bath, A. (1993). Application of the theory of reasoned action to the National Park Service's controlled burn. *Journal of Leisure Research, 25*, 263–280.

Brightbill, C. K. (1960). *The challenge of leisure.* Englewood Cliffs, NJ: Prentice-Hall, Inc.

Brown, B. A. and Frankel, B. G. (1993). Activity through the years: Leisure, leisure satisfaction, and life satisfaction. *Sociology of Sport Journal, 10*, 1–17.

Brown, B. A., Frankel, B. G. and Fennell, M. (1991). Happiness through leisure: The impact of type of leisure activity, age, gender and leisure satisfaction on psychological well-being. *Journal of Applied Recreation Research, 16*, 368–392.

Brown, J. D. (1991). Staying fit and staying well: Physical fitness as a moderator of life stress. *Journal of Personality and Social Psychology, 60*, 555–561.

Brown, P. J. (1970). Sentiment changes and recreation participation. *Journal of Leisure Research, 2*, 264–268.

Browne, M. A. and Mahoney, M. J. (1984). Sport psychology. *Annual Review of Psychology, 35*, 605–625.

Bruner, J. S., Jolly, H. and Sylva, K. (1976). *Play: Its role in development and evolution*. New York, NY: Basic Books.

Brunson, M. W. and Shelby, B. (1993). Recreation substitutability: A research agenda. *Leisure Sciences, 15*, 67–74.

Buchanan, T., Christensen, J. E. and Burdge, R. J. (1981). Social groups and the meanings of outdoor recreation activities. *Journal of Leisure Research, 13*, 254–266.

Bull, N. C. (1971). One measure for defining a leisure activity. *Journal of Leisure Research, 3*, 120–126.

Bull, N. C. (1982). Leisure activities. In D. J. Mangen and W. A. Peterson (Eds.), *Research instruments in social gerontology: Vol. 2, Social roles and social participation*. Minneapolis, MN: University of Minnesota Press.

Bultena, G. L. and Klessig, L. L. (1969). Satisfaction in camping: A conceptualization and guide to social research. *Journal of Leisure Research, 1*, 348–364.

Bultena, G. L. and Taves, M. J. (1961). Changing wilderness images and forest policy. *Journal of Forestry, 51*, 167–171.

Burch, W. R. (1965). The play world of camping: Research into the social meaning of outdoor recreation. *American Journal of Sociology, 69*, 604–612.

Burch, W. R. (1969). The social circles of leisure: Competing explanations. *Journal of Leisure Research, 1*, 125–148.

Burch, W. R. and Hamilton-Smith, E. (1991). Mapping a new frontier: Identifying, measuring, and valuing social cohesion benefits related to nonwork opportunities and activities. In B. L. Driver, P. J. Brown and G. L. Peterson (Eds.), *Benefits of leisure* (pp. 369–382). State College, PA: Venture Publishing, Inc.

Burger, J. M. (1992). *Desire for control: Personality, social, and clinical perspectives*. New York, NY: Plenum Press.

Burns, T. (1980). Getting rowdy with the boys. *Journal of Drug Issues*, 273–285.

Buss, A. R. (1979). *A dialectical psychology*. New York, NY: John Wiley & Sons.

Buss, A. H. (1989). Personality as traits. *American Psychologist, 44*, 1378–1388.

Bynner, J. and Ashford, S. (1992). Teenage careers and leisure lives: An analysis of lifestyles. *Loisir et Société/Society and Leisure, 15,* 499–520.

Calasanti, T. M. (1993). Bringing in diversity: Toward an inclusive theory of retirement. *Journal of Aging Studies, 7,* 133–150.

Caldwell, L. L., Adolph, S. and Gilbert, A. (1989). Caution! Leisure counselors at work: Long-term effects of leisure counseling. *Therapeutic Recreation Journal, 23,* 41–49.

Caldwell, L. L. and Andereck K. L. (1994). Motives for initiating and continuing membership in a recreation related voluntary association. *Leisure Sciences, 16,* 33–44.

Caldwell, L. L. and Smith, E. A. (1988). Leisure: An overlooked component of health promotion. *Canadian Journal of Public Health, 79,* 44–48.

Caldwell, L. L. and Smith, E. A. (1994). Leisure and mental health of high risk adolescents. In D. M. Compton and S. E. Iso-Ahola (Eds.), *Leisure and mental health* (pp. 330–345). Park City, UT: Family Development Resources.

Caldwell, L. L. and Smith, E. A. (1995). Health behaviors of leisure alienated youth. *Loisir et Société/Society and Leisure, 18,* 143–156.

Caldwell, L. L., Smith, E. A. and Weissinger, E. (1992). Development of a leisure experience battery for adolescents: Parsimony, stability, and validity. *Journal of Leisure Research, 24,* 361–376.

Call, J. (1970). Games babies play. *Psychology Today, 3,* 34–37.

Caltabiano, M. L. (1995). Main and stress-moderating health benefits of leisure. *Loisir et Société/Society and Leisure, 18,* 33–52.

Cameron, J. M. and Bordessa, R. (1981). *Wonderland: Through the looking glass.* Maple, ON: Belsten.

Campbell, A. (1980). *The sense of well-being in America.* New York, NY: McGraw-Hill.

Campbell, A., Converse, P. and Rodgers, W. (1976). *The quality of American life.* New York, NY: Russel Sage.

Carpenter, G. (1988, October). *Perceived freedom in leisure in middle adulthood.* Paper presented to the Leisure Research Symposium, Indianapolis, IN.

Carpenter, G. (1989). Life change during middle adulthood and valuing leisure. *World Leisure and Recreation, 31,* 29–31.

Carruthers, C. P. (1993). Leisure and alcohol expectancies. *Journal of Leisure Research, 25,* 229–244.

Carruthers, C. P. and Busser, J. A. (1995). Alcohol consumption and leisure participation. *Loisir et Société/Society and Leisure, 18,* 125–142.

Ceci, S. J., Peters, D. and Plotkin, J. (1985). Human subjects review, personal values, and the regulation of social science research. *American Psychologist, 40*, 994–1002.

Chalip, L., Csikszentmihalyi, M., Kleiber, D. A. and Larson, R. W. (1984). Variations of experience in formal and informal sport. *Research Quarterly For Exercise and Sport, 55*, 109–116.

Chalip, L., Thomas, D. R. and Voyle, J. (1992). Sport, recreation and well-being. In D. R. Thomas, and A. Veno (Eds.), *Psychology and social change* (pp. 132–156). Palmerston North, New Zealand: Dunmore Press.

Chambers, D. A. (1986). The constraints of work and domestic schedules on women's leisure. *Leisure Studies, 5*, 309–325.

Chaplin, J. P. (1985). *Dictionary of psychology*. New York, NY: Dell Publishing.

Chapman, A. J. and Foot, H. C. (1976). *Humour and laughter: Theory, research and applications*. New York, NY: John Wiley & Sons.

Chase, D. R. and Godbey, G. C. (1983). The accuracy of self-reported participation rates. *Leisure Studies, 2*, 231–235.

Cherrington, D. J. (1989). *Organizational behavior*. Needham Heights, MA: Allyn & Bacon.

Chick, G. E. (1987). Anthropology and leisure: Research and practical issues. In S. Parker and A. Graefe (Eds.), *Recreation and leisure: An introductory handbook* (pp. 5–9). State College, PA: Venture Publishing, Inc.

Chick, G. E. (1995). The anthropology of leisure: Past, present, and future. In L. A. Barnett (Ed.), *Research about leisure: Past, present, and future* (2nd ed.) pp. 43–64. Champaign, IL: Sagamore Publishing.

Chickering, A. W. (1969). *Education and identity*. San Francisco, CA: Jossey-Bass.

Chiriboga, D. A. and Pierce, R. C. (1993). Changing contexts of activity. In J. R. Kelly (Ed.), *Activity and aging* (pp. 42–59). Newbury Park, CA: Sage Publications.

Christie, J. F. and Johnson, E. P. (1983). The role of play in social-intellectual development. *Review of Educational Research, 53*, 93–115.

Chubb, M. and Chubb, H. (1981). *One-third of our time?* New York, NY: John Wiley & Sons.

Clark, S. M., Harvey, A. S. and Shaw, S. M. (1990). Sex roles, time and leisure in the Canadian family: Subjective and contextual dimensions. *Social Indicators Research, 23*, 35–50.

Clawson, M. and Knetsch, J. L. (1966). *Economics of outdoor recreation*. Baltimore, MD: Johns Hopkins Press.

Clough, P., Shepherd, J. and Maughan, R. (1989). Motives for participation in recreational running. *Journal of Leisure Research, 21*, 297–309.

Cohen, D. (1993). *The development of play*. London, UK: Routledge.

Cohen, E. (1979a). A phenomenology of tourist experiences. *Sociology, 13*, 179–201.

Cohen, E. (1979b). Rethinking the sociology of tourism. *Annals of Tourism Research, 6*, 18–35.

Cohen, E. (1988). Authenticity and commoditization in tourism. *Annals of Tourism Research, 15*, 371–386.

Cohen, E. (1991). Leisure—The last resort: A comment. In B. L. Driver, P. J. Brown and G. L. Peterson (Eds.), *Benefits of leisure* (pp. 439–444). State College, PA: Venture Publishing, Inc.

Coleman, D. (1993). Leisure based social support, leisure dispositions and health. *Journal of Leisure Research, 25*, 350–361.

Coleman, D. and Iso-Ahola, S. E. (1993). Leisure and health: The role of social support and self-determination. *Journal of Leisure Research, 25*, 111–128.

Coleman, J. S. (1961). *The adolescent society*. New York, NY: Free Press.

Colenutt, C. E. and McCarville, R. E. (1994). The client as problem solver: A new look at service recovery. *Journal of Hospitality and Leisure Marketing, 2*, 23–35.

Cook, S. W. (1976). Ethical issues in the conduct of research in social relations. In C. Selltiz, L. S. Wrightsman and W. Cook (Eds.), *Research methods in social relations* (3rd ed.) pp. 199–249. New York, NY: Holt, Rinehart and Winston.

Cosper, R. L. and Shaw, S. M. (1985). The validity of time-budget studies: A comparison of frequency and diary data in Halifax, Canada. *Leisure Sciences, 7*, 205–225.

Costa, P. T. and McCrae, R. R. (1985). *The NEO personality inventory*. Odessa, FL: Psychological Assessment Resources.

Costa, P. T. and McCrae, R. R. (1988). From catalog to classification: Murray's needs and the 5-factor model. *Journal of Personality and Social Psychology, 55*, 258–265.

Costa, P. T., McCrae, R. R. and Dye, D. A. (1991). Facet scale for agreeableness and conscientiousness: A revision of the NEO Personality Inventory. *Personality and Individual Differences, 12*, 887–898.

Coyle, C. P. and Kinney, W. B. (1990). A comparison of leisure and gambling motives of compulsive gamblers. *Therapeutic Recreation Journal, 24*, 32–39.

Crandall, R., Nolan, M. and Morgan, L. (1980). Leisure and social interaction. In S. E. Iso-Ahola (Ed.), *Social psychological perspectives on leisure and recreation* (pp. 285–306). Springfield, IL: Charles C. Thomas, Publisher.

Crandall, R. and Slivken, K. (1980). Leisure attitudes and their measurement. In S. E. Iso-Ahola (Ed.), *Social psychological perspectives on leisure and recreation* (pp. 261–284). Springfield, IL: Charles C. Thomas, Publisher.

Crawford, D. W. and Godbey, G. C. (1987). Reconceptualizing barriers to family leisure. *Leisure Sciences, 9*, 119–127.

Crawford, D. W., Jackson, E. L. and Godbey, G. C. (1991). A hierarchical model of leisure constraints. *Leisure Sciences, 13*, 309–320.

Creasey, G. L. and Meyers, B. J. (1986). Video games and children: Effects on leisure activities, schoolwork, and peer involvement. *Merrill-Palmer Quarterly, 32*, 251–262.

Creswell, J. W. (1994). *Research design: Qualitative and quantitative approaches.* London, UK: Sage.

Crompton, J. L. (1979). Motivations for pleasure vacations. *Annals of Tourism Research, 6*, 408–424.

Crompton, J. L. (1993). Rescuing young offenders with recreation programs. *Trends, 30*, 23–26.

Crompton, J. L. and Mackay, K. J. (1989). Users' perceptions of the relative importance of service quality dimensions in selected public recreation programs. *Leisure Sciences, 11*, 367–375.

Crosby, F. J. (1991). *Juggling: The unexpected advantages of balancing career and home for women and their families.* New York, NY: The Free Press.

Csikszentmihalyi, M. (1975). *Beyond boredom and anxiety: The experience of play in work and games.* San Francisco, CA: Jossey-Bass.

Csikszentmihalyi, M. (1981). Leisure and socialization. *Social Forces: An International Journal of Social Research, 60*, 332–340.

Csikszentmihalyi, M. (1990). *Flow: The psychology of optimal experience.* New York, NY: Harper Perennial.

Csikszentmihalyi, M. and Csikszentmihalyi, I. (Eds.) (1988). *Optimal experience: Psychological studies of flow in consciousness.* New York, NY: Cambridge University Press.

Csikszentmihalyi, M. and Graef, R. (1980). The experience of freedom in daily life. *American Journal of Community Psychology, 8*, 401–414.

Csikszentmihalyi, M. and Kleiber, D. A. (1991). Leisure and self-actualization. In B. L. Driver, P. J. Brown and G. L. Peterson (Eds.), *Benefits of leisure* (pp. 91–102). State College, PA: Venture Publishing, Inc.

Csikszentmihalyi, M. and Larson, R. W. (1984). *Being adolescent: Conflict and growth in the teenage years*. New York, NY: Basic Books.

Csikszentmihalyi, M. and Larson, R. W. (1985). *The experience sampling method: Towards a systematic phenomenology*. Unpublished manuscript: University of Chicago.

Csikszentmihalyi, M. and LeFevre, J. (1989). Optimal experience in work and leisure. *Journal of Personality and Social Psychology, 56*, 815–822.

Cumming, E. and Henry, W. (1961). *Growing old*. New York, NY: Basic Books.

Cunningham, P. H. and Bartuska, T. (1989). The relationship between stress and leisure satisfaction among therapeutic recreation personnel. *Therapeutic Recreation Journal, 23*, 65–70.

Curry, N. (1988). Enhancing dramatic play potential in hospitalized children. *Children's Health Care, 16*.

Curtis, J. E. and White, P. T. (1984). Age and sport participation: Decline in participation or increased specialization with age? In N. Theberge and J. Donelly (Eds.), *Sport and the sociological imagination* (pp. 273–293). Fort Worth, TX: TCU Press.

Cutler, S. J. (1977). Aging and voluntary association participation. *Journal of Gerontology, 32*, 470–479.

Cutler, S. J. and Hendricks, J. (1990). Leisure and time use across the life course. In R. H. Binstock and L. K. George (Eds.), *Handbook of aging and the social sciences* (pp. 169–185). New York, NY: Academic Press.

Cutler Riddick, C. (1985). Life satisfaction determinants of older males and females. *Leisure Sciences, 7*, 47–63.

Cutler Riddick, C., Drogin, E. B. and Spector, S. G. (1987). The impact of videogame play on the emotional well-being of senior center participants. *The Gerontologist, 27*, 425–427.

Cutler Riddick, C. and Gonder Stewart, D. (1994). An examination of the life satisfaction and importance of leisure in the lives of older female retirees: A comparison of blacks to whites. *Journal of Leisure Research, 26*, 75–87.

Dargitz, R. E. (1988). Angling activity of urban youth: Factors associated with fishing in a metropolitan context. *Journal of Leisure Research, 20*, 192–207.

Dattilo, J., Dattilo, A. M., Samdahl, D. M. and Kleiber, D. A. (1994). Leisure orientations and self-esteem in women with low incomes who are overweight. *Journal of Leisure Research, 26*, 23–38.

Dattilo, J. and Kleiber, D. A. (1993). Psychological perspectives for therapeutic recreation research: The psychology of enjoyment. In M. J. Malkin and C.

Z. Howe (Eds.), *Research in therapeutic recreation: Concepts and methods* (pp. 57–76). State College, PA: Venture Publishing, Inc.

Davidson, R. J., Goleman, D. J. and Schwartz, G. E. (1976). Attentional and affective concomitants of meditation. *Journal of Abnormal Psychology, 85,* 235–238.

Davidson, R. J., Schwartz, G. E. and Rothman, L. P. (1976). Attentional style and self-regulation of mode-specific attention: An electroencephalographic study. *Journal of Abnormal Psychology, 85,* 611–621.

Dawson, D. (1986). Unemployment, leisure and liberal-democratic ideology. *Loisir et Société/Society and Leisure, 9,* 165–179.

de Grazia, S. (1964). *Of time, work, and leisure.* New York, NY: Anchor Books, Doubleday.

deCharms, R. (1968). *Personal causation: The internal affective determinants of behavior.* New York, NY: Academic Press.

Deci, E. L. (1971). Effects of externally mediated rewards on intrinsic motivation. *Journal of Personality and Social Psychology, 18,* 105–115.

Deci, E. L. (1975). *Intrinsic motivation.* New York, NY: Plenum Press.

Deci, E. L., Connell, J. P. and Ryan, R. M. (1989). Self-determination in a work organization. *Journal of Applied Psychology, 74,* 580–590.

Deci, E. L. and Ryan, R. M. (1985). *Intrinsic motivation and self-determination in human behavior.* New York, NY: Plenum Press.

Deci, E. L. and Ryan, R. M. (1991). A motivational approach to self: Integration in personality. In R. Dienstbier (Ed.), *Nebraska Symposium on Motivation: Vol. 38. Perspectives on motivation* (pp. 237–288). Lincoln, NE: University of Nebraska Press.

Decker, J. M. and Crompton, J. L. (1990). Business location decisions: The relative importance of quality of life and recreation, park, and cultural opportunities. *Journal of Park and Recreation Administration, 8,* 26–27.

Deem, R. (1986). *All work and no play? The sociology of women and leisure.* Philadelphia, PA: Open University Press.

Degman, J. M. (1990). Personality structure: Emergence of the Five-Factor Model. *Annual Review of Psychology, 41,* 417–440.

Devereux, E. (1976). Backyard versus Little League baseball: The impoverishment of children's games. In D. Landers (Ed.), *Social problems in sport* (pp. 37–56). Urbana, IL: University of Illinois Press.

Devine, P. G., Hamilton, D. L. and Ostrom, T. M. (1994). *Social cognition: Impact on social psychology.* New York, NY: Academic Press.

Diener, E. and Crandall, R. (1978). *Ethics in social and behavioral research.* Chicago, IL: University of Chicago Press.

Diener, E., Emmons, R. A., Larsen, R. J. and Griffin, S. (1985). The satisfaction with life scale. *Journal of Personality Assessment, 49,* 71–76.

Diener, E., Larsen, R. J. and Emmons, R. A. (1984). Person x situation interactions: Choice of situations and congruence response models. *Journal of Personality and Social Psychology, 47,* 580–592.

Dimanche, F., Havitz, M. E. and Howard, D. R. (1991). Testing the involvement profile (IP) scale in the context of selected recreational and touristic activities. *Journal of Leisure Research, 23,* 51–66.

Dimanche, F. and Samdahl, D. (1994). Leisure as symbolic consumption: A conceptualization and prospectus for future research. *Leisure Sciences, 16,* 119–129.

Dindia, K. and Baxter, L. A. (1987). Strategies for maintaining and repairing marital relationships. *Journal of Social and Personal Relationships, 4,* 143–158.

Dinwiddie, S. A. (1993). Playing in the gutters: Enhancing children's cognitive and social play. *Young Children, 48,* 70–75.

Dishman, R. K. (1988). Determinants of physical activity and exercise for persons 65 years of age and older. *American Academy of Physical Education Papers, 22,* 140–162.

Dishman, R. K. (Ed.) (1994). *Advances in exercise adherence.* Champaign, IL: Human Kinetics.

Dorfman, L. T., Heckert, D. A. and Hill, E. A. (1988). Retirement satisfaction in rural husbands and wives. *Rural Sociology, 53,* 25–39.

Douse, N. A. and McManus, I. C. (1983). The personality of fantasy game players. *British Journal of Psychology, 84,* 505–510.

Driscoll, R., Davis, K. W. and Lipetz, M. E. (1972). Parental interference and romantic love. *Journal of Personality and Social Psychology, 24,* 1–10.

Driver, B. L. (1972). Potential contributions of psychology to recreation resources management. In J. F. Wohlwell and D. H. Carson (Eds.), *Environment and the social sciences: Perspectives and applications* (pp. 233–248). Washington, DC: American Psychological Association.

Driver, B. L. (1976). Quantification of outdoor recreationists' preferences. In B. Van Der Smissen (Ed.), *Research, camping and environmental education* (pp. 165–187). University Park, PA: The Pennsylvania State University Department of Health, Physical Education and Recreation.

Driver, B. L. and Brown, P. J. (1975). A socio-psychological definition of recreation demand, with implications for recreation resource planning. In *Assessing demand for outdoor recreation* (pp. 62–88). Washington, DC: National Academy of Sciences.

Driver, B. L. and Brown, P. J. (1984). Contributions of behavioral scientists to recreation resource management. In I. Altman and J. F. Wohlwill (Eds.), *Behavior and the national environment* (pp. 307–339). New York, NY: Plenum Press.

Driver, B. L., Brown, P. J. and Peterson, G. L. (Eds.) (1991a). *Benefits of leisure.* State College, PA: Venture Publishing, Inc.

Driver, B. L., Brown, P. J. and Peterson, G. L. (1991b). Research on leisure benefits: An introduction to this volume. In B. L. Driver, P. J. Brown and G. L. Peterson (Eds.), *Benefits of leisure* (pp. 3–11). State College, PA: Venture Publishing, Inc.

Driver, B. L., Brown, P. J., Stankey, G. H. and Gregoire, T. G. (1987). The ROS planning system: Evolution, basic concepts, and research needed. *Leisure Sciences, 9*, 201–212.

Driver, B. L. and Knopf, R. C. (1977). Personality, outdoor recreation, and expected consequences. *Environment and Behavior, 9*, 169–193.

Driver, B. L., Tinsley, H. E. A. and Manfredo, M. J. (1991). The Paragraphs About Leisure and Recreation Experience Preference scales: Results from two inventories designed to assess the breadth of the perceived psychological benefits of leisure. In B. L. Driver, P. J. Brown and G. L. Peterson (Eds.), *Benefits of leisure* (pp. 263–286). State College, PA: Venture Publishing, Inc.

Driver, B. L. and Tocher, S. R. (1970). Toward a behavioral interpretation of recreational engagements, with implications for planning. In B. L. Driver (Ed.), *Elements of outdoor recreation planning* (pp. 9–31). Ann Arbor, MI: The University of Michigan Press.

Dumazedier, J. (1967). *Toward a society of leisure*. New York, NY: The Free Press.

Dunn Ross, E. L. and Iso-Ahola, S. E. (1991). Sightseeing tourists' motivation and satisfaction. *Annals of Tourism Research, 18*, 226–237.

Dupuis, S. L. and Smale, B. J. A. (1995). An examination of relationship between psychological well-being and depression and leisure activity participation among older adults. *Loisir et Société/Society and Leisure, 18*, 67–92.

Eagles, P. F. J. (1992). The travel motivations of Canadian ecotourists. *Journal of Travel Research, 31*, 3–7.

Eagly, A. H. and Chaiken, S. (1993). *The psychology of attitudes.* Forth Worth, TX: Harcourt, Brace & Co.

Eckert, P. (1989). *Jocks and burnouts: Social categories and identity in the high school.* New York, NY: Teachers College Press.

Egli, E. and Meyers, L. (1984). The role of video game playing in adolescent life: Is there reason to be concerned? *Bulletin of the Psychonomic Society, 22,* 309–312.

Ekerdt, D. J. (1986). The busy ethic: Moral continuity between work and retirement. *The Gerontologist, 26,* 239–244.

Elder, G. (1974). *Children of the great depression.* Chicago, IL: University of Chicago Press.

Elkind, D. (1981). *The hurried child.* Boston, MA: Addison-Wesley.

Ellis, D. (1984). Video arcades, youth, and trouble. *Youth and Society, 16,* 47–65.

Ellis, G. D., Maughan-Pritchett, M. and Ruddell, E. (1993). Effects of attribution-based verbal persuasion and imagery on self-efficacy of adolescents diagnosed with major depression. *Therapeutic Recreation Journal, 27,* 83–97.

Ellis, G. D., Voelkl, J. and Morris, C. (1994). Measurement and analysis issues with the explanation of variance in daily experience using the flow model. *Journal of Leisure Research, 26,* 337–356.

Ellis, G. D. and Witt, P. A. (1994). Perceived freedom in leisure and satisfaction: Exploring the factor structure of the perceived freedom components of the leisure diagnostic battery. *Leisure Sciences, 16,* 259–270.

Ellis, G. D. and Witt, P. A. (1984). The measurement of perceived freedom in leisure. *Journal of Leisure Research, 16,* 110–123.

Ellis, G. D. and Witt, P. A. (1991). Conceptualization and measurement of leisure: Making the abstract concrete. In T. L. Goodale and P. A. Witt (Eds.), *Recreation and leisure: Issues in an era of change* (3rd ed.) pp. 377–395). State College, PA: Venture Publishing, Inc.

Ellis, G. D., Witt, P. A. and Aguilar, T. E. (1983). Facilitating flow through therapeutic recreation services. *Therapeutic Recreation Journal, 17,* 6–15.

Ellis, G. D. and Yessick, J. T. (1989). Toward person by situation research in therapeutic recreation. *Therapeutic Recreation Journal, 23,* 24–35.

Ellis, M. J. (1973). *Why people play.* Englewood Cliffs, NJ: Prentice Hall.

Ellis, T. and Richardson, G. (1991). Organizational wellness. In B. L. Driver, P. J. Brown and G. L. Peterson (Eds.), *Benefits of leisure* (pp. 303–329). State College, PA: Venture Publishing, Inc.

Elms, A. C. (1975). The crisis of confidence in social psychology. *American Psychologist, 30,* 967–976.

Emmons, R. A., Diener, E. and Larsen, R. J. (1986). Choice and avoidance of everyday situations and affect congruence: Two models of reciprocal interactionism. *Journal of Personality and Social Psychology, 51,* 815–826.

Endler, N. S. (1983). Interactionism: A personality model, but not yet a theory. In M. M. Page (Ed.), *Nebraska Symposium on Motivation* (pp. 155–200). Lincoln, NB: University of Nebraska Press.

Erikson, E. (1959). Identity and the life cycle: Selected papers. *Psychological Issues, 1,* 5–165.

Erikson, E. (1963). *Childhood and society.* New York, NY: W. W. Norton & Co.

Evans, S. T. and Haworth, J. T. (1991). Variations in personal activity, access to "categories of experience," and psychological well-being in young adults. *Leisure Studies, 10,* 249–264.

Ewert, A. W. (1993). Differences in the level of motive importance based on trip outcome, experience level and group type. *Journal of Leisure Research, 25,* 335–349.

Ewert, A. W. (1994). Playing the edge: Motivation and risk taking in a high-altitude wilderness-like environment. *Environment and Behavior, 26,* 3–24.

Ewert, A. W. and Hollenhorst, S. (1989). Testing the adventure model: Empirical support for a model of risk recreation participation. *Journal of Leisure Research, 21,* 124–139.

Eysenck, H. J. (1967). *The biological basis of personality.* Springfield, IL: Thomas Frewd.

Falk, J. H. (1995). Factors influencing African American leisure time utilization of museums. *Journal of Leisure Research, 27,* 41–60.

Farr, R. M. (1991). The long past and the short history of social psychology. *European Journal of Social Psychology, 21,* 371–380.

Feather, N. T. and Bond, M. J. (1983). Time structure and purposeful activity among employed and unemployed university graduates. *Journal of Occupational Psychology, 56,* 241–254.

Festinger, L. A. (1954). A theory of social comparison processes. *Human Relations, 7,* 117–140.

Festinger, L. A. (1957). *A theory of cognitive dissonance.* Stanford, CA: Stanford University Press.

Field, D. R. and O'Leary, J. T. (1973). Social groups as a basis for assessing participation in selected water activities. *Journal of Leisure Research, 5,* 16–25.

Fincham, R. and Rhodes, P. S. (1988). *The individual, work and organization.* London: Weidenfeld and Nicolson.

Fine, G. A. (1983). *Shared fantasy.* Chicago, IL: The University of Chicago Press.

Fine, G. A. (1987). *With the boys: Little league baseball and preadolescent culture.* Chicago, IL: The University of Chicago Press.

Fine, G. A. (1989). Mobilizing fun: Provisioning resources in leisure worlds. *Sociology of Sport Journal, 6,* 319–334.

Fine, G. A. (1993). The sad demise, mysterious disappearance, and glorious triumph of symbolic interactionism. *Annual Review of Sociology, 19,* 61.

Fishbein, M. (1980). A theory of reasoned action: Some applications and implications. In H. E. Howe and M. M. Page (Eds.), *Nebraska Symposium on Motivation*: Vol. 27 (pp. 65–116). Lincoln, NE: University of Nebraska Press.

Floyd, M. F. and Gramann, J. H. (1995). Perceptions of discrimination in a recreation context. *Journal of Leisure Research, 27,* 192–199.

Floyd, M. F., Gramann, J. H. and Saenz, R. (1993). Ethnic factors and the use of public outdoor recreation areas: The case of Mexican Americans. *Leisure Sciences, 15,* 83–98.

Floyd, M. F., McGuire, F. A., Shinew, K. J. and Noe, F. P. (1994). Race, class, and leisure activity preferences: Marginality and ethnicity revisited. *Journal of Leisure Research, 26,* 158–173.

Fodness, D. (1994). Measuring tourist motivation. *Annals of Tourism Research, 21,* 555–581.

Foster, R. J. and Jackson, E. L. (1979). Factors associated with camping satisfaction in Alberta Provincial Park campgrounds. *Journal of Leisure Research, 11,* 292–306.

Francken, D. A. and van Raaij, W. F. (1981). Satisfaction with leisure time activities. *Journal of Leisure Research, 13,* 337–352.

Franken, R. E. (1982). *Human motivation.* Monterey, CA: Brooks-Cole.

Frederick, C. J., Havitz, M. and Shaw, S. M. (1994). Social comparison in aerobic exercise classes: Propositions for analysing motives and participation. *Leisure Sciences, 16,* 161–176.

Frederick, C. J. and Shaw, S. M. (1995). Body image as a leisure constraint: Examining the experience of aerobic exercise classes for young women. *Leisure Sciences, 17,* 57–73.

Freud, S. (1933). *Introductory lectures on psychoanalysis.* New York, NY: W.W. Norton.

Freysinger, V. J. (1990). A life span perspective on women and physical recreation. *Journal of Physical Education, Recreation and Dance, 61*, 48–51.

Freysinger, V. J. (1994). Leisure with children and parental satisfaction: Further evidence of a sex difference in the experience of adult roles and leisure. *Journal of Leisure Research, 26*, 212–226.

Freysinger, V. J. (1995). The dialectics of leisure and development of women and men in mid-life: An interpretive study. *Journal of Leisure Research, 27*, 61–84.

Freysinger, V. J. and Flannery, D. (1992). Women's leisure: Affiliation, self-determination, empowerment and resistance? *Loisir et Société/Society and Leisure, 15*, 303–322.

Freysinger, V. J. and Ray, R. O. (1994). The activity involvement of women and men in young and middle adulthood: A panel study. *Leisure Sciences, 16*, 193–217.

Friedman, M. and Rosenman, R. H. (1974). *Type-A behavior and your heart.* New York, NY: Fawcett.

Friedman, M. and Ulmer, D. (1984). *Treating Type-A behavior and your heart.* New York, NY: Alfred A. Knopf.

Froelicher, V. F. and Froelicher, E. S. (1991). Cardiovascular benefits of physical activity. In B. L. Driver, P. J. Brown and G. L. Peterson (Eds.), *Benefits of leisure* (pp. 59–72). State College, PA: Venture Publishing, Inc.

Fromm, E. (1955). *The sane society.* New York, NY: Rinehart.

Fry, W. F. and Allen, M. (1975). *Make 'em laugh: Life studies of comedy writers.* Palo Alto, CA: Science and Behavior Books, Inc.

Frydenberg, E. and Lewis, R. (1993). Boys play sport and girls turn to others: Age, gender and ethnicity as determinants of coping. *Journal of Adolescence, 16*, 253–266.

Fryer, D. and Payne, R. (1984). Proactive behavior in unemployment: Findings and implications. *Leisure Studies, 3*, 273–295.

Galda, L. and Pellegrini, A. D. (1982). The effects of thematic-fantasy play training on the development of children's story comprehension. *American Education Research Journal, 19*, 443–452.

Gergen, K. J. (1973). Social psychology as history. *Journal of Personality and Social Psychology, 26*, 309–320.

Geva, A. and Goldman, A. (1991). Satisfaction measurements in guided tours. *Annals of Tourism Research, 18*, 177–185.

Giele, J. (1980). Adulthood as a transcendence of age and sex. In T. Sinclair, and E. Erikson (Eds.), *Themes of work and love in adulthood* (pp. 151–173). Cambridge, MA: Harvard University Press.

Gilligan, C. (1982). *In a different voice: Psychological theory and women's development.* Cambridge, MA: Harvard University Press.

Glancy, M. (1988). The play-world setting of the auction. *Journal of Leisure Research, 20,* 135–153.

Glass, D. C. and Singer, J. E. (1972). *Urban stress.* New York, NY: Academic Press.

Glynn, M. A. and Webster, J. (1993). Refining the nomological net of the adult playfulness scale: Personality, motivational, and attitudinal correlates for highly intelligent adults. *Psychological Reports, 72,* 1023–1026.

Godbey, G. (1988). The sociology of leisure: Past, present, and future research. In L. A. Barnett (Ed.), *Research about leisure: Past, present, and future* (pp. 35–44). Champaign, IL: Sagamore Publishing.

Godbey, G. (1994). *Leisure in your life* (4th ed.). State College, PA: Venture Publishing, Inc.

Goldberg, L. R. (1981). Language and individual differences: The search for universals in personality lexicons. In L. Wheeler (Ed.), *Review of personality and social psychology*, Vol. 2, (pp. 145–165). Newbury Park, CA: Sage Publications.

Goodale, T. L. (1990). Perceived freedom as leisure's antithesis. *Journal of Leisure Research, 22,* 296–302.

Goodale, T. L. and Godbey, G. (1988). *The evolution of leisure.* State College, PA: Venture Publishing, Inc.

Goodale, T. L. and Witt, P. A. (1989). Recreation non-participation and barriers to leisure. In E. L. Jackson and T. L. Burton (Eds.), *Understanding leisure and recreation: Mapping the past, charting the future* (pp. 421–449). State College, PA: Venture Publishing, Inc.

Gordon, C., Gaitz, C. M. and Scott, J. (1976). Leisure and lives: Personal expressivity across the life span. In R. Binstock and E. Shanas (Eds.), *Handbook of aging and the social sciences* (pp. 310–341). New York, NY: Van Nostrand Reinhold Company.

Goudy, W. J. and Myers, P. M. G. (1985). Retirement and leisure: A review of five books. *Leisure Sciences, 7,* 479–486.

Graef, R., Csikszentmihalyi, M. and Gianinno, S. M. (1983). Measuring intrinsic motivation in everyday life. *Leisure Studies, 2,* 155–168.

Graefe, A. R. and Fedler, A. J. (1986). Situational and subjective determinants of satisfaction in marine recreational fishing. *Leisure Sciences, 8*, 275–295.

Graham, D. F., Graham, I. and MacLean, M. J. (1991). Going to the mall: A leisure activity of urban elderly people. *Canadian Journal on Aging, 12*, 345–358.

Graham, R., Nilsen, P. and Payne, R. J. (1988). Visitor management in Canadian National Parks. *Tourism Management,* 44–62.

Gramann, J. H. (1995). Ethnicity, race, and outdoor recreation: A review of trends, policy, and research. Vicksburg, MS: U.S. Army Corps of Engineers, Waterways Experiment Station, Environmental Laboratory, Natural Resources Division.

Gramann, J. H. and Bonifield, R. L. (1995). Effect of personality and situational factors on intentions to obey rules in outdoor recreation areas. *Journal of Leisure Research, 27*, 326–343.

Greenberg, J. and Folger, R. (1988). *Controversial issues in social research methods.* New York, NY: Springer-Verlag.

Greenberger, E. and Steinberg, L. (1986). *When teenagers work.* Englewood Cliffs, NJ: Prentice-Hall.

Greeno, J. B. (1994). Gibson's affordances. *Psychological Review, 101*, 336–342.

Grieves, J. (1989). Acquiring a leisure identity: Juvenile jazz bands and the moral universe of "healthy" leisure time. *Leisure Studies, 8*, 1–9.

Griffiths, V. (1988). From playing out to dossing out: Young women and leisure. In E. Wimbush and M. Talbot (Eds.), *Relative freedoms: Women and leisure* (pp. 48–59). Milton Keynes, UK: Open University Press.

Grolnick, W. S. and Ryan, R. M. (1989). Parent styles associated with children's self-regulation and competence in school. *Journal of Educational Psychology, 81*, 143–154.

Gronlund, G. (1992). Coping with ninja-turtle play in my kindergarten classroom. *Young Children, 48*, 21–25.

Grubb, E. A. (1975). Assembly line boredom and individual differences in recreation participation. *Journal of Leisure Research, 7*, 256–269.

Guinn, R. (1980). Elderly recreational vehicle tourists: Life satisfaction correlates of leisure satisfaction. *Journal of Leisure Research, 12*, 198–204.

Gunter, B. G. (1987). The leisure experience: Selected properties. *Journal of Leisure Research, 19*, 115–130.

Gunter, B. G. and Gunter, N. C. (1980). Leisure styles: A conceptual framework for modern leisure. *The Sociological Quarterly, 21*, 361–374.

Gurin, G., Veroff, J. and Feld, S. (1960). *Americans view their mental health.* New York, NY: Basic Books.

Gutmann, D. (1975). Parenthood: A key to the comparative study of the life cycle. In N. Datan and L. Ginsburg (Eds.), *Life-span developmental psychology: Normative life crises* (pp. 167–184). New York, NY: Academic Press.

Gutmann, D. (1977). The cross-cultural perspective: Notes toward a comparative psychology of aging. In J. Birren and K. W. Schaie (Eds.), *Handbook of the psychology of aging* (pp. 302–326). New York, NY: Van Nostrand Reinhold.

Haavio-Mannila, E. (1971). Satisfaction with family, work, leisure, and life among men and women. *Human Relations, 24*, 585–601.

Haggard, L. M. and Williams, D. R. (1991). Self-identity benefits of leisure activities. In B. L. Driver, P. J. Brown and G. L. Peterson (Eds.), *Benefits of leisure* (pp. 103–119). State College, PA: Venture Publishing, Inc.

Haggard, L. M. and Williams, D. R. (1992). Identity affirmation through leisure activities: Leisure symbols of the self. *Journal of Leisure Research, 24*, 1–18.

Hamilton, J. A. (1981). Attention, personality, and the self-regulation of mood: Absorbing interest and boredom. *Progress in Experimental Personality Research, 10*, 281–315.

Hamilton, J. A. (1983a). Development of interest and enjoyment in adolescence. Part I: Attentional capacities. *Journal of Youth and Adolescence, 5*, 355–362.

Hamilton, J. A. (1983b). Development of interest and enjoyment in adolescence. Part II: Boredom and psychopathology. *Journal of Youth and Adolescence, 5*, 363–372.

Hammitt, W. E. (1980). Outdoor recreation: Is it a multi-phase experience? *Journal of Leisure Research, 12*, 107–115.

Harackiewicz, J. (1979). The effects of reward contingency and performance feedback on intrinsic motivation. *Journal of Personality and Social Psychology, 37*, 1352–1363.

Harlan, J. E. and Hawkins, B. A. (1992). Terminal illness, aging, and developmental disability: A therapeutic art intervention. *Therapeutic Recreation Journal, 26*, 49–52.

Harlow, H. F. (1950). Learning and satiation of a response in intrinsically motivated complex puzzle performance by monkeys. *Journal of Comparative Physiological Psychology, 43*, 289–294.

Harlow, H. F. and Harlow, M. (1962). Social depreciation in monkeys. *Scientific American, 207*, 137–146.

Harper, W. (1981). The experience of leisure. *Leisure Sciences, 4*, 113–126.

Harper, W. (1986). Freedom in the experience of leisure. *Leisure Sciences, 8*, 115–130.

Harvey, C. D. H. and Bahr, H. M. (1980). *The sunshine widows: Adapting to sudden bereavement*. Lexington, MA: Lexington Books.

Hastorf, A. and Cantril, H. (1954). They saw a game: A case study. *Journal of Abnormal and Social Psychology, 49*, 129–134.

Hatcher, M. (1988). What happens to the early retiree. *Career Development Quarterly, 37*, 184–190.

Havighurst, R. J. (1953). *Older people*. New York, NY: Longmans and Green.

Havighurst, R. J. (1972). *Developmental tasks and education*. New York, NY: David McKay.

Havighurst, R. J. and Albrecht, R. (1953). *Older people*. New York, NY: Longman, Green.

Havitz, M. E. and Crompton, J. L. (1990). The influence of persuasive messages on propensity to purchase selected recreational services from public or from commercial suppliers. *Journal of Leisure Research, 22*, 71–88.

Haworth, J. T. (1984). The perceived nature of meaningful pursuits and the social psychology of commitment. *Loisir et Société/Society and Leisure, 7*, 197–216.

Haworth, J. T. (1986). Meaningful activity and psychological models of non-employment. *Leisure Studies, 5*, 281–297.

Haworth, J. T. and Ducker, J. (1991). Psychological well-being and access to categories of experience in unemployed young adults. *Leisure Studies, 10*, 265–274.

Haworth, J. T. and Millar, T. (1986). Research note: Time diary sampling of daily activity and intrinsic motivation in unemployed young adults. *Leisure Studies, 5*, 353–359.

Hazel, K. L., Langenau, E. E. Jr. and Levine, R. L. (1990). Dimensions of hunting satisfaction: Multiple-satisfactions of wild turkey hunting. *Leisure Sciences, 12*, 383–393.

Heberlein, T. A. (1973). Social psychological assumptions of user attitude surveys: The case of the wildernism scale. *Journal of Leisure Research, 5*, 18–33.

Heckhausen, H. and Kuhl, J. (1985). From wishes to action: The dead ends and short cuts on the long way to action. In M. Frese, and J. Sabini (Eds.), *Goal-directed behavior: Psychological theory and research on action.* Hillsdale, NJ: Erlbaum.

Heider, F. (1958). *The psychology of interpersonal relations.* New York, NY: John Wiley & Sons.

Hendee, J. C. and Burdge, R. J. (1974). The substitutability concept: Implications for recreation research and management. *Journal of Leisure Research, 6,* 157–162.

Henderson, K. A. (1990a). An oral life history perspective on the containers in which American farm women experienced leisure. *Leisure Studies, 9,* 121–133.

Henderson, K. A. (1990b). The meaning of leisure for women: An integrative review of the research. *Journal of Leisure Research, 22,* 228–243.

Henderson, K. A. (1991a). *Dimensions of choice: A qualitative approach to recreation, parks, and leisure research.* State College, PA: Venture Publishing, Inc.

Henderson, K. A. (1991b). The contribution of feminism to an understanding of leisure constraints. *Journal of Leisure Research, 23,* 363–377.

Henderson, K. A. (1994). Broadening an understanding of women, gender, and leisure. *Journal of Leisure Research, 26,* 1–7.

Henderson, K. A., Bedini, L. A. and Schuler, R. (1995). Women with physical disabilities and the negotiation of leisure constraints. *Leisure Studies, 14,* 17–31.

Henderson, K. A. and Bialeschki, M. D. (1992). Leisure research and the social structure of feminism. *Loisir et Société/Society and Leisure, 15,* 63–77.

Henderson, K. A. and Bialeschki, M. D. (1993). Negotiating constraints to women's physical recreation. *Loisir et Société/Society and Leisure, 16,* 389–412.

Henderson, K. A., Bialeschki, M. D., Shaw, S. M. and Freysinger, V. J. (1989). *A leisure of one's own: A feminist perspective on women's leisure.* State College, PA: Venture Publishing, Inc.

Henderson, K. A., Bialeschki, M. D., Shaw, S. M. and Freysinger, V. J. (1996). *Both gains and gaps: Feminist perspectives on women's leisure.* State College, PA: Venture Publishing, Inc.

Henderson, K. A. and Rannells, J. S. (1988). Farm women and the meaning of work and leisure: An oral history perspective. *Leisure Sciences, 10,* 41–50.

Henderson, K. A., Stalnaker, D. and Taylor, G. (1988). The relationship between barriers to recreation and gender-role personality traits for women. *Journal of Leisure Research, 20*, 69–80.

Hendry, L. B., Shucksmith, J., Love, J. G. and Glendinning, A. (1993). *Young people's leisure and lifestyles.* London, UK: Routledge.

Henretta, J. C., Orand, A. M. and Chan, C. G. (1993). Joint role investments and synchronization of retirement: A sequential approach to couples' retirement timing. *Social Forces, 71*, 981–1000.

Herzog, A. R. and Rodgers, W. L. (1981). The structure of subjective well-being in different age groups. *Journal of Gerontology, 36*, 472–479.

Heywood, L. A. (1978). Perceived recreative experience and the relief of tension. *Journal of Leisure Research, 10*, 86–97.

Higgins, C., Duxbury, L. and Lee, C. (1994). Impact of life-cycle stage and gender on ability to balance work and family responsibilities. *Family Relations, 43*, 144–150.

Hildebrand, M. and Mannell, R. C. (1996). Leisure and the job satisfaction of teachers. In P. Stokowski and J. Hultsman (Eds.), *Abstracts of presentations: 1996 Leisure Research Symposium.* Arlington, VA: National Recreation and Parks Association.

Hilgard, E. R. (1962). *Introduction to psychology.* New York, NY: Harcourt, Brace and World, Inc.

Hill, M. S. (1988). Marital stability and spouses' shared time. *Journal of Family Issues, 9*, 427–451.

Hiroto, D. (1974). Locus of control and learned helplessness. *Journal of Experimental Psychology, 102*, 187–193.

Hirschman, E. C. (1984). Leisure motives and sex roles. *Journal of Leisure Research, 16*, 209–223.

Hogan, P. I. and Santomier, J. P. (1982). Stress and leisure activities. *Leisure Information Newsletter, 8*, 7–8.

Hogan, R. (1987). Personality psychology: Back to basics. In J. Aronoff, A. I. Rabin and R. A. Zucker (Eds.), *The emergence of personality.* New York, NY: Springer.

Holland, A. and Andre, T. (1994). Athletic participation and the social status of adolescent males and females. *Youth and Society, 25*, 388–407.

Holman, T. B. and Epperson, A. (1984). Family and leisure: A review of the literature with research recommendations. *Journal of Leisure Research, 16*, 277–294.

Holman, T. B. and Jacquart, M. (1988). Leisure activity patterns and marital satisfaction: A further test. *Journal of Marriage and the Family, 50*, 69–78.

Hooyman, N. and Kiyak, H. (1996). *Social gerontology* (4th ed.). Boston, MA: Allyn & Bacon.

Hormuth, S. (1984). Transitions in commitments to roles and self-concept change: Relocation as a paradigm. In V. Allen and E. Van de Vliert (Eds.), *Role transitions* (pp. 109–124). New York, NY: Plenum Press.

Horna, J. L. A. (1989a). The dual asymmetry in the married couples' life: The gender-differentiated work, family, and leisure domains. *International Journal of Sociology of the Family, 19*, 113–130.

Horna, J. L. A. (1989b). The leisure component of the parental role. *Journal of Leisure Research, 21*, 228–241.

Horna, J. L. A. and Lupri, E. (1987). Fathers' participation in work, family life and leisure: A Canadian experience. In C. Lewis, and M. O'Brien (Eds.), *Reassessing fatherhood: New observations on fathers and the modern family* (pp. 54–73). London, UK: Sage Publications.

Horney, K. (1937). *New ways in psychoanalysis.* New York, NY: W. W. Norton.

Houts, A. C., Cook, T. D. and Shadish, W. R., Jr. (1986). The person-situation debate: A critical multiplist perspective. *Journal of Personality, 54*, 52–105.

Hovland, C. I., Janis, I. L. and Kelley, H. H. (1953). *Communication and persuasion: Psychological studies of opinion change.* New Haven, CT: Yale University Press.

Howe, C. Z. and Qui, Y. (1988). The programming process revisited: Assumptions underlying the needs-based models. *Journal of Park and Recreation Administration, 6*, 14–27.

Howes, C. (1988). Peer interaction of young children. *Monographs of the Society for Research in Child Development, 53(1)*.

Hughes, F. P. (1991). *Children, play and development.* Needham Heights, MA: Allyn & Bacon.

Huizinga, J. (1955). *Homo ludens: A study of the play element in culture.* Boston, MA: Beacon Press.

Hull, R. B., IV (1991). Mood as a product of leisure: Causes and consequences. In B. L. Driver, P. J. Brown and G. L. Peterson (Eds.), *Benefits of leisure* (pp. 249–262). State College, PA: Venture Publishing, Inc.

Hull, R. B., IV and Michael, S. E. (1995). Nature-based recreation, mood change, and stress restoration. *Leisure Sciences, 17* , 1–14.

Hull, R. B., IV, William, P. S. and Young, K. Y. (1992). Experience patterns: Capturing the dynamic nature of a recreation experience. *Journal of Leisure Research, 24*, 240–252.

Hultsman, J. T. and Russell, R. V. (1988). Assessing the reliability of the measurement component of Neulinger's paradigm. *Journal of Leisure Research, 20*, 1–9.

Hultsman, W. Z., Hultsman, J. T. and Black, D. R. (1989). Hunting satisfaction and reciprocal exchange: Initial support from a lottery-regulated hunt. *Leisure Sciences, 11*, 145–150.

Hunter, P. L. and Whitson, D. J. (1991). Women, leisure and familism: Relationships and isolation in small town Canada. *Leisure Studies, 10*, 219–233.

Hutchison, P. and McGill, J. (1992). *Leisure, integration and community*. Concord, ON: Leisurability Publications, Inc.

Hutt, C. (1971). Exploration and play in children. In R. Herron and B. Sutton-Smith (Eds.), *Children's play* (pp. 231–251). New York, NY: John Wiley & Sons.

Ibrahim, H. and Crandall R. (1980). *Leisure: A psychological approach*. Los Angeles, CA: Hwong Publishing.

Ingham, R. (1986). Psychological contributions to the study of leisure—Part one. *Leisure Studies, 5*, 255–279.

Iso-Ahola, S. E. (1976). On the theoretical link between personality and leisure. *Psychological Reports, 39*, 3–10.

Iso-Ahola, S. E. (1977). Effects of team outcome on children's self-perception: Little League Baseball. *Scandinavian Journal of Psychology, 18*, 38–42.

Iso-Ahola, S. E. (1979a). Some social psychological determinants of perceptions of leisure: Preliminary evidence. *Leisure Sciences, 2*, 305–314.

Iso-Ahola, S. E. (1979b). Basic dimensions of definitions of leisure. *Journal of Leisure Research, 11*, 28–39.

Iso-Ahola, S. E. (1980a). *The social psychology of leisure and recreation*. Dubuque, IA: Wm. C. Brown Company Publishers.

Iso-Ahola, S. E. (Ed.) (1980b). *Social psychological perspectives on leisure and recreation*. Springfield, IL: Charles C. Thomas, Publisher.

Iso-Ahola, S. E. (1980c). A social psychological analysis of Little League Baseball. In S. E. Iso-Ahola (Ed.), *Social psychological perspectives on leisure and recreation* (pp. 171–218). Springfield, IL: Charles C. Thomas, Publisher.

Iso-Ahola, S. E. (1982). Toward a social psychological theory of tourism motivation: A rejoinder. *Annals of Tourism Research, 12*, 256–262.

Iso-Ahola, S. E. (1983). Towards a social psychology of recreational travel. *Leisure Studies, 2,* 45–56.

Iso-Ahola, S. E. (1986). A theory of substitutability of leisure behavior. *Leisure Sciences, 8,* 367–389.

Iso-Ahola, S. E. (1988). The social psychology of leisure: Past, present, and future research. In L. A. Barnett (Ed.), *Research about leisure: Past, present and future* (pp. 75–93). Champaign, IL: Sagamore Publishing.

Iso-Ahola, S. E. (1989). Motivation for leisure. In E. L. Jackson and T. L. Burton (Eds.), *Understanding leisure and recreation: Mapping the past, charting the future* (pp. 247–279). State College, PA: Venture Publishing, Inc.

Iso-Ahola, S. E. (1995). The social psychology of leisure: Past, present, and future research. In L. A. Barnett (Ed.), *Research about leisure: Past, present, and future research,* 2nd ed. (pp. 65–96). Champaign, IL: Sagamore Publishing.

Iso-Ahola, S. E. and Allen, J. R. (1982). The dynamics of leisure motivation: The effects of outcome on leisure needs. *Research Quarterly For Exercise and Sport, 53,* 141–149.

Iso-Ahola, S. E. and Crowley, E. D. (1991). Adolescent substance abuse and leisure boredom. *Journal of Leisure Research, 23,* 260–271.

Iso-Ahola, S. E., Graefe, A. R. and LaVerde, D. (1989). Perceived competence as a mediator of the relationship between high risk sports participation and self-esteem. *Journal of Leisure Research, 21,* 32–39.

Iso-Ahola, S. E., Jackson, E. and Dunn, E. (1994). Starting, ceasing and replacing leisure activities over the life-span. *Journal of Leisure Research, 26,* 227–249.

Iso-Ahola, S. E. and Mannell, R. C. (1985). Social and psychological constraints on leisure. In M. G. Wade (Ed.), *Constraints on leisure* (pp. 111–151). Springfield, IL: Charles C. Thomas, Publisher.

Iso-Ahola, S. E. and Weissinger, E. (1987). Leisure and boredom. *Journal of Social and Clinical Psychology, 5,* 356–364.

Iso-Ahola, S. E. and Weissinger, E. (1990). Perceptions of boredom in leisure: Conceptualization, reliability and validity of the Leisure Boredom Scale. *Journal of Leisure Research, 22,* 1–17.

Jackson, D. N. (1974). *Personality research form manual.* Goshen, NY: Research Psychologists Press.

Jackson, E. L. (1988). Leisure constraints: A survey of past research. *Leisure Sciences, 10,* 203–215.

Jackson, E. L. (1990). Variations in desire to begin a leisure activity: Evidence of antecedent constraints? *Journal of Leisure Research, 22*, 55–70.

Jackson, E. L. (1993). Recognizing patterns of leisure constraints. *Journal of Leisure Research, 25*, 129–149.

Jackson, E. L. and Burton, T. L. (Eds.). (1989). *Understanding leisure and recreation: Mapping the past, charting the future.* State College, PA: Venture Publishing, Inc.

Jackson, E. L., Crawford, D. W. and Godbey, G. (1992). Negotiation of leisure constraints. *Leisure Sciences, 15*, 1–12.

Jackson, E. L. and Dunn, E. (1988). Integrating ceasing participation with other aspects of leisure behavior. *Journal of Leisure Research, 20*, 31–45.

Jackson, E. L. and Henderson, K. A. (1995). Gender-based analysis of leisure constraints. *Leisure Sciences, 17*, 31–51.

Jackson, E. L. and Rucks, V. C. (1995). Negotiation of leisure constraints by junior-high and high-school students: An exploratory study. *Journal of Leisure Research, 27*, 85–105.

Jackson, E. L. and Searle, M. S. (1985). Recreation non-participation and barriers to participation: Concepts and models. *Loisir et Société/Society and Leisure, 8*, 693–707.

James, W. (1890). *The principles of psychology.* New York, NY: Henry Holt.

Jenkins, C. D., Zyzanski, S. and Rosenman, R. H. (1979). *Jenkins activity survey manual.* New York, NY: The Psychological Corporation.

Jensenscott, R. L. (1993). Counseling to promote retirement adjustment. *Career Development Quarterly, 41*, 246–256.

Johnson, R. C. A. (1978). Attitudes toward the use of designated versus non-designated urban recreation space. *Leisure Sciences, 1*, 259–269.

Johnson, R. L. and Brown, T. C. (1991). Beneficial economic consequences of leisure and recreation. In B. L. Driver, P. J. Brown and G. L. Peterson (Eds.), *Benefits of leisure* (pp. 385–391). State College, PA: Venture Publishing Inc.

Kabanoff, B. (1980). Work and nonwork: A review of models, methods and findings. *Psychological Bulletin, 88*, 60–77.

Kabanoff, B. and O'Brien, G. E. (1986). Stress and the leisure needs and activities of different occupations. *Human Relations, 39*, 903–916.

Kando, T. M. and Summers, W. C. (1971). The impact of work on leisure: Toward a paradigm and research strategy. *Pacific Sociological Review, July*, 310–327.

Kane, J. E. (1972). *Psychological aspects of physical education and sport.* London, UK: Routledge and Kegan Paul.

Kaplin, R. M., Sallis Jr., J. F. and Patterson, T. L. (1993). *Health and human behavior.* New York, NY: McGraw-Hill.

Karlis, G. (1990). Ethnic maintenance and recreation: A case study. *Journal of Applied Recreation Research, 15,* 85–99.

Kaufman, J. E., McBride, L. G., Hultsman, J. T. and Black, D. R. (1988). Perceptions of leisure and an eating disorder: An exploratory study of bulimia. *Therapeutic Recreation Journal, 22,* 55–63.

Keele, S. W. and Hawkins, H. L. (1982). Explorations of individual differences relevant to high level skill. *Journal of Motor Behavior, 14,* 3–23.

Kelley, H. H. (1967). Attribution theory in social psychology. In D. Levine (Ed.), *Nebraska Symposium on Motivation:* Vol. 15 (pp. 192–241). Lincoln, NE: University of Nebraska Press.

Kelly, J. R. (1972). Work and leisure: A simplified paradigm. *Journal of Leisure Research, 4,* 50–62.

Kelly, J. R. (1973). Three measures of leisure activity: A note on the continued incommensurability of oranges, apples and artichokes. *Journal of Leisure Research, 5,* 56–65.

Kelly, J. R. (1974). Socialization toward leisure: A developmental approach. *Journal of Leisure Research, 6,* 181–193.

Kelly, J. R. (1975). Life styles and leisure choices. *The Family Coordinator, Apr,* 185–190.

Kelly, J. R. (1977). Leisure socialization: Replication and extension. *Journal of Leisure Research, 9,* 121–132.

Kelly, J. R. (1978). A revised paradigm of leisure choices. *Leisure Sciences, 1,* 345–363.

Kelly, J. R. (1983). *Leisure identities and interactions.* London, UK: Allen and Unwin.

Kelly, J. R. (1987a). *Peoria winter: Styles and resources in later life.* Lexington, MA: Heath.

Kelly, J. R. (1987b). *Freedom to be: Toward a new sociology of leisure.* New York, NY: Macmillan.

Kelly, J. R. (1988). History and philosophy of leisure: Past, present, and future directions. In L. A. Barnett (Ed.), *Research about leisure: Past, present, and future* (pp. 19–33). Champaign, IL: Sagamore Publishing.

Kelly, J. R. (1993). Leisure-family research: Old and new issues. *World Leisure and Recreation, 35*, 5–9.

Kelly, J. R. (1996). *Leisure* (3rd ed.). Boston, MA: Allyn & Bacon.

Kelly, J. R. and Masar, S. (1970). *Leisure identities through a life course transition.* Unpublished Paper, University of Illinois at Urbana-Champaign.

Kelly, J. R. and Ross, J.-E. (1989). Later-life leisure: Beginning a new agenda. *Leisure Sciences, 11*, 47–59.

Kelly, J. R., Steinkamp, M. W. and Kelly, J. R. (1987). Later-life satisfaction: Does leisure contribute? *Leisure Sciences, 9*, 189–200.

Kelman, H. C. (1967). Human use of human subjects: The problem of deception in social psychology experiments. *Psychological Bulletin, 67*, 1–11.

Kerr, G. N. and Manfredo, M. J. (1991). An attitudinal based model of pricing for recreation services. *Journal of Leisure Research, 23*, 37–50.

Killinger, B. (1991). *Workaholics: The respectable addicts.* Toronto, ON: Key Porter Books.

Kilpatrick, R. and Trew, K. (1985). Lifestyles and psychological well-being among unemployed men in Northern Ireland. *Journal of Occupational Psychology, 58*, 207–216.

King, A. C., Barr Taylor, C. and Haskell, W. L. (1993). Effects of differing intensities and formats of 12 months of exercise training on psychological outcomes in older adults. *Health Psychology, 12*, 292–300.

Kirchmeyer, C. (1993). Nonwork-to-work spillover: A more balanced view of the experiences and coping of professional women and men. *Sex Roles, 28*, 531–552.

Kirkcaldy, B. D. (1989). Gender and personality determinants of recreational interests. *Studia Psychologica, 30*, 115–127.

Kirkcaldy, B. D. and Cooper, C.L. (1992). Work attitiudes and leisure pursuits: Sex differences. *Personality and individual differences, 12*, 737–745.

Kirkcaldy, B. D. and Furnham, A. (1991). Extraversion, neuroticism, psychoticism and recreational choices. *Personality and Individual Differences, 12*, 737–745.

Kirkcaldy, B. D., Shephard, R. J. and Cooper, C. L. (1993). Relationships between Type-A behaviour, work and leisure. *Personality and Individual Differences, 15*, 69–74.

Klausner, W. J. (1968). An experiment in leisure. *Science Journal, 4*, 81–85.

Kleiber, D. A. (1979). Fate control and leisure attitudes. *Leisure Sciences, 2*, 238–248.

Kleiber, D. A. (1985). Motivational reorientation in adulthood and the resource of leisure. *Advances in Motivation and Achievement, 4,* 217–250.

Kleiber, D. A., Caldwell, L. L. and Shaw, S. M. (1993). Leisure meanings in adolescence. *Loisir et Société/Society and Leisure, 16,* 99–114.

Kleiber, D. A. and Crandall, R. (1981). Leisure and work ethics and locus of control. *Leisure Sciences, 4,* 477–485.

Kleiber, D. A. and Dirkin, G. R. (1985). Intrapersonal constraints to leisure. In M. G. Wade (Ed.), *Constraints on leisure* (pp. 17–42). Springfield, IL: Charles C. Thomas, Publisher.

Kleiber, D. A. and Hemmer, J. D. (1981). Sex differences in the relationship of locus of control and recreational sport participation. *Sex Roles, 7,* 801–810.

Kleiber, D. A. and Kane, M. J. (1984). Sex differences and the use of leisure as adaptive potentiation. *Loisir et Société/Society and Leisure, 7,* 165–173.

Kleiber, D. A. and Kelly, J. R. (1980). Leisure, socialization, and the life cycle. In S. E. Iso-Ahola (Ed.), *Social psychological perspectives on leisure and recreation* (pp. 91–137). Springfield, IL: Charles C. Thomas, Publisher.

Kleiber, D. A. and Kirshnit, C. (1991). Sport involvement and identity formation. In L. Diamant (Ed.), *Mind-body maturity: Psychological approaches to sport, exercise and fitness.* New York, NY: Hemisphere.

Kleiber, D. A., Larson, R. W. and Csikszentmihalyi, M. (1986). The experience of leisure in adolescence. *Journal of Leisure Research, 18,* 169–176.

Kleiber, D. A. and Ray, R. O. (1993). Leisure and generativity. In J. Kelley (Ed.), *Activity and aging* (pp. 106–177). Newbury Park, CA: Sage Publications.

Kleiber, D. A. and Rickards, W. H. (1985). Leisure and recreation in adolescence: Limitation and potential. In M. G. Wade (Ed.), *Constraints on leisure* (pp. 289–317). Springfield, IL: Charles C. Thomas, Publisher.

Knapp, R. and Hartsoe, C. (1979). *Play for America: The National Recreation Association, 1906–1965.* Arlington, VA: National Recreation and Park Association.

Knopf, R. C. (1983). Recreational needs and behavior in natural settings. In I. Altman and J. F. Wohlwill (Eds.), *Behavior and the natural environment* (pp. 205–240). New York, NY: Plenum Publishing Corporation.

Knopp, T. B. (1972). Environmental determinants of recreation behavior. *Journal of Leisure Research, 4,* 129–138.

Kotash, M. (1987). *No kidding: Inside the world of teenage girls.* Toronto, ON: McClelland and Stewart.

Kubey, R. and Csikszentmihalyi, M. (1990). *Television and the quality of life.* Hilldale, NJ: Lawrence Erlbaum.

Kulka, R. A. (1979). Interaction as person-environment fit. In L. R. Kahle (Ed.), *New directions for methodology of behavioral science* (pp. 55–72). San Francisco, CA: Jossey-Bass.

Langer, E. J. (1975). The illusion of control. *Journal of Personality and Social Psychology, 32,* 311–328.

Langer, E. J. (1983). *The psychology of control.* London, UK: Sage Publications.

LaPage, W. F. (1974). Family camping trends: An eight-year panel study. *Journal of Leisure Research, 6,* 101–112.

Larsen, R. J., Diener, E. and Cropanzano, R. S. (1987). Cognitive operations associated with individual differences in affect intensity. *Journal of Personality and Social Psychology, 53,* 767–774.

Larson, R. W. (1978). Thirty years of research on the subjective well-being of older Americans. *Journal of Gerontology, 33,* 109–125.

Larson, R. W. (1990). The solitary side of life: An examination of the time people spend alone from childhood to old age. *Developmental Review, 10,* 155–183.

Larson, R. W. and Csikszentmihalyi, M. (1983). The experience sampling method. In H. T. Reis (Ed.), *Naturalistic approaches to studying social interaction* (pp. 41–56). San Fransisco, CA: Jossey-Bass.

Larson, R. W. and Kleiber, D. A. (1993). Structured leisure as a context for the development of attention during adolescence. *Loisir et Société/Society and Leisure, 16,* 77–98.

Larson, R. W., Mannell, R. C. and Zuzanek, J. (1986). Daily well-being of older adults with friends and family. *Journal of Psychology and Aging, 1,* 117–126.

Latane, B. and Darley, J. M. (1970). *The unresponsive bystander: Why doesn't he help?* New York, NY: Appleton-Century-Crofts.

Lawton, M. P. (1975). The Philadelphia Geriatric Center Moral Scale: A revision. *Journal of Gerontology, 30,* 85–89.

Lawton, M. P. (1993). Meanings of activity. In J. Kelly (Ed.), *Activity and aging* (pp. 125–144). Newbury Park, CA: Sage Publications.

Leary, M. R. and Atherton, S. C. (1986). Self-efficacy, anxiety, and inhibition in interpersonal encounters. *Journal of Social and Clinical Psychology, 4,* 256–67.

Lee, Y., Dattilo, J. and Howard, D. (1994). The complex and dynamic nature of leisure experience. *Journal of Leisure Research, 26,* 195–211.

Lee, Y. and Halberg, K. J. (1989). An exploratory study of college students' perception of freedom in leisure and shyness. *Leisure Sciences, 11*, 217–228.

Lefcourt, H. M. (1973). The function of the illusions of control and freedom. *American Psychologist, 28*, 417–425.

Lefcourt, H. M. (1976). *Locus of control.* New York, NY: John Wiley & Sons.

Lepper, M. R. and Greene, D. (1979). *The hidden costs of rewards.* New York, NY: John Wiley & Sons.

Lepper, M. R., Greene, D. and Nisbett, R. E. (1973). Undermining children's intrinsic interest with extrinsic reward: A test of the "overjustification" hypothesis. *Journal of Personality and Social Psychology, 28*, 129–137.

Lerner, R. and Busch-Rossnagel, N. (1981). *Individuals as producers of their own development.* New York, NY: Academic Press.

Lever, J. (1976). Sex differences in the games children play. *Social Problems, 23*, 478–487.

Levinson, D., Darrow, C., Klein, F., Levinson, M. and McKee, B. (1978). *The seasons of a man's life.* New York, NY: Alfred A. Knopf.

Lewin, K. (1935). *Dynamic theory of personality.* New York, NY: McGraw-Hill.

Lewin, K. (1947). Group decision and social change. In T. M. Newcomb and E. L. Hartley (Eds.), *Readings in social psychology* (pp. 330–344). New York, NY: Henry Holt & Co.

Lewinsohn, P. M. and Graf, M. (1973). Pleasant activities and depression. *Journal of Consulting and Clinical Psychology, 41*, 261–268.

Lieberman, J. N. (1977). *Playfulness: Its relationship to imagination and creativity.* New York, NY: Academic Press.

Likert, R. (1932). A technique for the measurement of attitudes. *Archives of Psychology, 140*, 1–55.

Linder, S. (1971). *The harried leisure class.* New York, NY: Academic Press.

London, M., Crandall, R. and Fitzgibbons, D. (1977). The psychological structure of leisure: Activities, needs, people. *Journal of Leisure Research, 9*, 252–263.

London, M., Crandall, R. and Seals, G. W. (1977). The contribution of job and leisure satisfaction to quality of life. *Journal of Applied Psychology, 62*, 328–334.

Long, J. (1987). Continuity as a basis for change: Leisure and male retirement. *Leisure Studies, 6*, 55–70.

Lopata, H. J. (1967). *Widowhood in an American city*. Cambridge, MA: Schenkman Publishing.

Losier, G. F., Bourque, P. E. and Vallerand, R. J. (1993). A motivational model of leisure participation in the elderly. *Journal of Psychology, 127*, 153–170.

Lounsbury, J. W., Gordon, S. R., Bergermaier, R. L. and Francesco, A. M. (1982). Work and nonwork sources of satisfaction in relation to employee intention to turnover. *Journal of Leisure Research, 14*, 285–294.

Lounsbury, J. W. and Hoopes, L. L. (1986). A vacation from work: Changes in work and nonwork outcomes. *Journal of Applied Psychology, 71*, 392–401.

Lounsbury, J. W. and Hoopes, L. L. (1985). An investigation of factors associated with vacation satisfaction. *Journal of Leisure Research, 17*, 1–13.

Lounsbury, J. W. and Hoopes, L. L. (1988). Five-year stability of leisure activity and motivation factors. *Journal of Leisure Research, 20*, 118–134.

Lounsbury, J. W. and Polik, J. R. (1992). Leisure needs and vacation satisfaction. *Leisure Sciences, 14*, 105–119.

Lundberg, G., Komarovsky, M. and McInerny, M. A. (1934). *Leisure: A suburban study*. New York, NY: Columbia University Press.

Lynd, R. S. and Lynd, H. M. (1929). *Middletown: A study in American culture*. New York, NY: Harcourt, Brace and World.

Lynd, R. S. and Lynd, H. M. (1937). *Middletown in transition*. New York, NY: Harcourt, Brace and World.

Lyons, R. F. (1985). Are we still friends? The impact of chronic illness on personal relationships and leisure. *Loisir et Société/ Society and Leisure, 8*, 435–465.

Lyons, R. F., Sullivan, M. J. L. and Ritvo, P. G. (1995). *Relationships in chronic illness and disability*. Newbury Park, CA: Sage Publications.

MacCannell, D. (1973). Staged authenticity: Arrangements of social space in tourist settings. *The American Journal of Sociology, 79*, 589–603.

MacCannell, D. (1976). *The tourist: A new theory of the leisure class*. New York, NY: Schocken.

MacNeil, R. D. (1995). Leisure programs and services for older adults. In L. A. Barnett (Ed.), *Research about leisure: Past, present, and future* (2nd ed., pp. 149–176). Champaign, IL: Sagamore Publishing.

MacNeil, R. D. and Teague, M. (1987). *Aging and leisure: Vitality in later life*. Englewood Cliffs, NJ: Prentice-Hall.

Madden, D. J., Pierce, T. W. and Allen, P. A. (1993). Linking retirement experiences and marital satisfaction: A mediation model. *Psychology and Aging, 8,* 508–516.

Madden, T. J., Ellen, P. S. and Ajzen, I. (1992). A comparison of the theory of planned behavior and the theory of reasoned action. *Personality and Social Psychology Bulletin, 18,* 3–9.

Maier, S. F. and Seligman, M. E. P. (1976). Learned helplessness: Theory and evidence. *Journal of Experimental Psychology: General, 105,* 3–46.

Major, W. F. (1994). *Serious running: An interpretive analysis.* Unpublished doctoral dissertation, University of Georgia, Athens, Georgia.

Maloney, T. L. and Petrie, B. M. (1972). Professionalization of attitude toward play among Canadian school pupils as a function of sex, grade, and athletic participation. *Journal of Leisure Research, 4,* 184–195.

Manfredo, M. J. (1992). *Influencing human behavior.* Champaign, IL: Sagamore Publishing.

Manfredo, M. J., Driver, B. L. and Brown, P. J. (1983). A test of concepts inherent in experience based setting management for outdoor recreation areas. *Journal of Leisure Research, 15,* 263–283.

Mannell, R. C. (1979). A conceptual and experimental basis for research in the psychology of leisure. *Loisir et Société/Society and Leisure, 2,* 179–194.

Mannell, R. C. (1980). Social psychological techniques and strategies for studying leisure experiences. In S. E. Iso-Ahola (Ed.), *Social psychological perspectives on leisure and recreation* (pp. 62–88). Springfield, IL: Charles C. Thomas, Publisher.

Mannell, R. C. (1984a). A psychology for leisure research. *Loisir et Société/ Society and Leisure, 7,* 13–21.

Mannell, R. C. (1984b). Personality in leisure theory: The self-as-entertainment construct. *Loisir et Société/Society and Leisure, 7,* 229–242.

Mannell, R. C. (1985). Reliability and validity of a leisure-specific personality measure: The self-as-entertainment construct. *Abstracts from the 1985 Symposium on Leisure Research.* Alexandria, VA: National Recreation and Parks Association.

Mannell, R. C. (1986). Problems, progress and usefulness of theory and research on leisure. In *Abstracts from the 1986 Symposium on Leisure Research.* Alexandria, VA: National Recreation and Park Association.

Mannell, R. C. (1989). Leisure satisfaction. In E. L. Jackson and T. L. Burton (Eds.), *Understanding leisure and recreation: Mapping the past, charting the future* (pp. 281–301). State College, PA: Venture Publishing, Inc.

Mannell, R. C. (1990). On the joys of research. In D. Dustin (Ed.), *Beyond promotion and tenure: On being a professor* (pp. 47–61). San Diego, CA: San Diego State University Institute for Leisure Behavior.

Mannell, R. C. (1991). The "psychologization" of leisure services. In T. L. Goodale and P. A. Witt (Eds.), *Recreation and leisure: Issues in an era of change,* 3rd ed., (pp. 429–439). State College, PA: Venture Publishing, Inc.

Mannell, R. C. (1993). High investment activity and life satisfaction among older adults: Committed, serious leisure and flow activities. In J. R. Kelly (Ed.), *Activity and aging* (pp. 125–145). Newbury Park, CA: Sage Publications.

Mannell, R. C. (1994). Constraints, leisure participation and well-being among older adults. In D. M. Compton and S. E. Iso-Ahola (Eds.), *Leisure and mental health*: Vol. 1 (pp. 79–97). Salt Lake City, UT: Family Development Resources, Inc.

Mannell, R. C. (1996). Approaches in the social and behavioral sciences to the systematic study of hard-to-define human values and experiences. In D. Dustin and B. Driver (Eds.), *Nature and the human spirit: Toward an expanded land management ethic.* State College, PA: Venture Publishing, Inc.

Mannell, R. C. and Backman, S. J. (1979). The effects of perceived freedom of choice and locus of control on transient 'leisure' experiences. In E. M. Avedon, M. Lelevre and T. Stewart (Eds.), *Contemporary leisure research.* Waterloo, ON: Ontario Research Council on Leisure.

Mannell, R. C. and Bradley, W. (1986). Does greater freedom always lead to greater leisure? Testing a person x environment model of freedom and leisure. *Journal of Leisure Research, 18,* 215–230.

Mannell, R. C. and Dupuis, S. (1994). Leisure and productive activity. In M. P. Lawton, and J. Teresi (Eds.), *Annual review of gerontology and geriatrics,* Vol. 14 (pp. 125–141). New York, NY: Springer Publishing Co.

Mannell, R. C. and Dupuis, S. (1996). Life satisfaction. In G. Birren (Ed.), *Encyclopedia of Gerontology*: Vol. 1 (pp. L6:1–6). New York, NY: Academic Press.

Mannell, R. C. and Iso-Ahola, S. E. (1987). Psychological nature of leisure and tourism experience. *Annals of Tourism Research, 14,* 314–331.

Mannell, R. C. and McMahon, L. (1982). Humor as play: Its relationship to psychological well-being during the course of a day. *Leisure Sciences, 5,* 143–155.

Mannell, R. C. and Reid, D. (1996). *The impact of changes in the workplace on employed and unemployed workers: Phase three of the "Changing Patterns of Work and Leisure Study."* Waterloo, ON: University of Waterloo.

Mannell, R. C. and Stynes, D. J. (1991). A retrospective: The benefits of leisure. In B. L. Driver, P. J. Brown and G. L. Peterson (Eds.), *Benefits of leisure* (pp. 461–473). State College, PA: Venture Publishing, Inc.

Mannell, R. C. and Zuzanek, J. (1991). The nature and variability of leisure constraints in daily life: The case of the physically active leisure of older adults. *Leisure Sciences, 13*, 337–351.

Mannell, R. C. and Zuzanek, J. (1995). Married with children: Family leisure in daily life and satisfaction with family life. In *Symposium on Leisure Research* (p. 16). Arlington, VA: National Recreation and Park Association.

Mannell, R. C., Zuzanek, J. and Larson, R. W. (1988). Leisure states and "flow" experiences: Testing perceived freedom and intrinsic motivation hypotheses. *Journal of Leisure Research, 20*, 289–304.

Manning, R. E. (1985). *Studies in outdoor recreation: A review and synthesis of the social science literature in outdoor recreation.* Corvallis, OR: Oregon State University Press.

Mansfeld, Y. (1992). From motivation to actual travel. *Annals of Tourism Research, 19*, 399–419.

Marcuse, H. (1964). *One-dimensional man.* Boston, MA: Beacon Press.

Martin, W. S. and Myrick, F. L. (1976). Personality and leisure time activities. *Research Quarterly, 47*, 246–253.

Marx, K. (1970). *The economic and philosophical manuscripts of 1844.* London, UK: Lawrence and Wishart.

Maslow, A. H. (1954). *Motivation and personality* (2nd ed.). New York, NY: Harper and Row, Publishers.

Maslow, A. H. (1968). *Toward a psychology of being* (2nd ed.). Toronto, ON: Van Nos Reinhold.

Maughan, M. and Ellis, G. D. (1991). Effects of efficacy information during recreation participation on efficacy judgments of depressed adolescents. *Therapeutic Recreation Journal, 25*, 51–59.

McAuley, E. and Rowney, T. (1990). Exercise behavior and intentions: The mediating role of self-efficacy cognitions. In L. VanderVelden, and J. H. Humphrey (Eds.), *Psychology and sociology of sport*, Vol. 2 (pp. 3–15). New York, NY: AMS Press.

McCarville, R. E., Driver, B. L. and Crompton, J. L. (1992). Persuasive communication and the pricing of public leisure services. In M. J. Manfredo (Ed.), *Influencing human behavior: Theory and applications in recreation, tourism, and natural resources management* (pp. 263–291). Champaign, IL: Sagamore Publishing.

McClelland, D. C., Atkinson, J. W., Clark, R. A. and Lowell, E. L. (1953). *The achievement motive*. New York, NY: Appleton-Century-Crofts.

McCormick, B. (1991). Self-experience as leisure constraint: The case of Alcoholics Anonymous. *Journal of Leisure Research, 23*, 345–362.

McCrae, R. R. and Costa, P. T. (1987). Validation of the five-factor model of personality across instruments and observers. *Journal of Personality and Social Psychology, 52*, 81–90.

McCrae, R. R. and John, O. P. (1992). An introduction to the five-factor model and its application. *Journal of Personality, 60*, 175–215.

McCullough, L. S. (1993). Leisure themes in international advertising: A content analysis. *Journal of Leisure Research, 25*, 380–388.

McDaniels, C. (1990). *The changing workplace: Career counseling strategies for the 1990s and beyond*. San Francisco, CA: Jossey-Bass.

McDonald, B. L. and Schreyer, R. (1991). Spiritual benefits of leisure participation and leisure settings. In B. L. Driver, P. J. Brown and G. L. Peterson (Eds.), *Benefits of leisure* (pp. 179–194). State College, PA: Venture Publishing, Inc.

McDougall, W. (1908). *An introduction to social psychology*. London, UK: Methuen.

McGuire, F. A. (1985). Constraints in later life. In M. G. Wade (Ed.), *Constraints on leisure* (pp. 335–353). Springfield, IL: Charles C. Thomas, Publisher.

McGuire, F. A. and Dottavio, F. (1987). Outdoor recreation participation across the lifespan: Abandonment, continuity, or liberation. *International Journal of Aging and Human Development, 24*, 87–99.

McGuire, F. A., Dottavio, F. D. and O'Leary, J. T. (1987). The relationship of early life experiences to later life leisure involvement. *Leisure Sciences, 9*, 251–257.

McGuire, F. A., O'Leary, J. T., Yeh, C.-K. and Dottavio, F. D. (1989). Integrating ceasing participation with other aspects of leisure behavior: A replication and extension. *Journal of Leisure Research, 21*, 316–326.

McIntosh, R. W. and Goeldner, C. R. (1990). *Tourism: Principles, practices, philosophies* (6th ed.). New York, NY: John Wiley & Sons.

McKay, S. (1993). Research findings related to the potential of recreation in delinquency intervention. *Trends, 30*, 27–30.

McKechnie, G. E. (1974). The psychological structure of leisure: Past behavior. *Journal of Leisure Research, 6*, 27–45.

McKechnie, G. E. (1975). *Manual for the Leisure Activities Blank*. Palo Alto, CA: Consulting Psychology Press.

McKenna, S. P. and Fryer, D. M. (1984). Perceived health during lay-off and early unemployment. *Occupational Health, 36*, 201–206.

McLeod, D. I. (1983). *Building character in the American boy: The Boy Scouts, YMCA and their forerunners, 1870–1920*. Madison, WI: University of Wisconsin Press.

McPherson, B. D. (1983). Socialization into and through sport involvement. In W. W. Widemeyer (Ed.), *Physical activity and the social sciences* (pp. 190–213). Ithaca, NY: Mouvement Publications.

McPherson, B. D. (1990). *Aging as a social process*. Toronto, ON: Butterworth.

McPherson, B. D. (1991). Aging and leisure benefits: A life cycle perspective. In B. L. Driver, P. J. Brown and G. L. Peterson (Eds.), *Benefits of leisure* (pp. 423–430). State College, PA: Venture Publishing, Inc.

Medrich, E., Roizen, J., Rubin, V. and Buckley, S. (1982). *The serious business of growing up: A study of children's lives outside of school*. Berkeley, CA: University of California Press.

Mehrabian, A. (1976). *Public places and private spaces: The psychology of work, play and living environments*. New York, NY: Basic Books.

Meir, E. I. and Melamed, S. (1986). The accumulation of person-environment congruences and well-being. *Journal of Occupational Behavior, 7*, 315–323.

Meir, E. I., Melamed, S. and Abu-Freha, A. (1990). Vocational, avocational, and skill utilization congruences and their relationship with well-being in two cultures. *Journal of Vocational Behavior, 36*, 153–165.

Meissner, M. (1970). The long arm of the job: A study of work and leisure. *Industrial Relations, 10*, 239–260.

Melamed, S. and Meir, E. I. (1981). The relationship between interests-job incongruity and selection of avocational activity. *Journal of Vocational Behavior, 18*, 310–325.

Melamed, S., Meir, E. I. and Samson, A. (1995). The benefits of personality-leisure congruence: Evidence and implications. *Journal of Leisure Research, 27*, 25–40.

Mercer, D. (1973). The concept of recreational need. *Journal of Leisure Research, 5*, 37–50.

Meyersohn, R. (1981). *Tourism as a socio-cultural phenomenon: Research perspectives*. Waterloo, ON: OTIUM Publications, Research Group on Leisure and Cultural Development, University of Waterloo.

Milgram, S. (1963). Behavioral study of obedience. *Journal of Abnormal and Social Psychology, 67*, 371–378.

Miller, S. J. (1965). The social dilemma of the aging leisure participant. In A. M. Rose and W. Peterson (Eds.), *Older people and their social worlds* (pp. 77–92). Philadelphia, PA: F. A. Davis Company.

Mischel, W. (1977). On the future of personality measurement. *American Psychologist, 32*, 246–254.

Mitchell, R. G. (1983). *Mountain experience: The psychology and sociology of adventure.* Chicago, IL: The University of Chicago Press.

Mobily, K. E. (1989). Meanings of recreation and leisure among adolescents. *Leisure Studies, 8*, 11–23.

Moghaddam, F. M. (1987). Psychology in the three worlds: As reflected by the crisis in social psychology and the move toward indigenous third-world psychology. *American Psychologist, 42*, 912–920.

Monat, A. and Lazarus, R. (1977). Stress and coping: Some current issues and controversies. In A. Monat and R. Lazarus (Eds.), *Stress and coping: An anthology* (pp. 1–11). New York, NY: Columbia University Press.

Monson, T. C., Hesley, J. W. and Chernick, L. (1982). Specifying when personality can and cannot predict behavior: An alternative to abandoning the attempt to predict single-act criteria. *Journal of Personality and Social Psychology, 43*, 385–399.

Montgomery, K. C. (1954). The role of exploratory drive in learning. *Journal of Comparative and Physiological Psychology, 47*, 60–64.

More, T. A. and Payne, B. R. (1978). Affective responses to natural areas near cities. *Journal of Leisure Research, 10*, 7–12.

Moriarity, T. (1975). Crime, commitment, and the responsive bystander: Two field experiments. *Journal of Personality and Social Psychology, 31*, 370–376.

Moscardo, G. M. and Pearce, P. L. (1986). Historic theme parks: An Australian experience in authenticity. *Annals of Tourism Research, 13*, 467–479.

Moscovici, S. and Zavalloni, M. (1969). The group as a polarizer of attitudes. *Journal of Personality and Social Psychology, 12*, 125–135.

Moss, M. S. and Lawton, M. P. (1982). Time budgets of older people: A window on four life-styles. *Journal of Gerontology, 37*, 115–123.

Moss, W. T. and Lamphear, S. C. (1970). Substitutability of recreational activities in meeting stated needs and drives of the visitor. *Environmental Education, 1*, 129–131.

Munson, W. W. (1991). Juvenile delinquency as a societal problem and social disability: The therapeutic recreator's role as ecological change agent. *Therapeutic Recreation Journal, 25,* 19–30.

Munson, W. W. (1993). Perceived freedom in leisure and career salience in adolescence. *Journal of Leisure Research, 25,* 305–314.

Murray, H. A. (1938). *Explorations and personality.* New York, NY: Oxford University Press.

Near, J., Rice, R. and Hunt, R. (1978). Work and extra-work correlates of life and job satisfaction. *Academy of Management Journal, 21,* 248–264.

Neugarten, B. L. (1977). Personality and aging. In J. Birren and K. W. Schaie (Eds.), *Handbook of the psychology of aging* (pp. 626–649). New York, NY: Van Nostrand Reinhold.

Neugarten, B. L., Havighurst, R. J. and Tobin, S. S. (1961). The measurement of life satisfaction. *Journal of Gerontology, 16,* 134–143.

Neugarten, B. L., Moore, J. W. and Lowe, J. C. (1968). Age norms, age constraints, and adult socialization. In B. L. Neugarten (Ed.), *Middle age and aging* (pp. 22–28). Chicago, IL: University of Chicago Press.

Neulinger, J. (1974). *Psychology of leisure: Research approaches to the study of leisure.* Springfield, IL: Charles C. Thomas, Publisher.

Neulinger, J. (1981). *The psychology of leisure, 2nd ed.* Springfield, IL: Charles C. Thomas, Publisher.

Neulinger, J. (1986). *What am I doing? The WAID: An introductory guide designed to help you measure and improve the quality of your life.* Dolgeville, NY: The Leisure Institute.

Neulinger, J. and Breit, M. (1969). Attitude dimensions of leisure. *Journal of Leisure Research, 1,* 255–261.

Nias, D. K. B. (1977). The structuring of recreational interests. *Social Behavior and Personality, 5,* 383–388.

Nickerson, N. P. and Ellis, G. D. (1991). Traveler types and activation theory: A comparison of two models. *Journal of Travel Research, 29,* 26–31.

Noe, F. P. (1969). An instrumental conception of leisure for the adolescent. *Adolescence, 4,* 385–400.

Noe, F. P. (1987). Measurement specification and leisure satisfaction. *Leisure Sciences, 9,* 163–172.

O'Brien, G. E. (1986). *Psychology of work and unemployment.* Toronto, ON: John Wiley & Sons.

Ogilvie, B. C. (1968). Psychological consistencies within the personality of high level competitors. *Journal of the American Medical Association, 205,* 780–786.

Ogilvie, B. C. and Tutko, T. (1985). Sport: If you want to build character, try something else. In D. Chu, J. Seagraves and B. Becker (Eds.), *Sport and higher education* (pp. 267–273). Champaign, IL: Human Kinetics.

Orne, M. T. (1962). On the social psychology of the psychological experiment: With particular reference to demand characteristics and their implications. *American Psychologist, 17,* 776–783.

Orthner, D. K. (1975). Leisure activity patterns and marital satisfaction over the marital career. *Journal of Marriage and the Family, 37,* 91–102.

Orthner, D. K. (1976). Patterns of leisure and marital interaction. *Journal of Leisure Research, 8,* 98–111.

Orthner, D. K. (1985). Leisure and conflict in families. In B. G. Gunter, J. Stanley and R. St. Clair (Eds.), *Transitions to leisure: Conflict and leisure in families.* New York, NY: University Press.

Orthner, D. K. and Mancini, J. A. (1980). Leisure behavior and group dynamics: The case of the family. In S. E. Iso-Ahola (Ed.), *Social psychological perspectives on leisure and recreation* (pp. 307–328). Springfield, IL: Charles C. Thomas, Publisher.

Orthner, D. K. and Mancini, J. A. (1991). Benefits of leisure for family bonding. In B. L. Driver, P. J. Brown and G. L. Peterson (Eds.), *Benefits of leisure* (pp. 289–301). State College, PA: Venture Publishing, Inc.

Osgood, N. and Howe, C. Z. (1984). Psychological aspects of leisure: A life cycle developmental perspective. *Loisir et Société/Society and Leisure, 7,* 175–195.

Ouellet, G. (Ed.) (1984). *Society and leisure* (Vol. 7). Sillery, PQ: University of Quebec Press.

Paffenbarger, R. S., Hyde, R. T. and Dow, A. (1991). Health benefits of physical activity. In B. L. Driver, P. J. Brown and G. L. Peterson (Eds.), *Benefits of leisure* (pp. 49–57). State College, PA: Venture Publishing, Inc.

Palmore, E. (1981). *Social patterns in normal aging.* Durham, NC: Duke University Press.

Paluba, G. V. and Neulinger, J. (1976). Stereotypes based on free time activities. *Loisir et Société/Society and Leisure, 3,* 89–95.

Parker, R. G. (1995). Reminiscence: A continuity theory framework. *The Gerontologist, 35,* 515–525.

Parker, S. R. (1971). *The future of work and leisure.* New York, NY: Praeger.

Parkes, C. M. (1972). *Bereavement: Studies of grief in adult life.* London: The Tavistock Institute of Human Relations.

Parks and Recreation Federation of Ontario. (1992). *The benefits of parks and recreation: A catalogue.* Toronto, ON: Ontario Ministry of Tourism and Recreation.

Parten, M. (1932). Social play among preschool children. *Journal of Abnormal and Social Psychology, 28,* 136–147.

Patrick, G. T. W. (1916). *The psychology of relaxation.* Boston, MA: Houghton Mifflin Co.

Patterson, I. and Carpenter, G. (1994). Participation in leisure activities after the death of a spouse. *Leisure Sciences, 16,* 105–117.

Pearce, P. L. (1982). *The social psychology of tourist behavior.* Oxford, UK: Pergamon.

Pedlar, A., Gilbert, A. and Gove, L. (1994). The role of action research in facilitating integrated recreation for older adults. *Therapeutic Recreation Journal, 28,* 99–106.

Pervin, L. A. (1968). Performance and satisfaction as a function of individual-environment fit. *Psychological Bulletin, 69,* 56–68.

Pervin, L. A. (1985). Personality: Current controversies, issues, and directions. *Annual Reviews of Psychology, 36,* 83–114.

Pervin, L. A. (1990). A brief history of modern personality theory. In L.A. Pervin (Ed.), *Handbook of personality: Theory and research* (pp. 3–18). New York, NY: The Guilford Press.

Pesavento Raymond, L. C. (1984). The effects of unemployment on the leisure behavior of unemployed steelworkers. *World Leisure and Recreation, 26,* 61–64.

Pesavento Raymond, L. C. and Kelly, J. R. (1991). Leisure and life satisfaction of unemployed North American urban minority youth. *Loisir et Société/Society and Leisure, 14,* 497–511.

Peterson, C. A. and Gunn, S. L. (1984). *Therapeutic recreation program design: Principles and procedures.* Champaign, IL: Sagamore Publishing.

Peterson, G. L., Driver, B. L. and Gregory, R. (1988). *Amenity resource valuation: Integrating economics with other disciplines.* State College, PA: Venture Publishing, Inc.

Petty, R. E. and Cacioppo, J. T. (1986). The elaboration likelihood model of persuasion. In L. Berkowitz (Ed.), *Advances in experimental social psychology*: Vol. 19 (pp. 123–205). New York, NY: Academic Press.

Petty, R. E., McMichael, S. and Brannon, L. A. (1992). The Elaboration Likelihood Model of persuasion: Applications in recreation and tourism. In M. J. Manfredo (Ed.), *Influencing human behavior: Theory and applications in recreation, tourism, and natural resources management* (pp. 77–101). Champaign, IL: Sagamore Publishing.

Piaget, J. (1954). *The construction of reality in the child.* New York, NY: Basic Books.

Piaget, J. (1962). *Play, dreams and imitation in childhood.* Boston, MA: Beacon.

Pieper, J. (1952). *Leisure: The basis of culture.* New York, NY: Pantheon Books.

Pierce, R. C. (1980). Dimensions of leisure I: Satisfactions. *Journal of Leisure Research, 12,* 5–19.

Pierce, T. W., Madden, D. J., Siegel, W. C. and Blumenthal, J. A. (1993). Effects of aerobic exercise on cognitive and psychological functioning in patients with mild hypertension. *Health Psychology, 12,* 286–291.

Pietropinto, A. (1986). The workaholic spouse. *Medical Aspects of Human Sexuality, 20,* 89–96.

Pittman, J. F. (1994). Work/family fit as a mediator of work factors on marital tension: Evidence from the interface of greedy institutions. *Human Relations, 47,* 183–210.

Pizam, A., Neumann, Y. and Reichel, A. (1978). Dimensions of tourist satisfaction with a destination area. *Annals of Tourism Research, 5,* 314–322.

Plog, S. C. (1972). Why destination areas rise and fall in popularity. *Paper presented to the Travel Research Association Southern California Chapter, Los Angeles.*

Podilchak, W. (1991a). Distinctions of fun, enjoyment and leisure. *Leisure Studies, 10,* 133–148.

Podilchak, W. (1991b). Establishing the fun in leisure. *Leisure Sciences, 13,* 123–136.

Pope, K. S. and Singer, J. L. (1978). *The stream of consciousness: Scientific investigations into the flow of human experience.* New York, NY: Plenum.

Price, R. H. and Bouffard, D. L. (1974). Behavioral appropriateness and situational constraint as dimensions of social behavior. *Journal of Personality and Social Psychology, 30,* 579–586.

Priest, S. (1992). Factor exploration and confirmation for the dimensions of an adventure experience. *Journal of Leisure Research, 24,* 127–139.

Provenzo, E. F. (1991). *Video kids: Making sense of Nintendo.* Cambridge, MA: Harvard University Press.

Przeclawski, K. (1985). The role of tourism in contemporary culture. *The Tourist Review, 40,* 2–6.

Ragheb, M. G. (1980). Interrelationships among leisure participation, leisure satisfaction and leisure attitudes. *Journal of Leisure Research, 12,* 138–149.

Ragheb, M. G. (1988). Leisure and recreation needs or motivations as a basis for program planning. *Journal of Park and Recreation Administration, 6,* 28–40.

Ragheb, M. G. (1993). Leisure and perceived wellness: A field investigation. *Leisure Sciences, 15,* 13–24.

Ragheb, M. G. and Beard, J. G. (1982). Measuring leisure attitude. *Journal of Leisure Research, 14,* 155–167.

Ragheb, M. G. and Griffith, C. A. (1982). The contribution of leisure participation and leisure satisfaction to life satisfaction of older persons. *Journal of Leisure Research, 14,* 295–306.

Ragheb, M. G. and Tate, R. L. (1993). A behavioural model of leisure participation, based on leisure attitude, motivation and satisfaction. *Leisure Studies, 12,* 61–70.

Ramos, C. I. and Folkers, E. (1994). The relationship of perception of time and attributes of leisure in daily experiences. *Leisure Studies, 13,* 140–147.

Rathunde, K. (1988). Optimal experience and the family context. In M. Csikszentmihalyi and I. Csikszentmihalyi (Eds.), *Optimal experience* (pp. 342–363). New York, NY: Cambridge.

Ray, R. O. (1979). Life satisfaction and activity involvement: Implications for leisure service. *Journal of Leisure Research, 11,* 112–119.

Reich, J. W. and Zautra, A. (1981). Life events and personal causation: Some relationships with satisfaction and distress. *Journal of Personality and Social Psychology, 41,* 1002–1012.

Reid, D. G. (1995). *Work and leisure in the 21st century.* Toronto, ON: Wall and Emerson, Inc.

Reid, D. G. and Mannell, R. C. (1993). Future possibilities: The changing patterns of work and leisure. In A. J. Veal, P. Jonson and G. Cushman (Eds.), *Leisure and tourism: Social and environmental change* (pp. 373–378). Sydney, Australia: University of Technology Sydney Press.

Reid, D. G. and Smit, P. (1986). Recreation participation patterns of the unemployed: A preliminary perspective. *Recreation Research Review, 1,* 43–49.

Reis, M. and Gold, D. P. (1993). Retirement, personality, and life satisfaction: A review of two models. *Journal of Applied Gerontology, 12,* 261–282.

Reissman, C., Aron, A. and Bergen, M. R. (1993). Shared activities and marital satisfaction: Causal direction and self-expansion versus boredom. *Journal of Social and Personal Relationships, 10,* 243–254.

Ricci, P. R. and Holland, S. M. (1992). Incentive travel: Recreation as a motivational medium. *Tourism Management, 13,* 288–296.

Riesman, D. (1950). *The lonely crowd.* New Haven, CT: Yale University Press.

Rigby, C. S., Deci, E. L., Patrick, B. C. and Ryan, R. M. (1992). Beyond the Intrinsic-Extrinsic Dichotomy: Self-determination in motivation and learning. *Motivation and Emotion, 16,* 165–185.

Ritzer, G. and Gindoff, P. (1992). Methodological relationalism: Lessons for and from social psychology. *Social Psychology Quarterly, 55,* 128–140.

Roadburg, A. (1983). Freedom and enjoyment: Disentangling perceived leisure. *Journal of Leisure Research, 15,* 15–26.

Roberts, J. and Sutton-Smith, B. (1962). Child training and game involvement. *Ethnology, 1,* 166–185.

Roberts, K., Lamb, K. L., Dench, S. and Brodie, D. A. (1989). Leisure patterns, health status and employment status. *Leisure Studies, 8,* 229–235.

Robertson, R. A. and Regula, J. A. (1994). Recreational displacement and overall satisfaction: A study of central Iowa's licensed boaters. *Journal of Leisure Research, 26,* 174–181.

Robinson, D. W. (1992). A descriptive model of enduring risk recreation involvement. *Journal of Leisure Research, 24,* 52–63.

Robinson, J. P. (1977). *How Americans use time: A social-psychological analysis of everyday behavior.* New York, NY: Praeger.

Robinson, J. P. and Godbey, G. (1993). Sport, fitness and the gender gap. *Leisure Sciences, 15,* 291–307.

Rogers, C. (1961). *On becoming a person.* Boston, MA: Houghton-Mifflin.

Rojek, C. (1989). Leisure and recreation theory. In E. L. Jackson and T. L. Burton (Eds.), *Understanding leisure and recreation: Mapping the past, charting the future* (pp. 69–88). State College, PA: Venture Publishing, Inc.

Rolston, H., III (1991). Creation and recreation: Environmental benefits and human leisure. In B. L. Driver, P. J. Brown and G. L. Peterson (Eds.), *Benefits of leisure* (pp. 393–403). State College, PA: Venture Publishing, Inc.

Romsa, G., Bondy, P. and Blenman, M. (1985). Modeling retirees' life satisfaction levels: The role of recreational, life cycle, and socio-environmental elements. *Journal of Leisure Research, 17,* 29–39.

Rosenthal, D. H., Waldman, D. A. and Driver, B. L. (1982). Construct validity of instruments measuring recreationists' preferences. *Leisure Sciences, 5,* 89–108.

Rosenthal, R. (1966). *Experimenter effects in behavioral research.* New York, NY: Appleton-Century-Crofts.

Ross, E. A. (1908). *Social psychology: An outline and source book.* New York, NY: Macmillan.

Ross, L. and Nisbett, R. (1991). *The person and the situation: Perspectives of social psychology.* New York, NY: McGraw-Hill Publishing Co.

Rotter, J. B. (1966). Generalized expectancies for internal versus external control of reinforcement. *Psychological Monographs: General and Applied, 80,* 1–28.

Rubenstein, C. (1980a). Survey report: How Americans view vacations. *Psychology Today, 13,* 62–76.

Rubenstein, C. (1980b). Vacations: Expectations, satisfactions, frustrations, fantasies. *Psychology Today, 14,* 62–66, 71–76.

Rubin, K. H., Watson, K. S. and Jambor, T. W. (1978). Free-play behaviors in preschool and kindergarten children. *Child Development, 49,* 534–536.

Russell, R. V. (1987). The importance of recreation satisfaction and activity participation to the life satisfaction of age-segregated retirees. *Journal of Leisure Research, 19,* 273–283.

Rutter, D. R. and Quine, L. (1994). *Social psychology and health: European perspectives.* Aldershot, UK: Avebury.

Ryan, R. M., Mims, V. and Koestner, R. (1983). Relation of reward contingency and interpersonal context to intrinsic motivation: A review and test using cognitive evaluation theory. *Journal of Personality and Social Psychology, 45,* 735–750.

Sakamoto, A. (1994). Video game use and the development of sociocognitive abilities in children: Three surveys of elementary school students. *Journal of Applied Social Psychology, 24,* 21–42.

Samdahl, D. M. (1988). A symbolic interactionist model of leisure: Theory and empirical support. *Leisure Sciences, 10,* 27–39.

Samdahl, D. M. (1991). Issues in the measurement of leisure: A comparison of theoretical and connotative meanings. *Leisure Sciences, 13,* 33–49.

Samdahl, D. M. (1992). Leisure in our lives: Exploring the common leisure occasion. *Journal of Leisure Research, 24,* 19–32.

Samdahl, D. M. and Jekubovich, N. J. (1993). Patterns and characteristics of adult daily leisure. *Loisir et Société/Society and Leisure, 16*, 129–149.

Samdahl, D. M. and Kleiber, D. A. (1989). Self-awareness and leisure experience. *Leisure Sciences, 11*, 1–10.

Schachter, S. (1964). The interaction of cognitive and physiological determinants of emotional state. In L. Berkowitz (Ed.), *Advances in experimental social psychology*: Vol. 1 (pp. 49–80). New York, NY: Academic Press.

Schaie, K. W. and Geiwitz, J. (1982). *Adult development and aging*. Boston, MA: Little, Brown and Co.

Schill, T., Beyler, J. and Sharp, M. (1993). Pleasure from activities and self-defeating personality. *Psychological Reports, 72*, 627–630.

Schlenker, B. R. (1984). Identities, identifications, and relationships. In V. Derlaga (Ed.), *Communication, intimacy and close relationships* (pp. 71–104). New York, NY: Academic Press.

Schmitz-Scherzer, R. (1976). Longitudinal change in leisure behavior of the elderly. *Contributions to Human Development, 3*, 127–136.

Schor, J. B. (1991). *The overworked American: The unexpected decline of leisure*. New York, NY: Basic Books.

Schreyer, R. and Driver, B. L. (1989). The benefits of leisure. In E. L. Jackson and T. L. Burton (Eds.), *Understanding leisure and recreation: Mapping the past, charting the future* (pp. 387–419). State College, PA: Venture Publishing, Inc.

Schurr, K. T., Ashley, M. A. and Joy, K. L. (1977). A multivariate analysis of male athlete characteristics. *Multivariate Experimental Clinical Research, 3*, 53–68.

Schwartzman, H. (1978). *Transformations: The anthropology of children's play*. New York, NY: Plenum Press.

Scott, D. (1991). The problematic nature of participation in contract bridge: A qualitative study of group-related constraints. *Leisure Sciences, 13*, 321–336.

Scott, D. and Godbey, G. C. (1992). An analysis of adult play groups: Social versus serious participation in contract bridge. *Leisure Sciences, 14*, 29–46.

Scott, D. and Willits, F. K. (1989). Adolescent and adult leisure patterns: A 37-year follow-up study. *Leisure Sciences, 11*, 323–335.

Searle, M. S. and Brayley, R. E. (1993). *Leisure services in Canada*. State College, PA: Venture Publishing, Inc.

Searle, M. S., Mactavish, J. and Brayley, R. E. (1993). Integrating ceasing participation with other aspects of leisure behavior: A replication and extension. *Journal of Leisure Research, 25*, 389–404.

Searle, M. S. and Mahon, M. J. (1991). Leisure education in a day hospital: The effects on selected social-psychological variables among older adults. *Canadian Journal of Community Mental Health, 10*, 95–109.

Seligman, M. E. P. (1975). *Helplessness: On depression, development, and death.* San Francisco, CA: Freeman.

Sessoms, H. D. (1986). "Of time, work, and leisure" revisited. *Leisure Sciences, 8*, 107–113.

Shamir, B. (1988). Commitment and leisure. *Sociological Perspective, 31*, 238–258.

Shamir, B. (1992). Some correlates of leisure identity salience: Three exploratory studies. *Journal of Leisure Research, 24* , 301–323.

Sharp, A. and Mannell, R. C. (1996). Participation in leisure as a coping strategy among bereaved women. In *Eighth Canadian Congress on Leisure Research* (pp. 241–244). Ottawa, ON: University of Ottawa.

Shary, J. M. and Iso-Ahola, S. E. (1989). Effects of a control-relevant intervention on nursing home residents' perceived competence and self-esteem. *Therapeutic Recreation Journal, 23*, 7–16.

Shaw, S. M. (1984). The measurement of leisure: A quality of life issue. *Loisir et Société/ Society and Leisure, 7*, 91–107.

Shaw, S. M. (1985a). The meaning of leisure in everyday life. *Leisure Sciences, 7*, 1–24.

Shaw, S. M. (1985b). Gender and leisure: Inequality in the distribution of leisure time. *Journal of Leisure Research, 17*, 266–282.

Shaw, S. M. (1992). Dereifying family leisure: An examination of women's and men's everyday experiences and perceptions of family time. *Leisure Sciences, 14*, 271–286.

Shaw, S. M. (1994). Gender, leisure, and constraint: Toward a framework for the analysis of women's leisure. *Journal of Leisure Research, 26*, 8–22.

Shaw, S. M., Bonen, A. and McCabe, J. F. (1991). Do more constraints mean less leisure? Examining the relationship between constraints and participation. *Journal of Leisure Research, 23*, 286–300.

Shelby, B. and Vaske, J. J. (1991). Resource and activity substitutes for recreational salmon fishing in New Zealand. *Leisure Sciences, 13*, 21–32.

Sheppard, B. H., Hartwick, J. and Warshaw, P. R. (1988). The theory of reasoned action: A meta-analysis of past research with recommendations for modifications and future research. *Journal of Consumer Research, 15*, 325–343.

Sherif, M. (1936). *The psychology of social norms.* New York, NY: Harper.

Sherif, M., Harvey, O. J., White, B. J., Hood, W. R. and Sherif, C. W. (1961). *Intergroup conflict and cooperation: The Robbers Cave Experiment.* Norman, OK: Institute of Groups Relations, University of Oklahoma.

Shin, W. S. (1993). Self-actualization and wilderness attitudes: A replication. *Journal of Social Behavior and Personality, 8,* 221–240.

Silbereisen, R. K., Noack, P. and Eyferth, K. (1986). Place for development: Adolescents, leisure settings, and developmental tasks. In R. K. Silbereisen, K. Eyferth and G. Rudinger (Eds.), *Development as action in context* (pp. 87–107). New York, NY: Springer-Verlag.

Singer, D. G. (1993). *Playing for their lives.* New York, NY: The Free Press.

Singer, J. L. (1973). *The child's world of make believe.* New York, NY: Academic Press.

Singer, J. L. and Singer, D. G. (1986). Family experiences and television viewing as predictors of children's imagination, restlessness, and aggression. *Journal of Social Issues, 42,* 107–124.

Skeels, H. M. (1973). Adult status of children with contrasting early life experiences: A follow-up study. *Monographs for Social Research on Child Development, 31,* No. 3, Serial No. 105.

Smigal, E. (1963). *Work and leisure.* New Haven, CT: College and University Press.

Smilansky, S. (1968). *The effect of sociodramatic play in disadvantaged children.* New York, NY: John Wiley & Sons.

Smith, E. A. and Caldwell, L. L. (1989). The perceived quality of leisure experiences among smoking and nonsmoking adolescents. *Journal of Early Adolescence, 9,* 153–162.

Smith, S. L. J. (1990a). A test of Plog's allocentric/psychocentric model: Evidence from seven nations. *Journal of Travel Research, 28,* 40–43.

Smith, S. L. J. (1990b). *Dictionary of concepts in recreation and leisure studies.* New York, NY: Greenwood Press.

Sneed, C. and Runco, M. A. (1992). The beliefs adults and children hold about television and video games. *Journal of Psychology, 126,* 273–284.

Sofranko, A. J. and Nolan, M. F. (1972). Early life experiences and adult sports participation. *Journal of Leisure Research, 4,* 6–18.

Spigner, C. and Havitz, M. E. (1992–1993). Health, recreation, and the unemployed: An interactive model. *International Quarterly of Community Health Education, 13,* 31–45.

Spreitzer, E. A. and Snyder, E. E. (1976). Socialization into sport: An exploratory path analysis. *The Research Quarterly, 47,* 239–245.

Spreitzer, E. A. and Snyder, E. E. (1983). Correlates of participation in adult recreational sports. *Journal of Leisure Research, 15*, 27–38.

Spreitzer, E. A. and Snyder, E. E. (1987). Educational-occupational fit and leisure orientation as related to life satisfaction. *Journal of Leisure Research, 19*, 149–158.

Staines, G. L. (1980). Spillover vs. compensation: A review of the literature on relationship between work and nonwork. *Human Relations, 33*, 111–130.

Stebbins, R. A. (1981). Science amators? Rewards and costs in amateur astronomy and archaeology. *Journal of Leisure Research, 13*, 289–304.

Stebbins, R. A. (1982). Serious leisure: A conceptual statement. *Pacific Sociological Reveiw, 25*, 25–72.

Stebbins, R. A. (1983). *The magician: Career, culture, and social psychology in a variety art.* Toronto, ON: Clarke Irwin.

Stebbins, R. A. (1992a). *Amateurs, professionals, and serious leisure.* Montreal, PQ: McGill-Queen's University Press.

Stebbins, R. A. (1992b). Costs and rewards in barbershop singing. *Leisure Studies, 11*, 123–134.

Stebbins, R. A. (1992c). Hobbies as marginal leisure: The case of barbershop singers. *Loisir et Société/Society and Leisure, 15*, 375–386.

Steers, R. M. and Porter, L. W. (1991). *Motivation and work behavior.* New York, NY: McGraw-Hill.

Stein, G. L., Kimiecik, J. C., Daniels, J. and Jackson, S. A. (1995). Psychological antecedents of flow in recreational sport. *Personality and Social Psychology Bulletin, 21*, 125–135.

Steiner, I. D. (1970). Perceived freedom. In L. Berkowitz (Ed.), *Advances in experimental social psychology, Vol. 5*, (pp. 187–248). New York, NY: Academic Press.

Steinkamp, M. W. and Kelly, J. R. (1986). Relationships among motivation orientation, level of leisure activity and life satisfaction in older men and women. *The Journal od Psychology, 119*, 509–520.

Steinkamp, M. W. and Kelly, J. R. (1987). Social integration, leisure activity, and life satisfaction in older adults: Activity theory revisited. *International Journal of Aging and Human Development, 25*, 293–307.

Stevenson, C. L. (1975). Socialization effects of participation in sport: A critical review of the literature. *Research Quarterly, 46*, 287–301.

Stewart, W. P. (1992). Influence of the onsite experience on recreation experience preference judgments. *Journal of Leisure Research, 24*, 185–198.

Stewart, W. P. and Carpenter, E. H. (1989). Solitude at Grand Canyon: An application of expectancy theory. *Journal of Leisure Research, 21*, 4–17.

Stewart, W. P. and Hull IV, B. R. (1992). Satisfaction of what? Post hoc versus real-time construct validity. *Leisure Sciences, 14*, 195–209.

Strauss, M., Gelles, R. and Steinmetz, S. (1980). *Behind closed doors*. New York, NY: Doubleday.

Strecher, V. J., DeVills, B. M., Becker, M. H. and Rosenstock, I. M. (1986). The role of self-efficacy in achieving health behavior change. *Health Education Quarterly, 13*, 73–81.

Stringer, P. F. (Ed.) (1984). *Annals of Tourism Research* (Vol. 11). New York, NY: Pergamon Press.

Strube, M. J., Turner, C. W., Patrick, S. and Perrillo, R. (1983). Type-A and Type-B attentional responses to aesthetic stimuli. *Journal of Personality and Social Psychology, 45*, 1369–1379.

Stryker, S. (1987). Identity theory: Development and extensions. In L. Yardley and T. Honess (Eds.), *Self and identity* (pp. 89–103). Chichester, UK: John Wiley & Sons.

Stuart, R. B. (1980). *Helping couples change*. New York, NY: Guilford.

Sullivan, H. S. (1953). *The interpersonal theory of psychiatry*. New York, NY: W. W. Norton.

Swanson, G. E. (1978). Travels through inner space: Family structure and openness to absorbing experiences. *American Journal of Sociology, 83*, 890–919.

Sylvester, C. D. (1985). Freedom, leisure and therapeutic recreation: A philosophical view. *Therapeutic Recreation Journal, 6*–16.

Szalai, A. (1972). *The use of time*. The Hague-Paris: Mouton.

Szinovacz, M. and Washo, C. (1992). Gender differences in exposure to life events and adaptation to retirement. *Journal of Gerontology, 47*, S191–S196.

Tang, T. L. (1986). Effects of Type-A personality and task labels (work vs. leisure) on task preference. *Journal of Leisure Research, 18*, 1–11.

Tang, T. L. (1988). Effects of Type-A personality and leisure ethic on Chinese college students' leisure activities and academic performance. *Journal of Social Psychology, 128*, 153–164.

Tarrant, M. A. (1996). Attending to past outdoor recreation experiences: Symptom reporting and changes in affect. *Journal of Leisure Research, 28*, 1–17.

Tellegen, A. and Atkinson, G. (1974). Openness to absorbing and self-altering experiences ('absorption'), a trait related to hypnotic susceptibility. *Journal of Abnormal Psychology, 83*, 268–277.

Tellegen, A., Lykken, D. T., Bourchard, T. J., Jr., Wilcox, K. J., Segal, N. L. and Rich, S. (1988). Personality similarity in twins reared apart and together. *Journal of Personality and Social Psychology, 83*, 268–277.

Thackeray, R. I., Jones, K. N. and Touchstone, R. M. (1974). Personality and physiological correlates of performance decrement on a monotonous task requiring sustained attention. *British Journal of Psychology, 65*, 351–358.

Theriault, J. (1994). Retirement as a psychological transition: Process of adaptation to change. *International Journal of Aging and Human Development, 38*, 153–170.

Thibaut, J. W. and Kelley, H. H. (1959). *The social psychology of groups.* New York, NY: John Wiley & Sons.

Tinsley, H. E. A. (1984). The psychological benefits of leisure counselling. *Loisir et Société/Society and Leisure, 7*, 125–140.

Tinsley, H. E. A. and Johnson, T. L. (1984). A preliminary taxonomy of leisure activities. *Journal of Leisure Research, 16*, 234–244.

Tinsley, H. E. A. and Kass, R. A. (1978). Leisure activities and need satisfaction: A replication and extension. *Journal of Leisure Research, 10*, 191–202.

Tinsley, H. E. A. and Kass, R. A. (1979). The latent structure of the need satisfying properties of leisure activities. *Journal of Leisure Research, 11*, 278–291.

Tinsley, H. E. A. and Tinsley, D. J. (1986). A theory of the attributes, benefits, and causes of leisure experience. *Leisure Sciences, 8*, 1–45.

Toffler, A. (1970). *Future shock.* New York, NY: Random House, Inc.

Toleman, W. (1909). *Social engineering.* New York, NY: McGraw-Hill Publishing.

Trafton, R. S. and Tinsley, H. E. A. (1980). An investigation of the construct validity of measures of job, leisure, dyadic and general life satisfaction. *Journal of Leisure Research, 12*, 34–44.

Triplett, N. (1897–1898). The dynamogenic factors in pacemaking and competition. *American Journal of Psychology, 9*, 507–533.

Tubesing, D. A. and Loving-Tubesing, N. (1991). *Seeking your healthy balance.* Duluth, MN: Whole Person Associates.

Tucker, L. A. (1993). Television viewing and exercise habits of 8,885 adults. *Perceptual and Motor Skills, 77*, 938–939.

Ulrich, R. S. (1984). View through a window may influence recovery from surgery. *Science, 224*, 420–421.

Ulrich, R. S. and Addoms, D. L. (1981). Psychological and recreational benefits of a residential park. *Journal of Leisure Research, 13*, 43–65.

Ulrich, R. S., Dimberg, U. and Driver, B. L. (1991). Psychophysiological indicators of leisure benefits. In B. L. Driver, P. J. Brown and G. L. Peterson (Eds.), *Benefits of leisure* (pp. 73–89). State College, PA: Venture Publishing, Inc.

Unger, L. S. (1984). The effect of situational variables on the subjective leisure experience. *Leisure Sciences, 6*, 291–312.

Unger, L. S. and Kernan, J. B. (1983). On the meaning of leisure: An investigation of some determinants of the subjective experience. *Journal of Consumer Research, 9*, 381–392.

Unkel, M. B. (1981). Physical recreation participation of females and males during the adult life cycle. *Leisure Sciences, 4*, 1–27.

Vallerand, R. J. and Bissonnette, R. (1992). Intrinsic, extrinsic, and amotivational styles as predictors of behavior: A prospective study. *Journal of Personality, 60*, 599–620.

Van Egeren, L., Sniderman, L. and Ruggelin, M. (1982). Competitive two person interactions of Type-A and Type-B individuals. *Journal of Behaviorial Medicine, 5*, 55–66.

Van Evra, J. (1990). *Television and child development.* Hillsdale, NJ: Erlbaum.

Vaske, J. J., Donnelly, M. P., Heberlein, T. A. and Shelby, B. (1982). Differences in reported satisfaction ratings by consumptive and nonconsumptive recreationists. *Journal of Leisure Research, 14*, 195–206.

Veal, A. J. (1989). Leisure, lifestyle, and status: A pluralist framework for analysis. *Leisure Studies, 8*, 141–153.

Veal, A. J. (1993). The concept of lifestyle: A review. *Leisure Studies, 12*, 233–252.

Veblen, T. (1899). *The theory of the leisure class.* New York, NY: Viking Press.

Virden, R. J. and Knopf, R. C. (1989). Activities, experiences, and envionmental settings: A case study of recreation opportunity spectrum relationships. *Leisure Sciences, 11*, 159–176.

Voelkl, J. E. (1990). The challenge skill ratio of daily experiences among older adults residing in nursing homes. *Therapeutic Recreation Journal, 24*, 7–17.

Vooijs, M. W. and vanderVoort, T. H. A. (1993). Teaching children to evaluate television violence critically: The impact of a Dutch schools television project. *Journal of Educational Television, 19*, 139–152.

Vroom, V. H. (1964). *Work and motivation.* New York, NY: John Wiley & Sons.

Wade, M. G. (1985). *Constraints on leisure.* Springfield, IL: Charles C. Thomas, Publisher.

Wahba, M. A. and Bridwell, L. G. (1976). Maslow reconsidered: A review of research on the need hierarchy theory. *Organizational Behavior and Human Performance, 15,* 212–240.

Wahlers, R. G. and Etzel, M. J. (1985). Vacation preference as a manifestation of optimal stimulation and lifestyle experience. *Journal of Leisure Research, 17,* 283–295.

Wankel, L. M. (1985). Personal and situational factors affecting exercise involvement: The importance of enjoyment. *Research Quarterly for Exercise and Sport, 56,* 275–282.

Wankel, L. M. (1993). The importance of enjoyment to adherence and psychological benefits from physical activity. *International Journal of Sport Psychology, 24,* 151–169.

Wankel, L. M. and Berger, B. G. (1991). The personal and social benefits of sport and physical activity. In B. L. Driver, P. J. Brown and G. L. Peterson (Eds.), *Benefits of leisure* (pp. 121–144). State College, PA: Venture Publishing, Inc.

Wankel, L. M. and Kreisel, P. S. J. (1985). Factors underlying enjoyment of youth sports: Sport and age group comparisons. *Journal of Sport Psychology, 7,* 51–64.

Wankel, L. M. and Sefton, J. M. (1989a). Factors distinguishing high- and low-fun experiences in ice hockey. *World Leisure and Recreation, Fall,* 29–31.

Wankel, L. M. and Sefton, J. M. (1989b). A season-long investigation of fun in youth sports. *Journal of Sport and Exercise Psychology, 11,* 355–366.

Warr, P. B. (1983). Work, jobs, and unemployment. *Bulletin of the British Psychological Society, 36,* 305–311.

Warr, P. B. and Jackson, P. R. (1984). Men without jobs: Some correlates of age and length of unemployment. *Journal of Occupational Psychology, 57,* 77–85.

Warr, P. B. and Jackson, P. R. (1985). Factors influencing the psychological impact of prolonged unemployment and re-employment. *Psychological Medicine, 15,* 795–807.

Watten, R. G. (1995). Sports, physical exercise and use of alcohol. *Scandinavian Journal of Medicine and Science in Sports, 5,* 364–368.

Wearing, B. (1990). Beyond the ideology of motherhood: Leisure as resistance. *Australian and New Zealand Journal of Sociology, 26,* 36–58.

Webb, H. (1969). Professionalization of attitudes toward play among adolescents. In G. D. Kenyon (Ed.), *Sociology of sport* (pp. 161–187). Chicago, IL: The Athletic Institute.

Weiner, B. (1986). *An attributional theory of motivation and emotion.* New York, NY: Springer-Velag.

Weir, L. (1928). *Parks: A manual of municipal and county parks.* New York, NY: A. S. Barnes and Co.

Weissinger, E. (1995). Effects of boredom on self-reported health. *Loisir et Société/Society and Leisure, 18,* 21–32.

Weissinger, E. and Bandalos, D. L. (1995). Development, reliability and validity of a scale to measure intrinsic motivation in leisure. *Journal of Leisure Research, 27,* 379–400.

Weissinger, E. and Iso-Ahola, S. E. (1984). Intrinsic leisure motivation, personality and physical health. *Loisir et Société/Society and Leisure, 7,* 217–228.

Weissinger, E. and Iso-Ahola, S. E. (1987). Relationship between Type-A behavior and self-reported leisure activity patterns. *Wellness Perspectives, 4,* 9–14.

Wells, A. J. (1988). Self-esteem and optimal experience. In M. Csikszentmihalyi and I. S. Csikszentmihalyi (Eds.), *Optimal experience* (pp. 327–341). New York, NY: Cambridge University Press.

West, P. C. and Merriam, L. C., Jr. (1970). Outdoor recreation and family cohesiveness: A research approach. *Journal of Leisure Research, 2,* 251–259.

Wheeler, R. J. and Frank, M. A. (1988). Identification of stress buffers. *Behavioral Medicine, 14,* 78–89.

White, R. W. (1959). Motivation reconsidered: The concept of competence. *Psychological Review, 66,* 297–333.

Whyte, L. B. and Shaw, S. M. (1994). Women's leisure: An exploratory study of fear of violence as a leisure constraint. *Journal of Applied Recreation Research, 19,* 5–21.

Wilensky, H. L. (1960). Work, careers, and social integration. *International Social Science Journal, 4,* 543–560.

Williams, D. R., Ellis, G. D., Nickerson, N. P. and Shafer, C. S. (1988). Contributions of time, format, and subject to variation in recreation experience preference measurement. *Journal of Leisure Research, 20,* 57–68.

Williams, D. R. and Schreyer, R. (1981). Characterizing the person-environment interaction for recreation resources planning. In *Proceedings of Applied Geography Conference.* Tempe, AZ: Association of Applied Geographers.

Williams, D. R., Schreyer, R. and Knopf, R. C. (1990). The effect of the experience use history on the multidimensional structure of motivations to participate in leisure activities. *Journal of Leisure Research, 22,* 36–54.

Williams, J. M. (1978). Personality characteristics of the successful female athlete. In W. F. Straub (Ed.), *Sport psychology* (pp. 249–255). Ithaca, NY: Mouvement Publications.

Willmott, P. (1971). Family, work and leisure conflicts among male employees. *Human Relations, 24,* 575–584.

Winefield, A. H., Tiggemann, M., Winefield, H. R. and Goldney, R. D. (1993). *Growing up with unemployment: A longitudinal study of its psychological impact.* London, UK: Routledge.

Witt, P. A. (1971). Factor structure of leisure behavior for high school age youth in three communities. *Journal of Leisure Research, 3,* 213–219.

Witt, P. A. (1988). Leisure programs and services for special populations: Past, present, and future research. In L. A. Barnett (Ed.), *Research about leisure: Past, present, and future* (pp. 127–139). Champaign, IL: Sagamore Publishing.

Witt, P. A. and Bishop, D. W. (1970). Situational antecedents to leisure behavior. *Journal of Leisure Research, 2,* 64–77.

Witt, P. A. and Ellis, G. D. (1984). The leisure diagnostic battery: Measuring perceived freedom in leisure. *Loisir et Société/Society and Leisure, 7,* 109–124.

Witt, P. A. and Ellis, G. D. (1985). Development of a short form to assess perceived freedom in leisure. *Journal of Leisure Research, 17,* 225–233.

Witt, P. A. and Goodale, T. L. (1981). The relationships between barriers to leisure enjoyment and family stages. *Leisure Sciences, 4,* 29–49.

Witt, P. A. and Goodale, T. L. (1985). Barriers to leisure across family stages. In M. G. Wade (Ed.), *Constraints on leisure* (pp. 227–242). Springfield, IL: Charles C. Thomas, Publisher.

Wortman, C. B. (1975). Some determinants of perceived control. *Journal of Personality and Social Psychology, 31,* 282–294.

Wright, R. A., Wadely, V. G., Danner, M. and Phillips, P. N. (1992). Persuasion, reactance, and judgements of interpersonal appeal. *European Journal of Social Psychology, 22,* 85–91.

Yoesting, D. R. and Christensen, J. E. (1978). Reexamining the significance of childhood recreation patterns on adult leisure behavior. *Leisure Sciences, 1,* 27–38.

Yoesting, D. R. and Burkhead, D. L. (1973). Significance of childhood recreation experience on adult leisure behavior: An exploratory analysis. *Journal of Leisure Research, 5,* 25–36.

Young, R. A. and Crandall, R. (1984). Wilderness use and self-actualization. *Journal of Leisure Research, 16,* 149–160.

Young, R. A. and Kent, A. T. (1985). Using the theory of reasoned action to improve the understanding of recreation behavior. *Journal of Leisure Research, 17,* 90–106.

Yuan, M. S. and McEwen, D. (1989). Test for campers' experience preference differences among three ROS setting classes. *Leisure Sciences, 11,* 177–185.

Yuan, S. and McDonald, C. (1990). Motivational determinates of international pleasure time. *Journal of Travel Research, 29,* 42–44.

Zajonc, R. B. (1965). Social facilitation. *Science, 149,* 269–274.

Zanna, M. P. and Rempel, J. K. (1988). Attitudes: A new look at an old concept. In D. Bar-Tal and A. Kruglanski (Eds.), *The social psychology of knowledge* (pp. 315–334). New York, NY: Cambridge University Press.

Zimbardo, P. G. (1973). On the ethics of intervention in human psychological research: With special reference to the Stanford prison experiment. *Cognition, 2,* 243–256.

Zimbardo, P. G. (1992). Foreword. In S. S. Brehm (Ed.), *Intimate relationships* (p. XIV–XVI). New York, NY: McGraw-Hill.

Zoerink, D. A. and Lauener, K. (1991). Effects of a leisure education program on adults with traumatic brain injury. *Therapeutic Recreation Journal, 25,* 19–28.

Zuckerman, M. (1979). *Sensation seeking: Beyond the optimal level of arousal.* Hillsdale, NJ: LEA.

Zuzanek, J. (1980). The work-leisure relationship in Soviet sociological discussion. *Canadian Slavonic Papers, 22,* 122–128.

Zuzanek, J. (1982). Leisure research in North America from a socio-historical perspective. In D. Ng, and S. Smith (Eds.), *Perspectives on the nature of leisure research* (pp. 170–186). Waterloo, ON: University of Waterloo Press.

Zuzanek, J. (1991a). Leisure research in North America: A critical retrospective. *Loisir et Société/Society and Leisure, 14,* 587–596.

Zuzanek, J. (1991b). Time-budget research: Methodological problems and perspectives. In E. J. McCullough and R. L. Calder (Eds.), *Time as a human resource* (pp. 243–250). Calgary, AB: The University of Calgary Press.

Zuzanek, J. and Box, S. J. (1988). Life course and the daily lives of older adults in Canada. In K. Altergott (Ed.), *Daily life in later life* (pp. 147–185). Newbury Park, CA: Sage Publications.

Zuzanek, J. and Mannell, R. C. (1983). Work-leisure relationships from a sociological and social psychological perspective. *Leisure Studies, 2,* 327–344.

Zuzanek, J. and Mannell, R. C. (1993a). Gender variations in the weekly rhythms of daily behaviour and experiences. *Journal of Occupational Science, 1,* 25–37.

Zuzanek, J. and Mannell, R. C. (1993b). Leisure behaviour and experiences as part of everyday life: The weekly rhythm. *Loisir et Société/Society and Leisure, 16,* 31–57.

Zuzanek, J. and Smale, B. J. A. (1992). Life-cycle variations in across-the-week allocation of time to selected daily activities. *Loisir et Société/Society and Leisure, 15,* 559–586.

A

B

S

W

About the Authors

Roger Mannell is a social psychologist and Professor of Recreation and Leisure Studies. Dr. Mannell completed his Ph.D. in psychology at the University of Windsor in 1977. He was Director of the Center of Leisure Studies at Acadia University in Nova Scotia before joining the University of Waterloo as a faculty member in 1979 and served as Chair of the Department of Recreation and Leisure Studies from 1990 to 1996. He has been a regular contributor to the social psychological study of leisure. In particular, he has been interested in social and personality factors that influence the nature of leisure experiences and in turn how these experiences affect the quality of life and mental health. His research has also included studying the impact of the changing relationship between work and leisure on the lifestyles of workers. He was the 1989 recipient of the Allen V. Sapora Research Award and in 1991 was awarded the Theodore and Franklin Roosevelt Research Excellence Award by the National Recreation and Parks Association. His leisure interests include reading, camping with his wife and five children, restoring an old house and coaching youth sports.

Douglas Kleiber is professor and head of the Department of Recreation and Leisure Studies at the University of Georgia. After undergraduate work in psychology at Cornell University he completed a Ph.D. in educational psychology at the University of Texas in 1972. He has held faculty positions at Cornell University, St. Cloud State University and the University of Illinois before moving to Georgia in 1989. At the University of Illinois, he served as director of the Leisure Behavior Research Laboratory from 1982 to 1987. Dr. Kleiber is a member and past president of the Academy of Leisure Sciences. His research is directed primarily to the influence of leisure on human development and adjustment across the life span. His nonwork interests include sailing with his wife, playing tennis with his son and daughter, and listening to the blues, sometimes alone.

✤ Other Books From Venture Publishing ✤

The A•B•Cs of Behavior Change: Skills for Working with Behavior Problems in Nursing Homes
> by Margaret D. Cohn, Michael A. Smyer and Ann L. Horgas

Activity Experiences and Programming Within Long-Term Care
> by Ted Tedrick and Elaine R. Green

The Activity Gourmet
> by Peggy Powers

Advanced Concepts for Geriatric Nursing Assistants
> by Carolyn A. McDonald

Adventure Education
> edited by John C. Miles and Simon Priest

Aerobics of the Mind: Keeping the Mind Active in Aging
> by Marge Engleman

Assessment: The Cornerstone of Activity Programs
> by Ruth Perschbacher

Behavior Modification in Therapeutic Recreation: An Introductory Learning Manual
> by John Dattilo and William D. Murphy

Benefits of Leisure
> edited by B. L. Driver, Perry J. Brown and George L. Peterson

Benefits of Recreation Research Update
> by Judy M. Sefton and W. Kerry Mummery

Beyond Bingo: Innovative Programs for the New Senior
> by Sal Arrigo, Jr., Ann Lewis and Hank Mattimore

Both Gains and Gaps: Feminist Perspectives on Women's Leisure
> by Karla Henderson, M. Deborah Bialeschki, Susan M. Shaw and
>   Valeria J. Freysinger

The Community Tourism Industry Imperative—The Necessity, The Opportunities, Its Potential
> by Uel Blank

Dimensions of Choice: A Qualitative Approach to Recreation, Parks, and Leisure Research
> by Karla A. Henderson

Effective Management in Therapeutic Recreation Service
> by Gerald S. O'Morrow and Marcia Jean Carter

Evaluating Leisure Services: Making Enlightened Decisions
> by Karla A. Henderson with M. Deborah Bialeschki

The Evolution of Leisure: Historical and Philosophical Perspectives, Second Printing
> by Thomas Goodale and Geoffrey Godbey

File O' Fun: A Recreation Planner for Games & Activities, Third Edition
> by Jane Harris Ericson and Diane Ruth Albright

The Game Finder—A Leader's Guide to Great Activities
> by Annette C. Moore

Getting People Involved in Life and Activities: Effective Motivating Techniques
> by Jeanne Adams

Great Special Events and Activities
> by Annie Morton, Angie Prosser and Sue Spangler

Inclusive Leisure Services: Responding to the Rights of People with Disabilities
> by John Dattilo

✤ Other Books From Venture Publishing ✤

✤ *Other Books From Venture Publishing* ✤

Quality Management: Applications for Therapeutic Recreation
    edited by Bob Riley
Recreation and Leisure: Issues in an Era of Change, Third Edition
    edited by Thomas Goodale and Peter A. Witt
Recreation Economic Decisions: Comparing Benefits and Costs, Second Edition
    by John B. Loomis and Richard G. Walsh
Recreation Programming and Activities for Older Adults
    by Jerold E. Elliott and Judith A. Sorg-Elliott
Recreation Programs that Work for At-Risk Youth: The Challenge of Shaping the Future
    edited by Peter A. Witt and John L. Crompton
Reference Manual for Writing Rehabilitation Therapy Treatment Plans
    by Penny Hogberg and Mary Johnson
Research in Therapeutic Recreation: Concepts and Methods
    edited by Marjorie J. Malkin and Christine Z. Howe
Risk Management in Therapeutic Recreation: A Component of Quality Assurance
    by Judith Voelkl
A Social History of Leisure Since 1600
    by Gary Cross
The Sociology of Leisure
    by John R. Kelly and Geoffrey Godbey
Therapeutic Activity Intervention with the Elderly: Foundations and Practices
    by Barbara A. Hawkins, Marti E. May and Nancy Brattain Rogers
Therapeutic Recreation: Cases and Exercises
    by Barbara C. Wilhite and M. Jean Keller
Therapeutic Recreation in the Nursing Home
    by Linda Buettner and Shelley L. Martin
Therapeutic Recreation Protocol for Treatment of Substance Addictions
    by Rozanne W. Faulkner
A Training Manual for Americans With Disabilities Act Compliance in Parks and Recreation Settings
    by Carol Stensrud
Understanding Leisure and Recreation: Mapping the Past, Charting the Future
    edited by Edgar L. Jackson and Thomas L. Burton

 Venture Publishing, Inc.
1999 Cato Avenue
State College, PA 16801

Phone: (814) 234-4561; FAX: (814) 234-1651